THE WESTERN TIME OF
ANCIENT HISTORY

This book examines the conceptual and temporal frames through which modern Western historiography has linked itself to classical antiquity. In doing so, it articulates a genealogical problematic of what history is and a more strictly focused reappraisal of Greek and Roman historical thought. Ancient ideas of history have played a key role in modern debates about history writing, from Kant through Hegel to Nietzsche and Heidegger, and from Friedrich Creuzer through George Grote and Theodor Mommsen to Momigliano and Moses Finley. Yet scholarship has paid little attention to the theoretical implications of the reception of these ideas. The chapters in this collection cover a wide range of relevant topics and approaches, and boast distinguished authors from across Europe in the fields of classics, ancient and modern history, and the theory of historiography.

ALEXANDRA LIANERI is Assistant Professor of Greek and Translation Theory at the University of Thessaloniki. She has written in the fields of the reception and translation of antiquity, the theory and history of historiography, translation theory, and the history of political thought. In addition to articles in these fields, she has co-edited the volume *Translation and the Classic* (2008), and is currently completing a monograph on the modern history of ancient democracy and co-editing a volume on the history of ancient philosophy.

THE WESTERN TIME OF ANCIENT HISTORY

Historiographical Encounters with the Greek and Roman Pasts

EDITED BY

ALEXANDRA LIANERI

CAMBRIDGE
UNIVERSITY PRESS

CAMBRIDGE UNIVERSITY PRESS
Cambridge, New York, Melbourne, Madrid, Cape Town,
Singapore, São Paulo, Delhi, Mexico City

Cambridge University Press
The Edinburgh Building, Cambridge CB2 8RU, UK

Published in the United States of America by Cambridge University Press, New York

www.cambridge.org
Information on this title: www.cambridge.org/9780521883139

First published 2011

A catalogue record for this publication is available from the British Library

Library of Congress Cataloguing in Publication data
The western time of ancient history : historiographical encounters with the Greek and Roman pasts /
edited by Alexandra Lianeri.
p. cm.
Includes bibliographical references and index.
ISBN 978-0-521-88313-9
1. History – Philosophy. 2. Historiography – Philosophy. 3. Historiography – Western countries.
4. Rome – Historiography. 5. Greece – Historiography. I. Lianeri, Alexandra.
D16.8.W398 2011
930.072 – dc22   2011001071

ISBN 978-0-521-88313-9 Hardback

Contents

UNFOUNDING TIME IN AND THROUGH ANCIENT
HISTORICAL THOUGHT

AFTERWORD

Acknowledgements

This volume is the product of a collaborative effort. It has depended upon the meticulousness, the acumen and the critical intelligence of the contributors, whose response to a semi-formed idea was creative and imaginative. I am also indebted to the translators and would particularly like to thank Chiara Ghidini, Neville Morley and Annie Osborne for their invaluable contributions, as well as the Hellenic Foundation and Leventis Foundation for funding used for the translations. This book began its life in the 'Ancient Histories and Modern Historicities' Craven Seminar of the Cambridge Classics Faculty, in which debates provided the kind of stimulation that is not easily found. I would like to thank Robin Osborne, Paul Cartledge and Geoffrey Lloyd for having listened, talked and read with exceptional commitment, for their subtly critical comments, and for insisting that theory must be mediated by style. Geoffrey Hawthorn asked the unthought questions and indicated the complexity of potential answers, while Oswyn Murray offered his insightful thoughts from the outset. John Dunn has been exemplary for me in combining historiographical inquiry with political reflection, and discussions with him have set high standards of learning and self-expectation. Bob Fowler's wise counsel has been invaluable and encouraging. The anonymous readers for Cambridge University Press provided astute and constructive critiques, aspects of which I still have to address. Michael Sharp was generous with his time and editorial advice, and had a dedication to lucid language, from which I often failed to learn. I am grateful to Linda Woodward for her meticulous reading and detailed corrections. I wish to thank Kostas Vlassopoulos for his perspicacious readings, for the pleasures of disagreement, and for never failing to leaven critical debates with good humour. Eftychia Bathrellou helped with her fine scholarly learning in classics and her incomparable good will. Angeliki Spiropoulou offered useful advice on the title. I would like thank

Yorgos Avgoustis for allowing me to benefit from his outstanding erudition and acumen, for inspiring discussions on all aspects of this work, and for his precious companionship. I am more grateful than I can say to my parents, Yorgos Lianeris and Eleni Lianeri, and my sisters, Christina and Ioanna, for their unfailing love and support.

Notes on contributors

PETER BURKE has retired from his chair in Cultural History, University of Cambridge, but remains a Fellow of Emmanuel College. His latest books include *Languages and Communities in Early Modern Europe* (2004), *What is Cultural History?* (2004), *Cultural Hybridity* (2009) and (with Maria Lucia Pallares-Burke) *Social Theory in the Tropics: Gilberto Freyre* (2008).

GIUSEPPE CAMBIANO is Professor of History of Ancient Philosophy at the Scuola Normale Superiore in Pisa. His books include *Il ritorno degli antichi* (1988, French tr. *Le retour des Anciens*, 1994), *Platone e le tecniche* (1991), *Polis. Un modello per la cultura europea* (2000, French tr. *Polis. Histoire d' un modèle politique*, 2003). His publications in English include 'Aristotle and the Anonymous Opponents of Slavery', in M. Finley ed. *Classical Slavery* (1987), 'Becoming an Adult', in J.-P. Vernant ed. *The Greeks* (1995), 'Philosophy, Science and Medicine', in K. Algra, J. Barnes, J. Mansfeld, M. Schofield eds., *The Cambridge History of Hellenistic Philosophy* (1999).

HOWARD CAYGILL is Professor of Cultural History, University of London and the author of *Art of Judgement* (1989), *A Kant Dictionary* (1995), *Walter Benjamin: The Colour of Experience* (1998) and *Levinas and the Political* (2002).

GIOVANNA CESERANI is Assistant Professor of Classics at Stanford University. She works on the classical tradition with an emphasis on the intellectual history of classical scholarship, archaeology and historiography since the eighteenth century. Her book *Italy's Lost Greece: Magna Graecia and Modern Archaeology* is forthcoming for Oxford University Press. Her recent publications include 'Wilamowitz and stratigraphy in 1873: A case study in the history of archaeology's "Great Divide"', in J. Nordblach and N. Schlanger eds., *Archives, Ancestors, Practices:*

Archaeology in the Light of its History (2008), and (edited with A. Milanese) *Antiquarianism, Museums and Cultural Heritage: Collecting and its Contexts in Eighteenth-Century Naples*, a special issue for the *Journal of the History of Collections* (2007).

JOHN DUNN has been a Fellow of King's College, Cambridge since 1966 and was Professor of Political Theory at Cambridge University from 1987 to 2007. Fascinated and dismayed by the vagaries of political fate across the modern world since childhood experiences in Occupied Germany, Iran and India, he is the author of *The Political Thought of John Locke* (1969), *Modern Revolutions* (1989, 2nd edn), *Dependence and Opportunity: Political Change in Ahafo* (1973) (with A. F. Robertson), *Western Political Theory in the Face of the Future* (1993, 2nd edn), *The Politics of Socialism* (1984), *Locke* (1984), *Rethinking Modern Political Theory* (1985), *Interpreting Political Responsibility* (1990), *The History of Political Theory* (1996), *The Cunning of Unreason: Making Sense of Politics* (2000) and *Setting the People Free: The Story of Democracy* (2005).

JONAS GRETHLEIN is Professor in Classics at Heidelberg University. He has written on Homer, Greek tragedy and poetry, ancient historiography and literary theory. His recent publications include *Littell's Orestie. Mythos, Macht und Moral in Les Bienveillantes* (2009) and *The Greeks and Their Past. Poetry, Oratory and History in the 5th Century BCE* (2010).

FRANÇOIS HARTOG is a historian. He is Professor and Chair of ancient and modern historiography at L'Ecole des hautes études en sciences sociales in Paris. His publications include *Régimes d'historicité, Présentisme et Expériences du temps* (2003), *Evidence de l'histoire. Ce que voient les historiens* (2005), *Anciens, modernes, sauvages* (2005), *Vidal-Naquet, historien en personne. L'homme-mémoire et le moment-mémoire* (2007).

ALEXANDRA LIANERI is Assistant Professor of Greek and translation theory at the Classics department of the University of Thessaloniki. She has written in the fields of the reception and translation of antiquity, the theory and history of historiography, translation theory, and the history of political thought. In addition to articles in these fields, she has co-edited the volume *Translation and the Classic* (2008), she is completing a monograph on the modern history of ancient democracy (forthcoming) and is co-editing a volume on the history of ancient philosophy (forthcoming).

NEVILLE MORLEY is Professor of Ancient Economic History and Historical Theory at the University of Bristol. His books include *Antiquity and Modernity* (2008) and *The Roman Empire: Roots of Imperialism* (2010), and he is currently leading a project on the modern reception and influence of Thucydides.

ULRICH MUHLACK was Professor of History and Theory and History of Historiography at the Johann Wolfgang Goethe-University, Frankfurt am Main, until his retirement in 2006. His publications deal with the theory and history of historical science, the history of political ideas of the modern period, and, in connection to that, of the Renaissance, Humanism and Absolutism.

OSWYN MURRAY was a Fellow of Balliol College, Oxford, teaching ancient history from 1968 to 2004; he is a Fellow of the Society of Antiquaries, the Royal Danish Academy and the Scuola Normale di Pisa. His books include *Early Greece* (²1993, tr. into six languages); and co-edited volumes: *The Oxford History of the Ancient World* (1986), *The Greek City from Homer to Alexander* (1990), *Latin Poetry and the Classical Tradition: Essays in Medieval and Renaissance Literature* (1990), *Paul Veyne, Bread and Circuses* (1990), *Sympotica: A Symposium on the Symposion* (1990, 1994), *In Vino Veritas* (1995), *Jacob Burckhardt, The Greeks and Greek Civilization* (1998), *Edward Bulwer Lytton, Athens: Its Rise and Fall* (2004), *A Commentary on Herodotus Books I–IV* (2007). He is the Founding Director of the website *Bibliotheca Academica Translationum* (http://bat.ehess.fr/).

ELLEN O'GORMAN is Senior Lecturer in Classics at the University of Bristol. She is the author of *Irony and Misreading in the Annals of Tacitus* (Cambridge, 2000) and of numerous articles on historical writing and historical understanding in antiquity and modernity.

STEFAN REBENICH is Professor of Ancient History and the Classical Tradition in the Department of History at the University of Bern. His recent publications include *Jerome. The Early Church Fathers* (2002) and *Theodor Mommsen. Eine Biographie* (2002; ²2007). He is currently working on the correspondence between Theodor Mommsen and Friedrich Althoff, to be published by the Bavarian Academy, and a biography of Wilhelm and Alexander von Humboldt.

ROSALIND THOMAS is a Fellow of Balliol College, Oxford. Among her publications are *Oral Tradition and Written Record in Ancient Athens*

(Cambridge, 1989), *Literacy and Orality in Ancient Greece* (Cambridge, 1992), and *Herodotus in Context: Ethnography, Science and the Art of Persuasion* (Cambridge, 2000). Her research interests include Greek law and the city-state, Greek historiography, Greeks and barbarians. She is currently writing on polis histories and the development of Greek historiography.

KOSTAS VLASSOPOULOS is Associate Professor in Greek History at the Department of Classics, University of Nottingham. His recent publications include *Unthinking the Greek Polis. Ancient Greek History beyond Eurocentrism* (Cambridge, 2007), *Politics: Antiquity and its Legacy* (2009). He co-edited with D. Geary, *Slavery, Citizenship and the State in Classical Antiquity and the Modern Americas* (Special Issue of the *European Review of History* 16:3, 2009).

MICHAEL STUART WILLIAMS is Lecturer in Ancient Classics at the National University of Ireland, Maynooth. He has recently published *Authorised Lives in Early Christian Biography: Between Eusebius and Augustine* (Cambridge, 2008).

Introduction

Unfounding times: The idea and ideal of ancient history in Western historical thought

Alexandra Lianeri

TIME AND CRITIQUE[1]

Any new interpreter must be aware of past interpreters: he who is not aware of past interpreters will still be influenced by them, but uncritically, because, after all, awareness is the foundation of criticism. The historian must therefore be able to account not only for all the data he possesses, but also for all the interpretations he is aware of.[2]

Such was the critical task posed by a master of the discipline of history, whose object of study was not the past as a realm that delimits certain events and actions, but historical thought in context:[3] the modes of speaking and writing through which the past locates itself within history and in doing so makes a claim to historical knowledge that both conditions and confronts that of the present. Readers of Arnaldo Momigliano's writings will remember his penetrating remarks about the critical role of the history of historiography in the field of historical research. The works of past historians, as this excerpt implies, do not enter the present fields of historical investigation as any other cultural product of the past. These works are undoubtedly part of the same historical matrix that gives rise to all other forms of cultural production. Yet, as an object of historical knowledge, past historical thought acquires a distinct relation to the subject of knowing constituting at once its precondition and its alternative. It is, at one and the same time, a material to be studied and part of the traditions and

---

[1] I am grateful to Yorgos Avgoustis, Paul Cartledge, Geoffrey Hawthorn, Geoffrey Lloyd, Robin Osborne, and Kostas Vlassopoulos for incisive comments on previous drafts of this introduction.

[2] Momigliano 1975a: 297.

[3] The term 'historical thought' is intended to cover a broader field of research than that designated by the term historiography. More specifically, the term includes forms of inquiry that engage with the past and its links to the present from the viewpoint of other disciplines and critical perspectives, such as the philosophy of history, but also literary writings, rhetoric, religious documents and so on. Still, as the notion does not imply an opposition between 'historiography' and 'historical thought', but rather suggests a broadening of the meaning of 'historiography', the two terms will henceforth be used interchangeably.

practices which allow us to engage with this material. This is the reason why critical engagement with history, as Momigliano observed, requires new interpreters to be aware of past ones. Understanding the history of historiography is a means of encountering the genealogical constitution of present forms of historical inquiry. It is the perspective from which we can grasp the historicity of categories that sustain the understanding of our object; and thus also grasp the difficulty in maintaining the division between subject and object of research.

The encounter with past historical thought underlines the fragility of this polarity between past and present historians, and their respective forms of writing and objects of study. What is the subject of modern histories of antiquity, when Thucydides is not only the key mediator of ancient historical 'data', but also the presumed father of history writing? Our relationship with past historians confronts us with what Michel de Certeau described as the primary task of the history of historiography, the task of

articulating time as the ambivalence that affects the place from which it speaks, and thus of reflecting upon the ambiguity of place as the work of time within the space of knowledge itself. (De Certeau 1986: 217)

Such an enterprise is critical in the sense that it shifts attention from the subject–object polarity to a plurality of authors and contracting parties of history. A hierarchy of knowledge is thus replaced by a mutual differentiation of subjects; and thus, from that moment, the particular place of the relationship that the present historian maintains with others introduces a dialectic of all places and therefore an experience of time.[4]

What is the aim of this critique when its object becomes the tradition which claimed to have laid the foundations of historical thinking, namely Western historical thought? More specifically, how does critique operate when its force is turned towards the historical locus of these foundations in Greek and Roman antiquity, and its modern establishment as the origin of both Western historiography and the possibility of understanding history as such?

In a series of lectures delivered in the early sixties, but published posthumously as a final – and still incomplete – historiographical testament, Momigliano offered a remarkable frame for beginning to answer these questions. While setting out to explore *The Classical Foundations of Modern Historiography*, he suggested that the critical task of this inquiry, at least with regard to Western history, must question the narrative line which begins with Greek and Roman historians, goes through Judeo-Christian

---

[4] De Certeau 1986: 217.

historiography, to end up in modern European historical thought. 'Greek historiography', he argued, 'was not naturally or inevitably destined to become the foundation of our Western historiography.' We would not have inherited the Greek tradition without the bold intervention of the Romans, and even so Greek historiography had to compete with the Hebrew tradition. Both Greek and postexilic Hebrew historians wrote against the background of the Persian Empire and bear traces of their common origins; while later, the Greek and Jewish traditions confronted one another in a battle that brought aspects of Jewish thought into Christian works, as in the ecclesiastical histories of late antiquity.[5] Equally, the 'modern' age, he went on, engaged with these conflicts and re-enacted them by setting, for instance, Roman historians against the Greeks, Thucydides against Herodotus, the classical tradition against ecclesiastical historiography and the whole matrix of ancient historians against the modern.[6] The foundational attributes attached to Greek and Roman historiography are therefore dually misleading. Not only was there no continuity between the ancient and the modern historiographical traditions, Momigliano says, but also the idea of a singular founding moment of (Western) historical consciousness is to be challenged. Far from offering a unified manifestation of the birth of historical thinking, Greece and Rome present a conversation among different traditions, including those which Western historians have systematically expunged from European lineages.

Momigliano's critique constitutes the starting point of this volume, which aims to explore the confrontation between ancient and modern European historiography by discussing configurations of Greek and Roman antiquity in Western conceptions of historical time. This investigation is centred on two distinct, yet interrelated, categories of time, which we could call 'the time of words of history' and 'the time of things of history' named through historiographical discourse.[7] The first of these time-frames pertains to genealogies of the discipline itself: the narrative timelines that established Greek and Roman historians as the origin of the tradition that was constituted, retrospectively, under the name of Western historical thought. The second relates to genealogies of the Western historical experience conceptualised in history writing: the timelines that go back to Greek and Roman antiquity as a foundation, whose construction safeguards the coherence of Western history. The key question raised by the book is a

---

[5] Momigliano 1990: 2.   [6] Momigliano 1990.
[7] On the 'words' and 'things' of history, see Rancière 1994: esp. 24–41 and Hayden White's foreword (1994) viii–ix.

historiographical one: what was ancient history, in the dual sense of *a 'historical' period* and *a mode of 'historical' understanding*, in relation to the dual temporality of Western 'historical' experience and 'historical' thought? Yet in attempting to answer this question, we shall see how historiographical narratives have been intertwined with certain philosophies of time and history, seeking to naturalise Western historical lineages by controlling the effects of time upon the limits of the place and of the object of historical knowledge.

The relation between these two timelines – the time of historical words and the time of historical things – is not addressed in Momigliano's writings. The turn of Western historiography towards its own history, evoked by him, entailed a critique which has left us uncertain as to the links between the founding position of Greek and Roman historians, crystallised over the Enlightenment and nineteenth-century modernity, and the appearance, in the same period, of engagements with Greek and Roman political and cultural history, the latter sustaining a philosophical reflection on the meaning of history as such and defining classical antiquity as the inaugural moment of a universal course of time. How do notions such as Voltaire's 'philosophy of history', Kant's 'idea of universal history from a cosmopolitan point of view', Herder's 'philosophy of the history of humanity', Humboldt's idea of a 'world history outside the circle of finitude', all of which approached classical antiquity as the starting point of a timeline centred on European history, relate to the inaugural position of ancient historians in the histories of Western historiography? How are these timelines inscribed into histories of antiquity? In other words, how does the starting point of a European history, which becomes the prototype for a history of humanity, relate to the starting point of an equivalent history of historical thought?

Momigliano's masterful critique of Western historiography offered scant theoretical consideration of these questions. Still his work became central to debates that have since challenged the positing of ancient 'data' within Eurocentric and exclusionist time-frames of social, cultural, political and economic history. We thus have today at least two historiographical models, which interrogate this conception of European antiquities, namely that of comparative and that of internal or immanent critique. The former of these models promises to deal with antiquity within the framework of comparative studies aiming to transcend Western historiography by setting Greece and Rome alongside other local and global configurations formulated outside Europe. Stemming from the encounter between historical, anthropological and postcolonial studies, such comparisons disclose the irreducibly local status of Greek and Roman histories by bringing them to confront other cultural lineages. The critical force of this enterprise, as Marcel Detienne has argued, among others,[8] lies in the juxtaposition of Western and non-western heritages, which must set forth a 'comparison of incomparables'. Comparative studies that focus merely on the European heritage, Detienne explains, cannot challenge notions and timelines – i.e. history, historicity, Europe, philosophy, rationality, progress, democracy – that have posited European history as the privileged epigone of the ancient Greek and Roman pasts. What is therefore needed is an expansion of these notions, which will be attained by locating antiquity within a global context. How does Greek and Roman historiography relate, for instance, to the *Shiji* of ancient Chinese historiography or the founding position of Vedic history in Indian historiography? What are the implications of such comparisons for the reconsideration of 'historical sense' as a category that designates diverse modes of engagement with the past, such as personal or collective memory? Since forms of popular participation in government can be encountered in pre-Babylonian Mesopotamia or the Indian assemblies of the sixth century BCE, Detienne asks, how do these early political formations challenge the consideration of 'democracy' as a Greek, and specifically Athenian, 'invention'?[9]

By contrast, the second model proceeds on the basis of categories formulated by the Western tradition. This perspective, which offers the key frame for this volume, finds its privileged articulation in the conflicts and diversity that characterise the Western historiographical heritage. Thus historians as different in their research areas and critical methodologies as Peter Burke, Anthony Grafton, J.G.A. Pocock, Joseph M. Levine and John W. Burrow have explored how the European 'sense of the past', to use Burke's expression, did not produce a homogeneous language, which would preclude the possibility of detaching Europe from the 'foundational' place of Greek and Roman history. On the contrary, the very act of constructing those foundations involved gaps, contradictions and inconsistencies, which allow us to identify disjunction and diversity at the core of what passes as a unified and unifying history and temporality. The concepts that linked antiquity to Western historical temporalities appealed to a

---

[8] Comparative studies of classical antiquity and non-European traditions have been pursued by a wide number of historians of antiquity and anthropologists including Moses Finley, members of the so-called Paris school, with which Detienne was affiliated, and especially J.-P. Vernant, P.-V. Naquet, L. Gernet and N. Loraux, as well as G. Lloyd and E. Wolf. For an overview see Detienne 2008; Gernet 1981; Cartledge 1996; Gernet 1981.

[9] Detienne 2008: xiii–xiv.

universality that was constantly threatened by what these concepts excluded and suppressed. Their putative act of founding European history was thus unfounded by considerations arising from the European tradition itself.

Both critical models have allowed us to understand that the history of Europe can no longer be seen as representing anything like a prototype of human history. It needs to be both 'provincialised', in other words to be viewed as one historical and historiographical trajectory among many, and located within a global and pluralised network of concepts and practices through which historians identify the course of time.[10] However, this development, at least with regard to the study of Greek and Roman history, has been imbued with a curious paradox. On the one hand, Greek and Roman antiquity has been deprived of the privileged locus of origin of a universal itinerary; on the other hand, critiques of Eurocentrism manifest a certain impossibility of *thinking* about ancient history without deploying certain categories and concepts, the roots of which are to be traced in the modern, Eurocentric historiographical traditions. Geoffrey Lloyd, in one of his comparative studies of Ancient Greek and Chinese practices of inquiry, describes this problem succinctly. He observes that the recognition of the distance that separates ancient conceptual categories from their present equivalents does not efface the need to ground our understanding in terms of the present – and these terms are the product of the modern European reception of the classical past. The word 'history', for instance, as a category that designates Greek *historia* or the ancient Chinese historiographical traditions not only effaces the foreignness of the original terms; it may also imply a false teleology which paradoxically assumes that both of these cultures were oriented towards modern ideas. Still these terms, Lloyd goes on, are the only means we have to understand ancient cultures. 'We cannot, on pain of distortion, impose our own conceptual framework. Yet we have to.'[11] To describe ancient Chinese historians *as* historians, alongside their Greek colleagues, acts to broaden and diversify the meaning and history of our notion of 'history'. But the use of a term that emerged out of European encounters with the Greek word – *history/historia* – obscures this diversity by the very move that identifies it. Comparisons of historiographical traditions cannot take place in a neutral site, which bears no traces of the meanings and timelines which set *historia* into European genealogies. It is not possible to simply tear the Greek and Roman traditions of historiography out of European temporalities and bestow on them a kind of

---

[10] On these issues see Chakrabarty 2000: 3 and Bayly 2004.
[11] Lloyd 2004: 2.

autonomy, which could then be reproduced on a theoretical level, as a move that allows us to conceptualise the local status of those traditions from a viewpoint that is not affected by their history.

This impossibility makes it necessary to consider how the terms deployed by comparative studies have not been the isolated products of local heritages that confront European legacies. They have themselves been constituted by the ways in which Europe, and European modernity in particular, has mediated the survival of Greek and Roman heritages beyond the limits of Europe. Concepts such as history, philosophy, rationality, citizenship, politics, democracy and other related ones all bear the burden of modern European discourses and history, even when they are used from the perspective of modernities that were formulated outside the Western tradition.[12] This means that (modern) European thought, as Dipesh Chakrabarty put it, is today no less indispensable than it is inadequate in helping us to provincialise Europe from the viewpoint of the 'periphery'. At the same time, Chakrabarty suggests, the European heritage, 'which is now everybody's heritage and which affects us all', has never manifested a unity of meaning either within or outside the boundaries of timelines posited as European. On the contrary, Europe's evocations of universality have provided a strong foundation, on which to ground, both in Europe and outside, studies of diversity and critiques of the oppressing and exclusionist implications of European unifying histories.[13] We may recall, for instance, how critiques of colonial uses of the ancient world have emerged precisely from appropriations of Europe's constructions of antiquity attempted by postcolonial theorists and critics.

Comparisons between 'European' antiquities and other historical formations can thus trace a transcultural constitution of concepts, in which Western historiographical languages are already entangled with alternative ones, and each of these traditions has been informed by the other. The same is true for the constitution of concepts that comprised Western historical thought. Modern Europe's confrontation with antiquity never established a singular idea of history and historical temporality.[14] Surely, the construction of a *European* sense of the past reveals a large measure of concern for historical foundations, which could unify Europe's temporal

---

[12] This is not to say that this use was founded on an act of transfer, nor to deny the forms of mediation and cultural translation involved in the various forms of appropriation of the Western heritage. On this issue see especially Chakrabarty 2000 and Liu 1995.

[13] Chakrabarty 2000: 16.

[14] On this diversity in relation to the development of categories and models in Western historiography see Burrow (2007) and Grafton (2007b) for categories of history in early modern Europe.

and spatial limits. Yet, on closer inspection, Western histories of antiquity and philosophies of history taking Greece and Rome as their starting point disclose a practice which never fully confirmed this unity, but which introduced into European thought a vision of the ancient past that became foundational by maintaining its peculiarity and resistance to modern times.

This book studies this co-articulation of disjunction and conjunction: a temporalisation of European history which displays at once division and interconnection, rupture and continuity. On the one hand, its aim is to trace the European attempt to spatialise time, to reduce the inevitable alteration of collective lives and cultures brought about by the passing of time to the limits of a space – Europe – which posited its unity by evoking a single ancient origin. On the other hand, it traces the time-frames which were left outside the apparent letter of this narrative, but nevertheless returned to it in the form of ruptures, antinomies and conflicts of traditions. Consequently the book narrates two different stories about antiquity and identifies two timelines that are intertwined with one another. The first is a story of beginnings and conclusions, of the classical foundations of historical time and their endpoint in the spatialised temporality defined as European or Western history. The second is a story that casts doubt over European history's capacity to fully appropriate antiquity. It is a story in which ancient history and historians not only escape the genealogies that link them to Western times, but also give voice to alternative temporalities, which resist inclusion into a uniform historical lineage.

THEORISING WESTERN TIME

This volume poses the question of how to account for the history of Western historical thought if time were to be considered a central concept in historiographical theory. Such a move requires us to rethink the terms in which time and history are understood. It requires, first and foremost, a repudiation of the notion of time as a quantifiable continuum, in which 'history' occurs as a web of events and actions. A historiographical focus on time implies a shift from a series of historical instances that follow one another to historical temporalities, in other words, to the multiple ways of experiencing and conceptualising time which take shape within history and through which history becomes meaningful. This transition defines time as a field in historical research, the incongruities of which posit the need to pluralise its name and to account for specificities that invite us to consider not a singular time, but many. As a consequence, the focus on temporalities entails that past ideas of time and history are not to be relegated to prefigured systems of periodisation, whose limits are set in advance by established temporal frames. On the contrary, those ideas are to be seen as constitutive of new frames for periodising which may challenge the periods of Western history and historical thought.

In this vein, François Hartog proposes a model for categorising periods in Western history, which is centred on what he calls 'regimes of historicity': shifting conceptions of historicity associated with specific affirmations of time's authority. Historicities articulated in Western historical thought, he argues, offer the perspective for making sense of the forms of authority through which the West has legitimised its historical unity. Thus, the period between classical antiquity and modern times – an endpoint marked by the experience and symbolic significance of the French Revolution – was defined by the authority of the ancient past and the dominant role of tradition in directing the present and the future, an idea of *historia magistra vitae*, as Cicero first put it. The self-positioning of the modern period transferred the locus of authority from the past to the future, which tended from that moment onwards to rule the present and calibrate the past: it was 'the measure of the past and the bearer of what must be'. Finally, the contemporary experience of a 'crisis of time' pertains to the recent disintegration of the authority of the future, predominantly within the old Europe, and a growth in power of the category of the present: the establishment of an all-encompassing present, which fabricates the past and future that it needs each day.[15]

But these newly defined and large-scale time-frames, as Burke points out, pose the question of the unity of the concepts of time that set their limits: how much diversity is compatible with the Western 'regimes of historicity'? Taking his cue from the early modern European engagement with antiquity Burke explores how the dominance of temporalities that deployed ancient history as an exemplar was challenged by traditions that denied the applicability of classical *exempla*, or even criticised the relevance of *exempla* in general. Exemplarity and anti-exemplarity co-existed as antagonistic temporalities, making the period 1530-1750 in European thought a field that resists unification under a single category of time. This diversity not only reveals a plurality of historicities formulated in the Renaissance, but also invites us to consider a broader theoretical problem, implied by Burke's critique of Hartog's model: how is it possible for our

---

[15] On this scheme see also Hartog 2003.

(narrative) histories of temporalities to avoid established conceptions of linear time? Can the history of conceptions of time move beyond the enfolding of multiple and mutually antagonistic historicities within a traditional scheme of succession and breaks?

Any attempt to answer these questions seems to me to have less to do with the positioning of breaks in the history of temporalities (as it is always possible to produce endless debates about emergent or co-existing temporalities) and more with the need to recognise that our focus on historical time is itself a historiographical choice, which necessitates a reflexive account of present categories. Hartog's account of the history of regimes is not a descriptive presentation of time-frames in Western history. It is set forth as a theory of history presupposing both the priority of temporalities in organising historical experience and a certain unity of articulations of time within the limits of a regime. This means that, while the different temporal relations Hartog identifies (i.e. past-, future- or present-oriented temporalities) are conceptualised in the frame of our research object, the notion of the 'regime' itself, as a unifying frame that makes these relations historically meaningful through selection and interpretation, is posed as a theoretical category, which is distinguished from debates about historical 'data'. Burke's account of Renaissance temporalities questions precisely this category, by suggesting a new interpretation of temporalities that comprise our object. More specifically, his analysis redefines the regimes of historicity as internally diversified realms, in which distinct temporalities and conceptions of history encounter one another.

Despite their differences, the two perspectives share an acceptance of the necessity of periodisation as such. Histories of 'regimes of historicity', as Burke's essay indicates, produce periodisations which unavoidably suppress the diversity of conceptions of time formulated within their limits. Still, Burke's deployment of the category of the period in order to delimit his object – the Renaissance's sense of the past – does not allow us to conclude that his critique implies a challenge to the practice of periodisation. In so far as we seek to link consciousness of time to the various manifestations of cultural and social history, his analysis implies, it is impossible to dispense with periodising. For a strict focus on the diversity of temporalities would ultimately amount to what Fredric Jameson has aptly described as a mere historiography of the break,[16] in other words, an endless series of concepts of time that remain unrelated not only to one another, but also to contextual articulations of social and cultural history.

---

[16] On this term see Jameson 2002: 29.

Burke's position rather takes us to a different direction. By defining regimes of historicity as constituted by distinct temporalities, without simultaneously abandoning the requirement, also posed by Hartog, to explore how these temporalities coexist, conflict with, or follow one another *at a certain moment in time*, it (Burke's position) enables us to inquire as to how this 'moment' is to be designated. This question generates an aporia which will concern us throughout this introduction and the rest of the book. If historical temporalities are to be seen as central to our narrativisations of history, or indeed, as Hartog suggests, as the key frame for making sense of past times, how are we to explain changes, differences and transitions in forms of consciousness of time? If a web of conceptions of time provides the limits of a regime, we need to account for the constitution of this network as well as the transition from one regime to another. But such an exploration would require us to contextualise conceptions of time and history in terms that no longer pertain to the regimes themselves, but stem from social and cultural history. Hence the aporia underlying any historiographical narrative that structures itself around shifting conceptions of time: if forms of temporal consciousness may be seen as providing a historiographical perspective that goes beyond narratives of social and cultural history, there is still a need to evoke these narratives in order to make sense of the specific articulations of this consciousness within the frames of certain historical (i.e. social and cultural) times.

Giuseppe Cambiano's chapter begins to engage with this aporia by exploring a succession of temporalities, from classical antiquity up until the modern period, which inscribe ancient philosophy into Western history. This investigation is posed as a critical enterprise: its aim is to challenge Western considerations of Greek philosophy 'as the starting point of philosophy, and even as the starting point of Western history, conceived of as a history shaped by philosophy'. But Cambiano's attempt to sustain this argument does not simply proceed through acts of negation and repudiation performed from the perspective of the present and directed against the constitution of Greek philosophy as a founding moment for Western philosophy and history. Rather, the chapter finds its critical standpoints in the fissures of the tradition it sets out to interrogate, in other words, in the shifting historiographical narratives that formulated and legitimised the relation between ancient philosophy and European history.

From this perspective Cambiano examines an astounding breadth of genres, including history, philosophy and rhetoric, in order to argue that temporalisations of Greek philosophy not only sustained, but also questioned its position as the origin of a tradition that was passed down in Western history. Greek writers of the classical period did not assign to philosophy an ethnicity and often recognised exchanges between Greek and Eastern wisdom at the very moment that they emphasised the cultural inferiority of foreigners in relation to a Greek world defined by *sophia*, wisdom and the love of learning. The Roman period confirmed the founding role of Greek philosophers and simultaneously shifted the horizon of the history of philosophy from the question of origin to the accessibility and availability of the Greek tradition beyond the time of its first elaboration: the problem of translating philosophy's founding moment and the possibility implied for 'translators' to choose their original and the modes in which they survive in history. Equally, certain Christian writers engraved classical antiquity into the history of Revelation and asserted its derivative character, but also its affiliation with the Hebrew tradition, while the modern period restated Greek philosophy as an inaugural moment for philosophy and Western history, while simultaneously dissociating itself from the classical past and asserting the priority of novel quests for knowledge. So with regard to the history of Greek philosophy, successive regimes of historicity not only change alongside other shifts in social and cultural history, but also stand far from attaining an internal unity. They figure less as coherent conceptual realms and more as encounters between opposing temporalities, each of which slides into the other as each also repudiates the other and posits it as an opponent. Cambiano's complex analysis invites us to consider these conflicts as articulations of broader oppositions manifested in the social and political sphere, which introduce into Western historical thought what its imaginary unity suppresses and excludes. But if alternative temporalities enter Western narratives through a return of what is excluded, how are we to account for their presence in the shadows of dominant regimes of historicity? And how does this presence qualify our periodisation of Western histories of historical time?

Howard Caygill turns to this question through an incisive reading of Momigliano's engagement with Jewish and Jewish–Christian oracular and prophetic historiography, and specifically his repudiation of the Nietzschean link between the vision of a messianic end of history and the *ressentiment* of 'pariah' groups. According to Caygill, Momigliano, unlike Nietzsche, defends such historiography in the name of a political theology, which is sensitive to the place of eschatological and messianic themes in the writing of history and the philosophy of history. Political theology – the inquiry into the relationship between politics and religion explored by Weimar Jewish intellectuals and crystallised in Carl Schmitt's 1922 *Politische*

Theologie – is not typically deployed as an intellectual frame for locating Momigliano's historiographical inquiries. However, as Caygill suggests, Momigliano was deeply immersed in this debate, and developed a fascination not only with the political theology of Rome and its dominion, but also with that of the enemies of Rome, and with the political theology of resistance. Starting from a negation of Nietzsche's and Weber's conviction that eschatological history pertained to the *ressentiment* of the powerless and subaltern groups – such as the Jews or Christians under imperial dominion – who were unable to pursue politics by the usual violent means, Momigliano offered new interpretations of texts such as the Book of Daniel and the Sibylline oracles, which reassessed the relationship between messianic and progressive temporalities, and even identified cases of their mutual compatibility. Most crucially, as Caygill points out, Momigliano affirmed that the notion of the messianic end of history, evident in the Book of Daniel, drew on and concomitantly transformed Greek historiographical ideas, and particularly the scheme of the succession of empires found in Herodotus, Ctesias and their successors. Christian conceptions of the past paradoxically deployed a Greek category – universal history, and especially the succession of universal empires crystallised in Polybius – to resist the imposition of Hellenism. Moreover, the Christian adoption of the Sibylline writings in the form of an underground reaction to political and social events of the Roman empire allowed Momigliano to identify a multilevelled merging of Jewish, Christian and Greek historiography, while encountering the foundational controversy of political theology: the relationship between the state and the forms of eschatalogical time.

The confrontation of progressive and eschatological temporalities, explored by Caygill's reading of Momigliano, indicate that regimes of historicity are broader and more complex than they at first appear to be; and that the times of Western history took shape by appropriating other temporalities, such as those of religion, through which they addressed conflicts taking place in the social and political realms. Regimes of historicity, as we learn from Hartog, are, indeed, centred on the affirmation of time's authority, that is, the evoked domination of a dimension of time – past, present or future – over others. This authority of time, however, is not reducible to historiographical relations, but pertains to the totality of a social experience of time. It is shaped by the multiplicity of temporalities which inform social and political relations and which constitute what Koselleck has aptly described as the 'experience of history': the product of the tension between diversified conceptions of time and the factuality of events which these conceptions serve either to make visible or to suppress and eradicate.[17] By the end of this introduction we shall see how the constitution of this experience by the encounter of dominant and subversive temporalities, pointed out by Momigliano, shapes the divided and contradictory articulation of the politics of time. At this point, however, we need to turn to the relation which was both key to understanding these contradictions and the means of introducing them into the Western temporalisation of antiquity, that between ancient and modern times.

ANCIENT HISTORY THROUGH MODERN TIMES

Antiquity, as a historiographical category designating the Greek and Roman past, has been closely tied to successive articulations of the notion of the modern. From the first uses of the term in the fifth century CE, when *modernus* was deployed by Cassiodorus to define a new time-frame associated with Christianity, in opposition to *antiquus*,[18] through the Renaissance's turn to antiquity to negotiate an exemplary temporality, to the aesthetic and political quests of modernity, voiced paradigmatically in Baudelaire's claim that among all relations into which modernity enters, its relation to antiquity is critical,[19] the concept of 'ancient times' was crucial to defining the novelty of historical experience and the principles of historical movement conveyed by the term modern. The semantic field defined by the opposition ancient vs. modern has not remained stable throughout its history. Yet it is possible to discern, through the various shifts in its meaning, a certain conjunction of the ideas of break and continuity, which emerged during the Renaissance, but came to be consolidated towards the late eighteenth century, as the distinct product of European modernity. The second part of this volume, 'Ancient History and Modern Temporalities', focuses on philosophical and historiographical articulations of this temporality over the eighteenth and nineteenth centuries. The essays included in it seek to shed light on the semantics and politics of the link between ancient and modern temporalities: the dual time-frame which asserted modern Europe's special bonds with ancient, or more specifically classical, times, while simultaneously affirming the moderns' distance from antiquity and perhaps the very inability of modernity to lay claim to beginnings.

The formation of this time-consciousness has been traced back to the fifteenth and sixteenth centuries in the political and historiographical

---

[17] Koselleck 1997.   [18] On this issue see Jauss 2005.   [19] Baudelaire 1964.

thought of the civic humanist tradition of the Italian city-states. As Eugene Rice and Anthony Grafton have argued, the medieval historian believed that his own historical epoch went back to the reign of Augustus (27 BCE– 14 CE), and never encountered the intellectual and imaginative gulf that had to be crossed if the ancient world was to be understood as a separate time zone. 'He regarded the Romans as his contemporaries,' as Rice and Grafton put it. It was Renaissance humanists who recognised the division of their era from the Roman empire, and the need to make new sense of the ancient languages and cultures by returning to the contexts in which they developed.[20] J. G. A. Pocock located this change in the forms of historicism that developed in the Italian city-states and for which the turn to antiquity defined political life, and life in the city-state in particular, as transcendent in terms of its aim to realise for citizens all the values that men are capable of realising, and particular, in the sense that it is finite, located in space and time.[21] Burke's chapter in this volume explores the same contradiction in Renaissance historiographical writings, which, on the one hand, idealised antiquity as a universal model and, on the other, turned to it antagonistically and with the intention of detaching them- selves from it. We must note, however, that the civic humanist endeavour confined this contradiction to a model of cyclical history, derived from Polybius, in which the distance between the past and the present found its place within a scheme of recurrence and rebirth.[22] The civic humanist turn to political antiquity recognised the finitude of the city-state in terms of its rise and fall as an exemplary regime.[23] Likewise, the Renaissance notion of history, alongside those of literature and the arts, served to delimit a new epoch by evoking the birth, demise and revival of an exemplary cul- tural production, in other words the history of the West from its founding moment in antiquity through the Middle Ages to the Renaissance itself. Thus, while both currents envisioned the imperative of modernity in terms of a break with the ancient past, they also reconfirmed the timelessness of that past as a classic model that is meant to survive its time by inserting it in the cycle of foundation, death and revival.

By the late seventeenth century and throughout the eighteenth ancient history was set against modern times in order to sustain explicitly the idea of unrepeatable, finite time. At the onset of this period, the *querelle des anciens et des modernes* offered the first serious challenge to the transhistorical ideal of antiquity and, simultaneously, the first resolution to the contradiction

---

[20] Rice and Grafton 1994: 81.   [21] Pocock 2003. See also Pocock 1968.
[22] On this issue see Jauss 2005.
[23] On the theme of 'rise and fall' see Pocock 1999-2005 vol. III (2003).

of a tradition that was required to be, at once, historically situated and universal. The outcome of the quarrel in both France and England was a new temporalisation of classical antiquity, which was encapsulated in the newly coined notion of the 'relative classic': the work or form of cultural production whose founding role on a universal level was deemed to pass through its specificity and its appraisal by standards pertaining to its age.[24] This coinage concluded the conflict by offering a common ground wherein the two combatants would meet with one another peaceably. It allowed both the *modernes* to challenge the claim that antiquity was unique in founding the course of history and the *anciens* to defend the divergence of the Greek and Roman past from the new cultural visions and political imperatives of modern Europe.[25]

Over the eighteenth century the tension between the quest for historicisation and the exemplary status of the ancients became explicit in both philosophies of history and histories of antiquity. This move took shape as a radical change in the meaning of the idea of history, described by Koselleck's seminal essay 'Geschichte' as the birth of the concept of history as a singularity which linked various historical temporalities under a master category, the notion of history itself (*Geschichte selber*). This formulation implied that history acquired an omnitemporal character,[26] which brought together the three dimensions of time – past, present and future – in the form of a unity, while, simultaneously, maintaining their distinction. Indeed the possibility of recognising temporal difference, as Koselleck notes, was founded on the very idea of a singular idea of history. The times of history existed on the condition that one single history also existed; and it was this paradox that added a moral and teleological meaning to the category of history, which was now seen as universal in scope and narrative in its mode of articulation in time.[27]

We can begin to grasp this move if we follow closely Kant's 1784 essay 'Idea for a universal history from a cosmopolitan point of view' (*Idee zu einer allgemeinen Geschichte in weltbürgerlicher Absicht*), in which the course of historical time is marked by the ancient Greek and modern European boundaries. Kant structures the essay around the problem of defining a universal temporality. What is the idea of history, he asks, that would reveal the guiding thread of human historical development? Given that history represents nature's rational plan for humanity, how

---

[24] Jauss 2005: 345 and Levine 1991.
[25] For further discussion of the concept of the 'relative classic' in relation to the history of the temporality of the classic see Lianeri and Zajko 2008.
[26] On this category see Ricoeur 2004: 300.   [27] Koselleck 1975.

can one trace this universal trajectory through and beyond the 'planless conglomeration of human actions'? In attempting to respond to these questions Kant describes this (philosophical) idea of history as centred on a singular European historical time going back to Greek history and historical thought:

For if one starts with Greek history (*Geschichte*), through which every older or contemporaneous history has been handed down or at least certified; if one follows the influence of Greek history on the construction and misconstruction of the Roman state which swallowed up the Greek, then the Roman influence on the barbarians who in turn destroyed it, and so on down to our times; if one adds episodes from the national histories of other peoples insofar as they are known from the history of the enlightened nations, one will discover a regular progress in the constitution of states on our continent (which will probably give law, eventually, to all the others). If, further, one concentrates on the civic constitutions and their laws and on the relations among states . . . if, I say, one carries through this study, a guiding thread will be revealed.[28]

Greek history, in the dual sense of events and historiographical narrative,[29] becomes a founding moment as the medium through which all other previous and contemporary traditions enter the trajectory that leads to the history of the modern European states. But this position presupposes that a certain notion of history would be distinguished not only from historiographical traditions outside Greece, but also from the diversity defining Greek historical consciousness. The establishment of Greece as the founding moment of a global time-frame implies the effacement of categories of historicity that have challenged this inaugural position. It is necessary for Kant to pose a division between the philosophical idea, which he traces back to the Greek past, and the categories through which Greek thinkers, as we discussed in relation to Cambiano's chapter, raise doubt over the status of a founding moment. A history of Europe going back to Greek antiquity has therefore to be grounded in a concept of time which transcends Greek historical temporalities and acts to reorganise them around the category of origin. By the same token, this history has to transcend the diversity manifested in all subsequent European encounters

---

[28] Kant 1998: 46.

[29] Since around 1750 the fusion of the German terms *Geschichte* and *Historie*, and the absorption of the latter by the former implied that 'Greek history' designates here the intermingling of historio-graphical language and factual history. In other words it is the dual frame of Greek historiography and historical facts that sustains Greece's inaugural position in Kant's account of the philosophy of history that would render meaningful the cosmopolitan course of historical time. On the mutual contamination of the two terms and the absorption of the meaning of the latter by the former after the mid-eighteenth century, see Koselleck 1975.

with any construction of the Greek past. But this act of transcendence would create a fissure between the diversity of time-frames manifested in the European historiographical traditions and the singular philosophical 'idea' that makes Greece the starting point of a global history. The founding moment of European history would thus be split by the contestation of temporalities which are formulated within its limits.

It is precisely this condition – the externality of the idea of history to historiographical temporalities that dispute the singular course of time – which makes Kant doubt the validity of his proposition. So just before attempting to delimit the history that derives from his 'idea', he questions not only the unity of this narrative, but also the possibility of its construction:

It is strange and apparently silly to wish to write a history in accordance with an Idea of how the course of the world must be if it is to lead to certain rational ends. It seems that with such an Idea only a romance (Roman) could be written.[30]

The term *Roman*, as Jacques Derrida noted, conveys here an idea of fiction or novel which undermines Kant's appeal to rationality and philosophical history.[31] Narrative fiction, is not simply an alternative to historiography that challenges the legitimacy of a singular course of history; it is the rift lying at the centre of the idea of unified and unifying European time. *Roman* is both the model for narrativising the rational course of history and the 'other' of history, the fiction that violates the boundaries of historical thought.

Kant's use of the term *Roman* crystallised a metaphor that was already implicit in Gottfried Leibniz's description of the history of humanity as God's novel and was to be used by Wilhelm von Humboldt, among others, to define the task of the historian as that of representing each historical incident as part of a narrative whole.[32] Humboldt, like Kant, set Greece as the starting point of that narrative in order to define the temporality of the present. As Stefan Rebenich notes in this volume, Humboldt's 1797 review of the eighteenth century was centred on the course of world history: 'Where do we stand? Which part of its long and arduous path has mankind covered? Is it on a course that leads to the final destination?' But this line of questioning, as Rebenich shows, indicates more an attempt to reformulate the self-positioning of the present, than a prompt to endorse

---

[30] Kant 1998: 46.   [31] Derrida 2002: 333.
[32] Koselleck 2004c: 35. Indeed, as Koselleck points out, even Ranke's declared intention to show the past as it actually was (*wie es eigentlich gewesen*) did not completely reject the value of that narrative; and while Ranke distinguished his task from that of deciphering the universal time of history and inferring from it the course of the future, he did not consider these perspectives as being in conflict with one another. Koselleck 2004c: 36.

an established position for it within historical time. For Humboldt, as for Kant, the present was in motion, mankind was changing, walking towards its transformation; and it was precisely this movement that dictated the need for a philosophy of history designating a direction. This correlation, the perception of shifting time and the need for normative categories that would orient the present, led to a turn to the Greek past which, according to Rebenich, veered between historicist particularity and idealising normativity. Thus Humboldt did not evoke Greece as a stable, timeless model that was to be imitated; but neither did he reduce antiquity to the imperatives and conditions of the present. His aim was rather to enlist antiquity in the cause of a vision, which was meant to overcome the status quo. Greek history thus became pivotal to the move, sustained by Humboldt, among others, which sought to establish in Germany, and through it in Europe, new conceptions of education and *Wissenschaft*, but also of nation, state and society. Introduced into the German tradition, as both national and European past, the Greek heritage not only provided an alternative to the Franco-Latin hegemony in Europe, which became central to German national identity, but also articulated the cultural demands of an emerging bourgeoisie seeking to establish its domination: the conception of education as the key to self-perfection, the definition of new links between education and freedom, and the establishment of liberal principles in institutional organisation and social relations.

The late eighteenth- and nineteenth-century shift from Rome to Greece[33] entailed a transformation of European genealogies and a repositioning of ancient history that was to sustain the new institutions of representative democracy and civil society, but also of European colonialism and imperialism. This move was closely linked to the concurrent development of the historicist *Wissenschaften* and the challenge it posed to exemplary uses of antiquity and its quick identification with modern practices, including the practice of history writing. Already in the eighteenth century, histories of ancient Greece, as Giovanna Ceserani argues, manifest narrative timelines that attest to this challenge. Ceserani suggests reconsidering periodisations of modern accounts of ancient Greek history: 'when did modern historiography of ancient Greece start?', she asks, observing how previous attempts to answer this question, including Momigliano's, have been centred on the nineteenth century and, above

---

[33] On this issue see Turner (1981), (1989) concerning Britain, Avlami (2000) regarding France and Butler (1935) pertaining to Germany. On Germany, see further the bibliography referred to in Rebenich's chapter in this volume.

all, on George Grote's critical disengagement from the narratives of Greek historians. Yet, as Ceserani suggests, the beginnings of the modern historiography of Greece need to be stretched back to the narrative histories of the eighteenth century, which, far from merely repeating, 'pillaging' ancient sources, deployed a narrativised chronology which posed a division between ancient and modern historians.

Kostas Vlassopoulos takes the question of the origin of modern histories of Greece a step further by perspicaciously noting that the very fact of writing these histories over the eighteenth century was far from being self-evident. The first Greek history ever to be written in the modern period was by Temple Stanyan in 1707, that is, more than three centuries after the Renaissance's turn to the classical tradition, and long after the canonical status of classical drama and poetry had led to attempts to imitate them and compose novel works on the themes provided by the ancient models. Moreover, he argues, it was not until after the French Revolution that Greek history emerged as an autonomous field of research. The frame that sustained this development was multidimensional and does not allow the dissociation of historiography from wider philosophical and political queries that defined the relation between ancient and modern European history. Among them Vlassopoulos, following Koselleck, considers forms of temporality which emerged during the period Koselleck called the *Sattelzeit*, a time of crisis in European history extending approximately between the mid-eighteenth and the mid-nineteenth centuries, and defined by accelerated changes and the pluralisation of conceptions of historical time. As Vlassopoulos points out, the coexistence of conceptions of continuity and discontinuity between the ancient and the modern world formulated during this period had a clear political dimension: it reaffirmed the Eurocentric directions of the modern historiography of antiquity by proclaiming both the uniqueness of the Greek past and the special link between that past and modern Europe.

Nineteenth-century historicism and the development of 'historical science', as Ulrich Muhlack argues, brought about a break from earlier views of antiquity by questioning its normative significance. Focusing on the reception of Herodotus and Thucydides in Germany, Muhlack explores how the new insight into the historicity of human life, the conception of the 'world as history' crystallised against the background of the French Revolution, implied the consideration of each epoch as 'immediate to God', as Ranke put it; and yet simultaneously as having its special tendency and its own ideal which was incomparable with and untranslatable into others. Ranke's position advocated a disengagement from the classical past, and classical historiography in particular, which had begun to take shape in the previous century. However, no one pursuing this break before Ranke remained free from the normative readings of Herodotus and Thucydides. Historians such as Creuzer, Niebuhr, Gervinus and Roscher, but also Heeren and Droysen, who measured Greek historians by the criteria of modern historical science, also gave them a paradigmatic significance: they cited Thucydides as an example of modern epistemological procedures and distinguished themselves from ancient writers only on the basis of a higher level of reflexivity or consciousness. Ranke took the final step: he collapsed normative and historical judgements by construing the Greek historians as protagonists of a problem that they solved in their own time and each new era has to solve in its own manner.

The conjunction of breaks and continuities formulated by nineteenth-century historicism in relation to antiquity was tied inextricably to what Koselleck described as the contemporary social experience of 'acceleration of time'[34] – the distinctly modern experience of incessant, rapid and potentially revolutionary change that took shape after the mid-eighteenth century and throughout the nineteenth in the context of a capitalist economy demanding constant changes in the field of production, and of radical social transformations and upheavals associated with the establishment of modern bourgeois societies. If modernity, as Marshall Berman wrote, implied finding oneself in an environment that promised growth and transformation of one's self and the world, and which, simultaneously, threatened to destroy everything one may have had, known or been,[35] then historicism may be viewed as the temporality that expressed this idea of perpetual disintegration and rebuilding. At the same time, the historicist consideration of events as products of both a particular time and place, on the one hand, and the course of their development, on the other, also offered a frame of stability operating as a form of control over the maelstrom of change experienced in the modern world. The very idea of a context in this historicist sense entailed the construction of a field in which transformation could be postponed and unity could be attained in the face of a society's inevitable fate of death.[36]

It was precisely this perception of time and history that established the idea of Europe as a frame that did not challenge the opposition between classical antiquity and modern times, but rather came to complete it. It is

---

[34] Koselleck 1975 and 2004c [1979].   [35] Berman 1983: 15.
[36] On the concept of 'fate of death' see especially Pocock 2003.

indicative that even Ranke, as Muhlack points out, did not merely declare the distinctness of Greek and Roman historians, but also compared himself to Thucydides and claimed that, although ancient historians could not be surpassed, since their achievement was specific to their age, he hoped to attain an equivalent standard in modern European historiography. It was the evocation of this standard that allowed historicism to legitimise the claims of European modernity to have set a universal model of historical thought.

Still, this claim already included an idea of discontinuity that was soon to undermine its coherence. By the end of the century, as Neville Morley argues, Nietzsche's challenge to historicism, and to the idea of historical knowledge as an end in itself, outlined an understanding of history that stressed the interlinking of past and future as this was mediated by the needs of the present. Focusing on the notion of the monumental, which Nietzsche defined in opposition to antiquarian and critical history, Morley explores how the 'preoccupation with the classics and the rarities of earlier times' came to be seen by Nietzsche as a mode of engagement with and articulation of power: an inspiration to men of power to perform great deeds and to the weak to subvert current forms of authority. But this encounter was, simultaneously, a means of effacing the untimeliness of the ancient past and its critical function in the present. While Nietzsche was alert to the risks of monumental historiography, he also recognised it as inescapable for a historiographical operation that turns to the past in order to act for the future. After the nineteenth century, as Morley suggests through a reading of Alois Riegl's and Michel Foucault's treatments of the monumental, Western historical thought has tended to suppress this necessity in favour of a critical model going back to a context-bound account of evidence that is presumably detached from the present. Yet such an approach, the chapter contends, does not, in fact, expunge the monumental from the realm of history writing, but rather obscures the historians' responsibility for their role in the construction or subversion of monuments, in other words, for the political, ethical and psychological consequences of bringing the past into the present.

The definition of monumental history as divided by the struggle between the 'powerful' and the 'weak' implied, by necessity, a radical uncertainty as to the outcome of the ensuing links between past, present and future. Even though Nietzsche stressed that the weak offer an inauthentic account of the monumental, wherein the turn to the great deeds of the past would become 'the theatrical costume in which they pretend that their hate for the powerful and the great of their time is a fulfilling admiration for the strong and the great of past times',[37] he accounted for their voice as an alternative to a dominant view of history. He thus admitted, even though indirectly, that no single encounter with the past can secure its domination over the present. By the same token no engagement with antiquity can establish a singular historicity that relates the ancients to a certain space and historical endpoint of the present. Instead, what Nietzsche anticipated was the indeterminacy of final contexts, the transitory temporalities which framed the sense of history over the twentieth century and which invited reflection on the historicity of every form of historicisation which links antiquity and modern times.

UNFOUNDING TIMES

What are the implications of critical historiography for the current study of Greek and Roman histories and historicities? In studying Greek and Roman accounts of time and history, the problem we must encounter is not only how to interpret concepts and practices which are different from our own, but also how to formulate our methodological engagement with this difference. Can we examine ancient historical thought without reducing the manifold temporalities embedded in it to a mere object of the historian's categories for which past consciousness would remain a thing to be identified, rather than an interlocutor that may challenge those categories? In pursuing an account of Greek historical thought centred on the polis, Katherine Clarke aptly observes the multiplicity of time-frames and positions from which history was constructed:

The answer to the question 'who had the right to tell the polis its past?' must be manifold: tragic and comic dramatists, orators, native and visiting historians, rhapsodes, exegetae, and statesmen all offered versions for the polis to reject or to accept through acclamation.[38]

The recognition of this plurality poses the need to expand and reformulate the meaning of categories deployed in order to understand the ancient historiographical traditions. Greek and Roman historical thought, Clarke suggests, remains irreducible to a genealogy that begins with Herodotus and Thucydides, and excludes all alternative historicities, including those indicating conflictual views of history within the limits of the polis.

The same diversity becomes evident if we approach ancient historians through the mediation of categories that interrogate the unity of Western historical thought. The book's third Part 'Unfounding Time in and

---

[37] Nietzsche 1983: 72.   [38] Clarke 2008: 370.

through Ancient Historical Thought' explores this diversity from a twofold perspective. On the one hand, it examines Greek and Roman ideas of history as defined by contradictions and conflicts that challenge the unity of the 'classical foundations' of modern historiography. On the other hand, it attempts to locate these contradictions within historical time and examine their constitution as products of a battle that inscribed into victories traces of defeated alternatives and notions of history that can still challenge the genealogies that established them as origins.

From this perspective, Rosalind Thomas focuses on Thucydides as narrator of radical social change and the collapse of society that he himself experienced in his own times. In opposition to other Greek writers and thinkers, who did not devote much attention to the breakdown of social order and *nomos* (custom and law), Thucydides' description of *anomia* (lawlessness) as the result of the plague and then the further stages of disintegration pertaining to *stasis* (civil conflict), suggests a focus on temporal breaks that not only reversed Greek theories of social cohesion and progress, but also presented strife as an alternative narrative frame to the established narrative of war. Thucydides, as Thomas suggests, approached *stasis* in terms of a universalism that offered a model for all time, while choosing to describe war in terms of *akribeia* – the detailed description of particulars that ensures historical accuracy. In doing so he not only set forth a coarticulation of historiographical models that were often construed as mutually oppositional by modern historians, namely universalising and particularist views of history, but he also questioned contemporary conceptions of war as the agent of social change. From Homer to Herodotus, war was the stuff of great narrative; and Thucydides' rivalry with his predecessors made him part of that tradition. At the same time, his studies of social disintegration offer insights into a view of history that transcends the limits of political temporalities and allows the theorisation of alternative views of time as well as the interlinking of historiographical and social times.

The complexity of the Greek historiographical tradition is also the subject of Jonas Grethlein's study of Herodotus' and Thucydides' stance towards exemplary uses of the past. This inquiry explores how the two historians break with other commemorative genres by deploying *exempla* for critical, rather than legitimising or glorifying, purposes, and by introducing into their narratives forms of action that challenge the temporalities of exemplary historiography. However, this challenge, Grethlein notes, needs to be distinguished from the forms of historicism that question the use of *exempla* after the eighteenth century CE. The ancient historians' questioning of examples stemmed from the recognition of the role of chance in shaping history, rather than a conception of the division between past and present. So both of them maintained a sense of historical continuity by embedding all changes that they took into account within the framework of what was already known. By contrast the modern critique of exemplary history expressed the feeling that the future is open and can be shaped, while contingency had to be construed not so much as chance, but rather as freedom to act.

The difference between ancient and modern forms of historicism not only challenges the unity of Western historiographical genealogies, as Grethlein aptly suggests; it also presents a temporalisation of history whose focus on chance as a force that lies beyond human capacities to shape the world may offer a necessary supplement and important limitation to the modern historiographical perception of history as controlled by human action.[39] The challenge posed by ancient history to modern historicities is also the subject of Ellen O'Gorman's insightful chapter, which returns to Roman deployments of repetition and exemplarity, and their difference from modern historical thought. The chapter juxtaposes ancient and modern notions of exemplarity, while deploying each tradition as the entry point into the critique of the other. It argues that modernity did not simply use the trope of exemplarity in order to configure a relation with the ancient past; rather modernity's relation with the past was marked by the difference between the ancient and the modern uses of this trope. This recognition of difference makes it possible to turn to the theory and practice of exemplary thinking in ancient Rome as a view on history that infuses the present with the complex temporalities of subjective pasts and futures, and can inform the ways in which political modernity, and Marx in particular,[40] engaged with exemplarity in an attempt to create new visions of the modern.

The exploration of temporalities which interrogate modern genealogical visions of antiquity by Michael Williams turns to Christian historiography, and particularly Sulpicius Severus' engagement with ancient history in his *Chronicle*, written at the turn of the fifth century CE. Sulpicius offered a historiographical perspective that highlighted what Williams calls 'authorial time', that is, the narrative temporalities for which the historian takes final responsibility, as opposed to the time-frames established by narrative structures posed by authoritative texts, such as the Scriptures. By bringing

---

[39] Bernard Williams attributes a similar role to Greek tragedy in which the 'horrors of the world' are presented as lying beyond human capacity to establish a moral order and which allow Greek tragedy to challenge and qualify the aim of moral philosophy to construe the world as safe for well-disposed people. See Williams 2006c.

[40] Cf. Prawer (1976) and Lekas (1988) on Marx's engagement with antiquity.

together the classical and the Christian pasts in a way that differed from the chronographical tradition of Eusebius and Jerome in that it integrated the two traditions into a single story, Sulpicius set aside all claims to priority of one of them over the other: Christianity filled the gaps in the classical past no more than the classical tradition could be used to supplement or even correct Christian history. This hybridity, while apparently sustaining the authority of Scripture in designating the course of history, gave rise to the significant claim that it was the language of the historian, as the product of guidance by biblical authors, but also as a medium that allows the rewriting of those authors, which had to be trusted.

Sulpicius' encounter with authoritative temporalities posed a question that became explicit in modernity's encounter with antiquity: what kind of authority is at stake when we formulate, contest or dispute established forms of historical time? How does change in the authority of time relate to breaks in the field of social history? Revolutionary breaks in history, as Giorgio Agamben observes, are never centred on merely changing the world; their aim is also – and perhaps predominantly – to change time.[41] But from which perspective is the connection between the two fields possible? This question invites us to return to the aporia which we examined as constitutive of all historiographical engagements with time: if the history of temporalities becomes central to the understanding of revolutionary breaks in social history, how can we understand breaks in the history of times?

We have so far introduced the idea of reversing the order in which we approach time in relation to social change: instead of coming to time through the observation of such changes and exploring forms of historical consciousness by placing them in specific social contexts, we began to see, on the one hand, how ideas of time offer a key perspective for making sense of such contexts and, on the other, how these ideas are themselves defined by a dynamic that relates to, but does not straightforwardly correspond with, social change. A characteristic of historical time, as Koselleck has noted 'is its constant reproduction of the tension between social history and its transformation on the one hand, and its linguistic articulation and processing on the other. All history feeds on this tension'.[42] This dual link can now be apprehended as an orientation of historical temporalities towards practice, towards a certain 'politics of time'. Dominant and marginalised temporalities formulated in antiquity as well as the rise and decline of concepts such as ancient history, classical or modern times

[41] Agamben 1993: 89.   [42] Koselleck 1998.

have been interventions within a field of antagonistic politics of time: the framework in which competing historiographies and philosophies of history have attempted to intervene in social history by engaging with established perceptions of the past and the visions of the future inherent in them.

To explore the diversity of conceptions of time that comprised Europe's relation to its past and to identify the mechanisms that reduced this diversity to a linear and presumably universal trajectory of historical thought is not only to pursue an alternative vision of time and history, but also to pursue a critical understanding of modern European imperialist politics. However, one final question remains: can the task of critique negate the modern quest to define a universal temporality without simultaneously abandoning the potential offered by the modern idea of universality to criticise local forms of domination, inequality and injustice? Ancient history as a time-frame that legitimised the West's appeal to a global historical and historiographical significance was conceivable only from a perspective that claimed to transcend its object, including all local historical temporalities produced in the context of that object. What Europe has defined as 'universal' has been no more than the projection of one or another aspect of our 'local' standards. Still this notion of universality has also informed a perspective from which critics of European domination, especially in postcolonial traditions,[43] but also within Europe, have criticised Western imperialism by demonstrating the parochial and non-linear status of every 'stage' of European genealogies. By indicating the parochialism of Europe's historical time-frames – i.e. classical antiquity, Renaissance, modern times – from the viewpoint of an inclusive global history, universality could thus break teleology apart.[44] Likewise, the idea of universality generated by modernity's turn to antiquity has sustained an ideal of humanity that has hitherto been indispensable to critiques of the West's violation of this ideal in historical practice.

We may certainly illuminate the ancient past by applying our own local standards to it, seeing it in ways that it may not have seen itself, just as the past may illuminate the present, enabling us to see ourselves as we might otherwise not have been able to. But if we want to stand in a political relation to that past, which seeks to criticise the forms of exclusion and injustice that have been sustained by it, can this criticism be reduced to an encounter between localities? Are not localities bound to thrust the self into explosive encounters with other people and other peoples, and to

[43] See Chakrabarty 2000: 254.   [44] On this issue see Osborne 1995.

undermine the ideal of universal human solidarity and interconnectedness? The idea of humanism that arose from the modern engagement with antiquity has not been – and does not have to be – the exclusive possession of an imperialist and colonial Europe. Greek and Roman histories, as Oswyn Murray observed, have not only entered European thought as tools of domination and oppression; they have also 'been fashioned and understood as a counter-culture and a refuge from the dominant world-view'.[45]

To engage with this dual legacy one must thus struggle to position oneself in the tension between two different temporalisations of antiquity. On one side, there is the universalising evocation of Greek and Roman history as the origin of a time-frame which legitimised the modern European imperialist and colonial enterprise; but which also helped to sustain ideas of human solidarity and interconnectedness that challenged Western historical lineages. On the other side, there are interruptions to Europe's unifying and imperialist genealogies: the counter-images of ancient history, which produced estranged and estranging visions of the ancient past and its links to the present. A critical history of Western historical times needs to encounter these directions as a twofold trajectory, whose parts cannot be separated from one another. It is on this condition that Western engagements with ancient and modern temporalities can offer a critique of Eurocentric historiographies of the Greek and Roman pasts. By highlighting the resistance of those pasts to unifying European narratives and the ruptures within the narratives themselves, a history of Western historical times can ground interpretations of the European past in what John Dunn called the problem of closing the context:[46] the consideration of the closure that inaugurates the historiographical operation by dividing past and present as a problem that needs to be posed anew and retrospectively, thus directing the history and politics of both past and present time.

---

[45] Murray 2001: 18.   [46] Dunn 1980a: 27.

Theorising Western Time: Concepts and Models

CHAPTER I

Time's authority

François Hartog

Time and authority: how does time have authority? This is the question I would like to address. In "What is authority?" Hannah Arendt shed much light on the link between authority and the past. Authority, she reminded us, is Roman in both word and concept, while Greek political philosophy never established such a concept. For the Romans, what mattered was the foundation's sacred nature: *auctores imperii Romani conditoresque*, as Pliny put it, the initiators, founders *and* guarantors of Roman power. If we look at the etymology, authority is that which serves to "augment" the foundation, *auctoritas* relating to the verb *augere* (to augment, grow, increase): it is what makes things grow. And in the absence of that first authority, that of the founding fathers, what stood yesterday and stands today is the *auctoritas majorum*.[1]

Pursuing these ideas, from the point of view not of authority[2] but of time, or rather the interrelation of the two, I would like to explore the links woven between types of temporality and types of authority.[3] Is authority necessarily linked to the past; can only the past create authority? Before now, coincidences have been identified between crises of or within time and questions of authority, but is there more to this than pure coincidence? Three questions arise here for the reader, with an inevitably programmatic, if not schematic appearance. Firstly, following on from Arendt about authority and the past: can we see the past as a source of authority, promoter and producer of authorities, and also as bearer, naturally, of that growth action (*augere*) that the etymology of the word conveys? Secondly, authority and the future: when, from the end of the eighteenth century onwards, the future became the dominant temporal category, did it not find itself taking on the same value of primacy that had until then been attached to the past? Lastly, authority and the present: in a time when

---

[1] Arendt 1972: 121–85.   [2] See Revault d'Allonnes 2006.
[3] For a first version of this idea see Hartog 2007: 23–33.

the present seems to have become an insurmountable horizon, is it not becoming established as a source, or even the only source, of authority? Does this authority given to time arise from what we might call an abuse of authority, or is it in the long run nothing more than different ways for the societies involved in history to live in their time and, above all, to find resources to act upon that time? The *tyranny* of the past has frequently been denounced, as has, still more recently, that of the future, while today is it not rare to take it out on the immediate, or simply the present?

THE AUTHORITY OF THE PAST AND *RESTITUTIO*

Authority and the past: this is the first association that comes to mind, being the most famous and the most ancient. The past is perceived as the compost of tradition and as a resource for a history based on examples and imitation, following the model of the *historia magistra vitae*. A few observations taken from different sources will suffice to remind us of their forms, and to inspire us to question their very simple evidence.

There is no shortage of pointers. Rome presents itself to us, as cradle and glorification of *auctoritas*: Rome, as according to Arendt, but above all according to Varro and Cicero. Authority thus conferred on the past would continue, more or less, until Tocqueville wrote up its death certificate in the aftermath of the French Revolution. "When the past no longer lights up the future, the spirit walks in darkness," he notes in his conclusion to *Democracy in America*.[4] Could we imagine Cato or Cicero risking a similar remark in the final stages of the Republic? First of all the category of future needs to have split away and gained a certain autonomy. Note, indeed, that Tocqueville writes "the future" ("l'avenir"): this is not about enlightening the present, but rather what is to come. The old regime of historicity was, precisely, when the past lit up a future continuation of the past, without repeating it or going beyond it. Then, the spirit did not walk in darkness.

This Rome is that of the *mos majorum*: *mos* is said to "lead to practice" (Varro). It is custom with the force of law, but without the need for a law. "We consider the right which has been consecrated by time (*vetustas*) to have been founded on custom, because it receives the consent of all without the sanction of a law."[5] This is the Rome which knew, amongst other things, how to conduct funerals for great people, with the role of emulation devolved to the masks of the ancestors, that were brought out for the occasion and formed part of the funeral procession. "Is there anyone

---

[4] de Tocqueville 1985, II: 399.   [5] Moatti 1997: 32.

who on seeing these images together would not be spurred on by such a sight?" notes Polybius, a good observer who knew how to appreciate the force of this ritual. Sallust also, more generally, recalled this mechanism of imitation:

I have often heard say that Quintus Fabius Maximus, Publius Scipion and other illustrious people of our city would tell how each time they looked at their ancestral portraits, their souls would be set ablaze by their honour. Probably, they said, it was not that the wax or clay had such properties, but that at the memory of things past a flame lit up in the hearts of these exceptional men and would not calm itself until their own honour had matched their reputation and glory.[6]

The contemplation of images and the solemn exhibition of them on the occasion of the mourning that strikes the family and so too the city, perpetuate the authority of the example. This is renewed, or rather, remains, on the horizon of the present day: in the present or in a past with which we find ourselves on an equal footing.

For Sallust, who has been reduced to a forced otium, the happy time of imitation or glorious imitation is no longer valid once it has been reduced to a forced *otium*, and the Republic is dying. Nowadays, in so far as there is still imitation, its object is the vices of the past: it is far less a case of competing with the virtues of our ancestors as with their riches and ostentatious expenditure. This crisis period is accompanied by the feeling of time passing, or time that has passed: *tempus fugit*. "Time (*vetustas*) wears away and carries away everything. That which we have seen as young and beautiful becomes old and ugly," writes Varro – including the Republic. Time dulls our memories and forgetfulness looms ahead. From then on there is a "time before" that grows ever more distant. It is here that we see the importance of the ancient approach and of a figure like Varro, precisely as an authority in a time of crisis, as a substitute: he picks up on what we knew before without ever having learned it, but that we no longer know. Yet beware, we must not succumb to the attractions of a simple *curiositas* regarding the past. Cicero affirmed time and again the value of the *auctoritas* of the past, precisely because we must keep imitation of the great examples in our view.

Livy believed that, in service to the *restitutio* policy wished for by Augustus, "each person should pay passionate attention to what life and customs were, for men and for their behaviour, in peace as well as in war, thanks to which the empire was born and has grown":[7] growth that brings primacy with it must justly create authority (again). In fact, Augustus presented

---

[6] Sallust, *Bellum Iug.* 5–6.   [7] Livy, *Ab urbe condita* 1.8.

himself as Rome's *restitutor*, re-founder, or new Romulus. His *Res gestae* witness to this in great detail. By restoring the ancient temples of the city, in particular, he was not concerned with heritage or with historical monuments, but with the legitimization of a new present order, taking his authority from a reconstructed past, or more exactly, a past newly consecrated by he who, as the great pontiff, is time's master. We can rely on Tacitus' judgement of this moment: "the ancient names were the same" but "once the political regime had been transformed, nothing, no part of the old customs remained intact any longer."[8]

Any process of *restitutio* is in its very intentions presentist, because its purpose is to act in and on the present time. Nevertheless, such an operation looks into the past (the founders' past, be they mythical or real) for the *growth* that it feels is necessary in order to become established. By making out of what has gone before it a past that serves as a resource and brings value and authority, it becomes an operation for times of crisis. It takes a gap (the previous Republic) as its starting point and derives part of its strength from that: the past's grandeur *vs.* the present's mediocrity. Then, whilst continually emphasizing that, it seeks to bridge the gap through transfer. The new beginning is a recommencing, and takes its strength, or its authority, precisely from being such. In the end, the *restitutio* can be seen as an operation that serves as *captatio* and *translatio* of the past authority onto that of the present, though on behalf of a past that it makes its own.

Christianity and the Church: authority and the past?

Rome provides a key example of the authority of the past, both for herself and for her later impact during the course of Western history. But she gives us authority in a complex and elaborate form, in which moments of crisis and questioning take root, and to respond to which we must apply a process like that of *restitutio*. To see a cruder version of this model, we can look at what Marcel Gauchet calls the time of the first religions, marked by "the absolute prevalence of a founding past and a sovereign tradition, which pre-exist all personal preferences and impose themselves irresistibly upon them as general law and common rule, forever valuable for everyone."[9] In such a model of holistic society, according to the definition proposed by Louis Dumont, "the exterior stands out as source, and the unchanging as rule."

---

[8] Tacitus, *Annales* 1.3.7.   [9] Gauchet 1985: 18.

What an upheaval Christian monotheism would introduce into this Roman pattern, since with it, within the space of a few centuries, a new age and a previously unseen authority were established. Does Jesus not appear as a rabbi who at once radically challenges the authority of the past and claims to represent it? Furthermore, summing up that past, he claims to fulfill it and to give it sense. All at once, the Book, which is now the Old Testament, finds its true authority, as a "preparation" for the coming of the Messiah. The Evangelists, Paul's Epistles, and more, consistently witness to this right up to Eusebius of Caesarea's *Evangelical Preparation*. From Moses to Jesus, from Law to faith, from the old manhood to the new, early Christianity never claimed to represent the model of *restitutio*, but that of *praeparatio*. The past is overtaken, remaining unfinished, and is preserved only in so far as it leaves itself open to interpretation in and by the present.

Is this, despite everything, a process of legitimizing the present? Surely; yet with the unbelievable assurance, or obstinate claim to proclaim the primacy of the messianic present that enlightens the past (and also the future). Once again, the past sees its authority confirmed, although according to the lines drawn and limits imposed by this conquering exegesis, always ready to cut between the letter and the spirit. It is not, as in the *restitutio*, the present that creates an allegiance with the past (in a more or less pompous or crafty manner), but the past that must (effectively) create its allegiance with the present. Conversion is not an empty word. Paul, the converted Pharisee, gave the strongest expressions of it from the outset, indeed the most violent and the most demanding.

With the Incarnation a new age opens up, in which the caesura between before and after can never again be bridged. This is precisely why all *restitutio* is now not only impossible, but absurd. Who would want to return to the ancient Alliance? The time that begins, opened up by the Passion and Resurrection, is conceived as an intermediate time that must last until the Second Coming. Hence it is of the present, but caught up in a tension between the 'already' and the 'not yet': everything has *already* been accomplished, but not everything has *yet* been concluded. It is also, says Augustine, the era of the world's old age: that of waiting, briefly we hope, for the end. Paul's words "forgetting what lies behind and straining towards what lies ahead" indicate the state of mind of the first communities. For the path that remains, faith in the risen Christ and the comfort of "do this in remembrance of me" should suffice. For the Eucharist is both a commemoration of that which having taken place once for all is now irreversibly past, and its repetition, realization, and *presentification*. So that, quite rightly, this past will never pass away, must never go by but will always remain present and active.

However, what happens to this when the wait grows longer, and when despite everything, the present of the life of Jesus becomes a past; when the last witnesses have gone, the apostles have disappeared and the Church becomes an institution? The weight of the *already* begins to increase, while the horizon of the *not yet* recedes. Faced with the numerous accounts that circulate and come to authorize sectarian practices, the Church is led to fix a canon of texts that will become its authority and will enable it to judge between orthodoxy and heresy. This had happened by the end of the fourth century. Even if the Church assigns itself the function, mission, and justification of being the authorized mediator of the word of God, nonetheless an apostolic age will take shape, a time of origins to which numerous reformers over the centuries, in particular Luther, would claim to return in a movement of *reformatio*. Thus legitimacy is found in the process of *restitutio*, to avoid forgetfulness and other divergences from the true tradition. More precisely, the pattern of *restitutio* combines with the ancient model of *historia magistra* as a source of examples for us to copy. The two converge in the imitation of Jesus. We claim to follow the past, and to rediscover it in its original purity, hence its indisputable authority; but at the same time this past is not entirely past, since each time we celebrate the Eucharist, Jesus is present and, indeed, the story of Salvation that he opened up to us has not yet been concluded. The return to the *already*, the reactivation of that *already* by the Church's mediation, with the aim of preparing us better for the *not yet*, is by no means backward-looking. The Church, as an institution, knows how to forge a link between past and present.

The humanists and the ancient past

The Renaissance period occupies an eminent position, because in it we see an entirely explicit revival of the Roman process of *restitutio*. If the issue at stake for the Italian humanists is not directly political power, as it was for Augustus, it is still no less important. The humanists present the revival of the Latin language and of the ancient monuments as a *restitutio* of Rome: a refoundation. More widely, through the fight for *belles lettres* and the defense of good study, this movement is about nothing less than the training and culture that a society chooses to make its goal. In which past will its elites find themselves; which part of history can they contemplate and imitate? We might think of Machiavelli taking Livy's first books as the object of his reflections.

Yet in this fight, there is one clearly defined opponent, the scholastic, and a much maligned time that they describe as the "intermediate period" or Middle Ages: an epoch of obscurity and ignorance over which we must somehow step, or that we must somehow sweep away, in order to reach the shining past of antiquity and cast light on the present. In denouncing the vices of contemporary education, Machiavelli urges one not to hesitate in turning to antiquity's example: "imitation seems impossible, as if heaven, the sun . . . and men were different from what they had previously been."[10] From Petrarch to Erasmus, the *studia humanitatis* are conceived *in actum* or *ad vitam:* for life and action. No question of a dead, book-based knowledge. Reading and publishing the ancient writers is carried out with a view to inviting the present day to rise to the heights of the antique past. If at this time we are "building on an ancient word,"[11] we are looking at a new world.

If the humanist *curiositas* leads towards recognition of the ancient past's *auctoritas*, this *restitutio* does not mean to challenge the Christian authorities, or at least not the authority of Christ and the Scriptures. But this same movement, in principle, aims to rediscover all the purity (and strength) of the apostolic period and the full authenticity of the antique texts. This is what Erasmus did in becoming editor of the Gospels. It is a matter of philology. We understand that the Church had nourished a certain sense of mistrust with regard to Greek and had been swift to condemn several of its practitioners and zealots.[12] Therein lay a serious threat for its magisterium, since a return to the written source could enable us to understand the spirit from closer up, indeed as close as possible. Furthermore, turning towards pagan authorities whilst sticking firmly within a Christian sphere of reference is a particularly delicate exercise. Is it enough to "Christianize" them, by suggesting allegorical readings of them, or to interpret them by, one way or another, taking up the exegetic techniques used by the Christians long beforehand to capture the Bible? Here, potentially at least, we can see conflicts of authority that are also conflicts of temporality: antique past *vs.* biblical past.

AUTHORITY AND THE FUTURE

To move on from the authority of the past, with the strategic process of *restitutio* – the instigator of links between past and present – to the authority of the future, fits into the Western tradition of moving away from the "already" and towards the "not yet": abandoning the "already" to enter into

---

[10] Machiavelli 1952: 378.   [11] Rico 2002: 41.   [12] Saladin 2000: 9–11.

the "not yet." The sky falls to earth; the golden age of mythology will no longer be behind, but ahead; we are not looking at making it come back, so much as making it happen. Yet, while the return to the "already" as practiced by the humanists dwelt within, and indeed attempted to enrich and reinforce a Christian frame of thought, the espousal of the "not yet" was to be accompanied by Europe's own great movement of secularization, or rather it is itself the very form of secularization. We were able pinpoint its successive stages or, rather, point out the breakdown that it proclaimed.[13] For Hans Blumenberg, in fact, modern times can neither be reduced to the secularization of matters until now theological, nor be seen to fizzle out through proclaiming their self-foundation. In any case, supporters of the secularization thesis, in which teleology takes the upper hand over theology and progress overcomes eschatology, delegitimize modernity, since that thesis would simply have deluded itself. On the contrary, we ought to take the desire for breakdown seriously, in which, according to Blumenberg, the legitimacy of modern times lies, without of course misunderstanding the gaps between aim and achievement.[14]

As far as time's authority is concerned, once people think that they are making history, they become responsible for their future. The future grows in power. The "not yet," to use that expression one last time, tends from that point onwards to rule that which is and to calibrate that which has been: it is the measure of the past and the bearer of what must be. But how can we give this "not yet," this future, shape and strength? How can we move towards it? This matter, we know, is not answered in one day, or in one place. Let us make do, for the time being, with a few points of reference amongst the many possible.

Francis Bacon's *Instauratio magna* of 1620 presents us with a case study. *Instauratio* and no longer *restitutio*, although *instaurare* implies at once restoration and renovation. In *Roma instaurata*, published in 1446, Flavio Biondo praised the pope for "restoring and remaking the crumbled buildings" (*instauras reficisque*), while he himself put his pen to service in this restoration-institution, describing both ancient and Christian Rome. In the Vulgate, it has been noted that this word is already used to describe the restoration of the Temple of Solomon. "It may well be that in using this word, Bacon was implying an analogy between his own project and the renovation of Solomon's temple."[15] We find the king of the Hebrews again in *The New Atlantis*, his last text, where the house of learning and wisdom is precisely named "The House of Solomon." There,

---

[13] Löwith 2002.   [14] Blumenberg 1999: 11–19.   [15] Zagorin 1998: 76.

we reach the heart of an unfinished utopian narrative, deemed to "prove" the excellence and welldoing of the wise ones' power. Everything rests on their ability to "observe" nature and people (the House is called "the very eye of the kingdom"), but time is not itself the vehicle of authority (the past surely not, or no longer, and the future not as such).

In the epistle dedicating his *Instauratio magna* to the king, Bacon uses the dual expression *regeneratio et instauratio scientiarum* to define his ambition. To illustrate it, he chose a frontispiece that shows the ship returning in full sail to pass through the Pillars of Hercules. In this, modern science's desire to break away seems to be fully affirmed, and it is then further reinforced in the legend of the inscription: *Multi pertransibunt et augebitur scientia*, "Many will make the crossing and thus will science be increased." Furthermore, we have noted that just at the moment in which he breaks his moorings with the past and with the authorities of the ancient world, Bacon in fact draws his authority from the most ancient of texts: the Bible. The motto turns out to be, in fact, a reworking of the verse in Daniel: "Many shall pass to and fro, and knowledge shall be increased." According to Anthony Grafton's accurate observation, "Bacon could imagine a new world, not only because he knew new facts, but because he had inherited the most vivid of visions of novelty from what he thought the oldest of books. He understood the future in terms of prophecy."[16] Here we are on a threshold. This involves letting go of the past, setting ourselves free from the Ancients, and launching ourselves into the unknown, reliant on our observation, but not yet assigning to the future itself a value of primacy.

In a longer-term perspective, a second example comes to us in the long-established couple of the Ancients and Moderns.[17] Their history is punctuated by numerous disputes, up until the total upturning described by Charles Perrault in his *Parallèle des Anciens et des Modernes* (1688). The authority of the Ancients is given a pounding and it is no longer a question of *restitutio*. One of the leading threads of this process follows the theme of perfection. We move from affirming the absolute perfection of the Ancients to considering the respective degrees of perfection of these and the others: the Ancients have their own particular perfection, as do the Moderns. Then, the connection will be made on the grounds of perfectibility,[18] before we come to reason quite simply along the lines of progress, as presented in all its ordering power by Condorcet in his *Tableau historique des progrès de*

---

[16] Grafton 1992: 217.   [17] Hartog 2005.

[18] The word 'perfectibility' is used by Rousseau in his *Deuxième discours* (1964 [1755]: 142). It does not appear until 1771 in the *Dictionnaire de Trévoux*, and until 1798 in that of the Académie.

l'esprit humain, where he eventually sets out the "table of future destinies of the human species." Time, as such, thus comes into the picture and becomes a fully fledged player. It is no longer a time that carries everything away, but one that carries away because it also contributes, it is pregnant with the future. From then on, that which has had its day must give up its place: the past is in the past because it has been left behind, and the future takes on, independently, an ever stronger authority. Beside illustrious figures like that of Plutarch, a new race of great men appears: that of the precursors, the visionaries, the solitary geniuses. Before his time, the great man (in romantic clothing) becomes a midwife to the future that history will one day recognize.

A final example of these transfers can be found in the changes brought by the notion of utopia, introduced by Thomas More in 1516. More's island of Utopia is a radical elsewhere. Playing on the word, something that no early reader of More failed to do, it is both a nowhere (*outopia*) and a place of happiness (*eutopia*), while at the same time being a never (*oudetopia*).[19] It is set neither within a past gone by (a miraculously preserved golden age), nor within a far-off future (a prefiguring of what England could one day become). Situated in the New World, since we are told that Raphaël Hythlodée took part in the Vespucci voyages, it is set up as an other space and constitutes a parallel world. Between the two islands, Hythlodée presents himself as a line of provisional union and a guarantor, while his speech is organized like a game of mirrors. We go from the same (the social state of England) to the other, and this fictional other (a Commonwealth in the true sense, without private property) reflects a new image back onto that same. Yet the perfect island of the Utopians cannot take a place in a linear representation of time any more than it can be placed into geographical space. It functions only in a present moment that is fundamentally achronic. Time is no vehicle of authority.

It does become such a vehicle, as we know, from the end of the eighteenth century, when the Moderns definitively detach themselves from the Ancients and transfer onto their future the primacy (the growth) that until then they had attached to the past. Utopian ideas also follow this progression, making room for perfectibility and opening up to the theory of progress. The first work to take these themes on board is *The Year 2440* by Louis-Sébastien Mercier (1740–1814). Published in 1771, this book, which responded to the public's expectations, was a great success in France and across Europe. In its title alone, it manifests a temporalization of

---

[19] More 1965.

utopia, writing it into the timeline of universal history.[20] We are no longer elsewhere, in a parallel world, but ahead: 700 years later. Through the mediation of dreams, the narrator in fact finds himself projected from the end of the reign of Louis XV, right into the year 2440. Utopia becomes a story of anticipation, presenting what has not yet taken place as already realized. Simple progress in reason leads to the end of absolutism, of fanaticism, and of intolerance. The Bastille has long since vanished; the dream ends with a visit to a ruined Versailles. Yet the Parisians of the twenty-fifth century know, too, that progress is still possible, "we are hardly half way up the ladder," they say to their strange visitor. Far from being unmoving and perfect, Mercier's utopia is aware of its development. In short, the future still has some authority in store.

From this point on, we play with opening up new times as we had played, since the sixteenth century, with opening up space in the New World. We located different spaces there, even utterly utopian ones; we will deploy different times, frankly futuristic ones. No one has expressed the opening of this new messianic time more confidently than Saint-Simon:

The imagination of the poets has placed the golden age at the cradle of the human race, along with the ignorance and coarseness of the early times; the iron age was far more deserving of such a relegation. The golden age of humankind is by no means behind us, it is ahead, it is in the perfection of social order: our fathers have not seen it, our children will reach it one day: it is up to us to pave the way for them.[21]

Perfection is no longer seen as that of the Moderns, not even that of the Enlightened: it is yet to come.

During the course of the nineteenth century, utopia is very present, but the term is often employed in a pejorative, even offensive manner (after 1848), to stigmatize dangerous social fantasies. Marx and Engels would oppose "utopian socialism" with their "scientific socialism." Time's authority is not everything; or rather, it is embodied in the struggle of the classes. Revolution is certainly seen as a grand futuristic promise, but it is driven by the need to construct itself as a regulated development, scientifically established out of a present of poverty and struggles, and leading towards the kingdom yet to come.[22] In this economy of time, the present is invited to outdo itself, to reform and eliminate itself, and all this more and more quickly, measuring itself against the yardstick of the future that has not yet arrived, but from which the light shines and authority floods in. Of course,

[20] Mercier 1971 (1771, see the 1786 edition for the definitive text). See also Trousson 1998.
[21] de Saint-Simon 1966, I: 247–8.   [22] Gauchet 2003: 118.

this authority reserved for the future is (already) responsible for, or reflects on, its instigators, theoreticians, or eulogists, those who are already men of the future (visionaries, revolutionaries, men of the avant-garde, artists who want to break away from the past). Confronting them, introduced as conservers of what is, or supporters of a return to the authority of the past, stand the Ancients, the backward looking, the partisans of Restoration and Reaction, the counter-revolutionaries, or simply the bourgeois whose time will soon be passed.

In this pattern that has just been outlined in which authority is transferred to the future, what becomes of the *restitutio?* Does this model whose strength and flexibility we have seen still have a place, and if so, by dint of undergoing what sort of change? An interesting response to this was provided in the French Revolution, when, hurriedly and under the pressure of events, it had to draw up a doctrine of its heritage. How can we in fact, in what seemed like the space of one day (between 1789 and 1792) have moved from elimination to conservation? From deleting all traces of an execrated past authority to preserving, conserving them? To conserving what, exactly? What will turn into a heritage. On the one hand, the past's masterpieces had somehow been waiting for this day (the day of the Free Nation), to fully deliver the message of freedom that these works had borne since their creation. On the other hand, at the same time as it is enabled to possess them, the regenerated present has a duty to *restore* these traces: it has only received them to look after them. Restore them to whom? To time, as their eminent owner, suggests Etienne Boissy d'Anglas.[23] If there is *restitutio*, it is carried out in the direction of the future. It is not about finding legitimacy through making what there was return, but of putting ourselves in a position from which we can give back what we have received. *Restitutio* becomes a matter of inheritance and cultural logic. It goes hand in hand with the development of a particular space, namely the museum. There, certain exhibitions of the past, above all works of art, are assembled, conserved, but also distinguished. In that space, they are finally taken out of ordinary time so as to enter into what becomes the eternity of art. They are consecrated by time's authority.

AUTHORITY AND THE PRESENT?

Lastly, we come to the third element, which unites authority and the present time. What kind of "growth" can the present as such (in itself) come to

---

[23] Etienne Boissy d'Anglas cited in Pommier 1991: 153–66.

bear? The authority of the past lived on by imitation, so well that the past was not really one single past, but joined together the *no longer* and the *still there* in the everyday facts of tradition. In this set-up, *restitutio* appeared as the process that allowed us to legitimize a new present by turning back to the authority of the past. *Restitutio* took its power precisely from the gap that it otherwise claimed to bridge. In emphasizing new beginnings, we set ourselves up to begin again, as Augustus refounded Rome.

With the period opened up by Christianity, comes a first example of the present loaded with authority. But the past retains a place, finding itself involved in serving this present in terms of *praeparatio*. We may have moved on from it, but we have also maintained it, by putting it back into its true place. As for the present itself, caught in the founding tension between the "already" and the "not yet," it is a messianic present in the process of being rewritten in a Story of Salvation (at any moment the "not yet" may rejoin the "already" in the final Coming). We have seen how *restitutio*, as the revival of the original and critical position (*reformatio*), nevertheless rediscovered a place and an efficacy there: such that the various reformers have never ceased to turn to it.

In order that, with modern times, the authority of the future can become established, we need to see some changes taking place. A perception of the past as a time long gone, left behind to the point of no return, results from our realization of a break with that past. It no longer has any relevance except in so far as it has produced precursors, and its surviving traits that subsist or resist are doomed to fade and disappear ever more quickly. There is no longer any question of returning to it: from now on if we learn, it is from the future. Thus Tocqueville, who looked at France from America, in other words from its own future, in order to grasp better the irresistible course of the movement towards equality, saw himself as a "lookout" who wanted to "dream of the future." A man of the Ancient regime, he knew better than most how to project himself into the future, how to learn to look *from* a viewpoint in the future. The voyage to America makes it possible to carry out a new experiment of *historia magistra*, a transfer of authority by which the future takes the place that up until then had been given to the past. Soon enough, the utopia of revolution and its many futuristic manifestos would bear thorough witness to this reversal. Henceforth, it is the present and no longer the past that is seen as preparing for the future. This is really its principal *raison d'être*; it has no consistency of its own, no authority. It is courier to the future.

This is what has become of the economy of time in the last thirty odd years. The authority of the future has disintegrated, first and foremost within old Europe. This is not the place to begin to describe such a broad phenomenon with its multiple components. To keep with the theme of time, we have seen the expression "crisis of time" first appear, and become more and more common.[24] The main feature of this crisis seems to be a growth in power to the category of the present, as if the present had become its own horizon, as if there was nothing left but the present, without past or future, or perhaps fabricating the past and future that it needs each day: an encompassing and omnipresent present. Tocqueville had already made a connection between the advance of democracy and a questioning of all structures of temporality:

Democracy not only makes man forget his ancestors, it also hides his descendants from him and separates him from his contemporaries; it constantly brings him back to himself alone and eventually threatens to shut him away completely within the solitude of his own heart.[25]

It is clear that democratic emancipation brought with it new relationships with time, beginning with the decline of the past's authority, to the profit of an authority conferred upon the future, as we have seen. Yet, today, the progress in individualism experienced by Western societies, with the many forms of disconnection that accompany it, coincides with a revocation of the future's authority. The future is no longer a promise but a threat, while there is now no question of trying to reactivate the authority of the past. Could this contemporary present become a vehicle for the primacy that was once conferred on the past and, more recently, on the future?

Having become a standard-bearing term, the present is what we must follow, or towards which we should devote our energies. We must have concern for the present, live in the present, observe it, understand it and explain it ever better and more quickly, in order to understand ourselves and to know how to respond immediately to its injunctions. Certain historians, practitioners of a "history of present time" see themselves as couriers of the present: in charge of "explaining the present to the present." *Urgency* is the element that is more and more imposed by a present become omnipresent. From now on, utopia is neither elsewhere nor ahead, no futurist mirror or mirage. Instead, it is repatriated in the present and resides, as Marcel Gauchet notes, in the gap between the principles that our societies uphold and the reality of their functioning. From it results the possibility of an infinite denunciation, caught between "that should be different" and "that could never be different."[26] In order to respond better still to the injunctions

---

[24] Hartog 2003.   [25] Tocqueville 1985, II: 10.   [26] Gauchet 2003: 120.

of the present, every person needs to be more and more flexible and mobile. Meanwhile politicians, who no longer have the time to be visionaries, never stop running after the present, running the risk of being transformed into a presentist contortionist, with the corresponding authority: ephemeral.

Are these few quick sketches sufficient to conclude, in a present that would create authority, indeed that would have itself sole source of authority? Probably not. Yet the route along which we have just come invites us, at the very least, to ask the question. In this, our own present, neither *restitutio* nor rupture, which are two inverse, symmetrical ways of structuring the past, the present, and the future, seem to have a place.[27] The first confers primacy upon the past, the second on the future. To us, only the present remains, with the diagnosis of crisis that is frequently posited, here and there: "crisis of time," "crisis of authority, and now simply crisis."

Translated by Anna M. Osborne

[27] *Restitutio* and rupture are not mutually exclusive. Real history has been seen to experience a mix of the two, for example during the French Revolution.

CHAPTER 2

Exemplarity and anti-exemplarity in early modern Europe

Peter Burke

The principal aim of this chapter is to discuss the relation between historical thought in the Renaissance and François Hartog's three regimes of historicity, thinking with and occasionally against his central concept. To anticipate the conclusion, the chapter will argue that historical thought and writing in early modern times (more or less 1350–1750) had distinctive characteristics of its own. It was a kind of regime within Hartog's spacious first regime, extending from Homer to Chateaubriand or from the *Achsenzeit* to the *Sattelzeit*.

One of the major features of this first regime is the idea of history as a storehouse of *exempla* offering a guide to life: *historia magistra vitae*, as Cicero wrote in his treatise *De oratore*. Like the late Reinhard Koselleck, Hartog argues that early modern European readers and writers believed in what he calls 'the authority of the past'.[1] Like their classical and medieval predecessors, these readers and writers believed in a usable past, claiming or assuming that history offered a repertoire of *exempla*. The assumption was abandoned after (and in part thanks to) the events of 1789, which offered the prospect of a future so different from the past that earlier models became irrelevant. Hence Koselleck speaks of the 'dissolution' (*Auflösung*) of the Ciceronian *topos* in the course of what he called the *Sattelzeit* of the late eighteenth century, the frontier zone between traditional and modern culture.[2]

For this reason, this chapter will focus on *exempla*, contrasting two views that coexisted in the early modern period. The majority of writers and readers – so far as the views of readers can be recovered – continued to recognise the value of examples from the past as guides to conduct in the present, thus supporting the narrative offered by Koselleck and Hartog. However, there was also a minority view – shared by some distinguished writers and thinkers – that denied or criticised the applicability to the

---

[1] Above, p. 34ff.   [2] Koselleck 2004a; Hartog 2003.

Renaissance and post-Renaissance of ancient *exempla* or even the relevance of *exempla* in general. The cases for exemplarity and anti-exemplarity will therefore be discussed in turn.

EXEMPLARITY

The first point to make is that the notion of *exemplum* is not as clear or simple as it may look. In the early modern period, the term had a range of meanings, ranging from 'example' in the modern sense, adduced to support a generalisation, to the better-known and more common moral meaning of an action worthy of imitation, whether for moral or for political reasons.

The second point is that the motives for reading and writing about the past cannot be reduced to the search for moral and political models. In his well-known survey of humanist historiography, Eric Cochrane notes that chronicles and histories might also be written for entertainment, or to praise the author's family or city, or to escape from the problems of the present.[3]

However, there can be little doubt that the Ciceronian phrase *historia magistra vitae* was a Renaissance *topos*, quoted again and again.[4] In Italy, for instance, the great historian Francesco Guicciardini copied out the famous passage from Cicero about the value of history and placed it at the beginning of the manuscript of his *Storia d'Italia*. In England, the title page of Sir Walter Raleigh's *History of the World* (1614) showed the figure of History (labelled with the Ciceronian phrase), holding up the world and treading down Death and Oblivion.

Magistra vitae was also a faithful summary of what Renaissance humanists in particular believed to be one of the main reasons for writing and reading history. History, like poetry, was viewed as a kind of applied ethics, offering both positive examples for readers to imitate and negative ones for them to avoid. The advantage of the concrete example was that it appealed to the emotions and so acted as a greater stimulus to virtuous action than a general precept. Petrarch, for example, wrote to his friend Giovanni Colonna that 'Nothing is more moving than the examples of famous men' (*Nihil est quod moveat quantum exempla clarorum hominum*).[5]

Again, the Florentine humanist Coluccio Salutati, for instance, presented history as a stimulus to virtue, or at any rate to the more ambiguous *virtus*: 'For we are incited by an *exemplum* and virtually impelled to virtue by

---

[3] Cochrane 1981: 13–17.   [4] Landfester 1972.
[5] Hartog, this volume, 'The humanists and the ancient past'; Stierle 1998: 583.

its stimulus' (*incitamur enim exemplo et quodam quasi stimulo ad virtutem impellimur*). For his part, Salutati's friend Leonardo Bruni suggested that reading history taught prudence, allowing the reader to learn at the expense of others, *ex alienis periculis*.[6]

Given these views, it is scarcely surprising to find that Plutarch's collection of biographies of Greek and Roman heroes should have been received with such enthusiasm during the Renaissance. It was studied in schools, in the famous school of the humanist Vittorino da Feltre in Mantua, for instance, in the leading Calvinist school in Geneva, the Academy, and in the schools of the Jesuits. It was translated into Italian, French, Spanish, English and German.[7] The life of Alexander by Quintus Curtius was translated into Italian, Spanish, French and English, and it seems to have been an inspiration to a number of rulers and commanders of the period.[8]

Again, the collection of memorable deeds and sayings compiled by Valerius Maximus was one of the classical texts most frequently printed and translated at the Renaissance. At least eight editions in Latin were produced in the 1470s alone, followed by translations into French (1485, 1548), German (1489, 1533), Spanish (1495) and Italian (1504, 1539).[9]

The translations of Valerius Maximus were accompanied by imitations that often copied his arrangement of examples by virtues such as *fortitudo* and the distinction between classes of example (in his case between Roman and non-Roman). In his *Exempla* (1507) Marcantonio Sabellico, for instance, historian to the Venetian Republic, separated 'pagan examples' (*ethnica exempla*) from Jewish and Christian ones, while the Venetian priest Giambattista Egnazio, in *De exemplis* (1554) separated Venetian examples from the rest, presenting doge Lorenzo Loredan, for instance, as an example of *fortitudo* and doge Francesco Foscari as an example of *patientia*. The interest in *exempla* seems to have been unusually strong among the Venetian ruling class, but it can be found virtually everywhere in Renaissance Europe.[10]

One might compare the function of books of this kind to that of narrative paintings (known in the Renaissance as *historiae*), representing and re-presenting famous *exempla* such as the clemency of Alexander, the continence of Scipio, the chastity of Lucretia, the bravery of Mucius Scaevola in placing his hand in the fire and so on.[11] Titian's Lucretia and the Alexanders by Veronese and Lebrun are only the most famous of many paintings of this kind. Such images were sometimes displayed in public places, for example,

---

[6] Landfester 1972: 58, 139.   [7] Bolgar 1954: 333, 354, 359, 520–3; Hartog 2005: 99–147.
[8] Bolgar 1954: 528–9.   [9] Bolgar 1954: 536–7; cf. Burke 1966: 135–52.
[10] Raines 2006: 199–208.   [11] Reumann 2006: 131–48.

Beccafumi's frescoes in the Palazzo Pubblico in Siena, or the various 'halls of illustrious men' in Italian cities, decorated with their portraits. Fiction too was often intended to be exemplary, with the advantage that in contrast to historical writing, the plot was tailor-made for the author's moral.

The historical practice of the early modern period suggests that the exemplary function of historical writing was taken seriously. Petrarch himself produced a collection of the biographies of famous Romans, *De viris illustribus*. Two Italian humanists, Antonio Beccadelli ('Panormita') and Galeotto Marzio, produced biographies of rulers, Alfonso of Aragon and Matthias Corvinus, that were structured on the *dicta-facta* model of Valerius Maximus. Moral and political generalisations, known as maxims or aphorisms, regularly recurred in these texts.

Humanist histories also devoted considerable space to what were known as 'characters', in other words moral portraits describing the virtues and vices of leading figures in the story. Francesco Guicciardini's characters of Alexander VI, Clement VII and Lodovico Sforza of Milan offer a famous example of a general trend, like Lord Clarendon's gallery of portraits of leading figures in the English Civil War, from Charles I to Oliver Cromwell via the Duke of Buckingham, the Earl of Strafford and John Hampden.

Biography, which also flourished in this period, was sometimes justi-fied in terms of exemplarity (a point that undermines Jacob Burckhardt's famous presentation of Renaissance biographies as a manifestation of 'indi-vidualism'). The Spanish bishop Antonio de Guevara's *Reloj de Principes*, a largely fictional biography of the Roman emperor Marcus Aurelius (first published in Valladolid in 1528 and often reprinted), advised Charles to take Marcus as a guide, master, friend, example and rival. Guevara must have known what appealed to his contemporaries, for his book was a great success, with French, Italian, English and Latin translations as well as numerous Spanish editions for the rest of the century.

Again, the French historian-magistrate Florimond de Raemond dedi-cated his edition of the memoirs of the soldier Blaise de Monluc to the nobility of Gascony with the remark 'ils vous y serviront de modèle, de mirouer et d'exemplere'. The title of the memoirs was the *Commentaires*, suggesting that Monluc in his turn had taken Julius Caesar as his model.

Looking at history from the reader's side, we find a good deal of evidence of the search for *exempla*. One of the authors of the popular genre of books on how to read history, Pierre Droit de Gaillard, in his *Methode en la lecture de l'histoire* (1579), called history 'vray miroir et exemplaire de nostre vie'.

Whether Montaigne should be regarded as a humanist is a matter of controversy. What we can say with confidence is that like the humanists, the early Montaigne, at least, believed that history should be read above all for its moral lessons (1.26). He loved Plutarch's book and he venerated some of the ancients, especially two Greeks, Epaminondas and Socrates. His interest in exemplarity is suggested by the fact that his *Essays* used the term *exemple* 165 times in the singular and 132 times in the plural. Indeed, Montaigne's early essays have been described as little more than chains of *exempla*.[12]

Anthologies of aphorisms taken from different historians and indexes of the aphorisms to be found in particular histories offer evidence of the interest that printers expected readers to take in a literary form that made explicit the lessons of exemplarity. An index of maxims or *gnomologia* was added to some editions and translations of the histories of Dionysius of Halicarnassus, Procopius, Curtius, Herodian and Zosimus, and, among moderns, Guicciardini.

It might be useful to distinguish three modes of reading during the Renaissance: rhetorical, moral and political. The rhetorical mode concentrated on the eloquence of the speeches delivered by leading figures in the story but invented by the historian, often anthologised and sometimes arranged according to rhetorical categories such as praise and blame, suasion and dissuasion. Here too *exempla* had a place. Writing on rhetoric in his *De copia*, Erasmus pointed out that quoting *exempla* was one mode of the amplification of a text.[13]

By contrast, both the moral and political modes of reading focused on maxims and the *exempla* that illustrated them. As the translator pointed out in the dedication to Guicciardini's *Hypomneses politicae* (1597), history teaches 'not by means of naked and cold precepts, but by famous and living examples' (*non nudis ac frigidis praeceptis, sed illustribus et vivis exemplis*). However, precepts were not despised either. One seventeenth-century English gentleman, Sir William Drake, whose voluminous notes on his historical reading have survived, may be described as a collector of maxims.[14]

The past was taken seriously as a guide to public affairs, offering concrete instances of prudence or imprudence. Machiavelli, discussing the relevance to his own time of the *exempla* discussed by Livy, went so far as to claim in the proem to his *Discorsi* (1532) that history repeated itself, that 'the world has always been the same' (*giudico il mondo sempre essere stato ad un medesimo modo*) and that successful political action followed general

---

[12] Stierle 1972: 195.   [13] van Moos 1988. Cf Lyons 1990; Jeanneret 1998: 569.
[14] Sharpe 2000: 201.

rules 'which rarely or never fail'. Guicciardini included many maxims in his history, maxims that were published separately after his death and also translated into Latin. No wonder then that Richelieu, Olivares and other statesmen owned so many history books.[15]

We can also follow the political uses of history through the records of speeches in assemblies. In the Polish parliament or Sejm of 1582, according to the papal nuncio, Livy was quoted as if he were scripture. In the House of Commons debates in 1621, which were recorded in particular detail, there were references to ancient Sparta (Lycurgus), the Roman Empire (Tiberius), the Norman Conquest and Richard II, suggesting that members knew their Plutarch and their Tacitus as well as their English history.

No wonder then that books on modern history were not infrequently seen, by official eyes at least, as too dangerous to publish. Take the case of Niccolò Contarini, for instance. Contarini was a patrician who became an official historian of Venice and ended his career as doge. After his death, the Council of Ten had to decide whether to publish his history. They consulted two advisers who reported that the history should not be published because 'It contains maxims revealing the secret principles on which the regime operates, and we really do not know whether it is a good idea to make these maxims public' ('Contiene massime molto intime del governo, che per verità non sappiamo se stia bene divulgare').[16] The history was not published until 1982.

Hence it was only prudent for Renaissance writers on prudence to confine their examples to ancient history. Hundreds of commentaries on the work of the master of prudence, Tacitus, were published in this period. These commentaries attempted to distil his wisdom into a few general statements and to use figures such as Tiberius or Sejanus as negative *exempla*.[17]

One of the humanists most concerned with the study of Tacitus was the Netherlander Justus Lipsius, who believed that the study of the late Roman Empire was particularly relevant in the 1570s because Europe's political history was going through a similar phase. When Lipsius read Tacitus on the emperor Tiberius, for example, he was reminded of the Duke of Alba and the cruel way in which he governed the Netherlands for Philip II. He was also the author of a famous textbook on politics (1589), which was sometimes published under the title *Monita et exempla politica*. It was effectively a collection of commonplaces or generalisations about political behaviour.

[15] Elliott 1984: 24.   [16] Cozzi 1958: 200.   [17] Burke 1969b; Luce and Woodman 1993; Soll 2000.

It seems, then, that we may speak of the belief in exemplarity as one of the main features of the first regime of historicity. It characterised what we might call the 'mentality' – a mixture of conscious beliefs and unconscious assumptions – of readers and writers over the *longue durée*, from classical antiquity itself to the Renaissance and beyond – it was, after all, in the eighteenth century that Lord Bolingbroke wrote his much-quoted sentence in his *Letters on the Study and Use of History* (1752) that 'history is philosophy teaching by example'.

Long after Bolingbroke, however, *exempla* were collected for the edification of children. In nineteenth-century French schools, history was expected to teach virtue as well as patriotism.[18] In the English-speaking world, the best-selling early twentieth-century *Children's Encyclopaedia* included 'the child's book of golden deeds'. These deeds offered what modern psychologists call role models – implying that even today, exemplarity has not completely lost its relevance.[19]

These examples add some nuances to the Hartog–Koselleck thesis according to which a new regime of historicity began in the late eighteenth century. As in so many cultural domains, we need to take account of *décalage*, 'cultural lag', or what Ernst Bloch and others have called 'the contemporaneity of the non-contemporary'. The theory of regimes needs to find a place for both continuities between regimes and for variation within them. The long second regime was not completely monolithic.

The first regime was not monolithic either. Attitudes to the past were not the same in classical, medieval and Renaissance culture. Medieval sermons, for instance, may have been full of *exempla*, but the examples that the faithful were exhorted to follow were religious ones, generally taken from lives of the saints. Renaissance *exempla*, in contrast, were generally secular.

However, the aspect of the Renaissance – or more generally, the early modern period, 1350–1750 – on which I should like to insist here is the fact that exemplarity could no longer be taken for granted. In the course of the period it became the subject of a vigorous debate.

ANTI-EXEMPLARITY

The humanists not only encouraged exemplarity, they also undermined it. As the American critic Timothy Hampton has claimed in a perceptive essay on this topic, 'Humanism needs and promotes exemplarity even as it subverts it.'[20] It might be more exact to say that one group of humanists,

---

[18] Boer 1998: 165.   [19] Bakker 2000.   [20] Hampton 1990: 16.

more philosophical in their interests, promoted exemplarity, while another group, more philological, subverted it, but certain individuals, as we shall see, were ambivalent.

The important point is that in the culture of the Renaissance what we might call the 'sense of exemplarity' coexisted with its opposite, the sense of anachronism. In other words, a view of the past as more or less homogeneous, so that ancient *exempla* and precedents were relevant to the present coexisted with the opposite view, that the past was culturally distinct and also distant from the present. The first view was probably the one held by the majority of the writers and readers of history, but the second, which I have described elsewhere as 'the Renaissance sense of the past' was not only more distinctive but also becoming more important in that period.[21]

Like many other groups in history, the humanists constructed a collective identity by contrasting themselves with the 'other', especially European culture in the centuries between antiquity and their own day. They invented the term 'Middle Ages' (*medium tempus, medium aevum*), just as they invented the terms 'Dark Ages', 'Gothic', and 'schoolmen' (*scholastici*), all labels which remained influential for centuries.

However, the sense of historical distance included, or more exactly came to include, ancient Greece and Rome. The story of the encounter of the humanists with the classical past is an ironic one. Ancient history was originally studied with enthusiasm in order to imitate the example of the Greeks and Romans. All the same, the more the humanists studied that ancient past, the more aware they became of the differences, discontinuities or as we might say, the cultural distance between their own time and earlier periods, not only the 'barbarous' or 'dark' Middle Ages, but antiquity as well.

In the case of their attitudes to antiquity one might speak of 'nostalgic distance', an awareness of difference joined with admiration and a desire to annihilate that difference. In the case of Renaissance attitudes to the Middle Ages it might be better to speak of 'ironic distance'. In practice, however the range of attitudes to the Middle Ages expressed by sixteenth-century Italians runs from the affectionate irony with which Ariosto rewrote the medieval romance in his *Orlando Furioso* to the contempt with which Vasari (at times, at least), dismissed Byzantine and Gothic art (which he described as the *maniera greca* and *maniera tedesca* respectively).

The humanist project of resurrecting the ancient world (like Augustus' attempt at *restitutio*) inevitably proved to be a failure. Indeed, it was

---

[21] Burke 1969a; 2001: 157–73.

essentially self-destructive. Some humanist students of Roman law, for instance (notably François Hotman in his *Anti-Tribonian* of 1567), came to reject it as irrelevant to their own time because institutions had changed so much over the previous thousand years.[22]

Language in particular was the domain in which humanists such as Lorenzo Valla, for whom philology was so important, discovered the remoteness of the past. It was, for instance, its linguistic anachronisms that allowed Valla to expose the so-called 'Donation of Constantine' as a later forgery.[23]

This discovery was at the same time a problem for humanists. Historians who wrote about the post-classical world faced a dilemma, either to use post-classical words like *mahometani*, which they generally regarded as 'barbarisms', or to find classical equivalents which were not altogether appropriate. The problem was discussed explicitly in the *Ciceronianus* (1528), a dialogue by Erasmus in which one of the characters remarks that if Cicero returned to earth today he would not write in the same way as he did in Roman times. The point was that the world had changed thanks above all to the coming of Christ.

The question was not a purely linguistic one and it was not seen as such. The fundamental problems were twofold: whether it is appropriate for people in one culture to imitate another and whether it is possible to formulate general precepts about human behaviour. Some leading humanists wrestled with these problems, pulled first one way and then the other.

Erasmus, for instance, was an enthusiast for Plutarch.[24] He made his reputation by publishing a collection of maxims taken from ancient writers, the *Adagia*. However, when he came to write a book of advice for Charles V, the *Institutio Principis Christiani*, Erasmus expressed his doubts about the propriety of Christians following examples from pagan antiquity. Where others cheerfully juxtaposed Biblical and classical *exempla*, Erasmus distinguished them.[25] Another difficulty raised by Erasmus was that of polysemy: a given exemplum, such as the death of Socrates, does not come with a single meaning or moral attached, but can be interpreted in a number of different ways.[26]

Guicciardini revealed a similar ambivalence, coining maxims but also undermining generalisations, especially in two texts that were not published in his own day, his *Ricordi* ('Reflections') and his *Considerazioni* ('Considerations' on the *Discourses* of his friend Machiavelli). In a now

[22] Pocock 1987b: 11–13.   [23] Gaeta 1955.   [24] Hartog 2005: 115–16.
[25] Hartog (this volume) 'Christianity and the Church'.
[26] Hampton 1990: 48–62; Jeanneret 1998: 571.

famous passage of the *Ricordi*, Guicciardini noted 'how mistaken are those who quote the Romans at every step', since 'one would have to have a city with exactly the same conditions as theirs' for their example to be relevant. Elsewhere he asserted that 'judging by examples [concrete examples rather than exempla] is extremely fallacious' ('E fallacissimo il giudicare per gli esempii'), because 'every tiny difference in the example can be the cause of a very great variation in the effect' ('ogni minima varietà nel caso può essere causa di grandissima variazione nel effetto').

Again, Guicciardini's *Considerazioni* criticised Machiavelli's generalisations on the grounds that they were 'put forward too absolutely' ('posto troppo assolutamente'). Guicciardini wished to make distinctions, 'because cases are different' (*perché i casi sono varî*), and human affairs 'differ according to the times and the other events' ('si varia secondo la condizione de' tempi ed altre occorrenzie che girano').[27] Incidentally, Koselleck did mention Guicciardini – as he did Montaigne – in his famous essay on *historia magistra vitae*, but still (in my view) continued to overemphasise the belief in the constancy of human nature and to underestimate the interest in circumstances during the Renaissance.[28]

Guicciardini himself was praised by some contemporary readers, such as the French soldier François de La Noue, in his *Discours Politiques et Militaires* (1587), precisely because he was careful to note the circumstances of events, in other words the differences in place, time and protagonist ('les circonstances des temps, lieux et personnes'). As La Noue remarked elsewhere, adapting a commonplace to his own purposes, a particular course of action does not suit all countries any more than a slipper fits all feet ('comme un soulier ne convient pas à tous pieds, aussi un fait ne se peut approprier a tous pais').[29]

Again, the Spanish political commentator Baltasar Alamos de Barrientos, in his *Tacito español* (1614), insisted that politics was an art not a science, and that the maxims of Tacitus had to be modified according to the situation or occasion. In his pamphlet *Of Reformation* (1641), Milton criticised the commentators who 'cut Tacitus into slivers and steaks', extracting maxims and applying them without regard for differences in circumstances.

The Renaissance critique of exemplarity was worked out most fully in two texts that have become literary classics, Montaigne's *Essais* and Cervantes' *Don Quixote*. Although he was closer to philosophical than to philological humanism, the later Montaigne – unlike his younger

[27] Guicciardini 1933: 8, 19, 41.   [28] Koselleck 2004a [1967]: 13, 23, 26.
[29] La Noue 1967 [1587]: 121n, 111.

self, discussed above – may be regarded, as a recent critic has suggested, as 'the exemplary figure of problematized exemplarity'.[30] In his essay 'On the education of children' (Book 1, ch. 26), while continuing to regard the study of Plutarch's *Lives* as necessary, Montaigne advised students to judge models rather than follow them, leading another critic to refer to his 'attempt to work out a type of posthumanist notion of exemplarity'.[31] The great problem was that *exempla* belong to a static world, while Montaigne saw the world as in constant motion.[32]

The later Montaigne agreed with Erasmus about the polysemy of *exempla* and with Guicciardini about the importance of circumstances (the *Essais* make 45 references to *circonstances*). For instance, in his final essay 'On experience' (Book 3, ch. 13), he argued that 'La vie de César n'a point plus d'exemples que la nôtre pour nous.' More generally, he claimed that no two men judge the same thing in the same way, that 'every *exemplum* limps' ('tout exemple cloche') and that it is 'simply foolish to chase after foreign *exempla*' ('c'est pure sottise qui nous fait courir après les exemples étrangers').

Like Montaigne, Cervantes seems to have been somewhat ambivalent towards exemplarity, making him an example of what has been called 'the co-presence of exemplarity and its crisis'. He published a collection of stories under the title *Novelas ejemplares* (1613), with a prologue explaining that each story offered 'some useful *exemplum*' ('algún ejemplo provechoso').[33] On the other hand, Don Quixote's failed attempt to lead his life on the model of the heroes of his favourite romances of chivalry implies the weakness of any attempt to base life on literature.[34] The second part of the novel has been interpreted as a story about 'the impossibility of exemplarity', especially the chapter in which Don Quixote expresses his awareness of 'the exemplar's alterity', notably the difference between himself and the great saints and knights of the past. What he does is 'to confront the limitations of humanist discourse and to narrate the failure of exemplarity, to underscore both exemplarity's value and its impossibility, to leave his reader caught between the nostalgic desire for a heroic model and the poignant awareness that such desire is madness'.[35]

Descartes' critique of attempts to follow historical exemplars is analogous to, and may even deliberately echo that of, Cervantes. At the beginning of his *Discours sur la méthode* (1638) Descartes argued that the study of history was not only futile but dangerous as well. His main attack was levelled at

[30] Stierle 1998: 585n; Stierle 1972 had already complained that Koselleck marginalised Montaigne.
[31] Hampton 1990: 134–9, at 139; cf. Stierle 1998.   [32] Starobinski 1985; cf. Hartog 2005: 119.
[33] Stierle 1998: 589.   [34] Hampton 1990: 237–96.   [35] Hampton 1990: 282–3, 296; cf. Stierle 1998.

the humanist principle of the dignity of history. His point was that writing history according to this principle involved leaving out trivial circumstances ('les plus basses et moins illustres circonstances'). It therefore encouraged readers 'to fall into the extravagances of the paladins of our romances' and to conceive plans that it was beyond their power to execute.[36]

We may now conclude that in the case of exemplarity during what we might call the 'long Renaissance', it seems useful to distinguish a strong argument with weak support from a weaker or more moderate argument with stronger support. The strong argument concerns the coming of what has been described as the 'crisis of exemplarity'.[37] It comes from literary historians, skilled at close reading and sensitive to the complexities of texts, but concerned only with a few outstanding writers, notably Petrarch, Erasmus, Machiavelli, Montaigne, Tasso, Shakespeare and Cervantes.

Looking at a wider range of texts, as a cultural historian must do, we find less evidence of crisis and more evidence of continuity. Indeed, we find that a majority of readers and writers still accepted the value of exemplarity. For this reason it might be advisable to avoid the dramatic word 'crisis' and to speak only of a critique of exemplarity, a critique that coexisted with its broad acceptance in early modern culture and even within individuals such as Guicciardini and Montaigne.[38]

However, the existence of the minority of critics is surely sufficient to make the period (1530–1750, though not 1400–1530) a distinctive one and inspires a more general question: how much variety in attitudes to the past is compatible with Hartog's concept of 'regime'?

---

[36] Descartes 1963: 574.

[37] Hampton 1990: x, 30, 240; Rigolot 1998: 557–64; cf. Stierle 1998 and Rigolot 2004. Hartog himself (2005: 119–23) now accepts this notion, at least for the last quarter of the sixteenth century. He argues that the crisis was overcome after 1600, but it returned in a new form at the time of the famous *querelle* between ancients and moderns.

[38] The notion of crisis is also rejected by Moos 1988 and Jeanneret 1998: 578–9.

CHAPTER 3

Greek philosophy and Western history: A philosophy-centred temporality

Giuseppe Cambiano

The idea that Greek philosophy should be conceived of as one of the constituting traits of Europe and, more generally, of the west, seems to be widespread nowadays both within and outside the academic world. Influential philosophers of the last century, such as Husserl, Heidegger or Popper, have advocated this idea, despite their radically different perspectives.[1] In the *Atlas* (1984) Jorge Luis Borges, who enjoyed shifting along remote times and spaces, from China to India or Iceland, expressed this widespread view with great force and clarity. In the chapter set in Greece and entitled "El Principio," he imagines two Greek men talking – maybe Socrates and Parmenides, but names are irrelevant as are the things they are talking about. What matters is that they agree on one thing alone: "They know that discussion is the non-impossible path for reaching a truth."[2]

Awakening from a dream, in which he dreamt that the *Encyclopaedia Britannica* had entries provided with conclusions, but without beginnings, Borges had realized that he was in Greece, ". . . where everything has begun, if indeed things, in contrast to the entries of the encyclopaedia dreamed, have beginnings."[3] It is legitimate to doubt that Greece has always been regarded as the original land of philosophy, and that philosophy has been its distinctive possession and defining feature, since this has been questioned by Greeks themselves. This idea is, rather, a historical construction, and one should ask why and in which historical contexts Greek philosophy came to be seen as the starting point of philosophy, and even as the starting point of Western history, conceived of as a history shaped by philosophy.

To deal with this problem, it is necessary to consider the history of Western perceptions of certain times and places. This history cannot be fully treated here, but it is possible to draw its outlines. We would have

---

[1] See Cambiano 1988.

[2] "Saben que la discusión es el no imposible camino para llegar a una verdad," Borges 1989: 415.

[3] ". . . donde todo ha empezado si es que las cosas, a diferencia de los artículos de la enciclopedia soñada, tienen principio," Borges 1989 : 419.

to analyze the expansion and contraction of such temporal and spatial coordinates, together with the ways in which these have been configured in the cultural history of the west. Here, however, I will focus on a few initial moments of this process, leaving its development and a more precise documentation to a wider research.

GREEK PHILOSOPHERS AND EASTERN WISDOM

In treating the relation between Greek philosophy and the eastern tradition it is not my intention to explore or document cultural or philosophical debts on the part of the Greeks of the archaic age to Egyptian and Mesopotamian culture,[4] but rather to identify which spatial and temporal coordinates were considered as relevant to the Greek envisioning of philosophy by the Greeks themselves. It will be necessary, of course, to take into account some variations in the meaning of philosophy as regards content, types of activity, and forms of life.[5] But it will also be necessary to distinguish between: (1) the notion, implicit or otherwise, that philosophy is present in the Greek world; (2) the view that philosophy is a feature strictly and solely Greek; (3) the notion that philosophy is a constituting trait of the Greek world, in the sense that it defines, alone or together with other factors, such as language, religion and political organization, what one should mean by Greekness. While evaluating assertions on philosophy made by the Greeks themselves, it will be necessary to keep in mind the above-mentioned distinctions. On this basis, different possible views, even with regard to ways of conceptualizing philosophy, will be assessed.

The impression one gains is that philosophers from the classical period did not assign to philosophy a connotation of ethnicity, even though some elements of this view emerge.[6] Sometimes Plato emphasizes the cultural inferiority not only of the Thracians or of the Scythians, but also of the Phoenicians and the Egyptians in relation to a Greek world characterized by the concept of *sophia* or the love of learning.[7] Generally, however, he does not exclude the possibility that philosophers can be found within barbarian populations – as are the ruling philosophers in his *Republic* – and

---

[4] On this issue see the research of F. M. Cornford, as well as West 1971 and Burkert 1992.

[5] On Greek philosophy as a form of life, see different approaches in Cambiano 1983 and Hadot 1995; see also Lloyd 2005: 9–34.

[6] On the issue of ethnicity in the Greek world, see Hall 2002, in particular 125–34. See also Konstan 2001.

[7] *Resp.* 4.435e–436a; *Laws* 5.747b1–d1; but see also 7.819a–e on Egyptian arithmetic. Older studies on the subject include Bidez 1945 (see Festugière's review in his 1971: 39–79) and Kerschensteiner 1945.

that they may have existed in the past.[8] One would think that such a premise would work as a guide for the remarks of Book 7 of the *Laws* on the regulations of citizens' journeys abroad and on the stay of foreigners in the cities, even though it is unclear from the context whether barbarians and barbarian countries are included or whether these regulations are envisioned first and foremost as applying to other Greeks. Under certain circumstances, it is lawful and even desirable for mature citizens to spend time abroad to observe norms and habits as well as *mathēmata* (951a4–952b9). Similarly, foreign observers can be welcomed within the city; an exchange of teachings is envisioned as a possibility and this openness to cultural exchanges (however limited) is contrasted with the closed attitudes of the Egyptians towards foreigners (953d8–e4).

In approaching such themes, Plato had the precedent of Herodotus having discussed foreigners such as the Thracian Salmoxis or the Scythian Anacharsis who, by traveling, had had contacts with the Greek world. Concerning Salmoxis, Herodotus (4.95–6) reported an account according to which he was a slave of Pythagoras, "not the weakest *sophistēs* among the Greeks," from whom he would have gained some Greek wisdom. However, Herodotus himself doubted this account, for he believed that Salmoxis had lived before Pythagoras. Thus, in 4.76, he introduced Anacharsis as being philhellenic and wrote that, after having observed (*theōrēsai*) much land and absorbed much *sophiē*, he had returned to his country, where he had been murdered because of his practice of Greek rites.[9] It is interesting to note that these two cases refer to the barbarians of the north, that is, foreigners that had been hellenized, while Herodotus does not mention any case referring to Egyptians going to Greece. Rather, it is Greeks who go to Egypt, like Hecataeus, to whom Egyptian priests boast the greater antiquity of their priestly order and learning, and speak about times when the gods used to live with humans (2.143–4). In general, Herodotus considers the Egyptians the most ancient people in the world, at least after the Phrygians (2.2), and admits that geometry came to the Greeks from Egypt, just as astronomy came from Babylonia (2.109). However, he does not provide Thales with any mediating role, even though he acknowledges his Phoenician birth (2.170.3); nor does he mention any trip to Egypt. The same goes for Pythagoras, even though, as Herodotus introduces the doctrine of the transmigration of souls, he does say that Egyptians were the first to support

[8] *Resp.* 6.499c–d. See also *Symp.* 209d6–e3, *Phaedo* 77e–78a, where the possibility of finding a charmer like Socrates also within the barbarians is not ruled out, even though later on Socrates is recognized as the only true charmer (84a–b).
[9] See Hartog 1980: 102–25 on Salmoxis and 82–102 on Anacharsis. See also Thomas 2001.

this doctrine and that several Greeks, whose names he chooses not to mention, presented it as if it were their own (2.123.2–3).[10] Herodotus, however, does not speak explicitly of Pythagoras' journey to Egypt. He mentions Solon's journey; but, according to this story, what Solon went to learn there were rules of taxation on citizens – which he later applied to Athens – and not doctrines of any kind (2.107). Moreover, when Solon went to Croesus in Lydia with the objective of *theōriē*, he, in fact, ended up not learning, but supplying an ethical lesson to Croesus, who knew of Solon's *sophiē* and of his "philosophizing" journeys in pursuit of *theōriē* (1.30.2). Despite the use of the term *philosopheōn* concerning Solon, none of these Herodotean narratives of journeys and cultural exchanges refers to philosophy as a distinct field of knowledge. Philosophy doesn't come across as an element of the Hellenic identity, which, according to Herodotus, consists of sharing the same blood, language, religious rites, and ways of life (8.144.2).

The first evidence of Pythagoras' cultural loan from Egypt is provided in the fourth century BCE by Isocrates in his *Busiris*, a text meant to show how to write the eulogy of a character, such as the Egyptian king Busiris, who apparently sacrificed strangers in order to eat them. Isocrates ascribes to Busiris a model form of political organization, which granted priests wealth and spare time (*scholē*). Wealth and spare time had allowed these priests to invent medicines to heal the body and philosophy to heal souls. Such a practice branches out in two directions, one concerning the development of laws, and the other the investigation of natural forces (21–2). In particular, Busiris had entrusted the eldest among the priests with the healing or reform of the most important things, while the younger ones had to devote themselves to the study of astronomy, calculation, and geometry (23). This system quite clearly resembles that presented in Plato's *Republic*. However, Isocrates does not mention Plato, but Pythagoras, who had gone to Egypt and had become a disciple of the priests, thus introducing their philosophy to Greece, along with their cultic practices. Hence his fame, which had drawn many disciples – so much so that even in these days those who claimed to be his disciples would be admired for their silence more than those whose highest reputation resided in their ability to speak (29; in 30 the expression "philosophy" of the Egyptians is used). Coming from a rhetorician like Isocrates, who bet everything on the ability to speak and saw in *logos* what distinguished not only man from animals, but also the Greeks from the barbarians (*Panathenaicus* 293), this eulogy cannot but

---

[10] See Burkert 1972: 126–8.

sound ironic. It is not a coincidence that he would present not Solon – an authoritative figure within Athens' political tradition – but Pythagoras as visitor and disciple of Egypt. Paradoxically, the prerogative of entrusting Egypt with the invention of philosophy has to be owed to an opponent of philosophy, a supporter of a form of panhellenism and, in the conflict against Persians, even an advocate of the cultural supremacy of Athens.[11]

The memories of the Herodotean journeys by Hecataeus and Solon as well as Isocrates' critique, are clear to the Plato of the *Timaeus*. Here Plato shares with Herodotus the conviction about Egypt's great antiquity, while he structures his narrative of Solon's meeting with the Egyptian priest in Sais in a manner similar to that of Herodotus, which carries out a comparison between the genealogies of Hecataeus, and the far more ancient genealogies of the Egyptians. The words Plato puts in the priest's mouth would echo for centuries in European culture, each time the existence of barbarian wisdom behind Greek philosophy would be affirmed. The Egyptian priest says: "you Greeks are all children, and there is no such thing as an old Greek" (*Tim.* 22b3–5, trans. H. D. P. Lee). This was due to the lack of historical and cultural memory on the part of the Greeks, a lack produced by periodical cataclysms which, the priest affirmed, had the effect of making the Greeks begin all over again like children (22b4). Egypt, instead, protected as it was by the river Nile, was immune to such devastations, and its time moved on in a linear and continuous manner. This is why in Egypt historical memory was retained and delivered in written form (22d–23b).

The differentiation between two types of temporality, one peculiar to Greece and the other to Egypt, must repudiate once and for all the indiscriminate ascription to Plato of a cyclical conception of time. Written cultural memory, the prerogative of Egypt, comes to reverse the temporal record of Egypt, since Egypt itself attests the existence of an archaic Athens dating from before the cataclysm, 1,000 years older than Sais, and characterized by a class of priests that were separated from others (24a2–5). This may be an allusion to the philosopher-rulers of the *Republic*. It was the goddess Athena, lover of war and *philosophos*, who chose the place where Athens was founded. Athena was guided in her choice by her will to see the city bloom with men gifted with her own capacities (24c4–d3). These words, put in Critias' mouth, an Athenian related to Plato himself, imply a connection between Athens – not the whole of Greece – and philosophy.

---

[11] On Isocrates' anti-Platonic debate see Eucken 1983: 172–212 and Livingstone 2001; see also Said 2001: 282.

Such a connection suggests the 'autochthonous nature' of Greek philosophy and its independence from a supposedly earlier Egyptian wisdom.[12] This notion suggests a profound detachment from Isocrates' insinuations. However, the *Timaeus* also hints at a connection between astronomy and the genesis of philosophy: the observation of astronomical phenomena would lead to the discovery of numbers and the notion of time, and would also give rise to research on the nature of the whole. It is from these sources, Timaeus says, that we have gained the *genos* of philosophy, the greatest good ever given to human beings by the gods (*Tim.* 47a4–b2). It is unclear whether the "we" used by Timaeus relates to humankind as a whole or to the Greeks alone. One interpretation of the passage came from a different dialogue, the *Epinomis*, usually ascribed to Philip of Opus.[13] Here wisdom is also conceptualized as a divine gift, consisting of the *epistēmē* guaranteed to mortals through number, the necessary condition for *sophia* (*Ep.* 976e–977c). The learning of number is made dependent on the observation of celestial phenomena, the regularity of which is founded on the relation between numbers (978b–979a). The novelty in Philip's account is that the first observer is considered to be a barbarian: it is the fairness of the summer season and the clarity of the sky that allowed celestial observations in Egypt and Syria. These observations subsequently spread everywhere else (986e6–987a6). Regarding this aspect, the author recognizes the inferiority of Greek geographical conditions and proposes a diffusionist model, which pertains to astronomy rather than philosophy. Yet he is also quick to affirm that whatever the Greeks acquire from foreigners is ultimately transformed by them into something nobler (987d9–e1).

Aristotle was also persuaded that the Egyptians were the most ancient human beings (*Pol.* 7.10, 1329b31–2). However, in the first book of the lost *De philosophia* (Diog. Laert. 1 proem 8), he affirmed that the Magi were more ancient than the Egyptians and mentioned that they had a dualistic form of religion. In discussing whether goodness should be at the beginning or the end, Aristotle described supporters of either alternative and identified the Magi as supporters of the view that goodness should be at the beginning, but without indicating that they were the first to formulate such a position (*Met.* 14.4, 1091b4–12). At the same time, in the first book of *Metaphysics* (1.1, 981b20–5) Aristotle stated that mathematical arts originated in Egypt, for it was there that the priestly class was allowed to enjoy *scholē*, as Isocrates had also noted. However, according to Aristotle, the true *sophia*, as the science of principles and causes, was superior to

---

[12] See the apt remarks made in Hartog 2002: 74–9.   [13] See Tarán 1975.

mathematics. When he talked of those who philosophized first, he referred to the Greeks and called Thales the founder (*archēgos*) of this type of philosophy – that is, of the investigation of nature (*Met.* 1.8, 983b20–1). Furthermore, Aristotle believed that the knowledge of causes had improved since the time of Thales, and this was why he could not be listed among the supporters of the view that knowledge reached its summit in the most ancient past: "the earliest philosophy is, on all subjects, like one who lisps, since it is young and in its beginnings" (1.10, 993a15–16, trans. W. D. Ross). The time of philosophy assumed by Aristotle is linear and has its starting point in Greece. He does not explicitly discuss possible precedents among other peoples.[14]

Aristotle was willing to admit the priority of Egyptians and Babylonians with regard to the observation of stars (*De caelo* 2.12, 292a7–9), but he did not extend such a priority to philosophy. Together with Egypt, as the cradle of wisdom, the world of Chaldaean Magi would find its place in the Platonic Academy and in Aristotle's Lyceum. It is interesting to note that even as far as this issue is concerned, an opposite line of dependences would be sometimes emphasized. Philodemus recorded an anecdote about a Chaldaean who, upon visiting Plato, admitted his musical incompetence.[15] The name of Zoroaster starts to circulate: references to him are attributed to the Platonic philosopher Hermodorus, to Eudoxus, to Xanthus of Lydia, and to Heraclides Ponticus. Calculations start to be made in order to show the great antiquity of Zoroaster and of the Persian Magi compared to the chronological data of Greek history.[16] Diffusionist views are introduced, which connect individual Greek philosophers with Egypt or with the Chaldaean world through the *topos* of journeys.[17] The Peripatetic philosopher Aristoxenus had already talked of Pythagoras' journeys to Egypt and to Babylonia, where he visited Zaratas the Chaldaean, who revealed to him a dualistic doctrine (fr. 13 Wehrli). Due to his Pythagoreanism, Aristoxenus must have included this information with a celebratory intent. Other key characters of Greek philosophy, such as Democritus or Plato, were also discussed in narratives of journeys outside Greece. According to Diogenes Laertius (9.34–5), some philosophers had stated that Democritus had not only traveled to Egypt, but also had contacts with the Indian gymnosophists. This assertion was a projection onto the past of the contacts

---

[14] See the critical approach in Spoerri 1959: 67–8 to the reconstruction effected by Werner Jaeger.
[15] *Acad.* 3.40 in Dorandi 1991, with the commentary on 220–2.
[16] See Bidez and Cumont 1973 [1938]. For a reconstruction and discussion see Festugière 1950: 19–44 and especially Momigliano 1975b.
[17] In general, see Montiglio 2005. On Plato's journeys, see Swift Riginos 1976: 61–9.

with those Indian sages that occurred during Alexander's expedition. Strabo (17.1.29) claimed that in Egypt he was shown the house where Plato and Eudoxus had resided for thirteen years. Plutarch even mentioned the name of the priest with whom Plato had engaged in philosophical discussions: Chonuphis (*De gen.* 7.578F).

It is impossible to confirm the reliability of these data on philosophical journeys. Moreover, the tendency of ancient biographers to infer facts from assertions made in the writings of authors about whom they researched must be acknowledged from the outset. In particular, it is difficult to reconstruct the problematic contexts within which these data, or pseudo-data, had been formulated in conditions of great ignorance as regards the oriental languages on the part of the Greek intellectuals. As Momigliano stated, "Zoroaster became a great master without hindrance because nobody really cared to know what he had been or what he had written or truly inspired."[18] In the Hellenistic world, news on the journeys of eminent philosophers in countries like Egypt or Syria, which were dominated by new monarchs, could contribute to the cultural prestige of the rulers of these countries, perceived as cradles of a very ancient wisdom from which the Greeks themselves had drawn. This might have well been the outcome of a work like *The Philosophy of the Egyptians* by Hecataeus of Abdera.[19] In these cases, the ascription of authority to whatever is most ancient could work to afford authority to those who presented themselves as having drawn upon ancient wisdom: in such cases the expansion of time, together with that of space, acquired a positive value.

We must not, however, forget the competitive and polemical context which characterized the relationship between different philosophical schools from the mid-fourth century BCE onwards. Proclus (in *Im R.* 2.109) reported that the Epicurean Colotes had believed that the Er of the final myth in Plato's *Republic* was in fact Zoroaster. In doing so, he emphasized the dependence of Plato on Zoroaster, if not necessarily accusing him of plagiarism. There were far too many divergences among various philosophical orientations to allow worries about the Greekness of philosophy in general, or willingness to defend or attack it. The positive or negative appeals to the dependence of certain philosophers on the wisdom of Egypt or Mesopotamia were elements of these inter-scholastic arguments. Moreover, it is interesting to note that – looking at the documentation available – these genealogies of Oriental wisdom did not involve the Epicureans – who used relationships of dependence polemically– or the Stoics, who had a

[18] Momigliano 1975b: 151–2; see also 7–8. [19] See Stern and Murray 1973.

non-Greek founder. In any case, even this type of literature on barbarian wisdom was in Greek, written by Greeks or by Hellenized barbarians and in a manner adapted to the expectations of a Greek audience. Alexander's expedition in the east would have disclosed the Indian world with its gymnosophists. Strabo (15.1.63–5) reports the account of one of Alexander's escorts, Onesicritus – who had listened to the teaching of Diogenes the Cynic – of his encounter with some of these Indian sages.[20] In these stories about encounters and conversations with the Brahmans, the greater antiquity of their wisdom or the assertion of a possible derivation of Greek philosophy from it is not at all central. More important is the comparison between the two worlds, carried out from a Greek perspective – a comparison which brought to the surface features associating these naked, frugal, and resistant sages with the Greek Cynics.

THE LOOK FROM OUTSIDE

The Roman conquest of Greece led the Greek intelligentsia to look at their philosophy with new eyes, and brought into the discussion those Romans who looked at Greek philosophy from the outside. Through this interaction, new ways of envisioning philosophy as something peculiarly Greek were elaborated – first of all, within Roman culture. The expulsion of philosophers from Rome – as, for instance, the expulsion of some Epicureans in 173 or 154 BCE – suggests that philosophy, or at least part of it, was perceived as something not Roman. On the occasion of the embassy of three philosophers from Athens in Rome in 155 BCE, it seems that Cato the Elder proposed to send them home, "in order that these men may return to their schools and lecture to the sons of Greece, while the youth of Rome give ear to their laws and magistrates, as heretofore" (Plut. *Cato Maior* 22.5–6, trans. B. Perrin). However, among other higher class Romans, or in the case of poets like Ennius, philosophy was increasingly accepted and fostered.[21] Rejection and acceptance, however, were both based on the premise that philosophy was something typically Greek. In the first century BCE, this premise was made explicit in some of the proems to Lucretius' *De rerum natura*. In the proem to book 1, Lucretius celebrates

---

[20] A shorter version is found in Plut. *Alex.* 65. Cf. Brown 1949, in particular 24–53. The *topos* of Alexander's conversation with the Brahmans and the gymnosophists goes on through antiquity, and not only in the so-called *The Romance of Alexander*. See Festugière 1971: 157–82. Cf. Muckensturm 1993.

[21] Data gathered and commented upon in Garbarino 1973; see also Ferrary 1988: 395–433, 539–45, 589–615.

the moment when *primum Graius homo* dared stand against a *religio*, which crushed human life as it was founded on fear (1.62–7). The adverb *primum* recalls the *topos* of the first inventor and points to something new: a new era marked by true philosophy. It is Lucretius who introduced this figure by locating himself at a later point in time in order to posit a form of continuity between the present and an originary moment of insight. Lucretius does not mention the name of the initiator, but he identifies him as Greek. He can do so, since, being Roman, he is located at a different space and speaks a different language. Ludwig Edelstein has maintained that Lucretius is not referring to Epicurus here, but to a whole group, namely to the first Greeks who investigated nature and criticized religion. He further suggests that Lucretius presents this account of the origins of philosophy as an argument against the prevalent view that these origins were Eastern.[22] Not so long before, the Stoic thinker Posidonius had suggested that the atomist theory was extremely ancient and dated back to a Phoenician man called Mochos of Sidon (Strabo 16. 2.24; S. E. *M.* 9.363). However, Lucretius is using the singular form of the noun *homo*, so it is difficult to think that he is not referring to a single individual. Some scholars have also thought that, within the Epicurean tradition, Lucretius was the first to emphasize the break represented by Epicurus in the history of civilization.[23] To be sure, neither in Hermarchus, nor in Diogenes of Oenoanda or in other Epicureans does an expression similar to *primum Graius homo* occur. It seems, however, that Hermarchus maintained that even the gods spoke; that they spoke Greek, and that all *sophoi* that have ever existed used the Greek language.[24] According to Clement of Alexandria (*Strom.* 1.15.67.1), Epicurus had affirmed that the Greeks were the only ones that were capable of philosophizing.

Lucretius' proem is rich with martial and agonistic metaphors identifying Epicurus as the winner who, thanks to his intellectual conquests, could deliver to us the loot of his victory (1.72–9). His achievement is not merely an individual triumph, since it concerns "us" as well: not only the Greeks, but also the Romans. According to Lucretius, there is a further *primus*, *Ennius noster* (1.117–19), who achieved a poetic conquest, and who represents a line of continuity which goes down to Lucretius himself. The thematization of the connection between Greece and Italy is clear. Lucretius emphasizes the difficulty of expressing the *obscura reperta* of

[22] Edelstein 1940.   [23] This thesis is explored in Furley 1978.
[24] Ermarco 1988: fr. 32, corresponding to Philod. *De dis/Peri theon* (*P. Herc.* 152/157), cols. 8.20–14.13, p. 36 (ed. H. Diels).

the Greeks in Latin verses, pointing out that Latin is a poorer language compared to Greek, and that to express many new things through new words is indeed a great challenge (1.136–9). Some scholars have thought that the name of Epicurus does not appear within the proem for a reason: since Epicurus did not have a good reputation in Rome, Lucretius chose – before mentioning his name – to provide the elements required for a proper understanding of his thought, lest the reader be deterred by his reputation from the effort of assimilating it.[25] However, it must be said that the name of Epicurus is not mentioned even in the proems to Books 3, 5, and 6. In the proem to Book 3, Epicurus is not mentioned, but Lucretius addresses him directly, stating again that he was a Greek and *primus* in shedding light. He calls him *Graiae gentis decus* and declares himself to be his follower, describing himself, however, as merely a *hirundo* contending with swans (3.1–6). From the simple qualification of *homo* in the first proem, he shifts to the appellation of *pater*: one who supplies "us" ("us" once again) with his precepts (3.9–13). The philosophy of Epicurus is true philosophy: it is Greek, since its author-inventor is Greek, but it can address non-Greeks as well, because it is true.[26] Here, Epicurus is given a *divina mens* (3.14–17), and for the first and only time in this same book Lucretius mentions his name explicitly – together with those of Ancus, Scipio, Homer, and Democritus – to emphasize the mortality of them all, Epicurus not excluded, who overtopped humanity with his genius, just as the sun, arising in the ether, extinguishes the stars (3.1042–4). In the proem to Book 5, Epicurus' name is not mentioned, but I believe that the different proems are built *in climax*. If Epicurus appeared as *homo* in the first and as mortal *pater* supplied with *divina mens* in the third, in the proem to Book 5 he appears as *deus*, as the *princeps* who found out the *ratio vitae* that is now called *sapientia* (5.8–10). In order to confirm Epicurus' divine nature, Lucretius compares his discovery with the discoveries attributed to Ceres or Bacchus, drawing the conclusion that men could live without the latter, but not without the freedom from darkness and fear given by Epicurus (5.13–21). From this perspective, it is legitimate to view this *homo* as a god (5.49–51). Even in the proem to Book 6 the name of Epicurus is not mentioned, but his praise accompanies the description of the city of Athens: a description that connects his wisdom to a particular place (6.5) and that stresses his mortality, placing him in a situation of plague in which all will die – a situation transcended by his divine discoveries, which outlive him (6.5–8).

---

[25] See for example Clay 1983: 97–8, 107.
[26] On the Greekness and the universality of the Epicurean message, see Sedley 1998: 57–9.

This means that the true philosophy of the Greek Epicurus transcends his mortality and is made available to those who are not Greek through the mediation of Lucretius.

Lucretius' discourse concerns all Greek philosophy, inasmuch as for him philosophy is identified with the one and only true philosophy of Epicurus. In Cicero, by contrast, the discourse, while becoming more general, tends to undermine the notion of philosophy as a unified whole, dividing the notion into a part concerned with the proper form of life and another concerned with techniques of thought and argumentation. In 59 BCE Cicero wrote to his brother Quintus – recently confirmed as proconsul of Asia – that, had he been appointed as governor of the Africans, the Spaniards, or the Gauls, i.e. of barbarian peoples, he would have had to rule with *humanitas*. However, since he happened to be the governor of a *genus* of men, the Greeks, who were believed to be the ones who had delivered *humanitas* to others, he should honour them with a special *humanitas*. Cicero is not ashamed to say that all which we have acquired – "we," Romans included – is owed to disciplines coming from Greece.[27] In his *De oratore*, completed around November 55 BCE, he discusses the place that philosophy should hold in the shaping of the perfect orator. It is accepted by all parties in the dialogue that philosophy is something Greek; the only question is whether philosophy can be compatible with Roman culture. Crassus sketches a history of *sapientia* in Greece: philosophical activity and oratorical skills were initially closely connected, but then *sapientia* was increasingly detached from political life, with writers such as Pythagoras, Democritus, Anaxagoras, and Socrates radically condemning oratory. Hence there was a useless and unreasonable laceration, leading to the rise of multiple philosophical schools in conflict with one another (*De or.* 3.15.56–19.73). Crassus hoped that this original link could be restored: Cato lacked no wisdom, except for this doctrine, "*transmarina* and *adventicia*," that is to say, he lacked only philosophy (3.33.135) which is foreign and imported (as Cicero will repeat in his *De republica* (3.3.5)).

There was no friction between Rome and philosophy – and philosophy could be assimilated and imported – because the part of philosophy concerned with practice and with life was a feature of the Roman tradition. Cicero declared himself to be philhellenic, but he never changed his view that Rome had no need to wait for Greek philosophy and teaching in order to equip itself with good laws and institutions, and to nurture

---

[27] *Ad Quintum fratr.* 1.1.27–8; see Ferrary 1988: 511–16.

men of extraordinary virtue.[28] The issue was merely one of acclimatizing Greek philosophy in its content and techniques. The problem was how to convey philosophical concepts in Latin. Cicero claimed, in this regard, that his works had merit, but he also thought that his writings had also worked against coarse prior efforts to popularize Epicurus' teaching in Latin prose (*Fin.* 2.15.49; 3.12.40; *Tusc.* 4.3–7). Unlike Lucretius, however, who acknowledged the poverty of Latin, Cicero claimed the superior richness of Latin compared to Greek (*Fin.* 3.2.5). At any rate, the act of translation was based on the possibility of transferring and effecting a connection with Greek philosophy. Greek philosophy had come first: philosophy, together with other arts, had been cultivated in Greece before Rome. Cicero used the anecdote told by Heraclides Ponticus on the invention of the term philosophy by Pythagoras – who had been the first to define himself as "philosopher" in distinguishing himself from the "wise man" (*Tusc.* 5.3.8–10). However, chronological priority did not imply exclusiveness. On the contrary, Cicero claimed that the points of view figuring in the *Epinomides* were developed in Rome and declared that he had always been persuaded that either "our" discoveries had been made more wisely or that "we" had improved whatever had come from Greece and had been deemed worthy of development (*Tusc.* 1.1.1). Selection, therefore, belonged to Romans, who would also improve whatever they chose from the Greek world. Cicero, being a translator, included philosophy among those parts of the Greek tradition that were worthy of re-elaboration. He did not follow the pattern of attributing superiority to those parts that came first. On the contrary, he encouraged people to tear from a currently "fading Greece" the *laus* in these studies, and take them to this *urbs*, Rome. This is how the medieval theme of the *translatio studii* came into being.

Plutarch (*Cic.* 5) reports that when Cicero returned to Rome from Greece he distanced himself from public life and received the nickname "Cicero the Greek" or Cicero the *Scholastikos*, the one attending philosophers' schools – pejorative terms used by the lowest classes of the Romans. Antonius, one of the protagonists of Cicero's *De oratore*, had already maintained that the orator should never present himself as *sapiens*, so as not to be judged as inept and as *Graeculum* (1.221). This pejorative term was supposedly also used in the oration that Dio Cassius (46.18.1–2) put in the mouth of Q. Fufius Calenus in his attack against Cicero. Both in Quintilian (11.1.35) and Tacitus

---

[28] *Rep.* 2.15.28–9; 3.3.6 and 3.4.7; *De finibus* 3.3.11; *Tusc.* 1.1.2; 4.3.5. The *topos* of the superiority of Roman virtue over the verbalism of Greek philosophers will continue; see Val. Max. 2.1.10; 2.2.2; Seneca, *Ep.* 104. 21–2; Quintil. 12.2.30 and the anecdote on the conversation between the Epicurean Cinna and the Roman Fabricius in Plut. *Pyrr.* 20.

(*Agr.* 4.3) there is evidence that, despite the example and arguments of Cicero, philosophical studies were still considered unsuitable for a Roman citizen. However, philosophy was not always seen as a foreign body. In Seneca, we witness the effacement of any spatial and temporal discontinuity with Greek philosophy. In *De brevitate vitae* (14.1–15.5), Seneca maintained that the ancient fashioners of "holy thoughts" had been born for our sake: for the sake of a posterity which included the Romans. "From no age are we shut out," he said: thanks to the labours of others, we are led to wonderful things, from darkness into light. We may argue with Socrates, doubt with Carneades, find peace with Epicurus. All the examples offered by Seneca are of Greek philosophers of the past; however, the horizon of discussion is not the question of the origin of philosophy, but rather its accessibility and availability beyond the time of its first elaboration, its ability to transcend its time. Seneca expresses this point through the metaphor of a dialogue with past philosophers implying the possibility of sharing their way of life. Seneca also uses the metaphor of clientage: despite the great chronological gap, it is possible for the Romans to become *clientes* of ancient Greek philosophers and receive their benefits. The advantage is that, unlike parents, the interlocutors of this dialogue can be chosen: the past makes them available to us. Starting from our small moment in time, it is possible, thanks to the mediation of Greek philosophers, to access that which is eternal and the common property of the best men. The life of the *sapiens*, Seneca concludes, has a great duration: all ages serve him as if he were a god. There is no barrier left between Rome and Greek philosophy; only a single chronological *continuum*.

GREEK PHILOSOPHY: BEGINNING OR DERIVATION?

How did the Greeks, now under the control of the Roman Empire, react to their loss of political centrality and to the fact that the Romans could not be considered merely as barbarians like others? Much has been said on this topic, especially since the so-called Second Sophistic (developed between the end of the first and the beginning of the third centuries) came to be considered not only as a literary phenomenon, but also as the product of political frustration and as a development linked to the assertion of a distinctively Hellenic identity on the part of the elites belonging to the Greek provinces within the Empire.

   Philosophy continued to be something undeniably Greek, in spite of Cicero's and Seneca's attempts acclimatize it to the Latin language. According to Plutarch, it was Athenian culture, after all, with Plato at its center,

that constituted Hellenic identity, rather than Roman citizenship.[29] However, as far as philosophy was concerned, the basis of comparison was not
Rome, where philosophy had arrived much later, but, once again, barbarian
wisdom. The *Lives of Philosophers*, written by Diogenes Laertius, who lived
at the beginning of the third century CE, begins with the statement that
some believe the activity (*ergon*) of philosophy to have originated in barbarians: Persians (Magi), Babylonians or Assyrians (Chaldaeans), Indians
(Gymnosophists), Celts and Galatians (Druids and Semnotheoi).

At issue are not specific teachings or modes of philosophizing, but
the very *ergon* of philosophy. Diogenes documents these philo-barbarian
theses through a variety of statements made in a variety of texts, from the
Magicus, ascribed to Aristotle, to Sotion, active around 200 BCE (1.1–2).
Diogenes also mentions several authors, who have described the way of
philosophizing of these peoples or the contents of their philosophies –
for the most part theologians or moral philosophers (1.6–7, 10–11) – and
have claimed the greater antiquity of the Magi or the Egyptians as far
as the discovery of philosophy is concerned (1.8–9). It is not important
here whether Diogenes had direct access to these texts or not.[30] But surely,
to acknowledge the greater antiquity of barbarian philosophy was one
thing, but to claim that Greek philosophy was dependent on barbarian
wisdom was another. Diogenes clearly rejected these pro-barbarian theses
and believed in the autonomy of Greek philosophy and the Greek origin
of philosophy proper.

In the first place, Diogenes reproached these authors for failing to consider the merits (*katorthōmata*) of the Greeks – from whom not only all
philosophy, but the whole of humanity originated – and for imputing
excessive merits to the barbarians. As a confirmation of this thesis, Diogenes considered the fact that Musaeus was born among the Athenians and
Linus among the Thebans, and that Musaeus was believed to be the son of
Eumolpus and the first author of a *Theogony* and a *Sphaera* – maintaining
that all things originated in one thing and returned to it upon their dissolution (1.3). Linus, instead, was the son of Hermes and the Muse Urania,
and he had composed a poem on cosmogony, writing about the sun and
the moon, animals and plants. Diogenes Laertius mentions the beginning
of these poems, from which Anaxagoras supposedly drew the *incipit* of his
own work. According to Diogenes, this was the way in which philosophy
(whose very name was not barbarian, but Greek) had arisen among the
Hellenes (1.4). In order to corroborate this last point, Diogenes mentions

---

[29] See Swain 1997; Preston 2001; and Said 2001, especially 287–93.   [30] See Spoerri 1959: 53–69.

the story of Heraclides Ponticus, according to which Pythagoras was the first one who called himself a philosopher, on the grounds that no man ought to be called wise, only the gods (1.12). It is likely that the original story of Heraclides (fr. 87, Wehrli), a platonic thinker active in the middle of the fourth century BCE, emphasized less the distinctively Greek nature of philosophy and more the difference between philosophy and *sophia*, and the primacy of contemplative life – a contribution to the academic debate of the time on whether one should prefer the active or the contemplative life.[31] This point of view, however, was opposed to that of Isocrates, who derived the philosophy of Pythagoras from Egypt. Diogenes Laertius deployed an anecdote to confirm his thesis on the Greek origin of philosophy and Heraclides was the only authority he adduced. He opposed those who cited Orpheus the Thracian – considered a very ancient philosopher – to affirm the barbarian origins of philosophy. Diogenes did not understand how a poet who had talked of the gods in such an unholy way, attributing passions and vileness to them, could be called a philosopher (1.5). In this fashion, he discredited the orphic theology, denied Orpheus the status of philosopher, and removed every connection between Orpheus the Thracian, a barbarian, and Musaeus or Linus, who were genuinely Greek. Even in the prehistory of 'proper' philosophy – which, following Sotion, Diogenes divided into two, specifically Greek, parts, ionic and italic– there were only Greek poets.

Diogenes provided the most explicit formulation of the Greek origin of philosophy in general (rather than of a particular school of philosophy). Yet he lost his battle. His argument showed that the central issue concerned theology: it was with regard to this subject matter that bridges with barbarian philosophies could be built, involving first and foremost two philosophers – Pythagoras and Plato. In the middle of the second century CE, Numenius of Apamea, while dealing with the problem of God, maintained that one ought to link the doctrines of Plato with those of Pythagoras. He also compared the doctrines of the more notable peoples – such as the Brahmans, the Jews, the Magi, and the Egyptians – and emphasized their similarity with those of Plato. The central issue was that of the immateriality of God (fr. 1a–b Des Places), but the inclusion of the Jews in the list was equally crucial. Numenius seemed to emphasize the similarity between Moses and the contents of Platonic philosophy, even though there is no proof that he would interpret such a similarity in a diffusionist

---

[31] For the context of Heraclides' tale and his interests in eastern wisdom see Gottschalk 1980: 23–33, 106, and 111–17.

way, in the sense of a derivation of Platonic philosophy from the teachings of Moses. Numenius' point of view was best expressed in the rhetorical question that would be quoted many times by the Church Fathers: "What is Plato if not an Atticizing Moses?" (fr. 8). The Jews appeared in the horizon of Greek philosophers already in the time of Theophrastus.[32] In the Hellenistic age, Hellenized Jews, especially in Alexandria, had started comparisons between the Holy Scriptures and Greek philosophy. Around 160 BCE Aristobulus maintained that Plato had read the Holy Scriptures and followed their precepts, and that Pythagoras had done the same before. There was a strong risk of anachronism: how could Pythagoras and Plato have read a text that had been translated into Greek only later, by the seventy translators under Ptolemy Philadelphus in Alexandria? Aristobulus replied that an earlier translation existed (Clemens, *Strom.* 1.22.150.1–3; Eusebius PE 13.12.1).[33] In the first century CE in Alexandria, Philo used the appellation 'philosopher' when referring to Abraham or Moses (*De gig.* 14.62; *De plant.* 6.24–7). However, in *The Life of Moses* (1.23), which was addressed to a Greek audience, he would claim that his hero had learnt not only the symbolic philosophy of the Egyptians and the wisdom of the Assyrians and the Chaldaeans, but also the disciplines of the Greeks. As a result, Moses received the whole Oriental and Hellenic wisdom, but this implied that the Hellenic wisdom, as the Oriental one, pre-dated him. Philo detected the presence of sages in Greece as well as in barbaric lands. He significantly isolated the group of Greeks from the barbarians, which included the Jewish Essaioi. Apart from the Indian Calanus, all the examples of good men that he mentioned were Greeks (*quod omnis probus* 73–5 and 93–130). Philo was not concerned to demonstrate a relationship of priority, unlike Flavius Josephus, who sought to show that the wisdom of the Jews preceded that of the Greeks in his *Against Apion* (1.2.7–14). Josephus knew that each population attempts to trace to older times their habits, institutions and activities, in order to prove that they did not imitate others (2.15.152). Drawing extensively on Hellenistic literature, he tried to show that the Greeks acknowledged that their first philosophers, such as Pherecydes, Pythagoras, and Thales, had been disciples of Egyptians and Chaldaeans. In particular, Pythagoras had not only learnt the Jewish doctrines, but he also followed them. The Greeks had been instructed by Moses on the principles of the virtuous life and on the nature of God (1.22.162–3; 2.11.168).

---

[32] The data are gathered and commented upon in Stern 1974; see also Momigliano 1975b.
[33] See Gruen 2001.

The Bible was not the only work of 'alien' wisdom available in Greek. There were works such as the *Chaldaean Oracles* – a poem in hexameters which has been called the "Bible of the Neoplatonists." The *Chaldaean Oracles* were ascribed to Julian the Theurgist, who lived under Marcus Aurelius and was the son of Julian the Chaldaean; but the original authors were thought to be the gods themselves: the oracle was indeed the traditional form through which gods spoke to men and provided revelations to initiates.[34] Another basic corpus of writings went under the name of Hermes Trismegistus, an ancient Egyptian master who was thought to have received revelations from the divine world.[35] In discourse 16 (1–2) Asclepius reported that Hermes, his teacher, told him that those who read his books in their original form would have found them simple and clear, but, had the Greeks attempted to translate them, everything would have seemed obscure, because the sense, which had preserved its integrity in the Egyptian language, would have been distorted in Greek. Asclepius convinced King Ammon to keep the text untranslated in order to prevent the divine mysteries from reaching them: "the Greeks have empty discourses which produce evidence, and the philosophy of the Greeks is only a hum of words." Paradoxically, such warnings were formulated in Greek and presented as translations from the Egyptian language. However, both the hermetical writings and the *Chaldaean Oracles* appear as documents of an ancient theological wisdom, one which had been revealed directly by the gods long before the Greeks began to philosophize.

Plotinus does not mention the *Chaldaean Oracles*, and only alludes to Egyptian hieroglyphs (*Enn.* 5.8.5–6). He does not make direct connections between Platonic philosophy, which for him was the original core of true knowledge, and Egyptian or Chaldaean theologies. His biographer, Porphyry, tells that Plotinus was determined to experience directly the philosophy of Persians and Indians and that he therefore joined Gordian in his expedition against Persia, but Gordian's defeat had made the project impossible to realize (*Plot.* 3). After refuting the Gnostics, Plotinus had passed on his mantle to Amelius and Porphyry, who wrote many refutations of the book of Zoroaster showing that it was spurious, a forgery of the sectaries who sought to attribute their doctrines to the ancient sage (ibid. 16). It is not clear which book this is. But this claim has led scholars to think that a lost book ascribed to him, the *Philosophy from Oracles*, had been composed before his encounter with Plotinus. In some of his writings, Porphyry makes

[34] See Lewy 1978; Saffrey 1990: 33–94 and Athanassiadi 1999.
[35] For issues related to Hermes, see Fowden 1986.

use, albeit limited, of the *Chaldaean Oracles*. In his *Life of Pythagoras* he mentions the periods spent by Pythagoras among non-Greek populations; and in his *De abstinentia* he applies without hesitation the term 'philosophers' to Egyptian or Judaic priests and to Brahmans. However, there is no proof that he – even if of Phoenician origin – would have had access to texts of oriental wisdom in the original languages: after all, his perspective was that of a Greek author who depends on Greek sources even if they are about non-Greek cultures.[36] In *Abbamon's Response to Porphyry's Letter to Anebos* – which Marsilio Ficino would entitle *The Mysteries of Egypt* – Iamblichus distinguishes three types of issues, addressed, respectively, in the teachings of Chaldaean sages, Egyptian prophets, and philosophers. These are theological, theurgic and philosophical issues, and each one of them requires different kinds of answers. Philosophical issues, however, will be solved according to the ancient steles of Hermes. Plato and Pythagoras had already analyzed these steles in detail (Iamb. *Myst.* 1.1.4–5; 1.2.5–7), as Iamblichus confirmed in his *Life of Pythagoras*, where he attributed to Pythagoras not only relationships with Phoenician and Chaldean sages, but even a twenty year sojourn in Egypt (*VP.* 1.2; 3.14; 4.18–19). It is tempting to think that Iamblichus meant by 'philosophers' the Greek philosophers, thereby distinguishing them from the Chaldaean sages and the Egyptian prophets. At any rate, he considers the language of sacred peoples – such as the Assyrians and the Egyptians – to be more suitable for sacred rituals and more ancient, since the Egyptians were the first who had the prerogative of communicating with the gods (*Myst.* 7.2.256–8). The immutability of sacred names is set against the mutability of the Greeks – according to a strategy that resembles that in treatise 16 of the *Corpus Hermeticum*. Greeks have no self-supporting basis, and they do not keep what they receive, but modify it due to their skill in finding words (7.6.259). All the writings transmitted under the name of Hermes, he maintains, have been translated from Egyptian by men who were not skilled in philosophy (8.4.265–7).

So the point of view of *Epinomides* got reversed. Greeks not only failed to improve, but they actually spoiled what they received from others, including theological and theurgic knowledge.[37] This assertion does not designate a gap between Oriental wisdom and Greek philosophy. Rather, Iamblichus affirmed the dependence of philosophy on Egyptian and Chaldaean wisdom, and its comparative imperfection. At the beginning of the fifth century BCE Syrianus, Proclus' teacher, supposedly wrote on *Orpheus,*

---

[36] See similar conclusions in Millar 1997 and Clark 1999.
[37] On theurgy in Iamblichus see Fowden 1986: 126–41. Armstrong 1987 tends to minimize the impact of the reference to Egypt.

Pythagoras and Plato's Symphony with the Chaldaean Oracles. Proclus insisted on the continuity between this ancient type of wisdom and Platonic philosophy, conceived of as the culmination of this line. In his *Platonic Theology* he identified several ways in which theological doctrines could be explained: the mode of symbols used by Orpheus; the mode of the Pythagoreans, consisting of images, in the sense that mathematical things are the images of divine things; the theurgic mode used by the Chaldaeans and, finally, the scientific mode of Plato (1.4.p.20.1–25). All Hellenic theology, he believed, shared the same father: Orphism. The sequence was Orpheus, Aglaophamus, Pythagoras, Plato.[38] However, Plato was defined as the guide gifted with divine intellect: Plato is certainly believed to be the heir of a tradition, but it is with Plato that theology got stripped of its mythopoetic elements and became *epistēmē* (1.5.p.25.24–6, 22).

GREEK PHILOSOPHY AND THE HISTORY OF REVELATION

By concentrating on military and political events, the historiography of Thucydides involved a new approach, which was different from Herodotus' focus on cultural aspects of non-Greek periods and countries. The events of philosophy – organized during the Hellenistic period according to the scheme of the succession of the schools – found chronological rhythms[39] which intertwined only indirectly with the time of historiography. Philosophers became the subjects of biographies and were included in historical narratives, but only as the protagonists of political or military events. In his *Hellenica*, Xenophon, who devoted many of his works to Socrates, mentions Socrates for his opposition to the decision to put the generals of the Arginusae battle on trial (1.7.15), but in Book 3, which describes the events occurring from 400 to 395 BCE, he never mentions Socrates' death. The narrative of Diodorus Siculus seems to represent an exception, for he wrote about the history of the Pythagoreans in Southern Italy. However, the events of this history matter politically for Magna Grecia (10.3–11 and 12.9.4). Mostly, Diodorus mentions the years of birth, activity, and death of philosophers, according to the annalistic scheme he adopted. Behind Diodorus' quotations were the chronographies, a genre developed during the Hellenistic age, starting with the *Chronicle* written by Apollodorus of Athens in the middle of the second century BCE. Chronographies were based on the philosophical model of the stages of life, and they calculated the birth date of an individual in accordance with the belief that a man would

---

[38] Brisson 1987 and Balthes 1999.   [39] Von Kienle 1961.

reach his intellectual *acmē* at the age of forty. Such a scheme allowed for the construction of synchronisms between different characters – such as Greek philosophers, historians, or poets – as well as their association with historical events. Apollodorus considered, for example, thinkers such as Thales, Democritus, and Socrates.[40] However, historical and philosophical events ran parallel and never really intertwined. The point of view of Christians on Greek philosophy implied, by contrast, a different temporal dislocation of philosophy itself, for the latter became part of, or at least interacted with, proper history – the history of divine revelation and salvation. This new perspective did not do away with traditional political-military historiography, which continued to flourish until late antiquity. However, it brought about the idea that there was indeed a more decisive and significant type of history and temporality beyond the histories and successions of empires. In Tatian, one of the first Christian apologists, the themes which will be recurrent later – and are in some cases attested in the Jewish tradition – are already present. In the first place, Tatian claims the chronological priority of the Scriptures over the doctrines of Greek philosophers. Tatian called Moses the "*archēgos*" – the same term used by Aristotle for Thales – "of every barbarian wisdom" and believed that he was more ancient than the very ancient Homer (29 and 31). This point was demonstrated through a long chronological argument (36–41) indicating that the Greco-Roman society, to which Tatian belonged, appreciated antiquity more than novelty. The point of view according to which truth is associated with antiquity was well established.[41] However, the issue is not simply one of chronological priority, but also of dependence and derivation. According to Tatian, Greek philosophers had derived their teachings from Moses and had altered his doctrine (40). One further element which will be extremely important as regards the Christian debate is the classification of Greek philosophers as arrogant, with their arrogance giving rise to the *diaphōnia* of their doctrines (2–3) – a sign that the latter held no truth, as the ancient Skeptics had already understood. Themes of this sort will be used by the Church Fathers, such as Justin, Clement of Alexandria, and Origen, albeit within different apologetic or polemical contexts.

Justin was also convinced that Greek philosophers had drawn from the Holy Scriptures and that, in particular, Plato had read them, without

---

[40] See Mosshammer 1979: 113–27.

[41] This point is widely reconstructed by Boys-Stones 2001, also as regards the pagan tradition and the development of the allegorical approach to ancient poetry and to its importance for the future of Platonism. On the use of the term philosophy in the Fathers see Malingrey 1961; cf. also Barnes 2002.

understanding them completely (*I Apol.* 44.8–9; 59.1 and 5; 60.1–6). How-ever, he was impressed at seeing how those philosophers, and Plato above all, had managed to get very close to the truth and the teachings of Christ. How could this be possible for philosophers who had lived before the revelation of Christ? No doubt, one could not conceive of a revelation meant expressly for them. Rather, Justin believed that in every man there existed "seeds of truth" (ibid. 44.10). In his *Second Apology* (8.1) he speaks of an "*empsychon* seed" implanted in all humankind, and introduces the notion of *logos*, which means both the power of reason that human beings are provided with, and Christ as Word. In this way, one could affirm that those who had lived without *logos* had been enemies of Christ, even though Christ had not yet appeared. By contrast, when philosophers had discov-ered or formulated truths, albeit in a somewhat partial or opaque manner, this happened because they spoke on the basis of a component of the universal *logos* present in them within the limits of their human capacity. Thus, they lived like Christians, while they were considered atheists in the eyes of the Greeks and were condemned. This was the case of Socrates, who had known Christ in advance thanks to that element of *logos* which resided in him (*I Apol.* 46.3–4; *II Apol.* 10.4–8; 13.3–5). However, their knowledge of truth could not be total, because totality became possible only thanks to Christ, who is the Logos (*II Apol.* 2–3; 13.6). In a different work, the *Dia-logue with Trypho* (2, 2.19; 7.1–2), Justin attacked those philosophical sects which were in conflict with one another, on the grounds that knowledge is one, but it is impossible to reach oneness without God and without Christ. This is why only prophets, who lived well before philosophers, could see the truth. The message of Jewish prophets and the revelation of Christ represented one unitary tradition.[42] The time of philosophy came to be included between the earlier time of Jewish prophets – from which it had drawn albeit partially – and the later one of the revelation of Christ. Greek philosophy therefore covered only one temporal segment of a wider event, and its time, in the best case scenario, could not but be a time of partial truths.

Clement of Alexandria will go one step beyond this, conceiving of Greek philosophy as a work of Providence. Obviously, true philosophy was due to divine revelation: "thanks to the Word – he said – the whole world has become Athens and Hellas" (*Protr.* 112.1; *Strom.* 11.112.2). However, Clement had to face few supporters of the theory that philosophy was the work of demons who sought to destroy humankind. He stands firmly

---

[42] On this issue see Boys-Stones 2001: 151–75 and on Justin in particular 184–8.

against this position, but believes that one cannot ascribe the discovery of philosophy to autonomous human intelligence: the Scriptures maintain that even the intelligence of men is a gift of God (*Strom.* 6.8.62.4). God is the cause of everything that is good and useful. He caused some things in a direct way, as for example, the revelation contained in the Old and New Testaments, and others in a mediated way – such had been philosophy, which could be called *theothen*, or coming from God (1.5.28.2; 6.17.156.4). In several passages from the *Stromata*, Clement dealt with philosophy as a gift of Providence to the Greeks, more than to men in general, as their specific property (*oikeia*) (1.19.1–2; 1.20.1; 6.5.42.1; 6.8.66.1). Philosophy had been given to the Greeks in order to educate them and prepare them for Christ, in the same way that the law had been given to the Jews with the same goal (1.5.28.3), "like rain on fertile soil" (1.7.37.1; 6.6.44.1). This means that there is a time for everything, a time that is established by Providence, not only a time for the spreading of the Gospel, for the law and the Jewish prophets, but also one for the philosophy of the Greeks. This is the theme of philosophy as a preparation for the Gospel, as if two strands, the Jewish and the Greek, converged towards this single terminal point.

This theme will continue to be significant also in the *Praeparatio evangelica* of Eusebius of Caesarea, composed when Christianity became the official religion of the empire under Constantine. Clement's peculiarity is represented by his theory that the propaedeuticity of Greek philosophy would function before and after Christ alike. Just like the *enkyklios paideia* helps and prepares for the study of philosophy, so philosophy prepares for the acquisition of wisdom, of the necessary knowledge of divine and human things. Such knowledge can only be achieved through revelation (*Strom.* 1.5.28.1; 1.5.30.1, and 32.4). Clement derives from Justin the theme of *Logos*, which is present in every man to a certain degree, and allows people to recognize certain truths, such as the existence of one God (1.13.57.2). However, he also believes that evangelical preaching had spread among all men, while philosophy had been confined to Greece alone, Providence granting it only to few men (6.5.42.3; 6.18.167.3). This view would be held later by Origen *(Contr. Cels.* 7.59–60), according to whom, if Plato had wanted his doctrines to benefit those who spoke Egyptian or Syrian, he would have learnt languages instead of remaining Greek. The Greekness of philosophers was a limit compared to the universality of the Christian message. Moreover, according to Clement, the truths accessible to philosophers had been necessarily partial and often confused. This had provided a space for the growth of conflicting philosophical sects, which had dismembered philosophy, just as the bacchantes had torn Pentheus apart, each of them claiming that their part of truth was the whole truth (1.13.57.1–6). In this sense, Greek philosophy appeared to Clement as a nut in which not everything is edible (1.1.7.3). However, truth is one, so it was possible to recompose these scattered limbs on the basis of Christian truth: I call philosophy – he said – not the Stoic, or the Platonic, or the Epicurean, or the Aristotelian, but whatever has been well said by each of those schools (*haireseis*), which teach righteousness along with a science pervaded by piety (*eusebēs epistēmē*) – this eclectic whole (*eklektikon*) I call philosophy what has not been corrupted by the intrusion of human reasoning (1.7.36.6). Christian revelation provided the criteria for appraising preexistent pagan philosophies, in order to lead them back to one single truth. In this operation, Clement gave Platonic philosophy a privileged position.

The preparatory function ascribed to philosophy could, however, allow for the recognition of its chronological priority and remove it from its connection with Divine Providence. This is why Clement used the theme already formulated in Jewish culture, according to which Greek philosophers had plagiarized the Scripture – a plagiarism that he compared to Prometheus' theft of fire (1.17.87.1–2). Clement devoted a large section of the fifth book of the *Stromata* to the plagiarism of the Greeks, comparing passages from Greek philosophers with passages from the Scriptures. The corollary of this thesis was the affirmation of the superior antiquity of the Jewish people and, more generally, of the barbarians, to the Greeks. As regards this point, Clement could draw on a variety of Hellenistic sources on the journeys of philosophers, and on the chronological arguments already used by Jewish authors such as Flavius Josephus.[43] The time of Greek philosophy had shortened again, leaving an opening which could be filled by barbarian wisdom, especially by the most ancient of all: the Jewish one. Celsus, a pagan author, in a work which has been lost, attacked Christians in the second half of the second century CE, tracing back Christian doctrines to Jewish culture. However, Celsus considered the Greeks as the true heirs of the authentic barbarian wisdom (Egyptians, Assyrians, Indians, Persians), from which the Jews were excluded. In this sense, Christianity seemed to be a threat to the Empire's unity, in so far as it was separated from the common tradition together with Judaism.[44] In the

---

[43] See Mortley 1980 and Boys-Stones 2001: 176–202.
[44] Origen, *Against Celsus* 1.2.14, and 21. On this point see Frede 1997 and 1999. For a general outline see Crouzel 1962.

following century, Origen, in his *Contra Celsum*, would object that better pagan authors, such as Numenius and others, had included the Judeans in the list of barbarian peoples possessing and transmitting wisdom (1.15). The decisive facts, however, were the chronological anteriority of Moses and the prophets – not only compared to Plato, but also to Homer, the oldest among the Greek authors (6.7, 13, 43) – and the plagiarism of Greek philosophers (7.30 and 7.59). Origen also believed that Greek philosophy could not claim any supremacy or originality arguing that the decisive breaks occurred outside the Greek tradition.

Greek philosophers, if anything, had been the inspiring sources of Christian heresies because of their theoretical disagreements. This point was debated for a long time in the works of Irenaeus of Lyon, and, above all, in the *Refutation of All Heresies* by Hippolytus.[45] It was a frequent theme in Tertullian; but here, the Greek tradition was presented within a history and genealogy of errors, rather than a history of truth. In the Latin Occident the priority of barbarian wisdom over that of the Greek philosophers was emphasized. This is what Lactantius argued when he cited Hermes Trismegistus – who was far more ancient than Plato and Pythagoras – in his *De ira Dei* 11 and returned to him several times in the *Divinae institutiones*. However, in this work Lactantius also effected a demolition of the myth about the connection between Greek philosophy and ancient wisdom. The faculty of searching things and examining what has been transmitted is a gift of God to all humankind; so, chronological priority does not entail any superiority of wisdom. It is not a matter of following the discoveries of the "ancients" *pecudum more*, like a herd (2.7). It is necessary to make a distinction between philosophy and wisdom. To confuse philosophy with wisdom, as both Lucretius and Cicero had done, was a fatal error. It was the same as bestowing man with *sapientia*, which is no human invention, but has its origin in God and as such was unknown to the warring philosophers. Truth is one, Lactantius emphatically remarked; God is one and *sapientia* must be one (3.2). Philosophers sought wisdom, but failed to find it. Yet wisdom ought to be somewhere. Philosophers like Pythagoras and Plato suspected that true wisdom concerned religion and so they set off to Egypt. Yet they did not have contact with the Judeans, the only ones who possessed wisdom. This does not mean that humankind lived without reason; *sapientia* and not philosophy represented the true beginning (*Div. inst.* 3.13–16). The very name "philosophy," introduced by Pythagoras, shows that at the time it is not considered to be wisdom. In this fashion, the myth according to

---

[45] Mansfeld 1992. On the First Fathers and the philosophy of barbarians see Waszink 1979.

which Plato would be an Atticizing Moses got destroyed. Divine Providence kept the Greeks from encountering the Judeans, so that they would not be able to know the truth, which would emerge in its due time with the advent of Christ (4.2). In this way, Lactantius claimed the posteriority of Greek philosophy, while, at the same time, distinguishing it from the far more ancient wisdom, that which had no need of the weapons of dialectic.

In the *De civitate Dei* Augustine formulated a different conception of the connection between philosophy and wisdom. He described philosophy as love for wisdom and explained that since wisdom belongs to God, the true philosopher is a lover of God (8.1). This did not imply that those who name themselves philosophers are all true philosophers, that is to say lovers of true wisdom. Augustine refers first and foremost of the Greek philosophers. He thus objects to those who believe that one of the reasons why Rome should be glorified is the existence there of philosophical schools:

Will our adversaries perhaps remind us of the schools of the philosophers and their disputations? In the first place, these are not Roman, but Greek; or even if they are now Roman because Greece herself has been made into a Roman province, they are still not the precepts of gods but the inventions of men. (2.7, trans. R. W. Dyson)

Then Augustine divides the field of philosophy according to the traditional Greek threefold system into physics, ethics, and logic, and makes use of the traditional schemes of the succession of the schools (8.2–4). In order to distinguish between true and false philosophers, Augustine uses the criterion of the congruency of their doctrines with Christian teaching. Unlike Clement, however, he does not talk in general about philosophy as a gift given by providence to the Greeks, but introduces the concept of providence only when it comes to doctrines which show such a congruency. The group of true philosophers, the lovers of God, is identified by Augustine with the Platonists who have made philosophical works all the more distinguished and famous by translating them (8.10). According to Augustine, for Plato to engage with philosophy was the same as loving God, whose nature is incorporeal (8.10). In this sense, Plato is the incarnation of the image that Augustine deems to be a true philosopher; but what he is interested in is the philosophical space shared by philosophy and Christian doctrines. In particular, he is interested in the notion of God, which should not be confined to Platonists alone, but should be extended to all Greek philosophers as well as to those among the barbarian peoples who had been held wise and philosophers, be they Atlantics, Libyans, Chaldaeans, Scythians, Gauls, or Spaniards (8.9). Augustine is concerned with finding doctrinal convergences, rather than establishing the genealogies and temporal sequences of a history of wisdom; and from this viewpoint Greeks and barbarians can be easily put side by side. However, he also raises the question of Plato's agreement with some doctrinal points of the Judeo-Christian tradition. He knows that some Christians, surprised by this agreement, believed that Plato had met the prophet Jeremiah during his trip to Egypt, and had read the book of prophets. On the basis of chronographic research – he probably drew on the *Chronicle* of Eusebius of Caesarea, translated into Latin by Jerome – Augustine exposed the anachronism of this thesis. For it appeared that Jeremiah prophesied almost one hundred years before the birth of Plato, while it was impossible for Plato to have read the Scriptures, which were translated into Greek only after his death under Ptolomaeus Philadelphus. Had Plato read the Scriptures, he could have done so only by using an interpreter and, thus, through oral transmission. Augustine does not exclude this last possibility, seeing the extraordinary convergence, for example, between passages in the *Timaeus* and in Genesis. He concludes with some caution: however Plato learnt about these things, whether from the books of his predecessors or because God appeared to him, his school seemed an entirely fitting partner for the discussion of issues of natural theology (8.11).

It had yet to be established which city the philosophers belonged to: if they belonged to the heavenly or the earthly one. The distinction raised the question of whether one lived according to God or to man. The Jews could not deny that some individuals, even among other peoples, belonged to the true Israelites not by earthly but heavenly fellowship: the prime example was Job, a stranger joining the people of Israel (18.47). However, Augustine did not use Greek philosophers as an example, and considered the dissent among philosophers as the fruit of the pride of each of them to appear wiser, rather than a follower of the doctrines of others, and as a typical expression of a city that worshipped demons. In this sense, even heresies, by reproducing the *diaphōnia* of the Greek philosophical schools, were the work of demons (18.41.51). In Book 18, devoted to the earthly city which was marked by division, Augustine, using mostly Eusebius,[46] established a series of synchronisms from Abraham until the end of the world. Greek philosophers were placed within this series. Augustine reports that Thales belonged to the time of Romulus and the succeeding natural philosophers to the time of Jewish captivity (18.24–5). Greek philosophers

---

[46] Markus 1988: 1–21.

were thus classified chronologically in reference to the two coordinates of Roman history and Jewish tradition, but reference to the latter coordinate was preferred. The issue was how to locate them with reference to sacred history. This allowed Augustine to affirm that at the time of the prophets, gentile philosophers in the proper sense of the term did not yet exist. The first to be called a philosopher was Pythagoras, who lived after the Jewish slavery had ended. Before the prophets only the theological poets had existed – Orpheus, Linus, Musaeus and a few others among the Greeks – but not even those preceded Moses, "our true theologian." In this way, Augustine resolved the issue of the chronological relationship between Jewish wisdom and Greek philosophy. However, the question of the relationship between the wisdom of Moses and that of the barbarians remained unsettled. Starting from a passage in The Acts of the Apostles (7.22), where it is stated that Moses had been instructed in all the sciences of the Egyptians, Augustine had to admit that Egyptian wisdom was older. However, even Egyptian wisdom turned out to be younger than the wisdom of another Jewish prophet, Abraham. Isis, who had given letters to the Egyptians, came long after Abraham, and after Noah (18.37–8). Generally, Augustine was opposed to the idea of an Egyptian wisdom that predated the wisdom of the patriarchs. He noted that the contents of Egyptian wisdom were confined to astronomy and other similar sciences that flourished with Hermes Trismegistus – long before the sages and philosophers of Greece, but after Abraham and Moses. He quoted a passage from the hermetic work *Asclepius*, translated into Latin by Apuleius, where Trismegistus seemed to foretell the advent of Christianity. However, it was clear that this prophecy came from a friend of the demons, for he deplored this event (18.23–4). Both Augustine's condemnation of the hermetic tradition and Trismegistus' engagement with antiquity were to become crucial to debates about the temporality and history of philosophy in the modern era.

THE *PRISCA THEOLOGIA* AND THE TIME OF GREEK PHILOSOPHY

In the patristic tradition, Greek philosophy was given only a small part within a larger universal history. This image was transmitted for centuries; and, even when connections between schools of thought or individual Greek thinkers were traced, these connections were always presented within the broader horizon of a history of revelation and salvation. In the Latin Middle Ages traditional chronographical schemes were kept and even the rediscovery of many works by Aristotle and of the lives of the

philosophers by Diogenes Laertius did not alter things significantly.[47]
Around the fifteenth century the revival of Greek texts and of the texts
written by the Greek Fathers helped focus the issue of the connections
between Greek philosophy and the wisdom of the barbarians, albeit in a
changed historical context. The most accomplished formulation was that
of Marsilio Ficino. In a letter of 1464 Franciscus Philelphus considered the
ideas of Plato as having their source in the teachings of Pythagoras, who in
turn received them from Zoroaster, "the most ancient of all philosophers,"
whose doctrines Pythagoras had learnt when he was with the Chaldaeans.[48]
Ficino, at least in his first writings, pointed towards a different direction.
In a short work dated in 1457, *Di Dio et anima*, he attributed to Hermes Trismegistus, "philosopho Egiptio più antico lungo tempo che' greci
philosophi," a notion of the divine substance characterized by three features – power, wisdom, and goodness – which prefigured the three persons
of the Trinity. Ficino found so great an affinity between Plato and Mer-
curius (who had lived many centuries before Plato), that he thought that
"el Mercuriale spirito" had been transformed into "nel pecto Platonico."
The teachings of both authors bore affinities with the doctrine of Christian
theologians.[49] It is not surprising, then, that in 1463, when Cosimo de
Medici commissioned Ficino to translate into Latin the Greek manuscript
of the hermetic writings (which lacks the last treatise, number xv), taken
from Macedonia to Florence around 1460, he managed to finish it in a
few months. Considering that the several treatises were in fact one single
oeuvre, he gave the whole work the title of the first treatise, *Pimander*.
Printed in 1471, this work had an extraordinary reception in Europe and
shaped the destiny of hermeticism. In the introduction to this translation,
Ficino presented a genealogy which combined motifs coming from several
sources, including Proclus: Hermes Trismegistus, called the *primus author*
of theology, then Orpheus, who initiated Aglaophemus, who was followed
by Pythagoras, and then Philolaus, the teacher of "our divine Plato." In
this way, Ficino constructed a single school of *prisca theologia*, a hexad
that began with Hermes Trismegistus, who had prophesied the advent of
Christ, and ended (*penitus absoluta*) with Plato.[50]

   It is a genealogy that Ficino was to present several times, but with
some important variations. In his *Theologia platonica*, completed in 1474,
the hexad is the same – with important magical and symbolic meanings

---

[47] For a general outline, see Piaia 1983.   [48] Republished in Hankins 1990, II: 515–23.
[49] See the critical edition of Kristeller 1937, II: 128–58; and I: clix–clx.
[50] Kristeller 1956: 221–47; Yates 1964: 14–16 and 20–83 on hermeticism and magic in Ficino; Garin
    1961: 143–54 and Garin 2006.

(6 were the days for creation, 6 the planets etc.) – but Philolaus disappears, as does the link between Pythagoras and Plato; his place is taken by Zoroaster, who is located at the top of the list, as the first theologian and the author of the *Chaldaean Oracles* (8.1). In *De christiana religione* (1474) Ficino sees in the will of Divine Providence the intention to leave no place on earth devoid of religion; his genealogy of wisdom is identical with that in his *Theologia*.[51] It was the traditional diachronic model, but it held no diffusionist value, because it did not postulate any direct relationship between those belonging to the "line" of wisdom – for example between Zoroaster and Hermes, or Hermes and Orpheus. The aim was rather to emphasize the concordance between these visions and the fact that the consummation of this *prisca theologia* was to be found in the Platonic writings. In his reply to the Hungarian Johannes Pannonius, Ficino explains his reasons for devoting his work to pagan philosophy.[52] Pannonius criticized this as vain *curiositas*. He could not see how the *renovatio* of the ancients – to which Ficino had contributed with his translations – would be of any use within the scheme of Providence, all the more because the contents of this ancient theology had nothing Christian about them. Moreover he accused Ficino of believing that the project he had embarked on was due to fate. Ficino conceived of his work as ordained by Divine Providence to strengthen the Christian religion. If religion was in such a bad state, he maintained in the prologue to the *De christiana religione*, this was because the ancient philosophical wisdom had been neglected. In his reply to Pannonius, Ficino deals with these themes again. Obviously, one could not demand the best of Christian wisdom from those who had lived before the advent of Christ. At the same time, one should not expect that philosophical intellects, relying as they do on reason alone, would join the Christian religion immediately and reject the impiety of, for example, Aristotelian philosophy. A preparatory philosophical training was crucial for them. Knowledge and illumination of ancient theology – of what he called *pia philosophia*, developed through the six stages explained above – were the two necessary elements of this training. Only by being acquainted with ancient theology, could modern thinkers be receptive to Christianity, which was the highest religion of all. In this way, Ficino went back

---

[51] On Proclus as source of Ficino's genealogy see Saffrey 1987. On the surfacing of Zoroaster, who replaces Hermes, see in particular Allen 1998: 29–42.

[52] The best analysis is in Allen 1998: 1–49, which provides also the edition of the two letters of Pannonius and Ficino. Many aspects of the letter to Pannonius are drawn from Ficino's introduction to his translation of Plotinus, published in 1492. On the issue of *prisca theologia* in Ficino see also Hankins 1990, I: 282–96 and II: 460–4.

to the traditional plan of making ancient philosophy ancillary to theology. The context for Ficino's *renovatio* of the ancients,[53] however, changed when at the beginning of the seventies millenaristic prophecies, horoscopes announcing the imminent derangement of Europe or the advent of peace and harmony started to be widespread. He believed that the new astral configuration could be perceived as a sign, but not as the cause, of such renovation. After all, the Magi had recognized the advent of the Lord from the stars. The outcome of Ficino' perspective, despite the changed historical and cultural frames, was nonetheless the compression of Greek philosophy, even in its more advanced peaks, represented by Platonism and his interpreters – Plotinus, Porphyry, Iamblichus, Proclus, and Ficino himself, now engaged in the translation of Plotinus – within a riverbed of much wider times and spaces, in which Greek philosophy constituted only a small segment, rather than the radical beginning of a historical world.

The temporal scheme provided by the *prisca theologia* enjoyed great success in Europe, certainly until the Platonists of Cambridge and even after.[54] In a climate now marked by the conflict between Protestants and Catholics, Agostino Steuco, librarian in the Vatican and connoisseur of Hebrew and Aramaic, minted the expression *perennis philosophia* for his homonymous work published in 1540, at the eve of the Council of Trent.[55] Steuco resumed Ficino's concordist theme, and once again made use of the *Chaldaean Oracles* and the theology of Hermes Trismegistus; but he belonged to different times, wherein the unity of the Christian world was breaking into pieces. He wanted to show the unifying effectiveness of the perennial philosophy which unanimously attested to the need to recognize and worship God and in which the best of Greek philosophy could be included. However, the unitary landscape had already started to crack. John Picus, Pico della Mirandola shared the Ficinian paradigm and concordist programme for some time, giving crucial weight to Jewish kabbalah, which he considered to have preserved the original wisdom given from God to Moses.[56] In this way, he expanded the sphere of texts that had transmitted wisdom before the time of Greek philosophers. But in his *Disputationes adversus astrologiam divinatricem*, completed in 1494 and printed in 1496, the tone changed:

As regards what Greek philosophers have rightly thought on natural philosophy, through rational demonstrations, no part of it was drawn from the Egyptians;

---

[53] See on this Vasoli 2006: 3–29 and 87–109.   [54] See Yates 1964 and especially Walker 1972.
[55] See Muccillo 1996: 1–72.
[56] Pico della Mirandola 1942: 142–4, 160, 170–2. Cf. Garin 1961: 231–40 and Grafton 1997: 93–134, in particular 115–26, 131–2.

only things relating to cult and astronomy have been taken from them. The proof of this is that, when it comes to astronomy and mysteries, we always see them mentioning the Chaldaeans and the Egyptians . . . but as far as philosophical arguments are concerned, we never see them [the Egyptians] mentioned in Plato or Aristotle. (12.3)

In this way, Pico distanced himself from Ficino and from the idea that the hermetic and Chaldaean literatures already contained the core of the philosophy of Plato and Aristotle. The drastic separation between Platonic philosophy and the Christian message in Florence at the time was likewise evident in the sermons of Gerolamo Savonarola. In a sermon on Exodus preached in 1498, against those who wanted to make "all of Plato Christian," he stressed

Plato is Plato and Aristotle Aristotle, and not Christian, because they are not, because there is as much difference between Plato and a Christian as there is between sin and virtue, and as much difference between Plato's doctrine and Christ's as between darkness and light. Philosophers are philosophers and Christians Christians.[57]

Greek philosophy started to be unanchored from the periods before and after its development, and got released from its status as knowledge derived from a more archaic wisdom and preparatory for the full revelation coming from God's initiative. Other factors contributed to this process of autonomization. I want to mention here only one philological component, by dealing with two cases skillfully reconstructed by Anthony Grafton. In 1579 Joseph Scaliger published an edition and commentary of Manilius' *Astronomica*. He considered this work as the repository of an ancient astronomical and astrological system derived from the Orient (probably Egypt), which had been lost and which Greek astronomers had later on rightly rejected, since it was full of mistakes, as Pico had already partially detected. Scaliger contrasted this work with the Greek geometrical models of the Ptolemaic astronomy. In this way, he could cast doubt on the assumption – based on the *prisca theologia* – that temporal priority entailed doctrinal superiority. Here, in fact, the reverse was the case. In a second revised edition of Manilius that appeared in 1599–1600, Scaliger added his *Prolegomena de astrologia veterum*, in which he maintained:

Although the Greeks taught many things in all areas of learning, everyone considers Greece to have been the teacher rather than the parent of the liberal arts, because she developed discoveries that were not her own but those of the Chaldaeans.

---

[57] Savonarola 1956, II: 290–1; see also predication xxv on Ezekiel dated to 25 February 1497 (Savonarola 1955, I: 329). On Savonarola and ancient theology see Walker 1972: 42–62.

Those who express this view seem to me either to forget the antiquity of the Greeks or to ignore their splendid literary achievements. (trans. A. Grafton)

Another excellent philologist, the Calvinist Isaac Casaubon, sensitive – as protestants usually are – to the differences between Christians and pagans who had not received a specific divine revelation, found in Cardinal Baronius' *Annales ecclesiastici*, which he was trying to demolish, the reference of pagan authors (Hermes Trismegistus among them) to the advent of Christ. Once he analyzed the texts of the *Corpus hermeticum*, he realized that their language and content, also because of the presence of anachronisms, could only have been written after the advent of Christianity. They recalled the age of the Fathers, drew from Greek philosophers, and contained no element of archaic Egyptian wisdom.[58] The tradition of *prisca theologia* was thus deprived of one of its primary texts. This move created space for the recognition of the distinctiveness of Greek philosophy without reference to any dependence upon Eastern wisdom.

In England, during the same years in which Casaubon was analyzing the *Corpus hermeticum*, Francis Bacon was preoccupied with finding a new way of understanding Greek philosophy.[59] The angle from which Bacon observed the past was no longer occupied by theology, but by natural philosophy. Since his *Temporis partus masculus*, written in 1602–3, Bacon had always maintained that each science must be grounded upon nature, rather than antiquity, and rejected the idea that the present should be considered as a continuation of the past. He knew that a claim that science had bloomed in antiquity would be useful in the attempt to persuade his audience and achieve consensus. Antiquity had authority, so advocating it could ensure a self-legitimizing predecessor. But this move, according to Bacon, was an imposture (*NO* 122).[60] Nevertheless, he believed that the present state of science was the same as it had been in ancient Greece: he talked repeatedly of natural philosophy, "which we have received from the Greeks" or which has "flown from the Greeks to us." The authority of Greece was still unquestioned.[61] And when he said "us," Bacon meant "the Western nations of Europe." This was an expression he explicitly used in his *Cogitata et visa* (17) and *Novum organum* (78), published in 1620. There is an ongoing debate on whether before 1700 a notion of Europe as a

---

[58] See Grafton 1983a: 180–226 and Grafton 1991: 145–61.

[59] The best research on the history of philosophy in Bacon is still the second chapter of Rossi 1957.

[60] For Bacon's works, I use the following abbreviations: *CV* = *Cogitata et visa*; *NO* = *Novum organum*; *RP* = *Redargutio philosophiarum*.

[61] See for example *CV* 13; *RP* 12 and 58.

collective identity existed.[62] In Bacon this sense of belonging seems present, but it is related to a science and a philosophy that he does not feel he can continue to share, a tradition that has not changed much since the Greeks and the Romans. Albeit under a negative sign, Bacon established a direct line between Greek philosophy and modern Europe. This allowed him to reconstruct the tradition that connected the Greeks to the present. In order to describe this continuity, he used the old model of the ages of life. Greek natural philosophy was the *pueritia* of science and shows the signs typical of childhood: verbosity and incapacity to generate (*CV* 13). Bacon mentioned the words of the Egyptian priest in Plato's *Timaeus* about the Greeks being always young, but he did not do so in order to claim or confirm the existence of an antecedent *prisca theologia*, whose roots lay in the Orient. On the contrary, he did so in order to emphasize that this age was immature and that this immaturity lingered on until the present time (*RP* 20; *NO* 71). Bacon evoked a well-known conception of antiquity: usually the Greeks were considered ancient compared to modern people, because they had come before. However, the truth was that modern people were in fact older, for the Greeks had remained children. One would expect more knowledge from the elders and a greater degree of judgement. Such qualities had been witnessed not in ancient Greece, but in modern times, thanks to the new geographical discoveries and technological inventions (*NO* 84). If there had been progress in the field of arts through the cooperation of many individuals, in science this had not occurred, and science had been arrested at the stage of Greeks' *pueritia* (*NO* 74).

Numerous writings circulating during his lifetime were for Bacon nothing more than "a portion of the philosophy of the Greeks," and of a philosophy which had not grown in direct contact with nature, but in "schools and cells:" "if you disregard these few Greeks, what do Romans or Arabs or our contemporaries have that does not come from the discoveries of Aristotle, Plato, Hippocrates, Galen, Euclid and Ptolemy?" (*RP* 10–11; *NO* 71). He believed that over the course of the several centuries elapsing between the Greeks and his own time there had been only three periods which had been productive as far as science is concerned, periods amounting to a total of five or six centuries: one with the Greeks, another with the Romans, and the last one with "us," the Western nations of Europe (*CV* 17, 392; *NO* 78). In addition, the political conditions of different historical periods were not irrelevant as regards the development of the philosophy of nature, and Bacon discerned a relation between political power and

[62] See Burke 1980: 24.

cultural flourishing. His historiography no longer consisted of a simple survey of synchronisms, as in the chronicle tradition. After the acceptance of the Christian faith, most minds had devoted themselves to theology, while natural philosophy had become the servant of other sciences and of theology itself (*CV* 6; *NO* 79–80). Theology, for Bacon, became a kind of impediment for the philosophy of nature instead of being its peak. But if Greek philosophy was still the nucleus of contemporary knowledge, then the analysis of the structural features of Greek philosophy could aid efforts to understand the reason for the absence of progress which had characterized the time of natural philosophy from ancient Greece to the present. Attention was thus shifted from doctrinal, especially theological, contents to the very modalities of philosophical activity. Such a shift entailed a totally different perspective, which should not be neglected, for theological contents had been the reference point for centuries in establishing the continuity of Greek philosophy with its possible Eastern precedents.

This point was developed by Bacon in his *Redargutio philosophiarum*, composed around 1608. First of all, Bacon tried to detect the historical conditions, the *nota temporis*, in which Greek philosophy was born and flourished. It was an age close to myths, devoid of history and of geographic knowledge, so much so that the Greeks celebrated as great enterprises the journeys of Democritus, Plato, and Pythagoras, which were only something like suburban promenades (*RP* 21–2; *NO* 72). It was in such a context, almost devoid of historical and geographical experiences, that philosophical activity developed in Greece. Bacon distinguished three types of philosophical activity: (1) that of the itinerant sophists, who claimed to transmit *sapientia* to adolescents for a fee; (2) that of those who opened schools in settled places, with auditors, disciples, and successors, and with original doctrines; (3) the activity of those who pursued truth far from the *pompa professoria* by conversing with few others and never disputing. These people would leave no school, only their writings. Representatives of the first type were the sophists described and criticized by Plato. Representatives of the second type were the founders of philosophical schools: Plato, Aristotle, Zeno, and Epicurus. Representatives of the third type were Empedocles, Heraclitus, Democritus, Anaxagoras, Parmenides, Xenophanes, Philolaus, and others. His thesis was that the first two types, even if they fought with each other, were in fact strictly interconnected. Therefore, Plato and Aristotle should be considered as sophists, for they wanted to have disciples. Greek wisdom was *professoria*, implicated in frequent disputes, which for Bacon was something inimical to the search for truth (*RP* 27–8; *NO* 71). Moreover, Bacon excluded Pythagoras from the second type, because, even though he had founded a school, it was a school full of traditions and superstitions. Pythagoras had mixed philosophy with theology, which was for Bacon the worst corruption of philosophy conceivable. Plato did something similar. He made a partial use of induction, but introduced fantastic and almost poetical elements in his philosophy in order to soothe the intellect (*RP* 36; *NO* 62, 65).

In this fashion, Bacon freed the field from the centerpieces of *prisca theologia* in Greece, for they were unproductive and dangerous for the philosophy of nature. But what was theology in Plato became dialectics in Aristotle, who, wanting to build the world starting from the categories, corrupted the philosophy of nature (*CV* 13; *RP* 29). By using his dialectical instruments, Aristotle acted towards his predecessors like an Ottoman despot with his family: with his refutations he progressively did away with all his opponents (*RP* 25). Freeing the field from opponents and predecessors, Aristotle was turned into a teacher, authority, and cult figure for the future, subjugating in this way many brains (*RP* 13, 35). This was the cost of professorial philosophy, as it developed in Greece. One should not mistake the consensus with regard to Aristotle's philosophy that lasted for so many centuries for proof that his doctrines were true. True consensus can only spring from free judgement, but those who supported Aristotle would only do so on the basis of his authority, rather than on the basis of an impartial analysis of his doctrines (*RP* 77). In spite of this, the loss of pre-Aristotelian texts was not to be attributed to Aristotle and the growth of his authority. Many of those texts, Bacon recalled, were still known in Cicero's time and under the Caesars. In fact, barbarians like Attila, Genseric, and the Goths helped Aristotle a great deal (*RP* 32–3, 37). Only the lightest wood survived this wreck, that is to say, Plato and Aristotle's works, while solid wood, that of the first philosophers, more attentive to nature and experience, and less tied to the dogmas of the schools, had sunk (*RP* 33, 39, 63; *NO* 71). But this did not mean that one should expect much from what had survived of these authors through quotations in the works of others – whether in the works of Aristotle, Lucretius, Cicero, Diogenes Laertius, or Plutarch – because those quotations, which were short and extrapolated from the harmonious whole to which they originally belonged, did not allow one to have an idea of the overall systems of the authors in question. However, Bacon believed that a collection of these passages would be useful, in order to realize the variety of opinions articulated in what can be considered to be the first and most meaningful steps taken by Greek philosophy.

Bacon meant to open a new path, an alternative to that of Greek philosophy – a path which entailed a new way of philosophizing. But he understood that his new programme would have been more easily accepted, had he chosen a type of antiquity which was older than that of Greek philosophy.[63] With this objective, he published in 1609 his *De sapientia veterum*. In this work he did not question the existence of divine revelation, or the idea that Moses had been instructed by the Egyptians, "one of the most ancient schools in the world." However, he did not refer to Jewish or Egyptian wisdom, but to the mythical heritage of ancient Greece. In his *Redargutio philosophiarum* (21) he described the age of the first Greek philosophers as an age close to *fabulae*, but he also stated that there had been divine men in those ancient days, gifted with superior knowledge. He knew that, had he turned to them, it would have been easier for him to persuade his audience that philosophy and the sciences had flourished thanks to the ancient sages long before the time of the Greeks. But he chose not to deal with the arcane contents of the fables written by poets, even though he did not think that the poets who transmitted them had also invented them.

It was this veil – which had been placed by poetic fables between the remotest antiquity and the most recent times – that he attempted to tear asunder in his *De sapientia veterum*. Bacon attempted to do so through the allegorical interpretation of thirty-one fables concerning nature or civil life, even though he was well aware of the possibility of different interpretations and of the risk of projecting onto them his own doctrines. However, his opinion was that mystery and allegory had been hidden in many of the fables written by ancient poets from the beginning. They were "almost golden relics and soft whispers of better times that had gone from the traditions of ancient descent to the bagpipes and flutes of the Greeks." In that ancient era, when all discoveries of human reason were new, "everything was full of fables, of riddles, of parables, of similes," and with these one tried to teach, not to conceal. It was a type of teaching suitable to minds still rough and incapable of refinement, which welcomed only what fell under the senses. Just as hieroglyphs are older than the alphabet, so the parables are older than rational arguments. Despite the comparison with the hieroglyphs, the myths that Bacon interpreted were Greek. They contained a wisdom which predated the Greek philosophers, but which was in accordance with the fundamental contents of Bacon's own programme. In spite of all, a new link with ancient Greece could still be re-tied.

---

[63] This is the thesis supported by Rossi 1957.

CONCLUSION

Bacon did not point towards Eastern precedents of Greek philosophy. For many centuries and even within the Greek world itself, the prevailing idea was that the time of philosophy was wider than that of Greek philosophy. Behind Greek philosophy a far more ancient alien wisdom was to be detected. There had been only few exceptions. In Rome, the focus on philosophy as something peculiar to Greece allowed the establishment of a much needed continuity between Greece and Rome, a continuity which would later define the links between the ancient world (Greece and Rome together) and the modern west. In the Greek world, the main exception to this tradition was Diogenes Laertius, according to whom philosophy was a Greek invention. Even Diogenes, however, stated that philosophy followed a story on its own, one which could not intertwine with history proper, that is to say political and military history. The Church Fathers were the first to include philosophy within a universal history, one marked by the relationship between God and men. Within such a sacred history, Greek philosophy had its precedent among the Jews. The theological perspective held by Christian authors implied that Greek philosophy could be seen not as a new beginning, but rather as instrumental and preparatory. Such was the main cultural landscape as regards the "Christian West" until the sixteenth century.

With Bacon, the center of attention shifted from theology to the Greek philosophy of nature, which came to mark the European philosophy and science of nature. It should not be inferred, however, that by welcoming the perspective of Bacon as well as the new science of nature, one would automatically be led into the seventeenth century, when the diffusionist models came to an alt. In fact, authors like Henry More and Ralph Cudworth – to remain in England – did approve of the mechanical/atomical philosophy restored by Cartesius, but traced it back to Democritus and to the Phoenician Moschus, identified with Moses. While Bacon meant to separate the new investigation of nature from the type of Greek philosophy that had ruled in Europe up to that moment, More and Cudworth aimed to include both physics and theology within the realm of a *perennis philosophia*. Even a fervent Baconian and anti-Aristotelian philosopher, like Joseph Glanvill, associated with the Royal Society (founded in 1660) and in favor of the new mechanical/atomical philosophy, continued to believe Greek learning to be merely a transcript of the Chaldaeans and the Egyptians. In 1690 William Temple would enter the *querelle* on ancient and modern learning. Against the image portraying modern thinkers as standing on the shoulders of giants, Temple emphasized how ancient Greeks and Romans also had their own giants, thus bringing back to the surface of debates the theme of barbarian wisdom (which by then probably included China as well) as the original source of Greek philosophy.

The one thinker who truly offered a new way of conceptualizing the relationship between Greek philosophy and Western identity was, in my opinion, Christoph August Heumann, in his *Acta philosophorum* (1715–26). Heumann detected a number of features which made it possible to distinguish philosophy proper from everything set outside its limits, thus providing a novel and "pure" notion of philosophy. He evoked Aristotle stating that philosophy was born out of "curiosity". It is curiosity that leads man to search for the truth and remove error, opens one's eyes and casts darkness away. Hence, philosophy cannot be based on human authority, nor can it be built on the quicksands of tradition. In this way, philosophy is incompatible with superstitions, obscure symbols, and hieroglyphs, and its main aspect is not initiating, but promotional. The priests belonging to the ancient peoples of the Orient, inclined as they were towards fake religions, could not be philosophers: it made no sense to talk about a "barbarian" or oriental philosophy. Only Greece could be the place where authentic philosophy started, as Diogenes Laertius had already detected. Among the necessary conditions for philosophy to flourish, Heumann included Greek forms of government, those who had developed the *libertas philosophandi*, and the secularization of the philosopher. Moreover, he also put an end to the label "pagan philosophers," since thinkers like Socrates or Cicero, who supported a natural theology that was distinguished from paganism, were philosophers who lived among pagans, rather than pagans. The time of philosophy had begun in Greece and could be continued in places where true religion (Christianity) had been purified. These places were the Protestant lands, which the *antibarbarus* Luther had freed from papal barbarity, one which tied superstition with violence and intolerance. In this fashion, Heumann elaborated the premises which would lead to different historical periodizations, and to the construction of positive and direct lines that linked ancient Greece to modern Europe.

Translated by Chiara Ghidini

CHAPTER 4

Historiography and political theology: Momigliano and the end of history

Howard Caygill

> Exodus may seem in principle simpler than messianism. It has often
> been opposed to messianism. But as is already evident from the work
> of Jewish medieval commentators, there is no less difficulty with the
> ideal of exodus than with that of the utopia at the end of the world.
> Yet there is a difference: apocalypse may be left to the responsibility
> of God, while, as Moses understood, exodus is the responsibility of
> heads of state, even if they are prophets.
>
> Arnaldo Momigliano, *Pagine Ebraiche*

In a typical aside in *Alien Wisdom: The Limits of Hellenization*,[1] Arnaldo
Momigliano provocatively links the historiography of the ancient and the
recent past. After describing the Stoic philosopher and historian Posidonius'
uncovering of 'mystical postures and bogus oracles among the supporters of
the slave king Eunus and the barbarous Mithridates', he observes ironically
that this ancient view lends 'some support to that candid Italian scholar
of unimpeachable erudition, Aurelio Peretti, who, in the year 1942, tried
to persuade himself (and if possible his readers) that no man of Indo-
Germanic blood could have protested against Rome: only Jews and other
Orientals scribbled sibylline oracles against the ruling power'.[2] The historiography of first- and second-century BCE Greek supporters of Roman
rule is linked to fascist historiography of the early 1940s by identifying the
shared assumption that uttering oracles against Roman dominion was the
prerogative of slaves, barbarians, Jews and Orientals. Equally characteristic
is Momigliano's immediate rebuttal of this assumption by citing a fragment from the history of Polybius' contemporary Antisthenes of Rhodes,
which relates that 'about 189 BCE the Roman general Publius became mad

---

[1] Originally presented as the Trevelyan Lectures at Cambridge in May 1973 and the A. Flexner lectures
at Bryn Mawr College, February–March 1974.
[2] Momigliano 1975b: 40; cf. Peretti 1943.

99

in the panhellenic sanctuary of Naupactus and began to utter oracles in good Greek about the end of Roman rule'. Here the uttering of oracles against Roman dominion is found, ironically, in the same Greco-Roman milieu frequented by Posidonius and Polybius, now attributed to a Roman general and, what is more, interpreted by Momigliano as an allegory of 'Hannibal, still living in Asia, if not Antiochus III himself'.[3]

This scholarly episode from *Alien Wisdom* is embedded within a broader intellectual context that shaped and informed Momigliano's inquiry into ancient and modern historiography. Posidonius and Peretti shared the assumption that oracular politics and prophetic historiography are rooted in the *ressentiment* of the powerless and were thus the prerogative of subaltern groups unable to pursue politics by the usual violent means. A version of this position was defended philosophically by Nietzsche in his *Genealogy of Morals* by means of the argument that the powerless, denied political or military expression, reacted by contriving resentful fantasies of the fall of the powerful and the end of history, even the end of the world. Exclusion from power prompts a reactive response to history that Nietzsche historically locates within certain currents of Judaism and early Christianity. Momigliano, however, consistently questions the implied equation between oracular politics, prophetic historiography and the *ressentiment* of 'pariah' groups, and most consistently in the case of Jewish and Christian oracular and prophetic historiography. He defends such historiography in the name of a political theology sensitive to the place of eschatological and messianic themes in the writing of history and the philosophy of history. His early and sustained interest in Weimar debates in political theology and messianism enabled him to develop an account of historical temporality able to do justice to both progressive and messianic philosophies of history and even to perceive cases of their mutual compatibility.

I

In *Alien Wisdom*, Momigliano continues his reflections on the significance of political prophesy by attributing Posidonius' and Polybius' silence regarding the oracles reported by Antisthenes[4] to their lack of religious

---

[3] Ibid. The general prophesied that a king from Asia would take revenge on the Romans for their oppression of the Greeks and that his prophesies would be confirmed by his being devoured by a wolf, as he duly was, leaving only his skull 'reiterating the prophesy of doom for Rome'. Momigliano interprets the testimony by identifying Publius with Scipio Africanus and the Asian king with Hannibal, while noting that the wolf and the skull 'are good Roman elements'.

[4] A source briefly mentioned by Peretti.

sensitivity: 'Religion was not the area of civilisation which Polybius and Posidonius found easiest to understand. It was better to talk politics.'[5] And yet, as Momigliano goes on to show, this insensitivity to religion meant that neither Greek historian was capable of understanding the internal political organisation of Roman dominion. In cooperating with Roman rule both 'left unexplored the most solid superstructures of the Roman-Italian complex' that encompassed 'law, honour and religion'. Concentrating exclusively on the ethos of the Roman ruling class and their techniques of conquest and rule codified in political and military organisation, neither 'asked a question about the justice of Roman rule nor about the real sources of her power'.[6] They were blind, in other words, to the political theology of Rome and the religious motivations that informed not only Roman institutions, but also what would become the imperial project of bringing justice to the entire world. Such insensitivity to the political theology of Rome, an account of which Momigliano presented to an English audience in his first lectures in exile in 1940, resulted not only in an underestimation of the sources of Roman power, but also of the pertinence of religious objections to it, in short, blindness not only to the political theology of rule but also to the modes of political and religious resistance that it prompted.

In his Cambridge lectures of January to March 1940 Momigliano explored the relationship between the themes of peace and liberty in Republican and Imperial Rome. The lectures were associated with a projected book *Liberty and Peace in Antiquity*, whose ambition was to analyse the development of these themes from the fifth century BCE to Augustine.[7] Informing Momigliano's study of the tension between peace and liberty through their transformation from Republican to Imperial and then Christian Rome is a particular understanding of the religious character of *pax* and *libertas*. Whether in the guise of Roman Republican liberty, *pax augusta* or the City of God, the political values of peace and liberty are inseparable from religion; they are situated by Momigliano within a particular understanding of political theology. Peace, liberty and justice informed the substructure of Roman institutions and were key to any understanding of the 'true functioning of political institutions'[8] that, as we have seen, in Momigliano's view, eluded Posidonius and Polybius. The reading of ancient history in terms of this political theology informed much of Momigliano's work; indeed whatever the textual or institutional detail under scrutiny,

---

[5] Ibid. 41. [6] Ibid. 48.
[7] The Cambridge lectures and other material from 1940 are available in di Donato's edition. See Momigliano 1996.
[8] Ibid. 142.

the problem of the relationship between politics and religion was always prominent. In his subsequent work, however, Momigliano developed a fascination not only with the political theology of Rome and its dominion, but also with that of the enemies of Rome, and inevitably with the political theology of resistance.

The conviction that religion and politics are inseparable is axiomatic for much of Momigliano's historical and philological work and may be traced to his interest in contemporary debates in political theology. His familiarity with the discipline of political theology that emerged in Weimar Germany and, more specifically with its critics, is evident from autobiographical comments in his work and with the remarkable series of late essays on Jewish critics of political theology that close his final collection of essays *Pagine Ebraiche*.[9] In the essay 'Gershom Scholem's autobiography' he locates himself as part of a generation 'who in the late twenties read German books and talked to German friends in Italy'.[10] He is indeed extremely well informed about debates concerning political theology among Weimar Jewish intellectuals including Rosenzweig, Benjamin, Scholem, Strauss and Löwith. He is also very sensitive to the political implications of these debates: in the opening paragraph to his 1986 Fondation Hardt address in Geneva – 'Some preliminary remarks on the "religious opposition" to the Roman Empire' – he emphasised how 'For my generation two books, both in German, and both reacting to the fascist-Nazi worldview, determined the interest in the religious situation of the Roman Empire: H. Fuchs, *Der geistige Widerstand gegen Rom in der antiken Welt*, 1938 and E. Peterson, *Der Monotheismus als politisches Problem*, 1935.'[11] With this characterisation of the debates, and their political context, that shaped his interest in 'the religious situation of the Roman Empire' Momigliano gives an almost exhaustive bibliography of the main protagonists of a debate concerning the meaning of political theology provoked by the work of Carl Schmitt from the early 1920s.[12] Benjamin, Löwith, Peterson and Strauss wrote constructive criticism of Schmitt, while Fuchs and Scholem

---

[9] In the moving Preface to this collection dated 'Hospital of the University of Chicago, July 1987', Momigliano describes the intellectual openness of the orthodoxy of his childhood, with his 'zio Amadio' a reader of the *Zohar*, an education at a convent school (absent on Saturdays and Jewish festivals), himself at eighteen looking to Spinoza's Deus-Natura for an alternative to the God of the prophets and the last letter from his father before he was murdered saying that he had found consolation in Spinoza and the Prophets.

[10] Momigliano 1987h: 210.   [11] Momigliano 1987c: 120.

[12] The only absence is the work of Ernst Kantorowicz who, in 1928, published the controversial *Kaiser Friedrich der Zweite* and after the war the influential *The King's Two Bodies: A Study in Medieval Political Theology* (1957); he is perhaps alluded to in the comment in the essay on Scholem 'followers of Stefan George were multiplying among the younger generation of German Jews'.

developed positions that were indirectly critical of Schmitt and his teacher Max Weber.[13] In order to understand and appreciate Momigliano's complex arguments concerning politics, religion and time in ancient historiography it is necessary to review this debate which shaped the course of his historical research.

The publication of Carl Schmitt's *Politische Theologie: Vier Kapitel zur Lehre von der Souveränität* in 1922 gave a name to a discussion already in course concerning the relationship between politics and religion. Schmitt's political theology stated the theological origins of the absolute claims of concept of sovereignty, and offered a theological justification of the state as the form of rule appropriate to the eschatological time of waiting.[14] The justification of the state in Schmitt's political theology left little room for a political theology of resistance.[15] The original stimulus of Schmitt's work came from his teacher Max Weber, and in particular the experience of the Munich Revolution of 1919, at which both Weber and Schmitt were present. Indeed the original formulation of political theology lies in Weber's sociology of religion elaborated in the essays that make up the *Gesammelte Aufsätze zur Religionssoziologie* and the chapter on religious groups in *Economy and Society*.[16] Weber sought not only to locate religious action according to distinct social groups (classes, status groups), but also to show how religious action in turn shaped such groups. His essay on the 'Protestant ethic and the spirit of capitalism' is an example of the complex interactions Weber saw taking place between social groups and religious orientations.[17] Another important historical example, one with which Momigliano would take issue, is that of the 'pariah groups' and the origins of the religions of salvation in an ethic of *ressentiment*.

While in Munich in the year of the revolutionary 'bloody carnival', Weber gave two seminal lectures as an *apologia pro vita sua*: 'Science as

---

[13] Walter Benjamin creatively applied some of Schmitt's ideas in *The Origin of German Tragic Drama* [1928] (2003), a compliment returned by Schmitt in his *Hamlet oder Hecuba: Der Einbruch der Zeit in das Spiel* (1956), still one of the most profound readings of Benjamin's work. The importance of Peterson's critique of Schmitt was emphasised by Jacob Taubes (see Taubes 1987 and 1993) and more recently by Giorgio Agamben (see Agamben 2007).

[14] The theme of waiting emerged at the end of Weber's two Munich lectures 'Science as a vocation' and 'Politics as a vocation' (Weber 1988). The former ends in the 'polar night' of despair, the latter with a citation from the Book of Isaiah 'He calleth to me out of Seir, Watchman what of the night? The watchman said, the morning cometh, and also the night: if ye will enquire, enquire ye: return, come.'

[15] Nevertheless, in his late work *Theory of the Partisan* (2007) [1975] Schmitt turned to the problem of resistance – it is profitably read alongside his reply to critics of his political theology (see Schmitt 1996). For Momigliano, however, Schmitt remained 'the chief speaker for a sort of theological Nazism'. Momigliano 1987d: 153.

[16] Weber 1971–2 and 1978.   [17] Weber 1992.

a vocation' and 'Politics as a vocation'. In the latter he describes a tragic tension at the heart of his political theology, one in which the state or 'monopoly of violence' requires legitimation drawn ultimately from religion. The 'driving force' of religion for Weber is 'the experience of the irrationality of the world' out of which has grown '[t]he Indian doctrine of karma and Persian dualism, original sin, predestination and the absent God'.[18] Violence (*Gewalt*) is a prime expression of the irrational course of the world, and its monopolisation in the modern state offers a potential source of immense irrationality in the violence of war. For this reason the monopoly of violence requires the legitimation of religion, but Weber underlines the instability of the alliance between religion and political violence: 'Even the ancient Christians knew very well that the world was ruled by demons, and that, whoever has anything to do with politics, that is to say, with the means of power and violence, makes a pact with demonic forces.'[19] Such a pact is indispensable for both state and religion, but threatens to undo the absolute claims of religion by its compromise with the demonic, or to make the exercise of violence in the name of religion ethically implacable. Schmitt learnt from Weber's lecture the necessity of a pact with demonic forces and developed the argument, with, against and perhaps even beyond Weber,[20] for an internal politico-theological legitimation of the state through the concept of sovereignty. It was the independent legitimation of the state that freed the political realm from the European confessional civil war unleashed by the Reformation. It was this aspect of Weber's argument that Schmitt would develop into an explicit political theology.

The notion of a religious refusal to enter into a pact with the demonic forces of the political is a recurrent theme throughout 'Politics as a vocation' – with references to the absolute ethics of Jesus' sermon on the mount, St Francis and Buddha, all of whom renounced the pursuit of salvation by means of politics. These 'religious virtuosi' earn Weber's Nietzschean admiration for their uncompromising affirmation of non-political values; less admired are those who practise 'mystical flight from the world' (*mystische Weltflucht*)[21] out of powerlessness and negation of the world. Their dreams of 'universal brotherhood' are, for a close reader of *The Genealogy of Morals* such as Weber, irremediably tainted with *ressentiment* and the reactive spirit of revenge. On this point Schmitt was in agreement with Weber, except that he had little time even for value-affirming religious

---

[18] Weber 1988: 554.   [19] Ibid.
[20] The first version of his *Political Theology* was published in a *festschrift* for Weber in 1922.
[21] Weber 1988: 560.

virtuosi who posed for him a threat to the legitimacy of the sovereign state. His critics, from Benjamin to Strauss, kept a distance from him and Weber on the issue of resistance, introducing eschatological and messianic themes into political theology.

In 'A note on Max Weber's definition of Judaism as a pariah religion' Momigliano took issue with Weber's understanding of political theology, and in particular with his interpretation of Jews as a pariah people and Judaism as a religion of *ressentiment*.[22] Weber's position is most clearly outlined in this passage from *Economy and Society:*

The factor of resentment (*ressentiment*), first noticed by Nietzsche, thus achieved importance in the Jewish ethical salvation religion, although it had been completely lacking in all magical and caste religions. Resentment is a concomitant of that particular religious ethic of the disprivileged which, in the sense expounded by Nietzsche and in direct inversion of the ancient belief, teaches that the unequal distribution of mundane goods is caused by the sinfulness and illegality of the privileged, and that sooner or later God's wrath will overtake them. In this theodicy of the disprivileged, the moralistic quest serves as a device for compensating a conscious or unconscious desire for vengeance.[23]

Weber thus reads the Psalms as 'replete with the moralistic legitimation and satisfaction of an open and hardly concealed need for vengeance on the part of a pariah people',[24] recognising also that they were probably written after the persecutions. While excepting the book of Job as an expression of 'aristocratic' religiosity Weber sees the 'hope for revenge' as suffusing 'practically all the exilic and postexilic sacred scriptures',[25] a compensatory hope expressed in the longing for the downfall of the powerful, the rise of a Messiah and the end of history in an apocalyptic war between the forces of good and evil.

Weber is careful to distinguish this view of a specific phase in Jewish history from Jewish history as a whole, insisting that 'to interpret *ressentiment* as the decisive element in Judaism would be an incredible aberration in view of the many significant historical changes that Judaism has undergone'.[26] Momigliano notes this in his otherwise implacable critique of Weber, referring to the latter's sympathy for the rationalism of Talmudic law and for the 'Messianic dimension' of Judaism. Yet Momigliano does not concede either that the Jews were a pariah people or that an ethic of *ressentiment* was inevitably associated with such religious groups, and especially not in the case of Judaism. He questions the very idea of a pariah group, the chronology of the transformation of the Jewish people into such a group,

---

[22] Momigliano 1987b.   [23] Weber 1978: 494.   [24] Ibid. 495.   [25] Ibid. 496.   [26] Ibid.

and asks, ironically, why the most extreme expression of religious *ressenti-ment* according to Weber and Nietzsche – Pauline Christianity – coincided with the call for a universalist overcoming of an alleged pariah status.[27]

Momigliano's critique of Weber is directed towards a revaluation of the history of Judaism, one with implications for the interpretation of the 'exilic and post-exilic' writings assigned to the alleged religion of *ressentiment*. Momigliano questions whether post-exilic Jews ever believed themselves to be powerless spectators of history: 'Believing Jews never gave up their sovereign rights and never admitted to being without political institutions of their own.'[28] Far from being reactive, Judaism can be understood in terms of the historical self-affirmation of a people. What is more, he sets out to show that this very affirmation was deeply indebted to concepts drawn from classical Greek historiography. The Messianic 'age' or 'dimension' was understood affirmatively as 'a promise of future rectification of present injustice: an effort to save the rationality of this world by finding a complement to it in a world to come', not as a reactive desire for revenge.[29] Momigliano's re-evaluation of the political theology of Judaism would have considerable implications for his interpretation of texts such as the Book of Daniel and the Sibylline oracles that would seem from a Nietzschean or Weberian standpoint to exemplify *ressentiment*.

Momigliano's reassessment of these writings proclaiming the end of history, specifically Roman history, may be situated within a current of messianic political theology that emerged in the 1920s as a direct critique of Schmitt and Weber, one which sought to free eschatology and messianism from the suspicion of *ressentiment*. Momigliano returned to the philosophical sources of his reassessment of prophetic historiography in his exquisite late essays on Strauss, prominent among which are those on Strauss, Benjamin and Scholem. The essays reflect on the hermeneutic situation of messianism and develop a number of connections between the oracular and the esoteric, messianism and the end of history, far removed from the hermeneutic principle of *ressentiment*. In the essay (and appended obituary) 'Hermeneutics and classical political thought in Leo Strauss', Momigliano identifies two hermeneutic principles at work in Strauss's historiography of political ideas. The first involves a critique of historicism

---

[27] Momigliano 1987b.   [28] Ibid. 235.

[29] Ibid. 237. Momigliano acknowledges Weber's appreciation of this dimension of Judaism, but does not ask if the 'complement' of a just world to come might not be vulnerable to being interpreted in terms of *ressentiment*. The work of Norman Cohn (1970) on chiliasm and political eschatology made precisely this judgement of ancient, medieval and modern messianic and quasi-messianic political movements.

and the sociology of knowledge, or the view that a text must be understood in terms of its context: Strauss proposes instead an approach to a text that assumes that its author was not only writing at or beyond the limits of expression of a past epoch, but also still has relevance for the present. The second principle is that a writer will not publicly or explicitly express all his thoughts, especially in periods of persecution.[30]

The use of discretion to the point of secrecy described in Strauss's apology for esoteric writing, *Persecution and the Art of Writing*, requires that the author would be read according to a 'particular technique of writing, and therewith to a peculiar type of literature in which the truth about all crucial things is presented exclusively between the lines'.[31] In the 1948 essay 'How to study Spinoza's *Theologico-Political Treatise*', Strauss argues that the critique of Jewish political theology presented in the *Treatise* is as much if not more directed to contemporary Christian theology and political institutions than it is to the critical exegesis of the Old Testament. Far from interpreting such esoteric writing as a resentful expression of the powerless Momigliano agrees with Strauss in regarding such secrecy as 'aristocratic' dedicated to the few who can see beyond the exoteric content.[32]

In his reading of Strauss, whose *Athens and Jerusalem* he describes as 'sibylline'[33] (not a term he uses lightly), Momigliano also hints at 'a secret position' that encompassed legal and messianic aspects of Judaism, even if presented in the guise of discussions of classical and modern philosophy. The key to unlocking this secret is to be found in Strauss's early Zionist writings, the milieu from which emerged his early Spinoza studies warmly referred to by Momigliano.[34] The link between Messianism, Zionism and Marxism, between the messianic hope forged in the exile preceding the Christian epoch and modern political projects, is made even more explicitly in the essays on Scholem and Benjamin. Esoteric writing is situated within a messianic horizon of expectation, one which was historically fused in the modern period with the Messianic figures of Sabbatai Zevi and Jacob Frank, whose antinomianism led to their conversions to Islam and Catholicism. In place of such examples that sought to complete Jewish history by intensifying the condition of exile, Zionism for Scholem offered an open messianic horizon, or in Momigliano's words, 'a collective phenomenon, Zionism has therefore become for Scholem the constructive answer to the

---

[30] 'Ermeneutica et pensiero politico classico in Leo Strauss' and 'In memoriam. Leo Strauss (febbraio 1977)', Momigliano 1987h: 189–99.

[31] Strauss 1980: 25.   [32] Strauss 1997.   [33] Momigliano 1987h: 197.

[34] Confirmed by Strauss's Zionist writings almost certainly unknown to Momigliano, but recently published in the collection Strauss 2002.

purely negative conversions to Islam and Catholicism of Zevi and Frank and many of their followers'. In place of the answers provided by Zevi and Frank, Zionism is understood as a form of messianism that opened questions: 'Zionism means to Scholem the opening of all the gates of the Jewish past.'[35] The deferring of all knowledge of the messianic end of history justified positions such as that of Walter Benjamin, who translated Messianic expectation into revolutionary Marxism, while maintaining an open horizon for questioning and interpretation. 'The revolution, precisely as with the Messiah in the tradition of rabbinic Judaism, was to be awaited and prophesied, but without any serious hope of ever seeing it.'[36] The time of waiting advocated by Benjamin does not, as in Schmitt, require stabilisation in the absolute claims of sovereignty, but rather an intensification of messianic expectation. In all these cases the interpretative principle at work is not *ressentiment*, but a messianic horizon, one which provides the link between oracles, prophesies and the end of history central to Momigliano's historiography.

II

The role played by a political theology of resistance and messianic expectation in Momigliano's historiography in general and his interpretation of the Sibylline oracles in particular may be highlighted by a contrast with the work of Peretti. The latter's reading of eschatology is indebted to a fascist inflection of Nietzsche's theory of *ressentiment*. Although departing with a warm reference to the same Fuchs who inspired Momigliano's research, praising *Der geistige Wiederstand gegen Rom in der antiken Welt* for its 'picture rich in chiaroscuri and interesting details',[37] his own interpretation of eschatological and messianic oracles is spectacularly lacking in nuance.[38] Peretti regards the Sibylline oracles as 'a ruthless weapon, fearful for its moral efficacy against an opponent who remained undefeated on the field of battle' or, to cite another of the many repetitious formulations, 'in the hands of Israel, the oracle became a weapon of combat'.[39] The oracles play a part in Peretti's obsessive scenario of a life and death struggle between Asia and Europe, East and West, in which the Jews are cast as the subversive representatives of a militant Asia. From this perspective, the Jewish Roman wars were not just police actions within Roman dominion, but rather 'the war of two worlds and two opposed and irreducible cultures, of two

---

[35] Momigliano 1987a: 262.   [36] Momigliano 1987h: 214.   [37] Peretti 1943: xiii.
[38] A lack of nuance ironically described by Momigliano as his 'candour'.   [39] Ibid. 23.

diverse imperialisms each equally set on world domination. It is the final and decisive battle between the universal empire of the dominators and the social revolution of the oppressed.'[40] Peretti sees the military defeat of this phantasmal Jewish bid for world dominion – a phantasm prominent in fascist and Nazi discourse and here projected onto ancient history – as prompting a change of tactics, with Judaism mobilising a subversive propaganda war through eschatology and the Sibylline prophesies. The military defeat of the Jews led to the opening of a propaganda front, which prophesied the end of the Roman Empire and even the end of the world, and which, as Peretti maintains, subsequently infiltrated early Christianity: 'The ideological contrast between Judaism and Rome, and the implacable hatred of the defeated for the armed power to which they did not know how to surrender, nourished the most bitter and ruinous invectives of the Jewish apocalyptic of early centuries of the Christian epoch.'[41]

For Peretti the Sibylline texts were diverted from their original role as vectors for Alexandrian Jewish missionary activity among the Greeks into a means for mounting devastating subversive attacks on the Roman state. As politics by other means, these eschatological texts, in Peretti's extravagant and ideologically charged judgement, posed an effective and credible threat to the very existence of the Roman Empire: 'A book like that of the Sibyl, in particular the third book of the Jewish Sibylline texts which predicts the imminent fall of the empire and the arrival of a king from the east, a king who would found a new kingdom and a new world order under the dominion of Asia, could not but be considered by the Roman authorities as a subversive book, a revolutionary work hostile to state and Emperor.'[42] In his conclusion, Peretti goes so far as to describe these texts not only as 'oriental propaganda', but also as a 'poison' released by a 'defeated and annihilated' Judaism 'with the desperation and the hatred of the mortally wounded mythical centaur into the veins of the western world'.[43] In this lurid scenario, the Sibylline texts are cast as accomplices in an attack 'against civilisation and humanity' and in the unwitting hands of Christians, concludes Peretti, continued to propagate 'the ancient judeo-oriental hatred against Rome, accelerat[ing] the ruin of the Empire and the failure of ancient civilisation'.[44] In this intensely ideological world

---

[40] Ibid. 19. Other examples 'The unnegotiable demands of a totalitarian state and the irreducible aversion of Jewish theology against Greco-Roman culture created an unhealable ideological contrast between the two worlds, the oriental represented by Judaism and the Western represented by Rome' (254), and 'The ambitious dream of an oriental Jewish empire shipwrecked in a sea of blood, in a war of extermination from which Judaism did not arise' (255).

[41] Ibid. 456.   [42] Ibid. 458.   [43] Ibid. 505.   [44] Ibid.

view, projecting fascist and Nazi paranoia concerning the East (USSR) and the allegedly subversive role of Jewish propaganda in the West onto ancient history, Peretti improbably attributes the fall of Rome and ancient civilisation to the subversive effects of an esoteric oracular and prophetic literature.

With Peretti the logic of *ressentiment* developed with such subtlety by Nietzsche and employed with discretion by Weber is driven to the point of delirium. Yet as Momigliano points out, the view that the resentful expressions of the weak are sufficiently powerful to destroy the strong, is implied throughout his otherwise learned interpretation of the Sibylline writings. Yet such an interpretation, which sees them as the dishonest expression of something else – 'oriental propaganda' – nevertheless misses the most salient feature of the oracular texts – their messianic horizon. One of the aims of Momigliano's studies in ancient history was to relocate and reassess such texts, and with them the place of Judaism in the ancient world and the relationship between progressive and messianic historiographies. The resistance to Imperial domination is seen to take place both within and without history: it is continuous with the history of a succession of empires developed by Greek historians, but also points to an imminent end to the sequence and the advent of a new, post-historical or messianic epoch.

In the lecture 'Prophesy and historiography', delivered at the University of Marburg in 1986, Momigliano presented a lapidary summary of his work on the Sibylline oracles: what distinguished them was their 'combination of historical and apocalyptic elements. In the last analysis they were an attempt made by Jews and Christians to interpret history at a time when an adequate form for doing so had still not been discovered'.[45] Their combination of historical and religious motifs expressed an original interpretation of Greek historiography, whose origins are visible for the first time in the Book of Daniel. Momigliano's interpretation attempts to do justice to the tense anachronisms of the latter text, not only between the first-person, almost fairytale narrative of the first six and the third-person prophesies of the last six chapters, but also between the *vaticinia ex eventu* (prophesies after the event) and the apocalyptic or messianic prophesies that accompany them. Already in antiquity the location of the narrative in late-seventh and early-sixth century Babylonia had been questioned, as well as the tension between prophesy and history, refined into a modern consensus, shared by Momigliano, in dating the first part to the third century and the second

---

[45] Momigliano 1987h: 115.

part to the 'Hellenistic' persecution of Jewish religion by Antiochus IV between 167 and 163.[46]

Momigliano sets the first half of the Book of Daniel within a constellation including the Books of Esther and Judith that for him formed part of a revival (or 'invention for the first time') of 'legends about the Babylonian and Persian periods' that encouraged 'faithfulness to the Mosaic Law in the new conditions'.[47] The closing of chapter six with Daniel's reward for his steadfastness to the law through Darius' recognition of the living God – with its very light eschatological hints – broadly confirms Momigliano's judgement that these books of the Bible show 'concern for the preservation of the Law, but no pressing anxiety. There is not in them that sombre atmosphere of a mortal struggle that we find in the second part of Daniel.'[48] For Momigliano the latter forms a new constellation with the apocalyptic and apocryphal books of Enoch, Jubilees and IV Ezra, parts of which he dates to the late second century, prior to the I and II Maccabees. Indeed, in so far as it predates these later apocalyptic texts, the second half of Daniel for Momigliano 'provides the first intimation of that apocalyptic interpretation of contemporary struggles which was to become an ordinary feature of the later rebellions of Jews against foreign rule'[49] and which for him would persist – with their literary expression in the Sibylline oracles – until the failure of Bar Kochba.

The importance of the Book of Daniel for Momigliano lies not only in its inaugurating a season of 'the apocalyptic interpretation of history', nor in its emergence 'from the confrontation with the Greeks about 165 BCE', but above all in its paradoxical use of a Greek invention – universal history – to resist the imposition of Hellenism. With respect to the latter, Momigliano makes the allusive comment that 'If II Maccabees reveals a true aspect of the activities of Antiochus IV by stressing the cooperation of Hellenizing Jews, this is something less than the whole truth.'[50] Momigliano makes an implicit parallel between the military resistance of the Maccabees to the profanation of the Temple, directed against the Seleucid dynasty, and Jewish Hellenisers and the resistance posed in the Book of Daniel. The very specific prophesies of the repurification of the Temple, and the end of the persecution, locate the composition of the text for Momigliano in 164, immediately after the restoration. Yet the Book of Daniel makes hardly any reference to the Maccabeans and does not share in II Maccabees' hostility

---

[46] For a report of Porphyry's fourth-century CE critique in *Against the Christians* and a review of modern debates, see Eissfeldt 1974: 517–20.
[47] Momigliano 1975b: 90. [48] Ibid. [49] Ibid. 112. [50] Ibid.

towards Hellenistic Jews. It is structured around the recognition of the world or a universal history of Empires:

He sees Jerusalem in the context of the struggle between Syria and Egypt and more generally within the framework of the kingdoms originating from the conquests of Alexander. The present struggle between Egypt and Syria is assuming in his eyes apocalyptic proportions. Syria or rather Antiochus, pollutes the Temple of Jerusalem on the eve of a final war which will give him victory over Egypt, but which will soon be followed by the deliverance of the Jews and by the Last Judgement.[51]

Far from being a compensatory, or reactive, expression of resistance, the historical vision of the Book of Daniel 'tells us something about the inner vision which inspired the enemies of Antiochus IV in facing battle and martyrdom' – a very different vision to the apologetic and non-messianic version presented in Maccabees.

What is more, the character of this vision is deeply indebted to Greek thought and in particular to the historiographical schema of the succession of Empires. In the lecture 'Biblical studies and classical studies' (1980), a sophisticated critique of postmodern historiography, Momigliano identifies the origins of the idea of the succession of Empires in Greek historiography:

The idea of the succession of the universal empires is to be found first in Greek historians from Herodotus to Dionysius of Halicarnassus, passing through Ctesias, Polybius, and that strange Roman disciple of the Greeks, Aemilius Sura, probably an elder contemporary of Polybius. It is a notion dependent on the basic Greek discovery of political history.[52]

While the Middle Eastern Empires registered the succession of rulers, only the Greeks – with the exception of the author of Daniel – used the schema of a 'succession of universal empires'. For Momigliano, the authors of Daniel 'got the idea from the Graeco-Macedonians who ruled the East after Alexander,' adding that 'about 250 BCE a Jew, either in Mesopotamia or in Palestine, got hold of the Greek idea of succession of universal empires and transformed it'.[53] It is the transformation, of course, of an account of past empires into one oriented towards the future, a transformation accomplished by placing history itself into the prophetic future and thus making the immediate future at once both continuous with and a break from the past.

Momigliano had examined the details of this paradoxical process of transformation in his lecture of the previous year 'The origins of universal

---

[51] Ibid. III.   [52] Momigliano 1987e: 8.   [53] Ibid. 9.

history'. The idea of the succession of four world empires emerges in Daniel's successful interpretation of the dream of Nebuchadanezzar in chapter 2 of the Book of Daniel. The giant image in the king's dream, with its head of gold, arms and chest of silver, belly and thighs of bronze, legs of iron and feet part iron, part clay is interpreted historiographically. Each part of the body and its associated metal figures a history of world Empire ranging from Babylonia, Media, Persia, Macedonia and its internal dissolution. What is remarkable is that the statue itself is shattered by a stone from heaven – in short, the new, transformative element to enter this Greek historiographic schema is the notion of a divinely motivated end of history. In Momigliano's interpretation,

> The stone smashes all the elements of the statue at the same time, including the golden head. It puts an eternal Jewish kingdom of God in the place of all the Empires of the past taken together. Thus the statue is not meant to represent a succession of empires, it rather symbolises the coexistence of all the past, as it had developed through a succession of kingdoms, at the moment in which all the past is destroyed by the divine stone and replaced by a new order.[54]

This messianic end of history is nevertheless dependent upon, even an outcome of, the Greek understanding of history. The apocalyptic fifth kingdom, the kingdom of God, in a sense both breaks with and concludes the succession of world empires.

Towards the end of his interpretation of the Book of Daniel in the light of the crisis that beset Judaism in the reign of Antiochus IV, Momigliano identifies 'the religious interpretation, the apocalyptic finale, [as] of course the specific Jewish contribution to the reading of the situation'.[55] He expresses admiration for the 'energy and independence with which the Jews turned Greek ideas upside down' as well as for the way in which 'the Book of Daniel turns a Greek summary of world-empires into a blueprint for the preparation of the Messianic age'.[56] Yet it is evident that for him this invention of the messianic end of history was only possible on the basis of Greek historiographical ideas. Momigliano thus arrives at the remarkable conclusion that 'the foundation of all this Messianic structure is provided by the scheme of the succession of empires which we found in Herodotus, Ctesias, and their successors'.[57] The notion of a messianic end of history that would become central to Judaism and Christianity is thus traced to its foundations in Greek historiography and its transformation in the course of a crisis in Hellenic and Jewish relations; that it continued and 'remained operative in Jewish thought' after the immediate crisis of Antiochus IV was

[54] Momigliano 1987f: 48.   [55] Ibid. 49–50.   [56] Ibid. 50.   [57] Ibid.

the historical result of the 'Jewish sibylline books and other apocalyptic writings'. In a further twist, the fusion of Greek historiography and Jewish messianism was propagated by the Jewish adoption of the Greek literary form of the oracle.

Although the Sibylline writings appear throughout Momigliano's authorship, as if in a prolonged and simmering controversy with Peretti, they are discussed at length and with particular effect in two essays from the 1980s: 'What Josephus did not see' of 1984 and, in his most explicit conversation with the tradition of political theology, the above mentioned 'Preliminary remarks on the "religious opposition" to the Roman Empire' of 1986. In the former Momigliano not only shows what Josephus did not see – the rise of the synagogue as the main locus of Judaism and Jewish apocalyptic sentiment and writing – but also explains *why* he did not see it. Josephus, for Momigliano, had prophetic aspirations: not only was Daniel 'one of his favourite seers of the past' but, more, 'it is impossible to suppress the feeling that somewhere in his conscience Josephus was equating himself with Daniel'.[58] But Josephus' identification would have been restricted to the Daniel of the first six chapters, who advocates an accommodation between loyalty to the ruling Empire and 'loyalty to the God of his fathers and to the law of the Bible'. Josephus seemed not to see the implications of Daniel's vision of the beasts, and the prophesy of the divine stone that signals the end of Empire and the messianic cessation of history. His distance from apocalyptic messianism is also a disdain for those forms of resistance couched in apocalyptic terms.

In 'What Josephus did not see' Momigliano describes how the apocalyptic messianism prompted by the Book of Daniel informed Jewish Sibylline writings until the second century CE. The predictions of the end of Imperial history with the fall of Rome are gradually adopted by Christians as Jewish messianism turns away from its complicated alliance with Greek philosophy of history. This turn coincides with the exhaustion of 'three messianic uprisings' and the abandoning by Jews of 'their messianic and eschatological hopes that had sustained them in their armed struggle against Rome'.[59] The increasing prominence of the synagogue and the Rabbis led to a turn away from the philosophy of history towards law and jurisprudence that culminated in the compilation of the *Mishnah* during the third century. In '"Religious opposition" to the Roman Empire' Momigliano firmly identifies the Sibylline texts as a technique of resistance, one destined to introduce a different and dissident sense of Imperial history. As

[58] Momigliano 1987g: 118.   [59] Ibid. 115.

a 'reflection on, or a reaction to, historical events', the Sibylline writings filled a 'historiographical gap' by undermining the successive narrative of Imperial history by imagining its end. Explicit forgeries in every sense, these texts, whether in Jewish or Christian hands, pursued 'the same spirit of critical evaluation of the past and visionary conjecture of the future. The very existence of the Jewish-Christian Sibylline Books is evidence for an underground reaction to the political and social events of the Roman Empire, an underground reaction which probably implies some exchange between Jews and Christians and certainly presupposes a Christian interest in what Jews thought about the Roman Empire.'[60] The role of messianic expectation in destabilising the history of empires and opening a period of waiting for the end of history continued to haunt Christianity, even while, according to Momigliano, it sought to situate itself within Imperial history.

With the issue of the Christian adoption of the Sibylline writings and through them the Greek historiographic idea of the succession of empires and its inflection towards the end of history, Momigliano returns to the classic, even foundational, controversy of political theology – the relationship to the state of the time of eschatological waiting. The early Christian view of the providential alignment of 'the monarchy of God, the destruction of the Jewish State, and the providential unification and pacification of the world under Augustus'[61] was consistent with Schmitt's view of necessity for an absolute state during the time of waiting, for security in the approach to the eschatological end of history. Against this view, Momigliano cites Erik Peterson's objection to Schmitt that 'Christological controversies of the fourth century effectively destroyed the doctrine of a correspondence between God's Kingdom and the Roman Empire', thus placing Christianity within an eschatological horizon beyond the history of Empire.[62]

When reviewing the debate between Schmitt and Peterson in the 'Disadvantages of monotheism for a universal state' Momigliano refers to the 'extraordinary complexities of this battle about political theology which has not yet come to an end'.[63] In a sense, his own work is a contribution to and a continuation of this debate. The terms of his inquiry into ancient and modern historiography are determined by the agenda of political theology. Central to this agenda is the intimate relationship between politics and religion and the role of each in the period of apocalyptic or messianic expectation. Momigliano's main contribution to this debate was to situate the emergence of the idea of a messianic end of history within Greek historiographic categories and to pay attention to non-official sources of

---

[60] Ibid. 140. [61] Ibid. 151. [62] 1987d: 153. [63] Ibid. 153.

historical understanding such as the Sibylline Books. By doing so he effectively broke down many of the implied distinctions between Greek, Jewish,
Roman and Christian cultures that informed debate in political theology.
In confronting political theology and historiography he was able to evoke
complex understandings of time at work in historical self-understanding
and historiography. The present is as much the outcome of the legacies of
the past as of the hopes for the future, even past hopes for the future. His
work should be read alongside that of Benjamin, Scholem and Strauss as
the extension and critique of political theology by means of radical historiography and the philosophy of history. In it historiography is situated
between continuity and interruption at a point where the 'critical evaluation of the past' makes, but is also made possible by, a 'visionary conjecture
of the future'.

Ancient History and Modern Temporalities

CHAPTER 5

The making of a bourgeois antiquity: Wilhelm von Humboldt and Greek history

Stefan Rebenich

"Where do we stand?" asked Wilhelm von Humboldt in his review of the eighteenth century.[1] "Which part of its long and arduous path has mankind covered? Is it on a course that leads to the final destination?"[2] The text is more than just a glimpse on the past: it expresses a borderline experience, around 1800, which had a profound influence on the perception of past and present in Germany.

In the middle of the eighteenth century Greek antiquity had been redis-covered. Greece became the foremost object of productive artistic recep-tion. At the same time, the exclusionist vision of classical culture associated with nobility began to end;[3] while the neo-humanist teaching at grammar schools and the scientific research at the universities concentrated equally on the study of Greece and Rome. The ancients were no longer time-less models, but historicized paradigms for *Wissenschaft*, literature, and the arts. Their works were still regarded as perfect, but also as historically con-stituted and therefore specific. The new German image of antiquity was characterized by a latent tension between classical aesthetics and enlight-ening historicism, and shifted between canonization of an idealized image of antiquity, on the one hand, and recognition of its interconnection with other cultures, on the other. These categories were paradigmatically artic-ulated in the work of Wilhelm von Humboldt. The aristocratic pupil of the classicist Christian Gottlob Heyne[4] from Göttingen made it possible for the hitherto aristocratic veneration of the classics to become a field of

---

[1] The works of Wilhelm von Humboldt to which I refer in the course of this chapter will be cited after his *Gesammelte Schriften*, vols. 1–17 published by the Royal Prussian Academy of Sciences (*Königlich Preußische Akademie der Wissenschaften*), Berlin 1903–36 (reprint 1967–8). The volume and page number will follow after the abbreviation *GS*. Volume and page numbers in brackets refer to the anthology: Wilhelm von Humboldt, *Werke in fünf Bänden*, ed. A. Flitner and K. Giel, Darmstadt 1960–81 (various reprints).

[2] Humboldt, 'Das achtzehnte Jahrhundert', *GS* II: 1 (1: 376).

[3] Cf. Walther 1998: 359–85.

[4] For Humboldt's studies in Göttingen see Sauter 1989; for Heyne's influence see Vöhler 2002.

inquiry with a scientific basis, and enabled the academic study of antiquity to ascend to a common leading discipline, which shaped lastingly the values and the curriculum of the class called the bourgeoisie.

But what was the bourgeoisie?

BOURGEOISIE: AN ATTEMPT AT A DEFINITION

It has long been acknowledged that conventional social parameters such as birth, education, occupation or economic resources are insufficient for attempts to define the bourgeoisie. A specific kind of lifestyle, a specific "culture" has to be added in order to reconcile the difference between the heterogeneity of social positions and the homogeneity of intellectual identities.[5] Thus, the bourgeois society is a model of acculturation, and contemporary historical research has specified numerous values and behaviours that determine the middle-class culture and mentality, the attitude of a citizen or simply the middle-class way of life (*Bügerlichkeit*):[6] education as "hope of redemption and entitlement to education,"[7] individual freedom, personal interest, development of personal talents, organization of society from within, orientation towards the common good, creativity and rationality, belief in progress, striving for material possessions, family as a private sphere, autonomy of literature, music and the plastic arts etc. Over the nineteenth century those values constituted a system of enduring behavioral arrangements in a way that despite different social bases the representatives of the bourgeoisie attained perfectly comparable lifestyles. In this context, middle-class intellectuals became the most important impetus of bourgeois culture and mentality. They were the part of the middle class that founded its claim to social excellence on the possession of knowledge and on a lifestyle, which was derived from this possession.

Current research mostly ignores the importance of European antiquity for the formation of the bourgeoisie, the emergence of middle-class

---

[5] Lepsius 1987: 96 states that "The socialised bourgeoisie corresponds to a specific kind of lifestyle, which can be described as a middle-class way of life (*Bürgerlichkeit*). The middle-class way of life and the bourgeoisie are in this respect corresponding terms without meaning entirely the same thing. The bourgeoisie denotes the socialisation of the middle classes, the middle-class way of life is the typical kind of lifestyle owing to this socialisation."

[6] Cf. the relevant passages in Nipperdey 1983; Wehler 1996 vv. 1 and 2. In addition cf. Conze, Kocka, Koselleck *et al.* 1985–1992; Engelhardt 1986; Hahn and Hein 2005; Kocka 1987; Kocka 1995; Lundgreen 2000; Maurer 1996; Riedel 1972; Schulz 2005; Vierhaus 1981; Vierhaus 1987 as well as Fahrmeir 2005a; 2005b; 2005c and Schmale 2005 with further references.

[7] Cf. Koselleck 2006.

intellectuals and for the genesis of a bourgeois culture as a whole.[8] Yet as will be argued, in early nineteenth-century Germany, antiquity as a historiographical construct and an idealized timeless projection contributed considerably to both the homogenization of the bourgeoisie and the constitution of middle-class mentality.[9]

THE INSTITUTIONAL FRAMEWORK

The importance of Wilhelm von Humboldt for the nationalization of the learned classes and the neo-humanist educational reform has been the object of debates in scholarly literature. The few months Humboldt worked as privy councillor and head of the section for cultural affairs and public education in the Prussian Ministry of the Interior, from February 1809 until April or June 1810,[10] make him, in the opinion of some scholars, the most influential minister for education and cultural affairs in German history.[11] In the midst of the collapse of Prussia, Humboldt demanded a reform of the school system, for which he fought in his two memoranda, the Königsberg and the Lithuanian plan for school organization.[12] Moreover, he advanced a successful application of the memoranda, which embraced ideas of Schelling, Schleiermacher, and Fichte, in the foundation of Berlin University.[13] It has been asserted that Humboldt has, apart from "the certainly significant achievement of founding the university in Berlin, accomplished nothing of importance in life."[14] Others suggest that his attempt at reform comprised an episode without consequences,[15] and it has been argued recently that the idea of a "Humboldt University" is, in fact, an invention of the late nineteenth and twentieth century.[16] Admittedly, it is indisputable that there were divergences between Humboldt's conception of an educational ideal and its practical implementation;[17] that reforms in the fields of *Wissenschaft* and education took shape before Humboldt's reform;[18] that older scholarly literature tended to idealize Humboldt;[19] and that making the "legend of Humboldt" (*Mythos Humboldt*) topical was of

---

[8] Cf. e.g. Hein and Schulz 1996: 10, where it is stated that the link between antiquity and bourgeois culture will "not be treated as an independent topic in this volume."

[9] Cf. also Kloft 1994: 17–23.

[10] Humboldt tendered his resignation on 29 April 1810 and the king acceded to his request on 14 June 1810. Cf. for Humboldt's work in the Ministry of the Interior e.g. Sweet 1980: 3–106.

[11] Cf. Berglar 2003: 81.   [12] *GS* xiii: 259–83 (iv: 168–95).

[13] Humboldt, "Über die innere und äußere Organisation der höheren wissenschaftlichen Anstalten in Berlin," *GS* x: 250–60 (iv: 255–66). Cf. Muhlack 2006a: 223–353; Bruch 2001: 63–77.

[14] Kaehler 1927.   [15] Menze 1975: 47f.   [16] Paletschek 2002; 2001.

[17] Benner 1995, who, moreover, portrays convincingly the development of Humboldt's theory.

[18] Neugebauer 1990.   [19] Cf. e.g. Spranger 1965 and 1928 [1909].

exceptional importance in numerous educational and higher-educational policy crises.[20] But it is also indisputable that Humboldt's reflections on the content and function of education and his ideas about the different kinds of teaching in school and university have displayed, after 1810, a continuous effect even beyond the scope of Cabinet politics. After Humboldt had been appointed head of the newly founded section for cultural affairs and education in the Ministry of the Interior, he was able to exploit the euphoria for reform, which prevailed in the devastated Prussian state after the military defeat, in order to give, in his term of office that lasted barely sixteen months, important impulses for the creation of a unified public school and university system, which reflected his ideas of a general education. Furthermore, he communicated his views to a large circle of friends by way of many personal as well as written contacts.[21]

For our objectives in this chapter it is particularly important that Humboldt's reform constituted a new understanding of antiquity. The historical point of reference that sustained his vision was Greek antiquity.[22] In encountering Greece Humboldt succeeded in bolstering the political demands of the bourgeoisie by means of his educational ideal, which amalgamated stimuli and notions of different provenance.[23] As Georg Bollenbeck has aptly put it, Humboldt effectively defined *Bildung*, education "as a general and harmonious development of an individual aptitude; as acquisition of the world from within without any specific purpose; as an unfinished process, result and standard mediated by 'culture'."[24]

ANTIQUITY AND BOURGEOIS CULTURE

Perfectibility: Education as a permanent process of self-perfection

Education was one of the central values of bourgeois mentality and culture. It facilitated the development of the individual and the progress of society. For Humboldt, the study of Greek antiquity helped the formation of the individual's personality, as in Greece there was to be found "an accomplished form," which "encouraged us to replicate it." Humboldt celebrated the Greeks' "refinement and accuracy of the mind," their "strength"

---

[20] Cf. Ash 1999.
[21] At this point I shall only refer to Jeismann 1996: vols. I and II. Cf. also Jeismann and Lundgreen 1987: vol. III; Bruch 1999: 29–57; Rüegg 1999; Ungern-Sternberg 2005; and Kraus 2008: 69–70.
[22] Cf. Flashar 1986; Jecht 2003: 85–139; Matthiessen 2003; Menze 1992; Quillien 1983; Rehm 1968: 229–54; Stadler 1959.
[23] For the traditions that Humboldt dealt with, cf. for instance Menze 1975: 9ff.
[24] Bollenbeck 1996: 147–8.

and their "dynamic power of imagination," their "agility and liveliness of emotion," their "prolific genius for the plastic arts and poetry," their "noble freedom of convictions," their "agreeable unity of temperament," and their "simple wisdom allowing them to live life impulsively and to enjoy it."[25] Yet he did not demand the reproduction of the ancient conditions. Instead, he advocated the creative examination of the Greek world with the intention of founding the individual personality on a historical individuality, which thus acquired transhistorical significance.

In the Greek character, as Humboldt explained, one could find "with utmost certainty of outline, all the richness of form, all the diversity of movement and all the intensity and liveliness of colours," the "formal facets of human purpose," which constitute

the appropriate proportion between receptiveness and independence; the deep fusion of the senses and the intellect; the protection of balance and harmony in the sum of all efforts; the tracing back of everything to the real, active life; and the portrayal in detail of every splendour in the whole assembly of nations and of the human race.[26]

The Greek character in its versatility and harmonic development has come closest to the "idea of a perfect human race" (*Idee der heilen Menschheit*), the "character of mankind in general", "which can be there and should be there in every situation, without taking into consideration individual differences."[27]

The neo-humanist educational programme that Wilhelm von Humboldt advanced in Prussia and Friedrich Immanuel Niethammer in Bavaria made Greek antiquity, which was viewed as noble and sublime, a central subject of grammar school instruction. The Greek language as a product of the Greek spirit and an expression of Greek character took absolute precedence, as it was believed that unity and diversity, senses and intellect, object and subject, world and disposition are harmonically connected by it, and it is an individual expression of the mind of the Greek people and its national character:

The Greeks are also distinguished by the peculiarity of a language reflecting brightly and clearly the essence of the entire population. . . . Through the poetic and prose works the liveliness and accuracy of the nation's linguistic meaning stands out, the

---

[25] Cf. Humboldt, "Das achtzehnte Jahrhundert," *GS* II: 25 (I: 402–3).
[26] Humboldt, "Über den Charakter der Griechen, die idealische und historische Ansicht desselben," *GS* VII: 613–14 (II: 69–70).
[27] Humboldt, "Über das Studium des Alterthums, und des griechischen insbesondere," *GS* I: 265 (II: 9).

genuine artistic love and the skill with which it treated an instrument that required greater agility, certainty of tactfulness and sensitivity of feeling, especially because of its perfection.[28]

Learning such a complexly structured language was meant not only to improve personal linguistic competence, but also to help the individual educate himself comprehensively and understand the world. By shaping the person, Greek language became an instrument for the appropriation of the world, which allowed one to appreciate the diversity of that world without utilitarian interests. Learning the Greek language, therefore, did not serve to imitate the spoken and written forms of a bygone age, but aimed at the "general and harmonic" development of individual aptitude in the present.[29] Consequently, education was an end in itself and simultaneously a permanent process of self-perfection: "The true purpose of man – not the one that changing inclinations dictate to him, but the one that the eternal unchanging common sense demands of him – is the highest and most proportioned formation of his powers into a whole."[30]

The university that Humboldt created to advance this purpose was based on an idealized image of the Greeks. His vision evoked the idea of education through *Wissenschaft*, which was, in turn, characterized by research without a specific purpose, the association of research and teaching, reflection on the whole, and the permanent endeavor to advance knowledge. *Wissenschaft*, in Humboldt's words, was "something not quite yet found and never totally attainable," which "was to be sought out for its own sake" and had to be practiced in "solitude and independence," namely, independence from political and social constraints.[31]

The search for truth and the striving for discovery for its own sake required an understanding of all fields of human knowledge. In the light of contemporary issues Humboldt opposed the specialization and fragmentation of education as well as the *Wissenschaft*, which led to the world not being understood as a whole anymore.

The mathematician, the naturalist, the artist, and frequently even the philosopher not only begin their work without knowing its true nature and without surveying

---

[28] Humboldt, "Über die Verschiedenheit des menschlichen Sprachbaues und ihren Einfluss auf die geistige Entwicklung des Menschengeschlechtes," *GS* VI: 112 (III: 145).

[29] Cf. Vierhaus 1972; Landfester 2001; and Walther 2005.

[30] Humboldt, "Ideen zu einem Versuch die Gränzen der Wirksamkeit des Staates zu bestimmen," *GS* I: 107 (I: 64).

[31] Cf. Humboldt, "Über die innere und äußere Organisation der höheren wissenschaftlichen Anstalten in Berlin," in *GS* x: 253, 255 (IV: 257, 259).

it in its completeness, but also, later on, only a few of them elevate themselves to a higher point of view and a more general overview of the work.[32]

Following Friedrich Schiller, Humboldt deployed Greek antiquity as an alternative to this present condition, which was frequently described as inadequate. For "the predominant trait" of the Greeks, he wrote, was "respect for and pleasure at symmetry and equilibrium, wanting to admit the most noble and sublime only there, where this is in harmony with the whole." As a consequence, the "disparity between inner and outer existence that frequently torments the present generation" was simply foreign to their nature.[33] The wide variety of the different areas of life which made modern man feel so very insecure, has not led to contradictions and conflicts in ancient Greece; instead differences were combined into a unit. This very harmony in the plurality of human existence has made the Greeks the "ideal we ourselves want to be and to which we aspire."[34]

The Greeks demonstrated that striving for education could never end and that it was a lifelong process of self-instruction.[35] Such concepts were directed against the class system of the *ancien régime*; while sustaining new educational elites that were no longer legitimized by birth and origin, but by performance and education.[36] The ideal of a higher education oriented towards Greek humanity was, in theory, available to all people,

as the most common day labourer and the finest educated person has to be initially made equal in his disposition, if the former is not to become callous unbefitting human dignity and the latter is not to become sentimental, chimerical and eccentric unbefitting the power of man.[37]

Yet, Humboldt's idea of education was by no means egalitarian. One had to be able to afford an education that served a purpose, but had limited practical usefulness. It was the rising bourgeoisie that could adopt Humboldt's ideal (through *Wissenschaft*) at the beginning of the nineteenth century. For this reason, the veneration of the Greeks established a central idea of education as a permanent process of self-perfection, which was vital to the cultural identity of middle-class society in Germany. The bourgeois world of the Greeks replaced the aristocratic vision of antiquity, already shaped by the French court's encounter with Rome. Education became

---

[32] Humboldt, "Theorie der Bildung des Menschen," *GS* I: 282–3 (I: 234).
[33] Humboldt, "Geschichte des Verfalls und Untergangs der griechischen Freistaaten," *GS* III: 198 (II: 102).
[34] Ibid. *GS* III: 189 (II: 92).   [35] Cf. Landfester 2001: 210–13.   [36] Cf. e.g. Nipperdey 1983: 59–61.
[37] Humboldt, "Der Königsberger und der Litauische Schulplan," *GS* XIII: 278 (IV: 189).

the actual and true title of nobility. From that point onward, the sign of bourgeois exclusionism was the sovereign mastery of the Greek language.

Normativity and historicity: Timeless magnitude and paradigmatic historicity

The Greeks revealed to Humboldt the "pure humanity of mankind fulfilled for its own sake." They "are to us what their gods were to them."[38] The Romans were merely perceived and accepted as conveyors of the Greek heritage. The adulation of the Greeks was accompanied by the debasement of the Roman tradition. "Provided that antiquity implies a form of idealism, the Romans are included only to the extent that it is impossible to separate them from the Greeks."[39]

Humboldt shared the conviction of his contemporary classicists that to understand oneself one needed to comprehend that which is foreign; and that one's own mind was to be discovered and educated in the frame of the debate with the person opposite and as part of the acquisition of another's intellect. In encountering Greece, Humboldt raised a crucial question for the German bourgeoisie: under which circumstances and conditions and with what aim could an individual and a nation appropriate and render accessible foreign traditions?[40] In responding to this question he emphasized again the importance of the Greek language, in which the Greek spirit manifested itself in its naturalness, power, and abundance. As he pointedly put it, "all genuine intellectual education" emerged "from the peculiarities of the Attic dialect."[41]

However, it was not only the language that had to be learned. Individuals were meant to grasp the Greek culture in its diversity and the Greek character in its totality. While Humboldt in principle granted every nation the opportunity to develop an individual character, he nevertheless argued that only Greek antiquity was of outstanding significance:

Through these traits the Greek character became the ideal of all human existence in as much as it could be maintained that these set out the pure form of human purpose, even if the implementation of this form could have happened in a different way afterwards.[42]

---

[38] Humboldt, "Über den Charakter der Griechen, die idealische und historische Ansicht desselben," GS VII: 609–16 (II: 65–72).

[39] Humboldt, "Geschichte der Verfalls und Untergangs der griechischen Freistaaten," GS III: 197 (II: 101); cf. "Über den Charakter der Griechen, die idealische und historische Ansicht desselben," GS VII: 610 (II: 66).

[40] Cf. Oesterle 1996: 307.   [41] Haym 1859: 134–5.

[42] Humboldt, "Über den Charakter der Griechen, die idealische und historische Ansicht desselben," GS VII: 613 (II: 69); cf. also GS I: 262–3 (II: 7–8.).

According to Humboldt, the study of such a character has to have a generally remedial effect on human education in every situation and in every era, "as, so to speak, the very same constitutes the basis of the human character in general."[43]

Humboldt's idealization of Greek antiquity was a late variant of the *Querelle des Anciens et des Modernes*, which, however, in the seventeenth century, had conveyed a largely Romanocentric image of antiquity.[44] Following Winckelmann, who had celebrated the "noble simplicity and calm greatness" of Greek works of art and had demanded the "imitation" (*Nachahmung*) of the Greeks in order to become great oneself,[45] Humboldt took delight in the emotionalism of the classical enthusiasm for all things Greek. Nevertheless, he did not speak out in favor of the imitation of the Greek historical paradigm, as this was in his opinion impossible: "To us the Greeks are not simply a useful historical people to know, but an ideal. Their authority over us is of a kind that arises particularly from their inaccessibility."[46]

Blind imitation could not lead the individual to harmoniously develop personal talents. What was needed was the continuous consideration of the idealized image of Hellas, which was not a historical place, but rather a Utopia, a "necessary illusion" (*nothwendige Täuschung*). Antiquity had passed and the modern world could not be deduced from the old one.[47] Normativity and historicity went side by side:[48] Humboldt did not want to portray the Greeks in their timeless magnitude anymore, but in their paradigmatic historicity. Consequently, Greece became the object of historical research, whose task was to describe the unique individuality of the Greek national character. The modern subject of the Classics – with which Humboldt had become acquainted as a student in Göttingen under Christian Gottlob Heyne and which Friedrich August Wolf with whom Humboldt corresponded intensively stood for – was responsible for the research into this individuality.[49] It could no longer be the sole task of Classics to edit and comment on the traditional texts of antiquity. It was rather necessary for those texts to be subjected to historical analysis and interpretation according to the rules of historical criticism of the

---

[43] Humboldt, "Über das Studium des Altertums, und des griechischen insbesondere," *GS* I: 275 (II: 19).
[44] Cf. especially Schmitt 2002.
[45] Uhlig 1988: 24.
[46] Humboldt, "Über den Charakter der Griechen, die idealische und historische Ansicht desselben," *GS* VII: 609 (II: 65).
[47] Cf. Humboldt to Goethe, 23 August 1804, cited in Humboldt 1960–81, V: 215–17. Cf. also Saure 2007: 12–13.
[48] Cf. Muhlack 1988: 179–80.   [49] Cf. Henze 1966 and Mattson 1990.

sources. Thus, classical philology became a historical discipline. And since antiquity was still regarded as the most distinguished object of historical interest, classical philology considered itself as the first amongst the historical disciplines. The question surrounding the conditions of the possibility of objective discoveries in history was discussed using ancient topics; and the principles of the newly constituted hermeneutics were applied to the philological historical analysis of Greek and Latin texts.[50]

As a result, Humboldt was at the forefront of a development, which historicized Greek antiquity and relativized its normative function. Over the nineteenth century the ideals of *Wissenschaft* and education drifted apart. In later years Humboldt not only concentrated on researching the ancient world, but also pursued universal historical objectives, at first intending to confirm the uniqueness of the Greek national character by drawing comparisons, and later without any explicit reference to the exceptionality of European antiquity. In his late linguistic studies, he distanced himself from every cultural hierarchy that privileged European antiquity.[51]

August Boeckh and Johann Gustav Droysen continued resolutely on the path set out by Heyne, Wolf, and Humboldt, at the end of which came the realization that the ancient world was only one epoch amongst others. The significance of their contribution, which initially made the Greeks its primary focus, cannot be underestimated when considering the development of a modern conception of history and its scientific methodology. In his speech to the academy held in 1821 and entitled "On the Task of the Historian" (*Über die Aufgabe des Geschichtsschreibers*) Humboldt advocated a historiography which brought to an end the mere enumeration of facts and stressed the powers of the mind and the imagination. These powers, he argued, were vital to discovering successfully the internal coherence of history and the laws of historical development. Humboldt addressed the ideas that structure history and make a fabric out of the material of facts. Ideas are, by their nature, "outside the circle of finitude;" they prevail in and dominate world history "in all their parts."[52] So it is the task of the historian, with his ability to imagine and his gift of deduction,[53] to uncover the transcendent ideas as the driving forces of history and to describe their effect in the immanence. "The duty of the historian, in his ultimate, but simplest resolution, is to portray the striving of an idea to win existence in reality."[54] In the transition from enlightened historiography to historicism

[50] Cf. Muhlack 1979: 232–6 as well as generally; Muhlack 1986 and Grafton 1983a.
[51] Cf. Messling 2008, especially 227–76.
[52] Humboldt, "Über die Aufgabe des Geschichtsschreibers," *GS* IV: 51–2 (1: 600–1).
[53] Humboldt, "Über die Aufgabe des Geschichtsschreibers," *GS* IV: 37 (1: 587).
[54] Ibid. *GS* IV: 56 (1: 605). Cf. also Süßmann 2000, especially 75–112.

Humboldt did not construct the unity of the past by portraying past events, but by describing ideas that the historian extracts from these events. The creative imagination of the historian was no longer stigmatized, but rather became the true condition of the possibility of historical discoveries.

The ancient paradigm furnished the bourgeoisie with the certainty that the passage of time could be influenced by historiography. The exclusive competence – and task – of historiography was to "enlighten the present about its future and therefore, about the historical moment to which it belongs and which it has to do justice to."[55] The citizen could, and had to, learn from antiquity how to exercise political and social responsibility. Historical reflection, which had its origin in Greek antiquity, thus became a central aspect of bourgeois culture.

The fundamental historicization of the ideas of mankind and the world as well as the unparalleled rise of historically oriented subjects at universities and in public perception characterized politics, society, and the mentality of nineteenth-century bourgeoisie. This dynamic process originated in the aestheticizing enthusiasm for Greek antiquity, the neo-humanist concept of education, the rational method of textual criticism, and the re-validation of historiography.[56] Humboldt contributed to the development of hermeneutics, which served as a theoretical concept to the study of history and antiquity of the bourgeois intellectual interpretation.[57]

Moreover the evocation of ancient Greece as an "ideal for comparison" (*Ideal zur Vergleichung*)[58] resulted in a critical assessment of Christianity, which, as Humboldt explained, was responsible for the decay of taste and scholarly culture in the period from the fourth to the mid-sixteenth century. Christianity has worn man down "in such a way that natural rest and undisturbed inner peace were lost to him forever ... By splitting his nature, it opposed human sensuality with a pure spirituality and filled man with ideas of poverty, humility, and sin that would now never disappear."[59] Humboldt contrasted the "barbaric times" that were "very fittingly named the Middle Ages" with the distanced and idealized Greek past.[60] In doing so, he broke with the idea, which had hitherto dominated the humanist tradition, that pre-Christian and Christian antiquity constituted a unity; and put in its place an exclusively pagan past, the study of which was to bring about the renewal of the present.

---

[55] Cf. Muhlack 1998: 276.
[56] Cf. in general Nipperdey 1983: 498–533 as well as for the development in the study of antiquity Rebenich 2008 and 2000 with further literature.
[57] Cf. Jaeger 1994: 65–85. [58] Humboldt, "Das achtzehnte Jahrhundert," *GS* II: 24 (I: 401).
[59] Ibid. Cf. Wilhelm von Humboldt to Goethe, 23 August 1804, in Humboldt 1960–81, V: 215.
[60] Wilhelm von Humboldt, "Das achtzehnte Jahrhundert," *GS*: II. 24 (I. 402).

Friedrich Paulsen has aptly described the consequences of this move:

The new age found the image of perfection within Hellenism rather than within Christianity: the image of the perfect human being rather than that of God incarnate . . . Hellenising humanism is a new religion, the philologists are its priests, the universities and schools its temple.[61]

Humboldt conceptualized a secular educational religion, which expedited the de-Christianization of society in the bourgeois world and led to a quasi-religious veneration of Hellenism.

Freedom and education of the individual: On the genesis of bourgeois society

Following Herder, Humboldt developed the term individuality in his studies on the ancient world.[62] From the French Revolution he deduced that in certain historical situations everything depends on individual abilities. The politician who seeks to change the world for the better has to create conditions that allow these abilities to develop freely. The historian, however, has to recognize and portray the individual abilities in their particular specific manifestation in the past epoch. The historical search for individuality has to be directed towards generality, which nevertheless manifests itself in the actions of individual people, as well as the language, the nation, and the state. This understanding of individuality emancipated the individual, who was no longer subordinate to a collective, but was understood in his exceptionality as a constituting part of generality.[63]

Every single person was entitled to individual rights and personal freedom, if he wanted to develop his talents and strive successfully for the appropriation of the world. Humboldt's demand to raise the individual to be independent, proactive, and responsible for himself presupposed individual rights and personal freedom and was directed at the state, which was the only institution that was able to guarantee these rights and this freedom.

For this education freedom is the primary and essential condition . . . The person educated like this would then have to become part of the state; and the constitution of the state, as it were, would have to measure itself taking him as an example. Only

---

[61] Paulsen 1921: 311.   [62] Cf. for the following Muhlack and Hentschke 1972: 80ff.

[63] The ideas presented here are also directed against Kost (2004) who argues that Humboldt had no part in the bourgeois discourse, aimed at establishing a community that was focussed on the individual.

as part of such a struggle would one be certain to hope for a true improvement of the constitution by the nation . . . [64]

Humboldt identified the liberation of the citizen to become a proactive human being as the foremost purpose of the modern state. Consequently, the state was not allowed to hinder the education of the individual, or intervene in the upbringing, religion, and morals, but had to accept freedom as the primary and essential condition of education and *Wissenschaft*. It was necessary, therefore, to restrict the effectiveness of the state.[65] The "state constitution" (*Staatsverfassung*) was merely "a necessary means" and "as it is inevitably associated with restrictions of freedom," nothing more than "a necessary evil."[66] Humboldt linked the new idea of the state to the new idea of education. The state was called to take in hand the education of the individual solely for the sake of the person himself and without pursuing any secondary aims linked to power and interest. At the same time, one would also expect that the new education, which was empowered by its inherent law, would inspire devotion to both the people and the state.[67]

Humboldt advocated the idea of active political participation of concerned citizens and integrated them into his model of a society that constituted itself as a community of citizens capable of controlling their own affairs independently. For Humboldt, though, the place for an individual's free activity was not the state, but the nation. He drew a sharp dividing line between the state and the nation. The state was responsible for internal and external security, while the nation was characterized by the voluntary cooperation of citizens in various areas. The citizen alone could establish the connection between state and nation by engaging in self-confident political activity. The "free interactions among the people of a nation," which "protects all possessions, the longing for which leads the people to form a community,"[68] anticipated the bourgeois conception of civil sphere that was partly separated from the state.[69] The purpose of this separation, according to Humboldt, was to secure an area for the citizens that would be largely free from state influence, as "the human race" (*das Menschengeschlecht*) has now "reached a level of culture, from which it could rise higher only by training the individuals. Therefore, all institutions that

---

[64] Humboldt, "Ideen zu einem Versuch die Gränzen der Wirksamkeit des Staates zu bestimmen," *GS* I: 144 (I: 106).

[65] Cf. Benner 1995: 55–67.

[66] Humboldt, "Ideen zu einem Versuch die Gränzen der Wirksamkeit des Staates zu bestimmen," *GS* I: 236 (I: 212).

[67] Schnabel 1948: 410.   [68] Humboldt, "Das achtzehnte Jahrhundert," *GS* I: 236 (I: 212).

[69] Cf. Sauter-Bergerhausen 2002; Spitta 2004.

may hinder this training and force people together in masses are more damaging now than ever before."[70]

Here Humboldt put past and present in a productive relationship to one another. Antiquity served as a point of reference, but no return to the ancient state of affairs was intended. In his theoretical considerations on the state, Humboldt left no doubt as to his conviction that the Greek *polis* and the Roman *res publica* represented an obsolete model:

> Those states were republics, their institutions of this kind were pillars of a free constitution that filled the citizens with enthusiasm, which let the detrimental influence of the restriction of individual freedom be felt less and did less damage to the energy of the character. As a consequence, the citizens enjoyed much greater freedom compared to us; and what they sacrificed they sacrificed to another activity, a share in the government. In our mostly monarchical states, all is completely different.[71]

In antiquity no distinction was made between state and society, and the citizen of the ancient city-state subordinated his individual freedom to the public good. Here Humboldt contrasted the political conditions prevailing in the monarchies of his time with the historical situation in antiquity. The discussion about the circumstances in antiquity led him to criticize contemporary state and society.[72]

Humboldt's image of antiquity served to construct and legitimize his idea of a modern state that guaranteed and promoted education and freedom. The study of antiquity had therefore a contemporary, eminently political dimension. The ancient examples explained the necessity to connect, in the present, bourgeois involvement and patriotism with the ideal of individual autonomy. Only such a state would be able to be strong that allowed its citizens personal and institutional freedom and ended the rule of one person over another. Freedom, in Humboldt's words, is "the necessary condition without which even the most soulful action is not able to produce salutary effects."[73] The concept of a politically active citizen and the model of a bourgeois society that shaped nineteenth-century discourse on liberalism, oriented themselves towards the ideal projection of political activity in the Greek city-states and the Roman Republic.[74]

---

[70] Humboldt, "Ideen zu einem Versuch die Gränzen der Wirksamkeit des Staates zu bestimmen," *GS* I: 142–3 (I: 105).
[71] Ibid. *GS*: I: 142 (I: 104–5).   [72] Cf. also Benner 1995: 58–9.
[73] Humboldt, "Ideen zu einem Versuch die Gränzen der Wirksamkeit des Staates zu bestimmen," *GS* I: 118 (I: 77).
[74] Cf. also Vick 2007.

A sense of affinity: The Greeks of the modern age

Humboldt recommended the study of the Greek nation in all its facets.[75] At first, however, he hardly had any interest in political history, as he thought he could recognize the character of a nation more easily in its literary, scholarly, and artistic achievements. Only the Wars of Liberation against Napoleon made him more sensitive to political events in the past and the present. In 1807, Prussia was devastated after the lost battles against Napoleon's army at Jena and Auerstedt. As an envoy to the Vatican, Humboldt was, at least physically, far removed from the political mood in his homeland. Apart from the linguistic studies he pursued in Rome, in a text that remained fragmentary he addressed the subject, which had to be of alarming relevance to a Prussian aristocrat: the "History of the Decline and Fall of the Greek Free States" ("Geschichte des Verfalls und Untergangs der griechischen Freistaaten").[76] In the foreword that preceded the introduction Humboldt justified his project:

[I have a] threefold purpose in mind: first of all, to imagine myself in a time where the deeply moving, but always engaging battle of better forces against overpowering violence was fought in an unhappy, but honourable way; secondly, to show that degeneration was only partly to blame for Greece's decline, but that the concealed reason actually was that a Greek person possessed a far too noble, delicate, free and humane nature to establish a political constitution in his time that by necessity limited individuality; thirdly, to arrive at a point of view, from which it is possible to comfortably survey the old and the new history in its entirety.[77]

The ways of inquiry that Humboldt had in mind for the history of the decline of Greece constituted nothing less than three different kinds of writing history. From a moving, aesthetic examination of the condition of Greece before the decline he wanted to reach, through the analysis of historical events, a point of view that revealed a universal historical view of past and present.

But what did the history of the decline and fall of the free Greek states demonstrate? Macedonians and Romans, the conquerors of Greece, were barbarians: "The better and nobler part succumbed and the brutish superior strength was victorious." Just as it happens nearly all the time, "barbaric peoples" defeated the "more educated ones," "one-sided, coldly calculating,

[75] Cf. Humboldt, "Über das Studium des Altertums, und des griechischen insbesondere," *GS* I: 257 (II: 2).

[76] Humboldt, "Geschichte des Verfalls und Untergangs der griechischen Freistaaten," *GS* III: 171–218 (II: 73–124).

[77] Ibid. *GS* III: 171 (II: 73).

restless nations their more humane neighbours, who dedicated themselves more faithfully and passionately to the activities of peace." Whoever does not descend "into despair" looks to "regain the freedom on the interior," which has been lost on the exterior.[78] And victorious Rome formed "in many respects, always the body into which Greece was supposed to breathe the soul."[79]

The actualization of the Greek history of decline is striking and the comparison between Hellas–Germany and Rome–France imposes itself perfectly. The history of postclassical Greece mirrored the most recent humiliation of Prussia by Napoleonic France. At the same time, Humboldt emphasized that Germans and Greeks were especially close:

The Germans have the indisputable merit to have faithfully comprehended Greek education at first and to have felt it deeply . . . Other nations have never been equally happy with this, or at least they have neither in commentaries, nor in translations, nor in imitations, nor eventually (what matters most) in the transmitted spirit of antiquity proven their intimacy with the Greeks in a similar way. A far stronger and closer bond, therefore, connects Germans to Greeks, than to any other, even much closer epoch or nation.

Humboldt goes on to write that Germany bears "an indisputable resemblance to Greece in her language, diversity of efforts, simplicity of mind, as well as her federal constitution and her latest fate."[80] Thus the fundamental arguments for spreading the idea of a Greco-German relationship were identified. The diversity of the Greek and German national character corresponded to the one-sidedness of the Roman and French one. Humboldt first gave his view on the "whim about the similarity of the Greeks and the Germans" in passing in a letter to Schiller dated 22 September 1795.[81] He repeated his idea that a "sense of affinity" existed between Germans and Greeks in other letters, until he developed it fully in his "History of the Decline and Fall of the Greek Free States" ("Geschichte des Verfalls und Untergangs der griechischen Freistaaten") published in 1807. Humboldt transformed the epochal comparison between antiquity and modernity, formulated in previous centuries, into a dual cultural comparison: on the one hand between ancient Greece and ancient Rome, and conversely between the cultural nation of Germany, which was equated with Greece,

---

[78] Ibid. *GS* III: 173–4 (II: 74–5).   [79] Ibid. *GS* III: 183 (II: 86).

[80] Ibid. *GS* III: 184, 185–6 (II: 87, 88–9). Cf. Leitzmann 1934: 42. "At the same time I cannot deny that I want to erect a memorial to the poor, shattered Germany, as, according to my long felt conviction, only when the German spirit is imbued with the Greek one, we have something, in which the human race can advance without standing still."

[81] Cf. Landfester 1996: 208–9 (with further references).

and the nation-state France, which he regarded as being in the Roman tradition. There was a need to respond to the military defeat of Prussia and to Napoleon's political triumph not only by means of educational, but also by means of cultural policy. The message that Humboldt promulgated in 1807 was that the barbaric "subjugator" was to be overcome culturally.[82]

Following Herder and German idealism's reception of antiquity, Humboldt propagated the concept of a culturally defined nation which renounces state integration, by having cultural cohesion at its disposal.[83] The idea of political unity was replaced by a consciousness of cohesion based on a shared cultural ground, which in turn substantiated the intellectual superiority of the politically fragmented nation. Humboldt's actualization of the dichotomy, which existed between the cultural nation of Greece and the nation-state of Rome, compensated for the Prussian political and military defeats and the dissolution of the Holy Roman Empire.

Humboldt thus invented a tradition that set forth the creation of a collective identity. Imagining the Greek past provided the German bourgeoisie with a welcome alternative to the Franco-Latin cultural hegemony in Europe. The Prussian aristocrats' national myth of the Greeks was directed against France and the "Gallomania" of the German nobility, against the absolutist state and its class system. This myth, which was spread by grammar schools and universities in Germany, was a key instrument in the protection of national identity and in the process of coming to terms with the present. The new myth of the relationship between Germans and Greeks, which originated in a certain historical situation, became part of the bourgeois endowment of national collective life with meaning and reinforced the idea of being a citizen of a superior cultural nation.[84]

EPILOGUE

The study of ancient, especially Greek, history in nineteenth-century Germany established new conceptions of upbringing, education and *Wissenschaft*, but also of nation, state, and society. Interpretations of the present and the past were closely interlinked. The present was not appraised on the grounds of antiquity. On the contrary, a utopian vision of the ancient past, constituted in the present, was projected back onto the past. Humboldt did not propagate a timeless model that was to be imitated, but imagined

---

[82] Cf. Fuhrmann 1979; Lohse 1997; Rüegg 1985 and 1978: 93–105.
[83] Cf. also Proß 1996 and Saure 2006.   [84] Cf. Landfester 1996: 211.

an ideal place, the examination of which was meant to help overcome the status quo.

The bourgeois conception of history, the rise of the historical *Wissenschaften* and the establishment of a theory of historical hermeneutics aiding the bourgeois creation of meaning had their origin in the study of antiquity. Greece (and to a lesser extent also Rome) was a pivotal point of reference and comparison in the definition of education, seminal to bourgeois society, as a permanent process of self-perfection; in the description of the relationship between freedom and education and in the link between individual, society, and state; finally in the discussion of the principles of social organization and structure. In the end, the idea of the cultural nation was developed through the dialogue with Greek antiquity. The idealized Greeks became a permanent part of German national culture, in which some scholars identified a "Tyranny of Greece over Germany."[85]

The image of the Greeks supported the productive comparison of modernity and classical antiquity. Humboldt advocated no unified and affirmative position regarding antiquity. Normativity and historicity characterized his vision of the past. His evocations of antiquity were critical of society and of contemporary issues. The absolutist world of men of estates was to be overcome for good and bourgeois social forms were to be realized. To Humboldt education was the basis for a comprehensive renewal of state and society; the identity of modern man was based on education. His ambitious concept of reform was applied to schools and universities. It made the German university an internationally effective paragon of a modern educational policy and instituted the rise of the historical *Wissenschaften*. Humboldt's ideal of antiquity was central to this process: it constituted the foundation for the study of the classics in the context of educational reforms that sustained nineteenth-century bourgeois culture. The emancipatory potential of Humboldt's image of antiquity, however, quickly got lost: there was fear that young people, by showing enthusiasm for Greek antiquity, could infect themselves with Republican ideas. In addition, there was competition from research into Germanic culture and the Middle Ages, inspired by romanticism.[86]

Humanist education not only offered an idea of freedom that was juxtaposed to the constraints of state and society; it also advocated taking refuge in a form of inwardness, which counteracted the bourgeois faith in progress,[87] and intensified the dichotomy between "culture" and

---

[85] Butler 1935.   [86] Cf. here as well as for the following Marchand 1996 and Sünderhauf 2004.
[87] Cf. also Bruford 1975.

"economy", and between "spirit" and "materialism."[88] Still, throughout the shaping of the German empire, an increasingly superficial concept of education came to be the basis of authoritarian institutions, which applied drill and routine to grammar schools. Contentment was attained by drumming in the verbs ending in -μι. In the class society of the nineteenth century the content of education no longer counted. What was important was the use of specific educational methods that could be used as effective instruments of exclusion. In universities classical education was triumphant and transformed Greco-Roman antiquity into an absolute – with a diminishing interest in the Middle East, and a neglect of the history of early Christianity.

At the same time, the historicization of antiquity marked the end of the idealized vision of the ancients. Humboldt and his contemporaries never left any doubt as to their conviction that Greek culture is the basis of a humanist education. Such a normative conception of antiquity was alien to the methodically professionalized study of antiquity, whose modern realism destroyed the special position of the Greeks upon which the German bourgeois intellectual had come to rely. After the mid-nineteenth century individual scholars, mostly academic outsiders such as Friedrich Nietzsche, opposed the established forms of classical education. They criticized a *Wissenschaft* of antiquity that only amassed highly specialized knowledge and tried, alluding to Winckelmann and Humboldt, to preserve European antiquity as a normative model, which was intended to have an educational function. Their efforts were characterized by a deeply rooted cultural pessimism implying a quest for far-reaching social and political changes.[89] Yet the profound shifts in bourgeois culture in the transition from the nineteenth to the twentieth century and the manifest competitiveness of different lifestyles and kinds of behaviour allowed only a minority to continue to believe in the educational and emancipatory potential of classical Greece.

Translated by Richard Brobson

---

[88] Ulf 2006: 67–79.   [89] Landfester 1988.

CHAPTER 6

Modern histories of ancient Greece: Genealogies, contexts and eighteenth-century narrative historiography

Giovanna Ceserani

When did modern historiography of ancient Greece start? The question is deceptively simple and betrays assumptions far more revealing than any straightforward answer. Its formulation implies distinguishing between ancient historians and modern ones. But this has long been a slippery endeavour, as Nicole Loraux's title *Thucydides n'est pas un collègue* of some years ago reminds us.[1] Ironically, in telling the history of historical practice, historians' chronology has often been fraught with issues of value and haunted by presentism. In fact, when the origins of modern historiography of the ancient world are sought, the divide between ancients and moderns is repeatedly left behind in favour of privileging some moderns above others. George Grote, the nineteenth-century British banker and political figure turned famous author of the *History of Ancient Greece* (1846–56), is the most frequently cited founder. Many of these claims, moreover, besides highlighting Grote's differences from previous moderns, reinforce this historian's foundational status by attributing contemporary value to his work. It has been well argued that his 'is the earliest history of Greece still consulted by scholars' and that his work has remained influential to most important twentieth-century historians of ancient Greece, including de Ste Croix, Momigliano, Finley and Hansen.[2] Such analyses have taught us a lot about the development of modern historiography of ancient Greece. But what else is lost by assimilating Grote's work to that of today's historians and by leaving out authors who preceded him?

The nineteenth century – the time of Grote – has long figured at the origins of modernity. Yet many recent insights into defining and understanding the moderns have come from approaches that take a longer perspective, reaching back to the late eighteenth century and well beyond. It is in this earlier period that narrative histories of ancient Greece began to be written. Their authors presented them as distinct from those of ancient times.

---

[1] Loraux 1980.   [2] Roberts 1994: 239 and Cartledge 2001: xvi–xvii.

Nevertheless, these early eighteenth-century histories have been written off by later historians. In fact, they have often provided them with a foil to define their own modernity. There is much to be learned, though, by reassessing both these early works and the process by which they were later dismissed and suppressed. These are the issues that this chapter, however briefly, sets out to explore. Peeling back the genealogy of Grote's foundational role is a good starting point. The claims for Grote's modernity, both in the shape they take today and in the way they were first formulated in his own times, point us to earlier eighteenth-century works. Attending to these hints in turn offers a rich view of how the origins of modern historiography on ancient Greece intertwine with a wider framework of modernity.

Arnaldo Momigliano's 1952 essay 'Grote and Greek history' has been crucial to recent presentations of Grote as a foundational figure. Grote was here conclusively depicted as master of evidence and political interpretation – his work combining 'passionate moral and political interests, vast learning and respect for the evidence'.[3] Momigliano also briefly but poignantly sketched the wider reception and impact of Grote's work, ranging from Germany to Italy, as well as contextualising his approach within British Radical and Utilitarian thought. Political philosophers and scholars of Victorian England have since expanded on these leads.[4] In studies of modern historiography of ancient Greece, on the other hand, Momigliano's essay has come to play a double role: it has provided the basic framework to assess Grote's *History* and at the same time it has served as proof of its foundational role and enduring influence in the discipline.[5]

To an extent, this double status reflects the essay which both situated Grote historically and appealed to his work to inspire contemporary historical practices. The piece was Momigliano's inaugural lecture at University College London, a university in whose foundation Grote played an important role. The essay spoke of a crisis in ancient history, especially Greek history, and proposed a way to overcome it. The same principles that Momigliano illustrated as those of Grote – that 'Greek History is central to the formation of the liberal mind, but in turn the liberal mind is religious in examining the evidence'[6] – were the ones along which he invoked progress in the historical study of ancient Greece in his own times. It was characteristic of Momigliano's approach, and fitting to his institutional link with Grote on the occasion of his inaugural lecture at

---

[3] Momigliano 1955a: 222.   [4] See Urbinati 2002; Turner 1981 and Jenkyns 1980.
[5] For example Cartledge 2001.   [6] Momigliano 1955a: 230.

University College London, to introduce future research directions by way of a retrospective examination of the discipline. Yet in order to further our understanding of the development of modern histories of ancient Greece, it is now time to move our emphasis away from Momigliano's inspired appreciation of Grote to his wider insights into the shaping of modern historiography.

Shortly before delivering his lecture on Grote, Momigliano published the essay 'Ancient history and the antiquarian' (1950). Here he first formulated the interpretation of the origins of modern historical scholarship that he revisited throughout his career.[7] This essay indeed set off one of the most influential lines of his work, one that has since been repeatedly reckoned with in modern intellectual history and that has been credited with launching the field of antiquarian studies.[8] Momigliano argued that modern history developed out of the eighteenth-century convergence of traditional historical narrative – what used to be linear accounts of mostly political events – and antiquarian research – scholarship devoted to systematic treatment of a variety of subjects that relied on the skills of paleography, epigraphy and the interpretation of archaeological material. This summary certainly reduces the rich texture of Momigliano's formulation which, at its most ambitious explained Western historiography from classical antiquity to the current age. It was though precisely the interplay between the simplicity and versatility of the dualistic structure of Momigliano's model that led to an extraordinary variety of applications.

By now, Momigliano's thesis has also undergone criticism and, more recently, has been itself placed in its historical context. On the one hand, the development of Momigliano's intellectual trajectory has been deftly mapped.[9] On the other, Momigliano has been aligned with twentieth-century interpreters of modernity, such as Koselleck or Benjamin, in whose work too, although in varied combinations, fragments or antiquarianism, the narrative and the political were major terms of analysis.[10] The intellectual historians engaged in these discussions had at times to remind their interlocutors that, despite the wider appeal of his thesis, the main scope of Momigliano's inquiry – one that explains both some of its chief features and its limitations – was the field of ancient history.[11] This conversely reminds

---

[7] See Momigliano 1955b; for latest formulation see Momigliano 1990: 54–79.
[8] See for example, Phillips 1996; Pocock 1999–2005 vol. I (1999a): 140–3 and vol. II (1999b): 1–25; and the essays collected in Miller 2007a.
[9] Most recently, Miller 2007b: 12–25; Di Donato 2007 and Grafton 2007b.
[10] Miller 2007b: 9, 51 and 2007c; Fumaroli 2007: 156.
[11] Miller 2007b: 31–3, 51 and Grafton 2007b: 101.

us that these wider debates still need to be brought to bear on studies of modern historiography of the ancient world. Momigliano's characteristic dualism is certainly present in his interpretation of Grote as the historian of Greece who brought together political and intellectual history, German scholarship and British narrative.[12] Yet following this essay Momigliano dived progressively deeper into the scholarship of the eighteenth and seventeenth centuries.[13] We risk losing these insights if we do not expand the net beyond the Grote essay to later developments in Momigliano's own work and others' discussions of it.

From the first time Grote discussed ancient Greek history in print, the eighteenth century played an important role in defining his image as innovator. His first foray into Greek history came in an 1826 review article of Henry Fynes Clinton's *Fasti Hellenici: the Civil and Literary Chronology of Greece* (1824). After appreciating in his first page the work's efforts at establishing chronology, however, Grote posed as the issue of true interest that of explaining what lay behind the grandiose and unparalleled cultural achievements that filled Clinton's tables of Greek history. Clinton's name in fact did not appear again in the following sixty-one pages. Grote rather turned to outline briefly his own thesis that Greek cultural success was owed to the ambition for individual excellence fostered by democratic institutions. By and large, the article moved to a lengthy and detailed criticism of William Mitford's *History of Greece* – of which the first volume was published in 1784 while the fifth and last appeared in 1810. Grote initially introduced Mitford offhandedly, as the author most often quoted by Clinton in reference to Greek society and institutions. But he quickly built him into his main target by stating his concern that the field of Greek history – for which democracy, he argued, was crucial – should be dominated by a work partial to kings.

Grote explained that Mitford's royal bias had infected both qualities needed in an historian, that of 'higher philosophizing powers' and that of 'trac[ing] out and report[ing] the facts of the period he selects'.[14] In the following pages, Grote extensively and in detail called into question Mitford's use of evidence and his political interpretations. These criticisms read also as converse guidelines for composing a 'good history of Greece' such as the one he called for in his conclusion.[15] This is precisely what Grote did in his *History of Ancient Greece*, with its rich scholarly effort rooted in German source criticism that allowed him, among other things, to

---

[12] Grafton 2007b: 104.   [13] Miller 2007b: 14–15, 178, and Grafton 2007b: 106.
[14] Grote 1826: 280.   [15] Grote 1826: 331.

reformulate the question of a Greek heroic age,[16] and its deep engagement of intellectual and political aspects of ancient Greek life. However, it took a long time for Grote to publish the first volume of the work he had envisioned in his 1826 critique of Mitford and even longer to finish it. Yet, when in 1846 the first volume was published, its advocates still pitted it against Mitford's *History*. Grote's most illustrious reviewers – John Stuart Mill and George Cornell Lewis, who knew him well from the circles of Utilitarian and Philosophical Radicals – heralded the opening of a new age in the history of ancient Greece: as Mill wrote, 'finally this was the end of the era of Mitford'.[17]

There was more, though, to this passing of eras. For one, Grote had a few fellow travellers in his overtaking of Mitford, such as the Cambridge don Connop Thirlwall and the novelist and political figure Edward Bulwer Lytton. Only recently have scholars recovered from oblivion and investigated their books – respectively the *History of Greece* (1835–47) and *The Rise and Fall of Athens* (1837) – an understanding of which is necessary to appreciate more fully the context from which Grote's own work, and its subsequent dominance, emerged.[18] But, the epochal passage from Mitford to Grote also appears more crowded if looking on its earlier side.

Indeed, more than Mitford preceded Grote, as Momigliano already pointed out. Despite the main focus on Grote, Momigliano's inaugural lecture at University College London put, however cursorily, the origins of modern Greek historiography back into the eighteenth century, stating that 'it is uncertain whether Greek history was invented in England or in Scotland'.[19] This uncertainty reflected the alternative posed by taking into consideration, beside Mitford's work, also the *History of Ancient Greece* by John Gillies. Chronological primacy between the two is elusive. Gillies published two years later than Mitford, in 1786, but at once put out his complete work in two volumes, while Mitford did not finish his own five-volume work until well into the nineteenth century. Momigliano claimed that it was in their writings that for the first time 'political discussion was embodied in a Greek history'.[20] These British historians inhabited, to an extent, similar worlds. Both travelled to Europe and moved within the orbit of philosophical history. Gillies was a Scot who resided for some time in Germany; Mitford visited France at length and was reputedly first

---

[16] Morris 2000: 83–4.   [17] In Roberts 1994: 246.
[18] See introductions by Oswyn Murray and Peter Liddel respectively in Lytton 2004 and Liddel 2007: ix–xxxii.
[19] Momigliano 1955a: 214.   [20] Momigliano 1955a: 215.

encouraged to write a history of ancient Greece by Gibbon. They both were wary of Athenian democracy and favoured monarchy.

There were also differences. Mitford was a barrister and a member of the House of Commons who published little beyond his Greek history. John Gillies was elected Royal Historiographer of Scotland upon William Robertson's death in 1793 and authored a number of works that involved Greek antiquity, ranging from a *View of the Reign of Frederic II of Prussia, with a Parallel between that Prince and Philip II of Macedon* (1789) to translations of Aristotle, Lysias and Isocrates, and a *History of the World from Alexander to Augustus* (1807). Momigliano found much innovation in Gillies' work, enough to call for a revision of 'ideas on the development of historiography in the nineteenth century'. He claimed Gillies as precursor to Niebuhr's discussion of Demosthenes and Philip and to Droysen's analogy between Macedon and Prussia.[21] He also thought Gillies had more 'political judgement' than Mitford and pointed out that this had been the opinion also of August Boeckh. Momigliano believed that Gillies' work was superseded by Mitford only 'because the latter's history was richer and more reliable in scholarly details'.[22] Mitford also surpassed Gillies in antidemocratic bias, which made him a better target for Philosophical Radicals. Yet, his absence from this debate and his neglected role in genealogies of Greek historiography since then are puzzling.

Gillies and Mitford considered together allow deeper readings of the contexts from which late eighteenth-century historiography of ancient Greece emerged. Recently Akça Ataç has showed how these works, while discussing Athens and Sparta, deeply engaged questions of empire of contemporary relevance.[23] Momigliano also analysed how Gillies and Mitford's political assessments owed much to their own times.[24] Gillies' comparison between Philip of Macedon and Frederick of Prussia was explicitly thematised in his work. Momigliano further highlighted how the age of revolutions was the major lens that coloured these authors' view of Greek history. In 1778 Gillies wrote that if a 'turbulent' government like that of ancient democratic Greece were to be established in 'a new hemisphere' – meaning the American colonies – 'might not the ancient barbarities be renewed; the manners of men be again tainted with a savage ferocity; and those enormities, the bare description of which is shocking to human nature, be introduced, repeated, and gradually become familiar?'[25] Mitford, looking back on the Greeks from the new vantage point of the French

---

[21] Momigliano 1955a: 217.   [22] Momigliano 1955a: 216.   [23] Ataç 2006.
[24] Momigliano 1955a: 215–17.   [25] Gillies 1778: lxiii.

Revolution, claimed that the testimony of the French events 'renders all the atrocious and before scarcely credible violence of faction among the Greeks probable, but almost make them moderate'.[26]

The passages highlighted by Momigliano not only show the present colouring the views of the past, but its impact on the very way the past is perceived. In both Gillies and Mitford one senses a new relationship to the past, shaped by late eighteenth-century events: what in ancient history seemed unheard of before became credible, in fact even pale in comparison with the new revolutions. The rupture is similar to the newly skewed parallel between modern and ancient revolutions that François Hartog explored in Chateaubriand's writing from the 1790s.[27] It is within the space created by this rupture that Reinhard Koselleck theorised the emergence of a sense of possibility, of acceleration of time, in fact the substance of progress that would constitute modern historicity.[28] Late eighteenth-century narrative historiography of ancient Greece can thus be seen to partake in important features in the development of modernity. But what to think about narrative histories of ancient Greece that appeared earlier in the century? Koselleck himself considered the changes brought about by the Revolution and the Enlightenment, the new sense of the past and what constitutes the political, as the result of processes that extend back into and can be explained only in the cultural, social and political dynamics of the early eighteenth century.[29] The eighteenth-century histories of ancient Greece that preceded Gillies and Mitford cannot be dismissed as pre-modern.

Momigliano highlighted already in the Grote essay that during the eighteenth century 'handbooks of Greek history were not uncommon on the continent, some of the most popular books being in fact vulgarizations translated from English into French, German and Italian' – as examples he quoted Diderot's translation of Temple Stanyan's *Grecian History* in 1743 and 'the rather low-level' 1774 compilation of Goldsmith.[30] In subsequent essays, Momigliano kept wondering what to make of these works. On the one hand, he clearly identified in the composition of such modern histories of the ancient world one of the major novelties of eighteenth-century historiography. On the other hand, especially for Greek history, he found it hard to answer the question of 'what value to attribute to schoolbooks?'; while resisting to judge them as derivative from the ancient sources, he saw them as limited to offering moral or political interpretation

---

[26] Mitford 1797, III: 670.   [27] Hartog 2003: 77–107.   [28] Koselleck 2004c, especially 9–42.
[29] See Koselleck 1988, especially 23–40 and 98–123.   [30] Momigliano 1955a: 215.

of the ancient evidence and found their merit possibly residing only in that 'there was nothing else'.[31] Since Momigliano, the judgement of these works as derivative and mostly conservative has been maintained by most scholars. But starting rather from Momigliano's open question, I would now like to take a closer look at these works, to begin at least to grasp their original contexts and to interrogate the role they have come to play in our accounts of the shaping of the modern turn to ancient Greece.

The earliest modern history of ancient Greece that Momigliano mentioned was that of Stanyan. A closer look reveals a more populated scenery. In 1707, the same year in which Stanyan put out the first volume of *The Grecian History*, a similar book, another first volume of a *History of Ancient Greece*, was published by Thomas Hind. Hind never brought out the second volume and has been long forgotten, but the coincidence of the title and date of publication of its project with that of Stanyan is tantalising. The story of Stanyan's second volume, finally published in 1739, more than thirty years after the first, brings into the picture another figure of early eighteenth-century historiography of ancient Greece, the Frenchman Charles Rollin. Rollin was the author of a twelve-volume *Histoire ancienne* (*Ancient History*), the first volume of which was published in Paris in 1730 and the last in 1738. That same year Rollin's work began to be translated into English, and this seems to have spurred Stanyan to complete his *History of Greece*, which, in turn, was translated into French in 1743. Momigliano did not mention Rollin, but this historian has since gained a space next to Stanyan in studies that deal, however briefly, with eighteenth-century historiography of ancient Greece. The works of Stanyan and Rollin are remembered as successful handbooks, but also quickly dismissed in similar ways, both judged as didactic and derivative, with Rollin in particular also being deemed politically conservative.[32] Studies of the French eighteenth century, on the other hand, have given Rollin more credit and so have recent insights in eighteenth-century views of the ancient past.[33] Moreover, in times closer to his own, Rollin elicited a variety of judgements. He was alternatively praised as the 'abeille de la Grèce' by Montesquieu and accused by Voltaire of merely putting into new words what others had already once said – an accusation that did not detain Voltaire himself from copying abundant segments of Rollin's work. These early eighteenth-century histories of ancient Greece warrant further investigation.

[31] Momigliano 1980a: 254.   [32] Roberts 1994: 154–7, 173–8; Ampolo 1997: 65–7.
[33] See Grell 1995: 7–17, 877–88 and Cambiano 2000: 271–4; Hartog 2005.

Rollin (1661–1741) was an educator with a history of clashes with institutional power. His career was chequered by his Jansenist sympathies that made even the funeral oration in his honour difficult to navigate for his colleagues at the Académie des Inscriptions et Belles-Lettres.[34] Twice elected rector of the University of Paris, his unorthodox religious beliefs, much disliked at Court, led to his dismissal after 1719. It was while forbidden to teach that Rollin turned to composing his published works. First was the 1727 educational treatise *Traité des études* (1726–31) – (translated in English as *Method of Teaching and Studying the belles lettres*) – in which Rollin advocated a larger role for both the vernacular and history in teaching practices. Rollin then published his own histories to remedy the weaknesses that he perceived in current curricula, the *Ancient History* first and later, in 1741, a *Histoire Romaine* (the *Roman History*). Recent studies praise the *Method* for its originality,[35] but it was the *Ancient History* that enjoyed greater success and had a much longer life, being reissued well into the nineteenth century.

The *Ancient History* reveals the tensions and constraints surrounding profane history in absolutist France, starting with its disorienting title. The work was titled in full – *Histoire Ancienne des Égyptiens, des Carthaginois, des Assyriens, des Babyloniens, des Mèdes et des Perses, des Macédoniens, des Grecs* – but it was in fact mainly a Greek history. Rollin finished with the other ancient peoples by half way through the second volume, while he dedicated the remaining eleven to the ancient Greeks – from the origins of Greek states to their subjection to Rome. That Rollin's interest was in Greek history is clear from his first mention of the project in his educational treatise, where he wrote of how necessary an ancient history in vernacular language was for the education of youth and specified that: 'Greek history is in even greater need of rescue than Roman history; the latter is in general better known... whereas we have almost no idea about the former.'[36] Yet, as the title shows, Rollin chose to present his Greek history within the traditional and reassuring framework of the succession of empires. Accordingly, throughout the entire work, each book is titled following the current reigning Persian king. In further nods to this traditional framework the origins of the Greek people are sought in Biblical migrations and the main historical junctures – such as Alexander's conquests – are explained with Daniel's prophecies.[37] To the tradition of Christian universal history Rollin also paid explicit tribute in the preface where, among his sources and models, the only modern he mentioned was Bossuet – the author of

---

[34] Gros de Boze quoted in Grell 1995: 7.   [35] Lombard 1998.
[36] Rollin 1728, I: 9. My translation for Rollin's French passages unless otherwise stated.
[37] See Rollin 1733–39, II: 503–5 and VI: 685–722.

the 1681 *Discours sur l'histoire universelle. Pour expliquer la suite de la religion & les changemens des empires.* He also here claimed that the value of profane history is that it reveals the working of divine providence.[38]

Within the constraints of this framework, Rollin organised a narrative of Greek history very closely based on ancient sources. About his much-decried dependence on sources, Rollin wrote that he was 'pillaging from everywhere, often without even quoting the authors that I copy, because sometimes I take the liberty to make changes to their texts'.[39] The adherence to ancient authors also affected the structure of his history. For example, when he first introduced Greece at the end of volume II, Rollin began by outlining Sparta's origins and its history down to the Messenian wars, then moved on to Darius' kingdom and here he included, on the model of Herodotus, an excursus on the Scythians. He then proceeded to the Greco-Persian wars and only at this point finally introduced Athens, thus opening another excursus into Athenian history from its origins down to the fifth century BCE. In consequence, Rollin's work grew much larger than originally planned – as he repeatedly lamented in each new volume's preface – and certainly offers the modern reader a rather confusing structure.[40]

But what was indeed new about Rollin is apparent from comparison with Bossuet's history. Bossuet's work – dedicated to the Dauphin to whom he was tutor – was divided into three parts: the first was taken up with the description of the twelve epochs of the world – from that of Adam and of creation to that of Charlemagne; part two followed the succession of religions from errors to the Revelation; and part three described the revolutions of Empire, regulated by Divine Providence, in turn dealing with the Scythians, Ethiopians, Egyptians, Assyrians, Medes, Persian, Greeks and the Roman Empire. In all, Greek history occupied eight pages out of the eighty-page long part III of the book, in which the Greeks are set between the Persians and Philip's conquest of Greece. In these few pages Bossuet emphasised the Greeks' love of liberty and country and how exercise of the body made them much stronger soldiers than the soft Persians. Of Greek governments – an oddity in a succession of empires – Bossuet only said that they were 'republics' and 'conducted their affairs in common and anyone could reach the highest honours'.[41] What Bossuet most underscored about the Greeks' political life was how their internal dissensions worked as one of the turning points in his narrative of succession of empire. He explained that the Persians repeatedly and unsuccessfully tried to exploit the Greek

---

[38] See Rollin 1733–39, I: i–xliii; Rollin also summarises Bossuet's work in VI: 722–3.
[39] Rollin, 1733–39, I: xxxviii.   [40] See for example Rollin, 1733–39, I: xxxix and III: i.
[41] See Bossuet 1976: 331–2.

lack of political cohesiveness. It was for Philip – the ruler of a united and absolutist state – to succeed in absorbing the Greeks in the Macedonian Empire and finally giving them unity and stability.

Rollin drew heavily on Bossuet's authority. In the *Ancient History* he indeed reproduced all of Bossuet's pages dedicated to the Greeks, in part as a coda to his own description of the character of the Greeks and the rest in closing the section on Alexander. Both Bossuet and Rollin brought a teleological Christian perspective to ancient history. In Rollin beyond the providential reading put forward in the preface, what prevailed was a concern for moral issues. The prominent lens through which Rollin viewed history was that of virtue corrupted by power, and this was the main approach that he tested in his Greek history. In the process, moreover, he carved an unprecedented space for Greek antiquity. Within this new space he also discussed at length, for example, the merits of the Spartan versus the Athenian constitutions, a topic that evaded the concerns of princely conduct advocated by Bossuet or Rollin's own moral concerns.

Rollin's projects did not fare as he hoped. His education proposal, despite being inspirational for late eighteenth-century school reform, was not taken up at the time.[42] The *Ancient History* also did not turn out as expected. It grew well beyond the originally planned five volumes to be completed in a school year. But, on the other hand, Rollin's history became tremendously successful, reissued well into the nineteenth century and translated into many languages, including Italian (1733–40), English (1738–40), Greek (1750), Spanish (1755–61), Portuguese (1773), German (1778) and even Bengali (1847). The work indeed gained audiences well beyond that of school children; Rollin's *Histoire ancienne* ended by counting among its fans men like John Adams, who, like many others before and after, familiarised himself with ancient history by reading Rollin.[43]

Stanyan's Greek history differed from Rollin's on many accounts. For one, Stanyan did not share Rollin's concern to conceal the novelty of his Greek history within the structure of a universal Christian one. When Stanyan put out his first volume in 1707 it was precisely the unprecedented nature of his enterprise that he most highlighted. He stressed the new challenges posed by making a single thread out of many, disparate ancient authors, with no established model to follow. Stanyan made this point by comparing his project to that of writing Roman history. A few years earlier, Jacob Tonson, Stanyan's publisher, had put out Laurence Echard's

---

[42] See Lombard 1998 and Morange and Chassaing 1974: 16–17.
[43] See Gribbin 1972: 611–22 and Winterer 2002: 19.

Roman History (1697) – a work that Momigliano credited with introducing the popular notion of history by revolutions.[44] Echard too in the preface made reference to the unprecedented nature and difficulties encountered in composing his Roman history. But Stanyan further argued how much more difficult it was to compose a narrative of Greek history than one of Rome. He thought Roman history easily captured by adopting the perspective of Rome, which always remained at the centre, while it assimilated through its conquests progressively more peoples into the Roman dominion. In Greek history, on the other hand, Stanyan wrote: 'it is no easy Task to marshal so many Events in due Order of Time, and Place, and out of them to collect an entire unbroken Body of History'.[45]

In the preface to his second volume – which took the narrative from the end of the Peloponnesian war to the death of Philip – Stanyan put forward a different claim. By the time this concluding volume came out in 1739, Stanyan had to contend with Rollin. From an emphasis on novelty Stanyan moved to differentiating his work from that of the Frenchman. He acknowledged reading Rollin, but denied any influence. He praised Rollin for his 'spirit of liberty', 'which is well suited to the subject, and which few of his countrymen . . . have attain'd to,'[46] but proceeded to criticise him for producing a disjointed narrative and for disrupting it with trite observations of moral character. Stanyan claimed that while Rollin's reflections offered useful moral lessons, his own work revealed the Laws of History 'such as naturally arise to the Reader from simple Relation of facts'.[47]

There was indeed little moralising in Stanyan's account. His 'relation of facts' was also independent of a universal history paradigm: it still placed the 'original' of the Greeks with biblical people, but swiftly left this topic behind after a mere couple of pages. Stanyan had a hard time with early Greek history, the period of Greek kings.[48] While in the preface he doubted with great scepticism the stories of the Greek heroes, this did not stop him from dedicating to this period his first section, 200 out of a total of more than 700 pages. Here Stanyan dealt in turn with the various Greek 'kingdoms' – Sicyon, Argos, Mycenae, Thebes, Sparta, Corinth and Athens. This section closed with the account of Hippias' expulsion from Athens. With this event, the time of legends gave way to that of history, the kingdoms made space for Greek 'commonwealths' and the narrative began to proceed strictly chronologically. Even a brief look at the contemporary volume by Thomas Hind shows Stanyan's narrative to

---

[44] Momigliano 1955b: 78.   [45] Stanyan 1707: [preface ii].   [46] Stanyan, 1739: [preface 6].
[47] Stanyan 1739: [preface 6].   [48] See Morris 2000: 80.

be indeed better articulated and more readable, with sections subdivided into chapters that quickly placed readers in context and led them clearly from one event to another. The facts of the narrative were mostly political and military. A comparison with Hind and Rollin shows the different emphasis in subject matter. Where, for instance, Hind delved at length in his introduction into the origins of the Greeks, Stanyan quickly left that topic for a geographical description – including a map – of ancient Greece and its resources. Stanyan's eight pages on Socrates, as another example, sharply contrasted with Rollin's sixty-page segment on this topic that was at the basis of many eighteenth-century treatments of the death of Socrates.[49]

When Diderot translated Stanyan into French in 1743, the French reviewers indeed lauded the book for its clear rendition of the political dynamics of the reversals of power among the various Greek states.[50] But what laws of history did Stanyan expect to emerge from his 'simple relation of facts'? The paratext – preface and dedication – helps to formulate an answer more than Stanyan's swift and cursory account. Stanyan, a government officer, and his publisher, Jacob Tonson, both belonged to the Whig intellectual circle of Horace Walpole, actively engaged in supporting the constitution resulting from the 1688 Revolution. Tonson, who had made a fortune with Milton's *Paradise Lost* and promoted Addison, founded *The Spectator*, established and was secretary of the Kit Cat Club, to which Stanyan belonged with Horace Walpole, Addison and Somers. Divining the growing taste of the public for the classics, he promoted new translations of Ovid – to which Stanyan contributed – and, alongside Stanyan's work, Echard's history of ancient Rome. Stanyan dedicated his Greek history to Lord Somers 'the defender of modern Liberty'. Liberty was a major theme of Stanyan's history: how the Greeks united to defend it from the Persians invaders, but lost it later, torn apart by their own internal wars and failing to maintain a balance among different states. The book, published in 1707 – the date of the Union – seems to be a cautionary tale for the British Kingdom as well as a reflection on the balance between various European powers.

Stanyan and Rollin's works remained dominant models up to the 1780s. Subsequent narrative Greek histories relied on, drew upon or combined the structure and claims of Stanyan or the style and richer information found in Rollin. Examples abound. British publishers created books that reassembled at will Rollin's volumes: for example, in 1737 a *History of the Arts and Sciences of the Ancients* and in 1750 a *History of Alexander*. Oliver

---

[49] Wilson 2007: 171.
[50] *Journal de Trévoux*, June 1747, 1137 and *Mercure de France*, August 1743, 1803.

Goldsmith's 1774 *Greek History* combined Rollin's prose with Stanyan's structure. Goldsmith's own contribution consisted mainly in his literary skills: the history reads as a novel, with a cliffhanger at every chapter ending, and displays an impressionistic style but not a single footnote. That Rollin – both the histories and the educational treatise – was a favourite source for Goldsmith is well attested in his other works, such as the *History of England* (1764) or the *History of Earth and Animated Nature* (1774).[51] Goldsmith's *History of Greece* was published posthumously without a preface to reveal its sources, but Stanyan and Rollin were obviously present.

But what to make of these works? The categories of school or hand books, derivative and conservative, within which these books are often understood, fall short at a closer look. In fact, Stanyan's French reviewers and many of Rollin's readers show that these texts were not just school books. Rollin had set out to write for schools but failed as his work became too unwieldy. Its eighteenth-century supporters and critics both attest that it was read and commented upon well beyond classrooms. Certainly these histories were eventually much used in schools and this seems to lie behind many of their nineteenth-century editions, as the heavily annotated copies in college libraries suggest. But these were not their primary or original contexts. Were these books derivative? Rollin certainly wrote plainly about his abundant use of ancient sources. Yet, writing off these books as not original runs the risk of applying retrospectively categories that belong to later times. It was precisely in the aftermath of books such as those of Rollin and Stanyan that one began to discuss what a derivative modern history of ancient Greece looked like and, for that matter, to call for alternatives. Two 1759 letters by Hume shed some light on the issue.

These letters were addressed to the Scottish historian Dr William Robertson days after the successful debut of the latter's *History of Scotland*. The subject at hand was which project Robertson should undertake for his next book following his recent success. Hume judged the topic of Emperor Charles V – which actually became Robertson's next and most influential book – a bad idea, because it 'would be the Work of half a Life'. Rather, Hume recommended 'the ancient History, particularly that of Greece': 'I think', he wrote, 'Rollin's Success might encourage you, nor need you be in the least intimidated by his Merit. That Author has no other Merit, but a certain Facility & Sweetness of Narration; but has loaded his Work with fifty Puerilities.'[52] Yet, two months later, after considering further the excellent historical narratives that survived from antiquity, Hume feared

[51] Friedman 1966: 332–5. [52] Hume 1759a: 47.

that they could indeed turn into a disadvantage for the aspiring modern historian: 'For what can you do in most places with these Authors, but transcribe & translate them? No Letters or State Papers from which you coud correct their Errors, or authenticate their Narration, or supply their Defects. Besides, Rollin is so well wrote with respect to Style, that with superficial people it passes for sufficient.' On the whole he thought, however, that a 'History of Greece till the death of Philip' 'woud be successful, notwithstanding all these discouraging Circumstances. The Subject is noble, & Rollin is by no means equal to it.'[53]

Hume's letter positions him clearly among the 'philosophical historians'. But it also holds other, more revealing elements. One well senses in Hume's concern for successful topics the flourishing market for history books in his times, on which, before the professionalisation of the discipline, authors more and more came to rely in lieu of earlier literary patronage practices.[54] These changes in status were accompanied by questions of methodology. While the classical model of the historian as political man writing history in his retirement from public life was in sharp decline, a clear successor was yet to follow. As J. G. A. Pocock put it: would one who studied, edited or rewrote past history be a historian at all?[55] Hume seems to be engaging some of these concerns. On the one hand, he thought Greek history in need of writing, but, on the other, was still uncertain about what could constitute its authoritative footnotes and scholarship.

Some twenty years later Gillies and Mitford offered possible answers. Their histories of Greece certainly show the marks of very specific political contexts – late eighteenth-century Revolutions and Frederick's ascent to power in Prussia, as highlighted by Momigliano, and British imperial politics, as argued by Ataç. But these works from the 1780s were also shaped by debates on practices of history such as those that emerge in Hume's letter. Gillies' and Mitford's histories counted as philosophical histories – contemporary reviewers disagreed as to what degree they were successful – and displayed learned footnotes well versed both in ancient sources and recent works such as Winckelmann's. These self-assured quartos did not discuss the novelty of writing a narrative of ancient Greece as much as the quality of their approaches, nor did they mention in prefaces Stanyan or Rollin. Indeed, in all of their volumes, Rollin alone appears but only very sporadically in some of Mitford's footnotes. Hume's letter, however, might contain a direct trace of the role played by the earlier works in the later eighteenth-century historiographical turn to ancient Greece.

[53] Hume 1759b: 48.   [54] See Kernan 1987: 62–117.   [55] Pocock 1999–2005, II (1999b): 8.

Dr Robertson did not pick up Hume's suggestion of a Greek history, but it was his successor as Scottish royal Historiographer, John Gillies, who did. Possibly also Gibbon's own suggestion to William Mitford originated from the same conversation about Dr Robertson's next project in which Rollin, as we have seen, was an important reference.

But Rollin and Stanyan were more than stepping stones to later works. Unravelling the genealogy of Grote's foundational role shows deeper connections than the linear succession that it suggests at first glance. Once we reach back to the very first modern narratives of Greek history, the initial, fraught question of when the modern historiography of ancient Greece began morphs into the more essential one of what went into its making. While in 1707 Stanyan underlined the unprecedented nature of his enterprise, he singled out a modern author who was helpful to his project. This was the French academician Jacques de Tourreil, who first translated Demosthenes' speeches into a modern language. Tourreil's volume was swiftly translated into English. This edition was, again, undertaken at the initiative of Tonson and with the involvement of Lord Somers' entourage, for which the rhetoric of freedom that Demosthenes deployed against Philip must have been of great interest. In presenting Demosthenes' speeches to his modern readers, Tourreil thought it necessary to provide a context, to make, in his words, his 'author understood', lest 'it will remain mere Greek to those who are not acquainted with the country'.[56] This came as a one hundred page long historical introduction. Here Tourreil elaborated an influential four-age division of Greek history and described in turn the rise and fall of Athens, Sparta and Thebes, leading to the showdown with Philip. It is in Tourreil's pages that one finds the first modern attempt at a narrative of ancient Greek events. Stanyan praised Tourreil for having 'distinguish'd the most remarkable Periods, discover'd the Genius and unravel'd the Interests of the Several States, and trac'd out the Steps by which they arriv'd at their Turns of Superiority'.[57] Rollin did not make much of his novelty, yet referred to Tourreil for his four-age division and as an authority on Pericles' support of the theatre and his role in initiating Athens' decadence.

Stanyan's claim that there was something novel at stake in Tourreil is worth closer consideration. Both Stanyan's rendering of his own challenges and his praise for Tourreil identify the novelty as the composition of a comprehensive narrative of ancient Greek history. This in turn directly

---

[56] Tourreil 1701: 7. On Tourreil's historical preface see Douhain 1910: 236–53.
[57] Stanyan 1707: [preface 10].

touches upon Momigliano's thesis for the origins of modern historiography with its dual weight placed on narrative and scholarship. It also reminds us that Momigliano, despite his more inclusive formula, in his inquiries into the formation of modern historiography, ended up privileging the antiquarian component over the narrative one.[58] Momigliano, it has been argued, was suspicious of current narrative studies.[59] There is also certainly a long tradition in taking the narrative component in Greek history for granted, as Hume seems to have done. Indeed, what can one say about it?

Koselleck has usefully emphasised the development of the narrative element in eighteenth-century historiography. He argued for its role in dismantling the model of exemplary history and in the elaboration of the concept of history *per se* that he attributes to modern historicity.[60] Rollin and Stanyan exemplify as well as complicate in important ways this trajectory of historical studies and its role in modern intellectual history. The narrative turn is strong in Rollin despite his confusing structure. In fact, Mitford wrote in a footnote that if only Rollin 'had avoided to interrupt and perplex his narrative with anecdotes, biography, and preaching, which might have been better thrown into an appendix, his book . . . might have maintained its reputation as the best epitome of Grecian history that has yet appeared'.[61] In Stanyan the narrative entails the shaping of a new form of history of ancient Greece – not surprisingly it seemed a functional school text even after the publication of Grote's history. With these early Greek histories something took shape that was different from both ancient texts and the modern tradition of universal histories. This appears in comparison with Bossuet but also with the twenty volumes British project of *An Universal History from the Earliest Account of Time to the Present* (1736–68).[62] Greek history occupies volumes VI, VII and VIII, edited by George Psalmanazar in the 1730s: a quick look at the structure shows how it was broken up into the histories of various city-states and disrupted by many chronological and geographical discontinuities. Paying due attention to Rollin and Stanyan allows us to examine the emergence of ancient Greece as an independent subject of history. Moreover, on the one hand, through analysis of Tourreil's role, it forces us to appreciate how these new forms had long, subtle roots in the practices of *ancien régime*'s academic cultures and the tradition of textual criticism.[63] On the other, we see how, differently than Rome – which became embedded in the Enlightenment project of understanding Europe's emergence from antiquity, to the Middle Ages and

---

[58] Phillips 1996: 303.   [59] Grafton 2007b: 104 and Miller 2007a.   [60] Koselleck 2004c: 34–5.
[61] Mitford 1797, III: 2.   [62] See Griggs 2007: 228–37.   [63] See Gossman 1968: 175–298 and 349–58.

onwards – Greece became a more disaggregated past, but one that could be returned to in utopian ways. Indeed this trajectory well illustrates how history for history's sake would replace the model of *historia magistra vitae* but also – in George Nadel's phrase – 'support other and perhaps less harmless delusions'.[64]

Resituating the early eighteenth-century narrative histories of ancient Greece within the genealogy of modern historiography of ancient Greece allows us to do many things. For one it can help establish new contemporaneities: Stanyan's words on lack of focus and clear boundaries in Greek history resonate with those of Momigliano in 1979[65] and indeed pertain to current efforts to undo some of the traditional fixtures of modern narrative Greek history, as shown in the work of Ian Morris and Robin Osborne.[66] Moreover, it points us to explore further the contexts of these works: what were the politics and what was the scholarship from which they were woven? What were the European intellectual networks that engendered this dialogue on ancient Greek history? For now, it certainly shows that the new moderns could easily distance earlier Greek histories as derivative, apolitical, naïve and conservative. But it was precisely their precedent that allowed the alternative 'Thucydides or Grote?' to be formulated in the aftermath of Grote's publication.[67] It was within the modern dialogue about ancient Greece initiated by these works that Grote could pass on the word to Thucydides as best commentator on Athens and report fully his Pericles' funerary oration in the pages of his own history of Greece, without being accused of merely repeating, 'pillaging', ancient sources the way Rollin did, but rather presenting his approach as an historicisation of antiquity for its understanding by the moderns.

---

[64] Nadel 1964: 315.   [65] Momigliano 1984: 133–4.

[66] See Osborne 1996 and Morris and Powell 2005.

[67] On this alternative as posed in the Shilleto controversy see Momigliano 1955a: 223 and Stray 1997. I thank Emma Dench, Miriam Leonard, Alexandra Lianeri and Corey Tazzara for various help in my work for this chapter.

CHAPTER 7

Acquiring (a) historicity: Greek history, temporalities and Eurocentrism in the Sattelzeit (1750–1850)

Kostas Vlassopoulos

The aim of this chapter is to look at the interconnection between the emergence of Greek history as an independent field, the construction of new temporalities and the discourse of Eurocentrism during what Reinhart Koselleck and the *Begriffsgeschichte* school have come to call the *Sattelzeit*.[1]

I would like to begin with two methodological reflections which, in my view, will be important for any further work on the subject. My first point is that the history of historiography cannot be simply another form of intellectual history. Most students of historiography study past historians, in order to elucidate the intellectual history of previous societies; they have studied how political, philosophical or cultural discourses or class concerns have manifested themselves in the study of history and how the study of history has contributed to these wider discourses. This is certainly legitimate; but in a sense, it is only one part of the story. For there is a crucial difference between studying the intellectual world of Michelet and that of Hegel or Hugo; between that of Herodotus and that of Plato or Sophocles. And the difference is precisely that Herodotus or Michelet are historians, colleagues.

When we study how they came to write history, how they constructed their historical subject or framed their historical narrative, this has implications for the way we as historians in the here and now pursue similar aims. The writing of history has never been and will never be a straight line from darkness to illumination; it has followed certain paths, while abandoning others; it has imposed certain ways of looking at the past, while pushing aside others; it has accepted certain metahistories, while eschewing others. This makes it dangerous to dismiss past scholarship as simply redundant, when it does not pose the same questions that we currently do. Therefore, the history of historiography must reflect on the current practice and context of historical writing. I see the history of historiography as the

[1] See Koselleck 1972.

anthropological conscience of historical writing; if the past is a foreign country, there are always reasons to learn from foreign or abandoned customs. A central argument of this chapter is that the emergence of ancient Greek history as an independent field and the construction of its temporalities have been fundamentally shaped by the discourses of Eurocentrism; if in a modern globalised world we are to write post-Eurocentric histories, the history of historiography will have to play a significant role in exploring ways of achieving such an aim.

My second point concerns the relationship between the history of historiography and the reception of antiquity. The reception of the classical tradition certainly has a glorious past, and one can enumerate many great works coming from this field.[2] But one essential problem with this approach is the usual lack of attention to genre, discursive context and vocabularies. Grote will serve as a good example of the issue at hand. Scholars have studied Grote with regard to his ideas on Athenian democracy or Greek philosophy;[3] this is fairly legitimate, and some of these works are indeed extremely stimulating. But it is important to emphasise what is lost in such an approach. For Grote did not write a treatise on the Athenian democracy or democracy in general; he inserted his treatment of democracy within what was then a very recent genre, i.e. a history of ancient Greece. And unfortunately, the study of the history of this genre is almost non-existent. How did Grote construct his historical narrative? What was his historical vocabulary? What were the larger metanarratives within which he inserted his work? How does his work on the history and politics of Greece compare to the contemporary work of Macaulay on the history and politics of Britain?[4] How does his narrative and image of Greek history contrast and compare with the contemporary work of Mommsen on Rome?

E. A. Freeman once pointed out that the history of Greece was different from other histories in being not the history of a polity, but a history of a system of polities; in this respect, he compared Grote's history of Greece with Sismondi's history of the Italian Republics of the Middle Ages;[5] nobody has ever tried to follow Freeman's point by investigating the particular narrative techniques and metanarrative contexts needed for writing Greek history, or comparing Grote's solution to that of Sismondi. Grote has been usually associated with Thirlwall, because of their common

---

[2] Rawson 1969; Roberts 1994.   [3] Demetriou 1999; Turner 1981.
[4] For a consideration of the relationship between Macaulay and the Utilitarians, to which Grote belonged, see Collini *et al.* 1983: 91–126.
[5] Freeman 1873.

opposition to Mitford's reactionary treatment of Athenian democracy. But otherwise their general metahistorical positions were quite different, Grote being a Utilitarian, Thirlwall belonging to the so-called Liberal Anglicans;[6] again, the divergences between a Utilitarian and a Liberal Anglican–Vichian approach to history have remained unexplored, buried under the focus on the reception of Athenian democracy.

Historical vocabularies and languages are equally neglected in current studies of the classical tradition. Periodisation is one of the most essential characteristics of historical writing. And yet, if one asks the simplest of questions 'when was periodisation in centuries first applied to Greek history? When did people first talk of fifth-century Athens?' he will find no answer (unless he is prepared to accept easy answers). This might be a basic issue in a history of historiography, but for current scholarship it seems to be uninteresting or useless.[7]

My point is that reception of the classical tradition, as currently practised, fails to take account of the genres and contexts of thinking and writing about the past. Looking at how different people in different times have written about Athens or Sparta says little, if we fail to take account of the contexts of discussion, their institutional setting, and the genres in which they are pursued. In this respect, one of the greatest failures of current scholarship is the abstraction of the study of Greek history from the wider contexts in which it was studied in the pre-nineteenth century period. By anachronistically projecting into this pre-nineteenth century period the treatment of Greek history as an independent field, we have largely missed its connections to the study of the Near East, the Bible, Universal history, the history of origins and the history of medieval and modern nations.[8]

CONTEXTS AND GENRES FOR GREEK HISTORY IN EARLY MODERN EUROPE

This chapter is divided in two parts. The first will delineate the contexts, genres and temporalities within which Greek history was studied from the Renaissance till roughly 1750. The second part will explore the changing landscape of contexts, genres and discourses and the emergence of new temporalities during the *Sattelzeit*. At the end of this period, Greek history had clearly become a distinct and independent field of study.

---

[6] Forbes 1952.   [7] For the *Jahrhundertrechnung* in modern historiography, see Burkhardt 1971.
[8] For a partial exception, regarding the study of Homer and the Bible, see Turner 1981: 135–86.

Let me start with an illustrative example. Friedrich von Raumer, known as the historiographer to the Hohenstaufen, reports the following episode from the year 1811, when he was still Hardenberg's secretary:

During counsel in Charlottenburg, Oelssen [section head in the Ministry of Finance] animatedly defended the preparation of a quantity of paper money so that debts could be paid. All argument to the contrary failing, I said with immense audacity (knowing my man): 'But Privy Councillor, do you not remember that Thucydides tells of the evils that followed from the circulation of too much paper money in Athens?' 'This experience', he concurred, 'is certainly of great importance' – and in this way he allowed himself to be persuaded, in order that he might retain the appearance of learning.[9]

The pun of the incident depended on the fact that by 1811 the assumptions behind Oelssen's attitude had become questionable, as Raumer's stance shows. But they can still serve as a good illustration of attitudes in the pre-1750 period. We can trace a number of issues here: the canonical status of classical texts; and the canonical status of the classical past. These two aspects were both based on and reinforced by two further issues: the identification of classical history with the texts of the classical historians; and a temporal continuum, which could accommodate different periods, but with no sense of fundamental historical discontinuities and irreversible changes.

The first issue is the canonical status of classical texts. On the level of form, these texts provided the genre models in poetry, drama, prose, philosophy, history, and, until the seventeenth century, even the sciences.[10] On the level of content, they provided myths, stories and exempla for pursuing discourses and discussions on man and nature and creating novel works, both fictional and non-fictional. Regarding history, classical texts came to set the models and the genres within which early modern Europeans came to write and think about history.[11]

We need not spend much time on why classical texts came to acquire a canonical status in early modern Europe. What is more important is that in the case of history, and in contrast with other fields of humanist scholarship, the canonical status of classical historical texts led to the complete absence of modern works on classical history.[12] It is important to emphasise that the first Greek history ever to be written in modern times was by Temple Stanyan in 1707,[13] more than three centuries after the Renaissance recovery

---

[9] Cited in Koselleck 2004c: 26.   [10] Grafton 1991.   [11] Momigliano 1980b, 1990.
[12] Momigliano 1966a: 6–8; 1977c: 254–6.
[13] *The Grecian History: From the Original of Greece, to the End of the Peloponnesian War*, 2 vols., London, 1707–39.

of the classical tradition. While the canonical status of classical drama or classical poetry led to attempts to imitate them and compose novel works on the themes provided by the classical texts, this was clearly not the case with history.[14] Until the eighteenth century, and even during that century, classical history for early modern Europeans was tantamount to the texts of the classical historians. Reading ancient history meant reading the ancient historians.

To an important extent we can seek the explanation in the neoclassical theory of history, which accepted readily the main theory of classical historiography. Thus, the classical tradition of history-writing[15] perceived history largely as a narrative of military and political deeds performed by great persons.[16] Ancient historians had narrated the political and military events of ancient Greece in an exemplary manner. If the task of the historian was to bear witness of the events in an exemplary narrative, whether personally, or through the living witnesses he has examined, little remained for moderns to do. The classical and neoclassical approach to historiography meant that the historian wrote mainly *Zeitgeschichte*. He functioned mainly as the narrator of his contemporary events and, to the extent that his work brought him to periods in the past, he based himself on what historians contemporary to these periods had written: from Diodorus to the eighteenth century the historian of times before his lifetime was seldom much more than an excerptor.[17]

Accordingly, the opportunities to present ancient history in a modern narrative were severely limited: early modern historians could write on periods of ancient history for which no ancient account survived,[18] or, from the eighteenth century onwards, they started writing compilations that would bring together into a single account all the stories preserved by the ancient historians.[19]

But there was another field in which ancient history could still be presented as part of historical narrative. This was universal history. The Christian version of universal history had evolved since late antiquity. It amalgamated the universal history of the ancients, and in particular the idea of the succession of empires,[20] and the tradition of sacred history that

---

[14] Highet 1949.   [15] Hicks 1996: 7–14.   [16] Burke 1969a; Levine 1991: 267–90.

[17] See the comments of Pocock 1987b: 1–29.

[18] E.g. J. Foy-Vaillant, *Imperium Seleucidarum, sive historia regum Syriae*, Paris, 1681; idem, *Historia Ptolemæorum Ægypti regum, ad fidem numismatum accommodata*, Amsterdam, 1701.

[19] Such is the work by Stanyan, and the first ancient history by C. Rollin, *Histoire ancienne des Egyptiens, des Carthaginois, des Assyriens, des Babyloniens, des Mèdes et des Perses, des Macédoniens, des Grecs*, Amsterdam, 1736.

[20] Fabbrini 1983.

was initiated by Eusebius.[21] But Greek history had a very limited role to play in this genre. Universal history in our period was mainly organised in two schemes: the one was the succession of the four empires; Greek history was treated as part of the history of the second empire (the Persian) and played a role in the history of the third one (the Macedonian); the other was the scheme of the three *aetates* (from Creation to Abraham, from Abraham to Jesus, from Jesus until the present).[22] In both cases, Greek history played a subordinate role, in the one to Rome, in the other to sacred history.[23]

If early modern Europeans had little use for Greek history in writing historical narrative, they left much space for it in a different genre and intellectual context. The ancient authors of history provided examples of noble conduct, ingenious stratagems and despicable actions, which could be exploited in non-narrative forms. The Plutarchean tradition of the *Parallel Lives* of great men was extremely popular in the early modern period, inviting comparisons between ancients and moderns; it was based on the perception of *historia magistra vitae*, whereby the past served as a rich field of *exempla* for modern use.[24]

But there also developed a wider form of *Parallèles*, comparing ancient phenomena with their modern equivalents. The political, social and economic life of Greek communities was directly available and relevant to early modern Europeans through the discourse of civic humanism. This discourse can be traced back to the ancient Greeks, and in particular to Aristotle, and was still evolving up to the eighteenth century.[25] It viewed the polis or *civitas* as a community of citizens, who are heads of households. The *civitas* could be governed in a variety of ways, depending on whether the governing element was an individual (monarchy), a few (oligarchy), many (democracy), or a mixed constitution;[26] and whether the governing element governed for the public benefit, or for its own sake (corrupted constitutions). The participation in the political community was dependent on political virtue, and the preservation of the community was equally dependent on the virtue of its members. But the political community was perennially threatened by the substitution of virtue for the particular interest of the citizens or of the governing element alone. This was the phenomenon of corruption, and each form of *politeia* was always susceptible to be transformed into each corrupt form or to a different form.

---

[21] Momigliano 1990: 132–52.   [22] Meyer-Zwiffelhoffer 1995: 256–67; Klempt 1960.

[23] C. Cellarius, *Historia Vniversalis: Breviter ac perspicue exposita in antiquam, et Medii Aevi ac Novam divisa*, Jena, 1696; C. Abel, *Historia monarchiarum orbis antiqvi*, Leipzig and Stendal, 1715.

[24] Grell 1993: 125–64.   [25] Pocock 1975a. But see now Nelson 2004.   [26] See Nippel 1980.

Therefore, the central concern of this paradigm was how to attain and retain civic virtue: the totality of relationships between humans, and between humans and things, were viewed through this looking glass. What we would call economic aspects was of interest only to the extent that they guaranteed or satisfied the political virtue of the citizens and the community. Political economy was still viewed until the end of the eighteenth century as the administration of the public household, in a way that could make the political community and its members as efficient as possible.[27] In the same way the multitude of *koinōniai* that form the political community were of interest only to the extent that they serve the autarchy and the good life of the community; the same holds true for the study of relations between polities. The paradigm was formed by selecting and focusing only on those aspects that can be administered or geared to the benefit of the political community.

Thus, the discourse of civic humanism blended what from the nineteenth century onwards would be seen as the three distinct fields of society, economy and the state, into the single whole of the polis or *civitas*. In so doing, and in presenting the *civitas* as a voluntary association of citizens, it gave politics the pre-eminent role: the image of the lawgiver, who constructs or reshapes the polity, was of crucial value. Therefore, the political history and experience of the ancients was readily available to early modern Europeans: their solutions to constructing a successful and virtuous polity, and in reforming a corrupted community, could be studied and potentially applied to modern problems. Also, in analysing the forms of polities on the basis of their governing element, it again allowed direct comparisons between ancient and modern democracies, oligarchies and monarchies. The history of ancient communities was used as a comparative standard for modern polities, even as arguments in contemporary political debates. Machiavelli's *Discourses on Livy*[28] was an early example of the use of the historical experience of the Greek and Roman polities, in order to draw conclusions about similar phenomena in the contemporary world.[29] Montesquieu was probably one of the last great followers of this tradition, and at

---

[27] People seem to have forgotten that for Adam Smith, still in 1776, 'Political economy, considered as a branch of the science of a statesman or a legislator, proposes two distinct objects; first, to provide a plentiful revenue or subsistence for the people, or more properly to enable them to provide such a revenue or subsistence for themselves; and secondly, to supply the state or commonwealth with a revenue sufficient for the publick services'; Smith 1976, book 4: 138, 1.

[28] *Discorsi sopra la prima deca di Tito Livio*, Florence, 1531.

[29] E. W. Montagu, *Reflections on the Rise and Fall of the Ancient Republicks Adapted to the Present State of Great Britain*, London, 1759; J. Symonds, *Remarks upon an Essay, Intituled the History of the Colonisation of the Free States of Antiquity, Applied to the Present Contest between Great Britain and her American Colonies*, London, 1778.

the same time pointing to novel directions.[30] Sparta and Athens provided a context for discussing the current issues and affairs of European societies, in issues such as the mixed constitution, the use of luxury, corruption or the role of education in society.[31]

But this is not the whole story. The rediscovery of classical texts during the Renaissance led to a huge effort to recover, emend and explicate these texts. The recovery, emendation and explication of classical texts created certain needs. It led to the emergence of textual criticism as an immensely important and prestigious field within humanist scholarship; but it also created the impetus for the emergence of antiquarian studies. It was not only necessary to have command of the language, to understand the forms of textual corruption and to master the techniques of textual emendation. Understanding of the text depended on understanding the political, social, cultural and religious background. But at the same time, it was precisely this background of the political, social, cultural and religious institutions and life of the ancient Greeks that was left out of the epistemic field of classical and neoclassical historiography.

Therefore, there emerged a new genre, called *Antiquitates*, which served a double role: as textual commentaries, enabling the reader and the scholar to emend classical texts and comprehend their true meaning;[32] and as accounts of those aspects of ancient life that were left out by canonical historiography.[33] What is important is that the evidence for these aspects of past life was concentrated in systematic accounts, organised around subject matter, and not according to time.[34] Partly, the reason was that the *Antiquitates* functioned as textual accompaniments, and therefore a systematic treatment was more useful and convenient. But more important was the fact that early modern scholars lacked a conceptual apparatus in order to narrativise these aspects and insert them into a temporal framework.[35]

---

[30] *Considérations sur les causes de la grandeur des Romains et de leur décadence*, Amsterdam, 1734; *De l'esprit des loix*, Leiden, 1748. I follow the interpretation of Meinecke 1972: 90–143. See also Cambiano 1974.

[31] See Rawson 1969 on Sparta; Roberts 1994 on Athens.

[32] See the characteristic title of a work as late as 1827: J. Robinson, *Archaeologia Graeca: Being an Account of the Manners and Customs of the Greeks . . . Chiefly Designed to Illustrate the Greek Classics, by Explaining Words and Phrases According to the Rites and Customs to Which They Refer*, 2nd edition, London.

[33] J. P. Pfeiffer, *Libri IV antiquitatum Graecarum gentilium sacrarum, politicarum, militarium et oeconomicarum*, Königsberg and Leipzig, 1689; J. Potter, *Archæologia Graeca: or, the Antiquities of Greece*, London, 1697. A large number of antiquarian works was collected in J. Gronovius, *Thesaurus Graecarum antiquitatum*, 12 vols., Leiden, 1697–1702.

[34] Momigliano 1966a.

[35] See Klempt 1960: 69–75; Bravo 1968: 29–40. Stanyan's history is a good example. He is interested in cultural history; but he has no way of narrating it, apart from introducing little notes about the eminent artists and thinkers that flourished in each period he deals with.

Political and military history had great men as actors and narrated events; but social, economic and cultural history could not function simply with great men as subjects of action,[36] and could not be organised only around events. It needed collective subjects and concepts of time that did not exist, either in the classical tradition that had survived, or in the *outillage mental* of early modern thinkers. In short, it needed a historical language in order to render them as objects of historical development and historical narrative.[37]

This is the reason that a central contradiction in the humanist study of antiquity from the Renaissance onwards remained unresolved.[38] While the purpose of the humanist agenda was to imitate antiquity, thus positing no fundamental historical difference between antiquity and modernity, the attempt to resurrect antiquity from its vestiges, in order to imitate it, revealed exactly how different antiquity was.[39] The efforts of philologists and antiquaries to reconstruct texts, coins and monuments were based on an understanding of the peculiarities of ancient institutions, practices and beliefs. To give just one example, the revival of Roman law was based on the belief that there existed no fundamental difference between Roman society and early modern Europe. But the application of Roman law necessitated the reconstruction of the texts and its exegesis; and this in turn necessitated the study of Latin language and Roman institutions and practices, in order to emend texts and understand their meaning. This study revealed in fact how different Roman society was from those of early modern Europe; some French lawyers and humanists (François Hotman, Andrea Alciato) of the sixteenth century came to accept this, and to argue that Roman law was inapplicable to their society.[40] The contradiction between relevance and *altérité* within Humanist scholarship remained unresolved, precisely because there was no conceptual apparatus that could narrativise these issues, and no discourse that could explain what constituted the basis of these differences and the source of historical change.[41] It still remains an open question to what extent and in what ways the development of

---

[36] Unless, of course, one was writing about great inventors of things, customs and institutions in the ancient tradition. This is probably why it was easier to write a history of learning and artists and scholars, than any other kind of social, economic or cultural history; and why this form of cultural history was the first to enter into narratives of ancient history.

[37] I am using the concept of historical language in a similar way to Pocock's (1987a) conception of political languages.

[38] Muhlack 1988: 165–70.   [39] See Grafton 1987; Levine 1991.   [40] Kelley 1970: 53–148.

[41] This is not to deny that there were efforts to construct such an apparatus. The French scholars and humanists of the sixteenth century are perhaps the best example; see Huppert 1970. But whatever explanation one is to give, their efforts did not manage to create a long-term historical paradigm.

Antiquitates influenced and interacted with the discourses of civic humanism and with narrative history.[42]

But if early modern scholarship lacked a social, economic or cultural
history of Greece, there was still a genre and context within which these
issues could be raised and treated. It is very difficult to give a name to this
genre and context: one could call it sacred history or history of the origins,
but neither term describes successfully enough the whole spectrum of issues
involved. The background to this genre was the crisis and reorientation of
sacred history in the aftermath of the Reformation and the religious and
cultural struggles of early modern Europe.[43] The controversies between
Catholics, Protestants and religious sceptics brought into sharp focus the
problems of a history of humanity based on the Biblical account:
the origins and spread of religion, learning and customs,[44] the migration
and colonisation of peoples and groups,[45] the rise and decline of states
and dynasties,[46] the beginning and duration of human history[47] and the
relationships and hierarchies between various peoples were main issues
in these controversies.[48] Unfortunately, the role of Greek history within
this intellectual context and genre has been largely left unexplored. To
many ancient historians the name of J. F. Lafitau[49] would be familiar as
an early attempt at an anthropology of the Greek world, thanks to the
work of Pierre Vidal-Naquet. But what remains clouded is the position
of Lafitau within the larger intellectual context that I have just described:
Lafitau used the religions of his contemporary savages and of the peoples
of antiquity to argue for the universality and naturalness of religion, and he
understood the similarities between modern savages and ancient peoples as
evidence for a migration.[50] It is easy to abstract Lafitau from his intellectual
context to score a point about modern anthropological approaches to
ancient Greece; but what we urgently need is a historical assessment of

---

[42] For such a study regarding Roman censors, see Parsons 2001.   [43] Hazard 1953.

[44] G. J. Vossius, *De theologia gentili, et physiologia Christiana, sive, De origine ac progressu idololatriæ*,
Amsterdam, 1641 ; A. Y. Goguet, *De l'origine des loix, des arts, et des sciences et de leurs progrès chez
les anciens peuples*, 3 vols., The Hague, 1758; P.-D. Huet, *Histoire du commerce et de la navigation des
anciens*, Paris, 1716.

[45] R. Cumberland, *Origines gentium antiquissimæ: or, Attempts for Discovering the Times of the First
Planting of Nations*, London, 1724; E. Fourmont, *Réflexions critiques sur les histoires des anciens
peuples*, Paris, 1735.

[46] G. Hornius, *Arca Noae. Sive historia imperiorum et regnorum a conditio orbe ad nostra tempora*,
Leiden, 1666.

[47] N. Freret, *Défense de la chronologie: fondée sur les monuments de l'histoire ancienne, contre le système
chronologique de M. Newton*, Paris, 1728.

[48] Manuel 1959; Rossi 1984.

[49] *Moeurs des sauvages américains, comparées aux moeurs des premiers temps*, Paris, 1724.

[50] Lemay 1976.

the contribution of this early modern context and genre to the study and use of Greek history.[51] The crucial question, and one largely unexplored, is the relationship between antiquarian studies of the social, economic and cultural aspects of Greek history and the treatment of these subjects in the history of origins.[52]

Finally, there is the subject of the temporalities used in order to render Greek history a discursive subject. Until about the 1750s, early modern thinkers had a limited number of temporalities available in order to construct their subject. The one can be described as historical recurrence;[53] the other as succession. Both of them were inherited from antiquity. The temporality of succession presented a linear pattern that linked antiquity with the present in a continuum. The concept of the translation of empire from the Assyrian monarchy to the Romans and even up to the Holy Roman Empire of the German nation is a good example of this temporal pattern.[54] The temporality of historical recurrence exploited a variety of modes: the pattern of birth, acme, death; the pattern of rise and fall; the pattern of constitutional *anacyclosis*; the pattern of liberty and tyranny. It used a vocabulary in which corruption, renovation and revolution played a key role.[55] It was this temporality of historical recurrence, along with the belief in the constancy of human nature, which rendered Greek history as directly relevant to the historical experience of early modern Europeans. This should not be confused with a lack of a sense of historical anachronism.[56] The point is, though, that until the 1750s early modern Europeans were still depending on temporalities inherited from antiquity to construct their historical accounts; it was only after the 1750s that new temporalities for the study of ancient history were invented.

We have so far presented a number of different contexts in which Greek history was discussed and studied in early modern Europe: the discussion of classical texts; *Antiquitates*; Plutarchean exemplary works; the discourse of civic humanism; universal history; and the history of origins. This was the situation before modern scholars started producing their own accounts of Greek history and before the construction of Greek history as an independent field through the emergence and consolidation of a number of new approaches, the most influential of which was the German *Alter-tumswissenschaft*. This was part of larger developments: the reformulation of the European discourses during the *Sattelzeit*;[57] the revolution that

---

[51] A rare example: Nippel 1990.   [52] See the case of slavery in Deissler 2000.   [53] Trompf 1979.
[54] Fabbrini 1983.   [55] Schlobach 1980; Goulemot 1996.   [56] See Burke 1969a.
[57] Koselleck 2004c.

transformed historical thinking and historical writing during the same period;[58] and academic, educational and institutional changes that created new forms of organising and disseminating knowledge.[59] This story has not been told yet. What I intend to do here is to deal with only one part of it, but a crucial one: the construction of the new temporalities that allowed the emergence of Greek history as an independent field and shaped the course of its study.

THE RETHINKING OF ANTIQUITY AND NEW TEMPORALITIES: 1750–1789

During the eighteenth century, the picture we have presented underwent a variety of changes. The transformation of the wider European discourses, which were associated with the main current of the Enlightenment, and the diverse parallel, or counter-currents, changed profoundly the context of thinking about Greek history. If it was not until after the French Revolution that Greek history emerged as an independent field, it is still the case that the changes during the eighteenth century shaped to a large extent what was to follow.

Some people came to argue that antiquity was fundamentally different from modern times and defined it on the grounds of how it differed from modern societies. This created a whole discourse on how antiquity was different, why it was so, and why it had not developed in the same way as modern Europe had. At the same time, others came to see antiquity as particularly relevant: its history could provide examples of how to reform society during the great crisis of the late eighteenth century.[60] Equally, Greek history came now to be written as a narrative, in order to foster arguments in contemporary political debates. Others came to value Greek history for different reasons: precisely because it was different from contemporary society, and allowed the discovery of alternative forms of expression and feeling. From this perspective, they came to discover how the field of history could be expanded in order to encompass social, cultural and economic history. They discovered the collective subject of the *Volk*; and the temporal concept of the *Zeitgeist*. Finally, others came to discover new, 'secular' temporalities, within which history could be narrated: they discovered that history could be seen as moving through distinct stages; and they discovered new metahistories. The emergence of Greek history as

---

[58] Blanke and Rüsen 1984; Iggers 1968; Peardon 1933.   [59] Grafton 1983b; Marchand 1996.
[60] For this crisis, see Venturi 1989; 1991.

an independent field during the *Sattelzeit* was shaped by all these different developments.

During this period emerged a completely new way of approaching antiquity. This was the idea that there was a complete and insuperable gap between antiquity and modernity. This attitude had diverse sources. One was the famous *Querelle des anciens et des modernes*, which had taken place from the end of the seventeenth until the first two decades of the eighteenth century.[61] In this debate, the *modernes* had come to argue, against the essence of humanism, that modernity had come to surpass antiquity in many, if not all, fields of learning and technology. The debate had no clear winners; but a consensus was more or less reached, in which it was recognised that modernity had surpassed antiquity in the sciences and technology, but was still behind in the creative arts. The importance of the *Querelle* lay in that it was the first construction of a notion of modernity in opposition to antiquity.

But the gap was soon to grow wider. During the eighteenth century, many thinkers came to believe that their age was experiencing developments that were unique and differentiated it from all past history. The cessation of bloody civil and religious wars, commercial expansion, and the advances of science were seen as symptoms and causes of a larger process. There emerged what has been described as 'the Enlightened narrative': a narrative of how the spread of commerce since the end of the Middle Ages had destroyed the feudal relations of dependence, diffused property, created a stable system of states and introduced order and good government, and thus liberty and the security of individuals.[62]

Seen in this perspective, the ancient republics ceased to be valuable *exempla*. They were based on agriculture and slavery; their *raison d'être* was war and conquest; the community had absolute right over its subjects, without recognising individual rights; thus, their political quarrels took the form of bloody civil wars and political stability was impossible.[63] The old paradigm of civic humanism came to be seen as irrelevant: the changes in property and manners, the role of commerce and civility, created a new form of society, economy and state, in which the virtue of the citizen was irrelevant.[64] The debate on the populousness of ancient nations is a good example.[65] The issue was long treated by antiquarians; but it was also of direct interest in contemporary debates about the desired density of population and the measures needed to achieve it. David Hume's contribution

---

[61] By far the best account is Levine 1991.   [62] See Pocock 1999–2005, vol. II (1999b).
[63] See Guerci 1979; Avlami 2001.   [64] Pocock 1975b; 1985.   [65] See Cambiano 1984.

to the debate illustrates nicely the new perspective of the *modernes*: he showed that the debate on ancient populations was not simply a matter of numbers; instead it involved the whole social structure of ancient and modern societies.[66] He argued that slavery, constant warfare, brutal civil wars, and the low volume of trade, which were essential characteristics of ancient Greek polities, were unfavourable to high populations; therefore, free labour, political stability and the expansion of trade, which characterised modernity, proved that modern societies had larger populations.

Thus, for the first time some thinkers attempted to think in a systematic way about the differences between antiquity and modernity; they also tried to discover and show the structural interconnections between the various features of ancient societies, and their modern counterparts; finally, some of them, belonging to the Scottish school of moral philosophy and conjectural history (Adam Ferguson, John Millar), tried to discover a scheme of historical development that would explain how the world had passed from antiquity to modernity: ancient societies were incorporated in these schemes as part of a less developed, agricultural stage, before the commencement of the modern commercial one.[67] And of course modern European societies appeared as the pinnacle of the developmental process under examination. Thus emerged a new way of thinking about antiquity: a new temporal framework and a new, Eurocentric, standard of comparison.

But others felt that antiquity was still directly relevant for contemporaries and refused to accept this fundamental gap. It would be superfluous to refer here extensively to the works of people such as Rousseau or Mably.[68] In fact, their work did not contribute anything novel to the study of Greek history. What is important to note though, is that the politicisation of Greek history in the decades before the French Revolution had ultimately important repercussions. The use of the models of ancient republics by the French revolutionaries created heightened reactions; as we shall see in the next period, the liberal and conservative reaction to the Revolution forced the universal acceptance of the axiom that there existed a clear gap between antiquity and modernity. More relevant here is that, paralleling the politicisation of Greek history by Rousseau and Mably, some English scholars started writing narrative histories of Greece for the first time, as

---

[66] 'Of the populousness of ancient nations', in *Political Discourses*, London, 1752.
[67] Schneider 1988.
[68] J. J. Rousseau, *Discours sur si le rétablissement des sciences et des arts a contribué à épurer les mœurs*, Paris, 1751; Abbé de Mably, *Observations sur l'histoire de la Grèce*, Genève, 1766. See Grell 1995: 449–553.

arguments in the contemporary political debates.[69] In the eyes of these thinkers, the history of Athens and Sparta presented arguments to defend or attack democracy, popular sovereignty or monarchy.

Meanwhile, there emerged a new evaluation of Greek history in Germany, along with a new historical language.[70] The currents that contributed to this were diverse, but they all shared an opposition to the main thrust of the Enlightenment:[71] a stress on the field of experience and feeling, instead of rationality (Hamann);[72] on national character, instead of the universalising principles of the Enlightenment (Herder); on simplicity and originality, instead of subtlety and artificiality (Rousseau);[73] and a resistance to the secularising tendencies of the Enlightenment. 'The feelings and traditions, which bound a people together, and which were expressed in their culture, were not rationally grounded, nor to be rationally justified. Such feelings and traditions sprung from a common language, a common heritage of customs, a common facing of the exigencies of life in a particular locale.'[74] The concept of the *Volksgeist*, the living psychic unity of a nation, was their discovery: it allowed the construction of a new historical subject; a new actor in historical narrative.

At the same time, other people discovered the concept of *Zeitgeist*; the most renowned among them being Giambattista Vico.[75] Vico tried to save Sacred history from the attacks of sceptics, who used the historical traditions of Babylonians, Egyptians and Chinese, narrating histories much older than allowed by the Bible, in order to challenge it.[76] They were mistaken, argued Vico, because they imputed their own assumptions and ideas to periods that were very different. Instead of the wise lawgivers and statesmen, which pagan annals credited with the beginnings of their history, in reality the early stages of nations were characterised by savagery and ignorance. Only gradually did the nations manage to move towards civilisation; each particular phase of their history was autonomous and different, having its own institutions, practices and values. In this way Vico discovered the historicity of each society and each different historical period.

A new language was now created that allowed scholars to write about culture in its totality, in its historical development, and with a historical actor at its centre.[77] These developments coincided and interacted with the contemporary re-evaluation of Greek culture and history in Germany:[78]

---

[69] See below.   [70] Trevelyan 1934.   [71] Berlin 1979.   [72] Manuel 1959: 283–309.
[73] Fuhrmann 1979.   [74] Mandelbaum 1971: 56.   [75] Grafton 1999.
[76] See Rossi 1984: 168–87.   [77] Schaumkell 1905.   [78] Butler 1935; Rehm 1968; Marchand 1996.

the discovery of the history of Greek art;[79] the discovery of the Homeric and the Archaic as distinct historical periods;[80] the new evaluation of mythology, religion and social institutions.[81] This combination would bear fruit in the coming period.

The seventy years from the French Revolution to the 1850s witnessed the radical readjustment of European debates and the formation of Greek history as an independent field. These two processes are directly connected. The so-called 'twin revolutions', the French Revolution and the Industrial Revolution readjusted the European political, economic and social discourses.[82] The French Revolution put inescapably on the agenda the issue of the nature of the political community and the rights of its members.[83] For the first time in many centuries people felt that they could rebuild society from scratch; the Jacobin attempt to reshape French society, and its demise, fuelled a huge debate on the nature of society and its institutions, the form and nature of social change, the relevance of the past for the present and the attainable future of humanity.[84] Moreover, the Revolution saw the development of nationalism as a potent political force and it helped reshaping perceptions of identity and belonging and collective destinies.[85]

The Industrial Revolution had equally important consequences. The west was now in a position to bid for unchallenged world supremacy due to the great advancement of its technology, productivity and power;[86] these monumental changes impressed so much the (European) people of the time that they tried to explain this successful Western bid for world supremacy. All the great nineteenth-century thinkers strove to explain 'the rise of the west'. Many different answers have been attempted. What they all shared was a belief that a comparison of the successive stages of the west (antiquity – Middle Ages – modernity) would enable scholars to understand its rise.[87] At the same time, the rise of the west was accompanied by the fall of the east. The east was now finally relegated to a position of eternal stagnation, outside history proper; the west owed nothing to the east, but

---

[79] J. J. Winckelmann, *Geschichte der Kunst des Alterthums*, Dresden, 1764. See the brilliant remarks of Bravo 1968: 51–63.

[80] See the works of Vico, Herder and Wood, among others, culminating in F. A. Wolf, *Prolegomena ad Homerum*, Halle, 1795; see Simonsuuri 1979; Grafton 1981.

[81] E.g. C. G. Heyne, *Opuscula academica collecta*, 6 vols., Göttingen, 1785–1812; see Wohlleben (1992); see also Levine 1991.

[82] For the 'twin revolutions', see Hobsbawm 1962.   [83] Livesey 2001.

[84] Koselleck 2004c. See also Vidal-Naquet 1979; Avlami 2000.   [85] Thiesse 1999; Thom 1995.

[86] Wolf 1982.   [87] Blaut 1993.

had advanced by its own internal dynamic.[88] Racial theories, such as the discourse on the Indo-Europeans, served to intensify this gap.[89]

These historical changes affected the study of ancient history. We have already seen how during the eighteenth century diverse groups of thinkers came to argue in favour of a radical discontinuity between antiquity and modernity. Now, the Jacobin use of antiquity to reshape contemporary society gave added importance and urgency to the issue.[90] A group of French liberals, the so-called *Idéologues*, tried to argue that the invocation of ancient models by the Jacobins was fatally wrong, because it misinterpreted both antiquity and modernity.[91] Antiquity could not be imitated by the moderns, because social, economic and political structures had fundamentally changed. The liberty of the ancients, centred on citizen participation and based on agriculture, slavery and small polities, could not be imitated in the world of the moderns, based on commerce, free labour and large states; therefore, only the liberty of the moderns was relevant, centred on the individual enjoyment of property, freedom of conscience and the rights of the private sphere.[92] Antiquity was therefore totally different from modernity and the only way to understand it was by its own means. Antiquity was a wholly different structure from the structure of modernity and one had to show how every aspect of antiquity fitted together to form this different structure.

Because the *Idéologues* argued forcefully that antiquity had no relevance for modernity, French historians focused their interest on what seemed to matter: the Revolution, the Middle Ages and the national history of France, in an attempt to understand what should be retained and what should be dismissed from the past and how that past threw light on the present.[93] Consequently, there was very little work concerning ancient history and almost nothing concerning Greek history.[94] But the great contribution of the *Idéologues* to the study of ancient history bore fruit later through the work and influence of a fellow soul, namely Fustel de Coulanges. What needs to be stressed for the time being is that, since the *Idéologues*, French

---

[88] See the classic Said 1978. Also Chakrabarty 2000.

[89] Poliakov 1974; Olender 1992. Concerning Greek history, Bernal 1987: 317–99.

[90] Baker 2001; Vidal-Naquet 1990; Hartog 2000.

[91] See Vidal-Naquet 1979; Hartog 2000; Avlami 2000, 2001.

[92] C. F. Volney, *Leçons d'histoire*, Paris, 1795; P.-C. Levesque, *Études de l'histoire ancienne et de celle de la Grèce*, Paris, 1811; B. Constant, *De la liberté des Anciens comparée à celle des Modernes*, Paris, 1819. See Vidal-Naquet 1979.

[93] For French historians in the first half of the nineteenth century, see Crossley 1993.

[94] It was not before 1851, when V. Duruy published his *Histoire grecque*, that the first work on Greek history appeared. See Avlami 2000.

ancient historians have shown a particular interest in a structural study of antiquity that shows the interdependence between its various aspects and its difference from modernity; an approach that we can describe as distantiation. Their main interest has not been how actual people have shaped and changed their history, but how structures have shaped the behaviour and attitudes of ancient people.[95]

But not everybody was convinced about this radical discontinuity. German historians were equally adamant that the misapplication of ancient models was fatal. In fact, the ancestor of German ancient historians, B. G. Niebuhr, wrote with the explicit aim in mind of refuting the demand of the French revolutionaries for an agrarian law that would limit and redistribute property; a demand that revolutionaries legitimated by appeal to the reforms of the Gracchi. Niebuhr showed that the Gracchan reforms pertained to the public property of *ager publicus*, and not to the sacrosanct private property.[96] But in the attempt to do so, he discovered the importance of source criticism: one could not trust the accounts of ancient historians as such, and source criticism was necessary to show which reading of the ancient historians was correct. A further step was the realisation that one could actually write an account of ancient history, which did not depend on the priorities and aims of the ancient sources.[97] The crucial question was then, in Momigliano's words, 'how are we going to proceed, where we cannot be guided by the ancient historians?'[98] The aim was to give life to antiquity, to present an account of how ancient people shaped and changed their lives. This approach can be described as actualisation.[99] In the exemplary words of Mommsen, the task of the historian was

to take down the Ancients from the imaginary high heels, from which they appear to the mass of the public, and to shift them into the real world of the reader, where there was hate and love, sawing and hammering, imagination and lies – and therefore the consul had to become a mayor.[100]

These thinkers came to argue that the categorical distinction between antiquity and modernity was rather misleading. There had been important changes during the long span of antiquity. Moreover, these changes were coherent enough to divide ancient history into distinct periods. Finally, these periods were not unique to antiquity; rather, they were recurrent

[95] On the tradition stemming from the French approach, see Di Donato 1990 in respect of Glotz, Gernet and Vernant.
[96] See Momigliano 1982: 225–36.   [97] Muhlack 1988.
[98] Momigliano 1980b: 33. For the debates and questions emanating from the challenges put to classical models of historiography, and the attempts to create new models, see Hicks 1996; Phillips 2000.
[99] Walther 2001.   [100] Cited in Schneider 1990: 427.

stages in the history of every nation, civilisation and society. This was an elaboration of the Vichian theory of historical cycles and was followed by many German historians and their followers in other countries.[101] Thomas Arnold called for 'a more sensible division of history than that which is commonly adopted of ancient and modern':

> The largest portion of that history, which is commonly called ancient is practically modern, as it describes society in a state analogous to that in which it is now, while on the other hand much of what is called modern history [he means the Middle Ages] is practically ancient, as it relates to a state of things which has passed away.[102]

Thus, although accepting that there is a larger, universal frame of development, they argued that every nation and every society passed through successive stages of birth, adulthood and maturity.[103] Antiquity was not homogeneous: it had passed through successive stages, each with its own characteristics. One could still see similarities between antiquity and modernity: but they were similarities between equivalent stages of antiquity and modernity.[104] Thus, the Homeric age was seen as the Greek Middle Ages, the archaic period as similar to early modern Europe, the classical resembled the nineteenth century, and the Hellenistic period was seen as the equivalent of late nineteenth – early twentieth century imperialist Europe.

Interestingly enough, though many thinkers fostered the approach on theoretical grounds, and it was applied to Roman history by Niebuhr and Mommsen, it was not applied to Greek history until the last decades of the nineteenth century, with the work of Beloch and Meyer.[105] Indeed, from Niebuhr onwards the majority of German historians turned their attention to Roman history for two generations.[106] We have learnt in the last few decades how misleading their modernist assumptions for the nature of the ancient economy and society have been. What has seldom been grasped is that their attempt to actualise their narratives of ancient history was revolutionary and valid, despite the fallacy of their modernist assumptions. The overthrow of modernism, followed by the dominance of an approach

---

[101] For the theory, and its English adherents, see Forbes 1952: 12–65.
[102] *Thucydides*, Oxford, 1830, vol. 1: Appendix 1, 636.
[103] A somewhat similar idea, the biological metaphor of phases of birth, acme and decline, is more general and could in fact easily be accommodated with all three different approaches. The Viconian approach is quite different, though not necessarily contrary.
[104] Turner 1981: 25–30.
[105] Characteristically, Arnold wrote a Roman history but no history of Greece.
[106] Yavetz 1976; see also Turner 1989 for the opposite development in Britain.

influenced by the French structuralist distantiation, should accordingly be viewed with mixed feelings.

The last approach can be described as evolutionist or developmental. There were indeed many different sources of this approach.[107] One was Scottish conjectural history;[108] another, related to the first one, were the evolutionary schemes deriving from the sociology of Saint-Simon and Comte;[109] and, finally, there were the various philosophies of history that followed in the wake of Herder.[110] Probably the best indication of why all these currents should be seen together, is that Marxism, another developmental approach,[111] was equally influenced by all three of them.[112] I will focus here on the philosophies of history, simply because they present my point more clearly. They had strong philosophical overtones. Yet, the fact that nobody subscribes to these nowadays, should not obstruct from our view the real influence of this approach. In every philosophy of history, each society or civilisation is viewed from the perspective of how, or what, it has contributed to the larger process at hand (whether the development of the Spirit, Civilisation, the West, the State, Capitalism, etc.), and only to the extent that it has done so.[113]

Combining a Christian perception of a linear history moving towards redemption, and the argument of the *modernes* that the world was actually advancing, the new philosophies of history were showing not Greeks borrowing from Orientals or any other primeval source of wisdom and civilisation, but each society and civilisation building upon the foundations of their predecessors and thus leaving them behind for ever: thus, the Greeks built upon the Orientals and superseded them, the Romans upon the Greeks, etc.[114] This perspective had a double effect. It meant that Greek history was inserted as part of a process that was clearly Eurocentric. Greek history existed as an independent field only as a stage in the larger Eurocentric development: otherwise, later periods of Greek history were

---

[107] Mandelbaum 1971: 41–138, argues, convincingly in my view, that they should be treated together.
[108] Meek 1976.
[109] Here one has to include nineteenth-century evolutionist anthropology; see Burrow 1967; Stocking 1987. For the approaches to Greek history of Condorcet and Comte, see Garlan 2000; Fedi 2000 respectively.
[110] J. G. Herder, *Ideen zur Philosophie der Geschichte der Menschheit*, Riga–Leipzig, 1784–91; F. von Schlegel, *Philosophie der Geschichte*, Vienna, 1828; G. W. F. Hegel, *Vorlesungen über die Philosophie der Geschichte*, Berlin, 1837. See Bravo 1968: 140–68.
[111] It has of course to be said that not all forms of Marxism are developmental. For a superb defence of an alternative form of Marxism, see Thompson 1978.
[112] On Marxism, temporalities, and ancient history, see, with caution, Lekas 1988.
[113] See in general Sampson 1956.   [114] Bernal 1987: 196–201. See also Levine 1995; Gascoigne 1991.

subsumed under the Roman Empire. The history of Greek communities after the classical period had no interest *per se* and was not studied from a Greek perspective.[115] When later Droysen, under the heavy influence of Hegel's philosophy of history, came to invent the concept of *Hellenismus* as a new stage in the development of world history, the history of Greek communities in the last three centuries BCE was subsumed within this new stage.[116] It also meant that Greek history was considered to have a unity, only to the extent that it was such a stage in the Eurocentric progression; no other conception of Greek history was admissible.

The new philosophies of history created, therefore, a radical distinction between an ancient Orient, which had remained static, and a Greece, which came now to be totally separated and inserted, under certain terms, in the Eurocentric narrative. In a sense, the belief in the existence of two different entities, the east and the west, can be traced back to the ancient Greeks. The discourse started thousands of years ago; but until the nineteenth century, the Orient could still be seen as superior to the west in a number of respects or as a model to be followed by the west. The Industrial Revolution and the imperialist run of the long nineteenth century created a fundamentally new perception of the differences between the east and the west. All the great thinkers of the nineteenth century strove to explain what separated the east and the west and explained their allegedly divergent paths. Greece then was critical, in being the original and primeval west. It had nothing to do anymore with the east. Antiquity came to be restricted to the Greeks and the Romans: the Near-Eastern societies and cultures were to be excluded from the *Altertumswissenschaft*.[117] The invention of the Indo-European racial discourse helped further to sever the links with the east: the Eastern contributions and connections were systematically minimised and denigrated.[118] Greek history then was withdrawn from accounts of universal history: it acquired its own beginning and end.

Thus, we can see how three temporalities of antiquity and Greek history emerged. The one posed an unbridgeable gap between antiquity and modernity; it constructed antiquity as a homogeneous and unified entity, on the basis of how it differed from modernity; and it largely saw no developmental link between antiquity and modernity: the emergence of

---

[115] For the effects created on the study of the ancient Near East by this passing the torch approach, see Larsen 1989.

[116] See Bravo 1968; Canfora 1987; Wagner 1991.

[117] For F. A. Wolf's exclusion of the Near East from his conception of antiquity, see Meyer-Zwiffelhoffer 1995: 249–50.

[118] Bernal 1987: 189–399.

modernity was usually attributed to some fundamental discontinuity that took place in Europe in the late Middle Ages.[119]

The second approach was more positive to the idea that antiquity was not a homogeneous entity. It distinguished between different periods within antiquity, and argued that every ancient society had seen phases of development and change; it argued that the best way to understand them was by comparing different periods of antiquity with their counterparts in modern times. This approach was more historically sensitive; but what marred it ultimately, was again its Eurocentric and modernist angle: historical change and development could be seen only in the terms posed by change and development in modern European history: the expansion of trade, the emergence of the bourgeoisie, the decline of superstition, etc. The German modernist current followed this approach and fell with the demise of its theoretical foundation.

The third approach (evolutionism as articulated in the philosophy of history) created the long-term narrative into which Greek history was inserted, and helped to set the terms on which Greek history would become an independent field. It ensured that Greek history existed as an independent field only to the extent that it formed a stage in the larger Eurocentric process. In the archaic and classical periods, when it existed as an independent field, it was abstracted from the larger Mediterranean and Near-Eastern background of which it formed part; in the later Hellenistic and Roman periods, it was subsumed under the stages of *Hellenismus* and Rome.

The three different approaches were not always mutually exclusive. Herder discovered both national individuality *and* a philosophy of history which saw nations from the perspective of how they contributed to the process of universal history;[120] Fustel was adamant on the unbridgeable gap between antiquity and modernity, and engaged in a structural analysis of ancient society, and yet saw the modern world emerging out of antiquity as a result of a series of revolutions;[121] the Liberal Anglican followers of Vico and Niebuhr could see both recurring stages of national development in all periods of history *and* a Universal progression of history.[122] There was, and still is, plenty of space for ambiguities and contradictions here.

I hope the above exploration has managed to show how Greek history acquired a historicity, the different temporalities that were constructed and

---

[119] E.g. Smith 1976 [1776], Book 3: iii. The work of Moses Finley is probably the best example of the continuation of this approach until the present. In Finley's case, the influence of Hume is quite strong.
[120] See the classic of Meinecke 1972 [1936]: 322–61.   [121] Momigliano 1970: 333–7.
[122] Forbes 1952: 55–86.

employed to emplot it and the meta-historical concerns which influenced this process. As I remarked in the methodological reflections in the beginning of this chapter, this conclusion has direct implications for the modern study of Greek history.[123] We still have not managed to extricate ourselves from the Eurocentric temporalities constructed during the *Sattelzeit*. This is certainly not an easy task, and in the effort to deal with its challenges, the study of the historiography of the period under study here, has much to offer.

[123] See Vlassopoulos 2007.

CHAPTER 8

Herodotus and Thucydides in the view of nineteenth-century German historians

Ulrich Muhlack

The development of modern historical science in Germany from the beginning of the nineteenth century brought about a sharp break from earlier views of classical antiquity. From the Middle Ages via the Renaissance to the Enlightenment, antiquity, whether in a narrow or a wider sense, whether through imitation or delimitation, had been ascribed normative significance, whereby it eclipsed all other epochs. With the emergence of modern historical thought, which disputed the validity of transhistorical values, the foundations of this view were undermined. The new insight into the historicity of human life, the 'world as history', brought into being through the experience of the tremendous dynamism of the French Revolution and the consequent political-social struggles, now admitted only individual phenomena which had value solely in themselves. In this view, all epochs were fundamentally the same; each was, as Ranke famously put it, 'immediate to God', each had 'its special tendency and its own ideal',[1] was incomparable and untranslatable; none should be elevated or denigrated in comparison to the others. It was thus inevitable that antiquity lost its exclusive position and became just one epoch among others, of merely historical significance.

However, antiquity was still held in high esteem even among these German historians. There were two reasons for this. Firstly, it became a preferred object of study for the new forms of historical investigation. Modern historical science began with the historicisation of classical antiquity, and it proceeded from the inherited conception of that period. A paradigmatic work like Niebuhr's *Römische Geschichte* arose from a classical theme which was developed ever more into a historical one; classicism here became the vehicle or medium of historicisation, which pointed the way for the modernisation of historiography.[2] It needed, one might say, the traditional authority of antiquity to deliver the new historical thought which then

---

[1] Ranke 1971: 60–1.   [2] Essential works on this issue are Heuß 1981; Walther 1993.

brought about its downfall. Secondly, this fully historicised antiquity was nevertheless regarded as especially significant. It offered not only models of exemplary historicising but also possessed considerable relevance for the present. Most importantly, one could see in antiquity the emergence of certain basic forms from which all later developments could be deduced. Friedrich August Wolf, the founder of the historical science of antiquity (*Altertumswissenschaft*), spoke of the 'diversity of forms of political organisation' which were encountered in antiquity 'in their more simple forms'; he referred to 'several moments in ancient, especially Roman, history, without more detailed knowledge of which not even the development and consequences of the greater events of the future can be understood correctly', and saw in the 'building of our knowledge and arts ... still many traces of its Greek and Roman origins';[3] his great pupil August Boeckh considered 'the culture of the Greeks and Romans' to be 'the basis of our whole education'.[4] Antiquity's standing was no longer established on a normative basis but on a genetic one: namely, its fundamental contribution to the development of the present. This view became a commonplace of the time; even Ranke's *Weltgeschichte*, which appeared from 1881, was built on it.

Antiquity not only appeared in a new light as the object of study of historical science. There was also a strong ancient element in historians' self-understanding, through the influence of Greek and Roman historiography. Besides using the ancient texts as sources for ancient history, one looked closely at their historiographical concepts in order to clarify one's own scientific concept; one measured them by one's own criteria and thus felt prompted to make those criteria sharper and more precise. Ancient historiography functioned, at least to some degree, as a kind of midwife of modern historical science. Generally, this dealing with ancient historiography becomes a learning exercise, because it makes it clear that the transition from normative to historical judgement could not be taken for granted but involved a long drawn-out process of transformation, in which the old and the new appeared for some time less in radical opposition than in the most varied combinations.

Only certain ancient historians were referred to regularly in this debate. In a diary entry of 1850, Ranke named only three: Thucydides, Tacitus and Herodotus.[5] The order was carefully considered: Thucydides was for him the greatest historian of all, not to be surpassed;[6] Tacitus was in his way a 'master' and stood alongside Thucydides among the 'great exemplary

---

[3] Wolf 1985: 123–4.   [4] Boeckh 1877: 21.   [5] Ranke 1964: 242.   [6] Ranke 1971: 82.

authors for all time';[7] Herodotus was the first historian, from whom 'all narrative derived'. Ranke's view corresponded to the prevalent valuation. Thucydides in particular had become since the turn of the nineteenth century a positively fashionable author, as the one most suited to play a role in debates about the theoretical foundations of modern historical science. However, anyone who concerned himself with Thucydides could not ignore his predecessor; any judgement about the one contained or implied a judgement about the other. This is the context in which we shall consider the analysis of Herodotus and Thucydides by German historians. Tacitus can be ignored, because he belonged to another line of debate and so merits separate consideration. It may be added that this article examines only a selection of the historians who might be considered; the choice is certainly not completely random, but seeks to grasp as precisely as possible the basic tendency of the discussion. There is no attempt at evaluating the positions advocated in this discussion against the current state of research; that lies well beyond the terms of inquiry.

The nineteenth century had not of course discovered the two Greek historians. They were well known into late antiquity, passed into oblivion in the medieval west but became accessible again during the Renaissance and thereafter were the object of persistent interest.[8] This was never greater than in the second half of the eighteenth century. The nineteenth-century debate at first remained largely within the traditional context, but finally reached a conclusion which distinguished it from the whole of the earlier history of their reception.

This history was of course anything other than unified or uniform. Herodotus and Thucydides, each in himself and both in relationship to one another, were from time to time evaluated differently, depending on the context in which they were considered. There was not only movement between high estimation and devaluation, praise and censure and balanced and polemical judgement, but also changes in the criteria by which such judgements were reached. These differences were in turn qualified by the fact that both these Greek historians – they were always regarded as 'historians' – were seen in the light of a general theory of historical writing which from antiquity to the eighteenth century was taken entirely for granted.

---

[7] Ranke 1975: 412. Cf. Ranke 1971: 69: 'People like Thucydides and Tacitus are unsurpassable, the most elevated.' The following citation is from Ranke 1964: 242.

[8] On the history of their reception in general see Schadewaldt 1982: 9ff. and 223ff.; Meister 1990: 40–1, 61–2 and 205; Kelly 1998, *passim*. For the better researched *Nachleben* of Thucydides, see especially Meineke 2003: 480–94.

The core of this theory is familiar enough: the equation of historical writing with a literary genre.[9] Cicero called *historia* a *munus oratoris*, and this was how he spoke of it in *De oratore*.[10] Everything centred therefore on historiographical representation. The task of the historian was the production of a work of literary art, and firm principles were established which were equivalent to the artistic rules of historiography. Nevertheless, it was not a matter of a free linguistic game; unlike other literary genres, historical writing was awarded a specific *auctoritas* or authority,[11] which regulated its literary–artistic means. At its heart stood the demand for truth: the historian, unlike the poet, ought not to invent anything and, unlike the orator, ought not to take sides; he was forbidden to report falsehoods or to conceal truths, or to allow himself to be governed by favour or enmity;[12] the *lux veritatis* must illuminate his work.[13] However, the critical point was that this truth existed not through itself but only through historiographical representation, and could only be discerned in this way. Truth was established in the literary work of art that the historian produced, fixed on the rules which he followed therein. This literary performance had such dead weight that differences between historiography and other literary genres once again receded in importance; Quintilian placed historical writing alongside poetry, describing it simply as *carmen solutum*, poem in prose, and advised orators to participate in the *historicus nitor*, the lustre of the historian.[14]

Herodotus and Thucydides were included within this horizon at an early stage. They were seen as the founders of the genre; the rules of historiographical art were to a great extent drawn from their works, which were then evaluated according to that template. Cicero coined for Herodotus the well-known phrase *pater historiae*, Father of History:[15] *qui princeps genus hoc ornavit*;[16] he put Thucydides as Herodotus' immediate successor, without distinguishing between them in a qualitative sense.[17] In his view, they did not stand at the beginning of a historical process, in and through which the genre of historiography had developed, but appeared rather as the discoverers of the genre which thereafter remained unchanging in its essentials.[18] Especially, Herodotus and Thucydides were seen to have developed different possibilities of the genre, in a clearly exemplary manner. Cicero gave equal praise to the entertaining *eloquentia* of Herodotus and the instructive

---

[9] Cf. Keßler 1982.
[10] Cicero, *De oratore* 2.9.36 and 13–15.55–64; the quotation is from 2.15.62.
[11] Quintilian, *Institutio oratoria* 10.1.102.   [12] Cicero, *De or.* 2.15.62–3.   [13] Ibid. 10.9.36.
[14] Quintilian, *Inst.* 10.1.31, 33.   [15] Cicero, *De legibus* 1.1.5.   [16] Cicero, *De or.* 2.13.55.
[17] Ibid. 2.13.56.   [18] See Schadewaldt 1982: 13.

dicendi artificium of Thucydides;[19] Quintilian expressed himself in similar terms.[20] There was some debate elsewhere over which of them deserved the higher praise. Dionysius of Halicarnassus tended to give precedence to Herodotus: in his work there is a unity of form and content which Thucydides lacks.[21] In contrast Lucian placed Thucydides above Herodotus: the latter entertained his readers with fables, the former sought through truth to provide them with something of use.[22]

In the early modern period, the predominant view tended towards the judgement of Lucian. The most important figure here was Jean Bodin and his work *Methodus ad facilem historiarum cognitionem* of 1566. Bodin was not a writer of history, and he had no literary interest in historiography. He was a jurist and politician; his work, inspired by the wish to strengthen royal power in France, aimed to lay the foundations of a comparative science of law of all times and peoples. Histories were to supply him with material; the *Methodus* indicated how *cognitio* might be achieved, and began with a critical examination of the entire historiographical tradition. Bodin read histories not as works of art but as sources of factual information for his political–juristic inquiry, and he did not conceal that he thus had the least regard for authors who concentrated too much on rhetorical–aesthetic effect. Nevertheless he retained the traditional generic concept of historiography. In so far as he offered a critique, it took place within the established framework; he did not wish to set *rei veritas* against *eloquentia*, but rather to establish a correct relationship between them.

In this account, Thucydides gets the nod ahead of Herodotus. Bodin expressly refuses Herodotus the Ciceronian title of *historiae pater*, so as to award it to Thucydides instead: 'Thucydidi verissimo historiae parenti.' Thucydides had for him all the qualities of a reliable historian: he had taken part in the Peloponnesian war about which he wrote, possessed political and military expertise, had gathered information from everywhere, was, although sent into exile by the Athenians, impartial, and surrendered himself to the judgement of those who had themselves experienced the war. Thucydides thus offered *rei veritatem* and thereby *historiae fidem*, and this with appropriate *brevitas*. Bodin's only criticism, and that indirect, was of the speeches, because they went beyond the *historiae modum*. Herodotus

---

[19] Cicero, *De or.* 2.13.55–6. Cf. *Orator* 12.39.
[20] Quintilian, *Inst.* 10.1.73: 'Historiam multi scripsere praeclare, sed nemo dubitat longe duos ceteris praeferendos, quorum diversa virtus laudem paene et parem consecuta. densus et brevis et semper instans sibi Thucydides, dulcis et candidus et fusus Herodotus: ille concitatis, hic remissis adfectibus melior, ille contionibus, hic sermonibus, ille vi, hic voluptate.'
[21] Dionysius of Halicarnassus, *De Thucydide*; on Herodotus, 5 and 23.
[22] Lucian, *Quomodo historia conscribenda sit* 42, 53–4.

was quite different. Bodin did not reject him completely, conceding that the later books of the *Histories* had a certain informative value. However, in general Herodotus seemed to him to embrace an excess of *eloquentia*, which, in order to please, did not shrink from inventions and fables and so missed the proper task of the historian.[23]

When Thomas Hobbes published his English translation of Thucydides, his interest was similarly juristic and political. He described Thucydides as 'the most political historiographer that ever writ'; his absolutist views, which he shared with Bodin, led him to praise the Greek historian as the enemy of democracy and the spokesman for monarchy.[24] From this perspective he ascribed to Thucydides a perfect combination of 'truth and elocution'.[25] The reasons he gave for identifying 'truth' were roughly the same as those which Bodin had listed: Thucydides lied neither consciously nor unconsciously; he was incorruptible and thought only of posterity; he maintained strict neutrality; Hobbes especially emphasised that Thucydides wrote the history of his own time and so could form it from primary sources.[26] Unlike Bodin he also discussed Thucydidean 'elocution': he commented on 'disposition' and 'style' and found everything excellent, even the speeches; he sought to refute the objections which Dionysius of Halicarnassus had put forward, point by point.[27] Above all, Hobbes was certain that Thucydides was both the founder of history and had achieved the highest possible level in it.[28] Herodotus fell short of him in every respect: he wrote about ancient events 'of which it was impossible for him to know the truth', and served up 'fabulous narrations' with which he satisfied the entertainment needs of the masses.[29]

This high valuation of Thucydides remained unquestioned among British intellectuals. David Hume's well-known remark expressed this: 'the first page of Thucydides is the commencement of real history'.[30] Kant cited this in one of his essays on historical philosophy and so popularised it in Germany.[31] His comments echoed Bodin's view that the trustworthiness of Thucydides was guaranteed to a great extent through the approval of his well-informed audience, and raised this to a basic law of historiography: 'Only an educated audience, which has continued uninterrupted from its beginning until our time, can authenticate ancient history.'[32] In his reference to Greek historians, Kant could assume that he was expressing a view which was widespread amongst the German 'educated audience'.

[23] Bodin 1967: 49–50 and 318.   [24] Hobbes 1966/1843, I: viii and xvii.   [25] Ibid. xx.
[26] Ibid. xx–xxi and xxiv.   [27] Ibid. xxi ff.   [28] Ibid. vii.   [29] Ibid. xxiv.
[30] Hume 1963: 419; cited by Meineke 2003: 487 and 492.
[31] Kant 1985: 437.   [32] Ibid. 36.

A German translation of Thucydides' work had appeared only a few years earlier, placing the discussion on a new footing;[33] the publisher wished 'that many German readers may through such a charming history of antiquity be entertained in a socially beneficial manner',[34] thus moving the literary character of the work ostentatiously into the foreground. This translation was taken as authoritative well into the twentieth century.

In the second half of the eighteenth century, however, people in Germany also began to turn more frequently to Herodotus; the genre-specific context in which such recourse had taken place since antiquity stood out once more, virtually ideal-typical or paradigmatic. The impetus came from new efforts to develop universal history under the sign of enlightenment, inspired by the British *Universal History* and Voltaire's *Essai sur les moeurs*. If any of the German writers deserves to be singled out, it is the Göttingen historian Johann Christoph Gatterer: not because he ever produced a work that was in any way definitive, but because in his many attempts he clearly identified the problems which had to be solved in universal history. There were two: one of substance and one of form. It was a matter on the one hand of the collection of a vast amount of material, far surpassing any earlier endeavours in this field, and on the other hand of the incorporation of this material into a well-ordered representation. The goal was thus once again the production of a historiographical work of art, and the task was to establish or clarify the rules according to which one should proceed.

Gatterer regarded it as generally agreed that a new writer of history 'must first study and imitate the good models of the ancients, and only then can venture something of his own with confidence'.[35] The Greek and Roman historians could not be copied straightforwardly in the present; that was excluded by the change in circumstances. However, they offered an idea of the basic structure within which one had to work, and so one had to start with their advice. Thus Gatterer considered it necessary to consult Herodotus: the universal historian of antiquity was to teach the universal historian of the present about the construction of a universal history. Gatterer wrote a large treatise 'On the plan of Herodotus'; he found the work to be organised around 'the central history' of the conflict between Greece and Asia, which included the 'events of other nations' in suitable places as 'incorporated episodes'; he aimed to illuminate this composition from book to book, chapter to chapter. Since 'we now have a quite different location in the world', one could 'not employ the plan of Herodotus in its entirety: but the theory of this plan, the method of inclusion, as is

---

[33] Heilman 1760.   [34] Ibid. publisher's foreword.   [35] Gatterer 1990: 621.

fitting for the extent of history in our days and for our individual European history, must always be important for us'.[36] A glance at Gatterer's universal-historical writing shows how time and again he attempted by means of this method to transform the variety of individual information into a unified representation and above all to bring the diachronic and synchronic into a common order. The model of Herodotus was so significant to him that he believed he could overlook traditional objections 'against the trustworthiness of Herodotus', which seemed to him 'not without ground'.[37] The quality of the historiographical representation ranked above the validity of the facts it communicated. The traditional conception of the literary nature of historiography was never more strongly held than by this author at the end of the early modern period.

The process of historicisation which set in from the end of the eighteenth century drove out this conception of the genre. The 'world as history' did not allow itself to be bewitched by the rules of historiographical art; indeed, it was not to be understood in literary terms. Rather, it brought an entirely new reality into view, which could be grasped only with the greatest empirical precision; it was necessary – to quote another well-known phrase of Ranke's – to say 'wie es eigentlich gewesen', how it really was.[38] It was thus a matter not of art but of knowledge, of historical thought and history as science; and, because the number of possible objects of interest in the progress of the ages was in principle infinite, it was a matter of history as research or, better, as a never-ending process of research. Historiography was given the task of depicting the current results of this process; it changed from a literary event to a research report, and stepped from the realm of historiographical aesthetics into the realm of the logic of historical research.

Admittedly the traditional rules of the genre had not wholly lacked a scientific aspect. Historians were placed under obligation to the truth and expected thereby to produce reliable knowledge; this was the only reason why a reader like Bodin had any interest in historiography. However, the truth which was demanded stood only in relation to the artistic form in which it was published; it was a function of representation. The development of modern historical science was synonymous with the idea that historical truth tore off its fetters, so to speak, and established itself as absolute; this emancipation accompanied a tremendous radicalisation of what was understood by truth. Henceforth historiographical representation became a function of the truth, that is to say of historical research. It

[36] Gatterer 1767: 47–8.   [37] Ibid. 47.   [38] Ranke 1824: vi.

is exciting to see how this 'paradigm change' affected subsequent work on Herodotus and Thucydides, or became gradually manifest in it.

Any overview should begin with the young Georg Friedrich Creuzer. In later years, Creuzer caused a sensation above all through his writings on the religious history of antiquity. During the theological and philological studies which he followed in Marburg and Jena between 1791 and 1799 and concluded with a *Habilitation* on ancient history and Greek and Roman authors, he became filled or stamped with the great intellectual currents in Germany at that time. The late Enlightenment and the new humanism were as familiar to him as Idealism and early Romanticism. He perceived himself as standing at a point of departure, in which everything came together to bring forth a new understanding of history. It is significant, therefore, that the budding ancient historian made his debut with a little book about Herodotus and Thucydides,[39] which he soon followed with a monograph on Greek historical writing as a whole,[40] and it is still more significant that in both works he moved initially along largely traditional paths.

In the first treatise Creuzer engaged directly with an ancient debate. He began with a judgement of Lucian about the different degrees of trust-worthiness of Herodotus and Thucydides (*Hist. conscr.* 42), discussed the remarks of Thucydides (1.22) which Lucian had referred to, and developed from these philological findings a general comparison of the two historians. He thus demonstrated that he followed the same rules of historiography as Lucian. His development of the theme also showed how far Creuzer followed the old approach; he presented the differences between Herodotus and Thucydides, as the earlier rules of the genre required, in terms of literary and aesthetic conceptions. He perceived in Herodotus' work 'a certain cheerfulness', a 'youthful brightness':[41] 'a history in the epic manner', which wished 'to entertain in a friendly fashion'.[42] In contrast Thucydides seemed to him 'strict and earnest', full of 'knock-down statements from experience':[43] entirely concerned about 'dialectically sharp certainty and the demand of lectures that were fully planned and calculated';[44] this last point referred to Thucydides' speeches. This characterisation, in outline and even in detail, was scarcely distinguishable from those of earlier authors.

Creuzer's second book pointed in this direction even with its title: *The Historical Art of the Greeks*, meaning the literary – aesthetic art of Greek historiography. Creuzer structured the book around headings which he called

---

[39] Creuzer 1798.   [40] Creuzer 1803.   [41] Creuzer 1798: 47 and 109.   [42] Ibid. 104 and 109.
[43] Ibid. 48.   [44] Ibid. 126.

'the internal conditions of possibility of any history': 'critical research, ordering, judgement, and language'.[45] This sequence indicated an ascending line from the establishment of 'truth', which was the 'essence of all history', via the composition of the assembled material, which stood 'in the closest connection to the opinion and judgement of the writer of history', to the cultivated prose, which was 'the most appropriate form of expression for history' and at the same time stood for the highest form of language overall.[46] 'The historical style' was therefore the perfect epitome of historical writing in general,[47] and it provided Creuzer with the criterion for making a final judgement about Herodotus and Thucydides. Herodotus once more stood for 'epic' historiography, Thucydides for 'demegoric', that is historical writing concentrated on the 'public pronouncements' of those involved. They were the founders of these two forms, which Creuzer regarded as principal forms of historiography; in addition he identified the 'dramatic' form, which he saw beginning with Xenophon.[48] It does not require any long-winded explanation to appreciate that this way of thinking corresponded in every respect to views that were commonplace up to that time.

There was no contradiction for Creuzer in the fact that in both books he developed motifs and arguments that betrayed the modern historian and presented the two Greek historians in a new perspective. At the very beginning of the first work he emphasised that, although he set out from Lucian, he knew himself to be different from him: he remarked 'how far the standpoint, from which even the most thorough critics among the Greeks regarded the historical works of their nation, differs from our own'.[49] This 'standpoint' was none other than the historical sense, which the present possessed to a greater extent than antiquity, or the Middle Ages or the early modern period, and which first made possible a disassociation from the 'most thorough critics of the Greeks'. Previously unknown aspects of Herodotus and Thucydides became visible, or familiar aspects appeared in a different light. The two historians became, in one way or another, the objects of a far-going historicisation.

The first stage was that Herodotus and Thucydides ceased to be timeless archetypes of historical writing, entirely unconnected to one another, and became the initiators of a development, linked by a genetic connection. This was the 'development of history' among the Greeks,[50] which Creuzer saw beginning before Herodotus and continuing beyond Thucydides: a

---

[45] Creuzer 1803: 43.   [46] Ibid. 43, 113 and 240.   [47] Ibid. 237.   [48] Ibid. 318–19.
[49] Creuzer 1798: v. Cf. the harsh judgement on Dionysius of Halicarnassus, 48–9 and 86ff.
[50] Creuzer 1803: 32.

process of the history of the genre, which led from the 'epic singer' via the 'historical poet' and 'logography' to the development of 'history' in its different branches.[51] This process did not happen in isolation, but was at all times conditioned by the course of history in general. From the 'end of the heroic period'[52] to the formation and fortification of city-states, a change in 'culture'[53] took place which encouraged the emergence of historiography. What Creuzer understood by 'culture' is shown by his characterisation of 'Ionic culture', which he saw as decisive for 'the first sprouting as much as for the later development' of history.[54] It encompassed the 'climate of Ionia', the geographical 'situation of its cities', its 'political constitution' and 'great power' arising as a consequence 'of internal strife and revolutions', 'prosperity' and 'refinement of external life' through 'trade' and 'industry', 'inner cultivation' though 'art and science', 'spirit of liberty' and 'wisdom of experience'.[55] 'Ionic culture' existed in the interaction of all these relationships and factors. Creuzer also presented it under the label of 'youthful Greek spirit';[56] *Kultur* and *Geist* in these senses were familiar concepts to the historical thought of the late Enlightenment and early Romanticism. Historiography grew up on this soil: the 'wisdom of experience' of the Ionians promoted a sense for 'what had gone before', which elevated itself above the unbridled 'fantasy' of the heroic period and located itself within 'bounded reality', without abstaining from 'delighting' its audience;[57] in place of poetry, which pursued a 'game with legends', history finally stepped in, holding firmly 'to reality'.[58]

Creuzer classified Herodotus and Thucydides in this double historical context. Both had their places in the history of the genre of historiography, which indicated the different 'levels of culture'[59] on which they found themselves. Herodotus became the 'epic' historian because his experience of reality was still coloured strongly by religion, as he proved in his work above all through 'the great mass of oracular pronouncements' which 'according to the religious convictions of the historian were truly divine revelations';[60] that matched the 'spirit of the time', filled by 'the ruling religious concepts'.[61] In contrast Thucydides advanced to 'demegoric' historical writing, because as 'in the strongest sense a public writer of history' he concentrated only on 'the great events of state',[62] which he accounted for not through oracles but through the speeches of those involved;[63] that corresponded to 'important changes in the situation of the Greek states and men'.[64]

---

[51] Ibid. 24, 29 and 40.   [52] Ibid. 36.   [53] Ibid. 32.   [54] Ibid. 32–3.   [55] Ibid. 33ff.
[56] Ibid. 37.   [57] Ibid. 38, 40 and 204.   [58] Ibid. 38.   [59] Creuzer 1798: 96.   [60] Ibid. 54.
[61] Ibid. 96.   [62] Ibid. 68.   [63] Ibid. 56–7.   [64] Ibid. 108.

This historical classification meant that both authors were deprived of any unmediated relevance to the present. Creuzer understood them as individual cases, who were *sui generis* and must be understood in their peculiarity. A crude normative rapport, as had previously been usual, was thus excluded. However, they were relevant because they were protagonists in a process which led up to the present and from which modern historical science originated. They had in their time laid foundations on which the historians of later periods could build; one stood in this respect on their shoulders.

However, Creuzer noticed almost in retrospect a chasm between modern historians and the two Greek historians – and ancient historiography in general. He identified the reason for this as 'the development, completely opposed to the Greeks, of modern scientific culture',[65] which seemed to him to consist of a turning away from the 'ideas of the ancients about historical language and representation'.[66] Here he hit upon the decisive point: the change from historiographical art to history as science, which established the writing of history as a function of historical research. He explored this change in two aspects, one material and one methodological. He noted on the one hand 'a new higher standpoint for the examination of humanity', from which 'a history of humanity of a broader scope would be made possible', and on the other hand a perfection of critical source analysis.[67]

There were precedents for the 'new examination of humanity' and the new concept of a 'history of humanity' in the universal history of the Enlightenment, from the *Universal History* to Gatterer. Creuzer, how-ever, referred above all to Herder, who had so emphasised the concept of 'humanity', over and above the internal and external boundaries of the Enlightenment writing of universal history, that it became identical with the concepts of individuality of modern historical thought. 'Humanity' meant in this sense nothing other than that equal right was due to every human being, every human phenomenon and every human event in the eyes of the historian.[68] This equal right required in turn a maximum degree of objectivity. The perfection of critical source analysis noted by Creuzer arose from this necessity; without it, the requisite objective knowledge was unachievable. 'Humanity' and critical source analysis thus went hand in hand; they were the two sides of the process of the 'scientificisation' of history.

[65] Creuzer 1803: 255.   [66] Ibid. 241.   [67] Ibid. 258–9.
[68] Creuzer 1798: 118–19. He refers to Herder's *Briefe zu Beförderung der Humanität*, 10th collection, Letter 121; new edition, Herder 1991: 735.

In neither aspect were Herodotus and Thucydides completely removed from the needs of the present. As far as 'humanity' and 'history of humanity' were concerned, Herodotus offered through the universal conception of his *Histories* starting points in which one could recognise one's own problem. Gatterer had already sought 'in a work, which has the form of universal history'[69] enlightenment about the 'plan' of his own world history, admittedly still within the conventional framework of historiographical art. Herder took the next step, when he laid claim to Herodotus for his postulate of a universal sense of objectivity: 'Thus nothing remains to history solely and eternally but the spirit of its oldest writer, Herodotus, the unrestrained mild sense of humanity. Impartially he sees all peoples and shows each in its place, according to its customs and usages.' Creuzer, who adopted this passage of Herder, declared this 'sense of humanity' to be Herodotus' 'chief contribution': 'for he thus became the historian of humanity', as he said in a further allusion to Herder. At the same time he distinguished Herodotus from Thucydides, who remained within 'the field of vision of his people',[70] but had judged impartially and in that respect 'in fact (although without clearly thought intention) takes the higher standpoint of humanity'.[71]

As far as critical source analysis was concerned, however, Thucydides took precedence. Ever since antiquity, Herodotus' inclination towards fabulous stories had been criticised and the trustworthiness of Thucydides, founded on the study of sources, praised. Creuzer had, as a result of his scientific premises, a still sharper view. Already in his first work he chose the different credibilities of the two historians as a starting point, in order from there to approach the principles and circumstances which explained this difference; and there was no concealing which of them gained first place: for 'in this treatise historical criticism is attributed to Thucydides'.[72] In the second book all this was set out more precisely: Herodotus stood 'on a middle rank between logography and credible history'[73] while Thucydides brought 'research and criticism' to a level whereby he became the 'most decisive critic of antiquity';[74] Creuzer even allowed the Thucydidean speeches to pass with reservation as a 'faithfully transmitted document'.[75]

However, Creuzer placed considerable weight on the fact that these kinds of approaches were very distant from what modern historians had achieved. The 'historian of humanity' and the 'most decisive critic of antiquity' were in their own time and in fact throughout the whole of antiquity exceptions:

[69] Gatterer 1767: 47.   [70] See n. 68.   [71] Creuzer 1803: 284.   [72] Creuzer 1798: 88.
[73] Creuzer 1803: 111.   [74] Ibid. 262 and 276.   [75] Ibid. 275.

Herodotus' sense for humanity 'must have remained always hidden from
the Greeks',[76] as Thucydides 'stood above them in more correct historical
concepts'.[77] In the present, however, both the history of humanity and
critical source analysis had reached dimensions which were unimaginable
within the horizon of antiquity. The modern 'historian of humanity' not
only possessed positive knowledge quite different from that of Herodotus,
who provided many 'proofs' of his 'deep ignorance'.[78] He also contributed
to 'a world of abstract ideas', in which the concept of 'humanity' and all
its implications had been brought for the first time into consciousness.[79]
This 'historical idealism', this clear insight into the historical equality of
all human beings, which 'is of a philosophically abstract nature' (that is to
say, derived from an act of reflection), was absent from both Herodotus
and Thucydides,[80] and was an achievement of the modern German mind
(*Geist*) from Herder to Goethe.[81] The same was true of critical source
analysis. For Creuzer, however much he stressed in Thucydides the 'great
and intensive strength of the critical spirit', 'the true critical method, if
this is understood as an activity supported through the historical auxiliary
sciences and led by clearly thought-through scientific laws' was 'exclusively
the possession of the moderns':[82] 'a young and tender plant, which could
flourish only in the most recent times and mainly, perhaps only, under
German skies'.[83] Here too it was a matter of a genuinely new creation, and
an achievement of the German mind.

For Creuzer these achievements were beyond question; nothing could
be further from his mind than to hark back to earlier times. However,
there was one respect in which he criticised or regretted the progress of the
moderns, and he referred repeatedly to this turning-point: the shift from
history as art to history as science. He accepted the turn towards history
as science, but objected to the turn away from history as art. He remarked
upon the lack of 'aesthetic development' of modern historical writing: 'we
have not progressed in historical representation to the same degree'.[84] The
'ever-growing wealth of ideas', the immense richness of universal–historical
knowledge, the giant mass of critically ascertained facts have 'chained up
the spirit of representation', or rather grown over it.[85] Instead there was 'the
demand for a certainty that went beyond experience', which led 'to mis-
judgement about the nature of history' and thereby about its appropriate
artistic form:[86] speculative philosophy of history instead of historiographical representation – here he has the emerging German idealism in his sights.

---

[76] Creuzer 1798: 119.   [77] Ibid. 121.   [78] Ibid. 120.   [79] Creuzer 1803: 257.
[80] Ibid. 261.   [81] Creuzer 1798: 123.   [82] Creuzer 1803: 259.   [83] Creuzer 1798: 88.
[84] Creuzer 1803: 255 and 258.   [85] Ibid. 258.   [86] Ibid. 259.

Of course these developments also had their innate causes and could not easily be reversed.[87] However, Creuzer yearned to combine the great mass of ideas and facts which the new historians had produced into representations of 'an artistic kind'.[88] History as science should be transformed into 'aesthetic or artistic research' and thereby developed into historiographical art.[89] The example of Johannes von Müller seemed to him to prove that this was possible. It also demonstrated that historiographical art did not have to be invented from scratch but that there were ancient models: none of the modern historians has 'understood the artistic development of the history of the Greeks more deeply'.[90] Creuzer wanted the rules of historiographical art deriving from the Greek historians to be revived, or at any rate their basic direction to be restored. Herodotus and Thucydides were of particular interest to him in this connection; they had produced principal aesthetic forms of historiography, which could not be disregarded even in the present. Accordingly Creuzer introduced Herodotus and Thucydides first of all in the context of the traditional rules of the genre. All the tendencies which he followed towards historicisation and thereby the scientification of history reached their limits here. History as science came to life with him in the guise of history as art.

This connection between 'modern' historical science and 'ancient' historical art can be observed in German historians well into the nineteenth century. When Barthold Georg Niebuhr reached the middle of the revision and continuation of his *Römische Geschichte*, one of the great models of modern historical research, the desire awoke in him for creating a historiographical representation in the style of the ancients: 'it was for me a charming idea, when this scholarly work, through which the material will be produced, is completed, to write a wholly narrative history of the Romans, without examination, proof and scholarliness; as one would have written it 1800 years ago'.[91] He shared the literary-aesthetic nostalgia of Creuzer, and outdid him in his valuation of Thucydides: the Greek had 'reached the highest level possible in the writing of history, both from the perspective of definite historical reliability and from that of living representation'.[92] Thucydides was both historiographical artist and analyst of sources, and Niebuhr referred time and again especially to the former. Already in his youth Thucydides had 'refreshed' him.[93] During the

---

[87] Ibid. 255.   [88] Ibid. 261.   [89] Ibid. 254.   [90] Ibid. 254–5.

[91] Niebuhr 1981–1984, IV: 117.

[92] Niebuhr 1847–51, II: 42. Cf. Niebuhr 1827: 198, where especially 'the perfect sense of the great writer for appropriateness', for 'elevated' as for 'light' tones is praised. On Niebuhr's consideration of Thucydides in the context of his historical thought see Montepaone 1994.

[93] Niebuhr 1926: 243; cf. Walther 1993: 305.

preparation of the second edition of the *Römische Geschichte* the founder
of 'demegoric' historiography became fundamental: 'I have just completed
a speech which comes from the heart, as if I had spoken it before my people, after the Thucydidean model.'[94] Herodotus was regarded less highly.
Niebuhr spoke of him as 'a real writer of history'[95] who preceded Thucydides without attaining his level. He treated him generally as a source
whose reliability he had to evaluate. He found him usable in many cases
and so considered it reasonable 'to praise him anew',[96] but could not avoid
'placing him in a disadvantageous light'; measured by contemporary scientific standards 'the ancient historian' seemed to him not even comparable
'with a well-taught lad of our own days'. Nevertheless he took for granted
the literary value of Herodotus, whom he named in the same context 'the
beloved and respected writer of antiquity', as if to relativise his judgement
of the critic and researcher.[97]

In the case of Georg Gottfried Gervinus, a historian of the younger
generation held himself even more firmly within the bounds of historiographical art. Gervinus had studied from 1826 to 1830 with Friedrich
Christoph Schlosser at Heidelberg, who gave equal weight in his teaching
to the connection between history and the present and between political and literary history. Thereafter Gervinus belonged to the political
school of nineteenth-century German historical science, and first to its
national-liberal wing: a political historian, for whom political engagement
and scientific work formed a dialectic unity. His idea of Herodotus and
Thucydides was formed against this background, wherein the latter clearly
commanded the field. Gervinus concerned himself with Thucydides at an
early stage, and set down his views in 1832 in his *Historische Briefe*.[98] He
denied that 'the character of Thucydides' work was to be found in the
criticism that rules there', and found it rather in the relationship between
the author and the events of his time; it was typical of Thucydides 'that
only in the huge upheaval did he gather his experience and his knowledge
of men and of human relations and made a habit of deep observation';
his critical sense too derived from this.[99] Thucydides became the model of
a political historian, as Gervinus himself wished to be. Herodotus could
not keep pace; Gervinus granted him, against the prevailing view, a certain
'critical side', but not the political interests through which critical research
would reach its goal.[100] Accordingly he denounced the scholarliness of the

---

[94] Niebuhr 1981–4, II: 128; cf. Walther 1993: 535–6 and 569–70.
[95] Niebuhr 1847–51, I: 385.   [96] Niebuhr 1981–4, I: 432–3.
[97] Niebuhr 1828: 133.   [98] Gervinus 1838: 93–115. Cf. Hübinger 1984: 36–7.
[99] Gervinus 1838: 114.   [100] Ibid. 99.

Alexandrian period; it was 'too far distanced from the original sources of Greek life'.[101] With such judgements, Gervinus distinguished himself from other contemporary scientific views. Thucydides and Herodotus functioned as badges or ciphers for different directions in the emergent modern historical science.

It was nevertheless not by chance that Gervinus at the same time resorted to a historiographical art whose rules were anchored in traditional doctrine. A political historian of his type obviously required some literary-rhetorical means in order to be persuasive, and it was convenient to procure these from the inherited categories. Gervinus certainly understood his *Grundzüge der Historik* of 1837 as guidelines for a literary genre, comparable with other literary genres.[102] His opening question was: 'How is it that no *Historik* could ever win a place beside the *Poetik?*'[103] He discussed 'historical art' and distinguished it from the 'method of historical research' which served merely as preparation for it.[104] A central theme was 'the different forms of historical writing', which were reduced to 'two primary forms'.[105] The first was a matter of recording the 'objective' course of events in chronological succession; this extended from 'genealogy' via 'chronicle' to 'history of one's own people', and was labelled 'chronological'. The second involved the 'subjective' assessment of what had happened; this extended from 'memoir' to 'pragmatic history-writing', and was called 'pragmatic'.[106] The task every time was 'perfection in itself', 'a unified whole', 'unity of the plan', 'combination of the parts into a whole':[107] 'the unified and total effect of the work of art'.[108] How this was to be achieved could be learnt from the poet; just like him, the historian had to select 'material' which was 'capable' of such an effect;[109] here the subordination of 'research' to 'art' is blatant. The 'primary forms' of historical writing recurred again and again, and each time the same task was set; the external relationships changed but the internal laws of historical writing were immutable; no historian could escape them. In this text there was scarcely any mention of Herodotus. When he was mentioned, he was assigned to the middle stage of 'chronological' history.[110] Much more prominent was Thucydides, whom Gervinus presented as the most mature representative of this historiographical style; he was comparable to Machiavelli in the 'pragmatic' tradition.[111]

Gervinus had a student who initially went further along this road: Wilhelm Roscher. The founder of the older Historical School of German

---

[101] Ibid. 114–15.   [102] Gervinus 1962.   [103] Ibid. 49.   [104] Ibid. 50.   [105] Ibid. 84.
[106] Ibid. 58, 68–9 and 84.   [107] Ibid. 63.   [108] Ibid. 92.   [109] Ibid.   [110] Ibid. 69 and 80.
[111] Ibid. 84 and 90.

economic thought began his academic career with a project called *Klio,
Contributions to the History of the Historical Art*. He planned 'monographs'
on selected historians from classical antiquity in order to exemplify the
legitimacy of this 'history', in which the system of 'historical art' was
set out. The first volume would be devoted to Thucydides, the second to
Herodotus and Xenophon, the third would deal with 'the five great Roman
historians', Caesar, Cicero (as letter-writer), Sallust, Livy and Tacitus.[112]
Roscher thus wished as it were to continue the *Historik* of Gervinus,
especially in his recourse to the appropriate ancient authors; he said of the
'study of the ancients' that it was 'for the historian just as unavoidable as
it is for the artist'.[113] This was an aesthetic–classicising plan *par excellence*,
entirely along traditional lines.

Roscher wrote, or at any rate published, only the volume on Thucydides,
which appeared in 1842. He opened with 'Prolegomena' which related to
the whole project; they provided an outline 'of the aesthetics of historical art in general' and thereby explained the theoretical premises for the
planned case studies. Through rearrangement and combination he turned
the concepts developed by Gervinus into a new set of generic rules, without
changing anything fundamental. Roscher recognised 'three stages of any
artistic activity' which constituted an order of development: 'gathering of
material', 'internal assimilation' and 'reproduction'. Three 'stages of development of the historical art' corresponded to these: 'chronicle', 'memoir'
and 'artistic history'.[114] The whole was a cyclical process which led from
'chronicle' via 'memoir' to 'artistic history' and from 'artistic history' via a
period of decline back to 'chronicle', whereupon a new cycle began.[115] The
'corresponding stages of development of different nations' made analogies possible between different national traditions in historiography.[116]
Comparison with classical historiography showed that contemporary historiography 'of the Roman and German peoples' had reached the stage
of 'artistic history' and therefore needed to be trained through ancient
'artistic history'.[117] As the 'highest model of this type' Roscher offered
Thucydides.[118]

The sole aim of the Thucydides book was to present this 'highest model'.
Roscher proceeded firmly according to the theory set out in the 'Prolegomena'. Thucydides' achievement lay in the fact that he proceeded
from 'collection' via 'assimilation' to 'reproduction', and thereby developed 'chronicle' and 'memoir' into 'artistic history'. Roscher accordingly

---

[112] Roscher 1908: 383; Roscher 1842: vii.   [113] Roscher 1842: ix.   [114] Ibid. 48 and 58.
[115] Ibid. 6off.   [116] Ibid. xii.   [117] Ibid. 48.   [118] Ibid. 58.

considered in succession Thucydides' study of sources, his conception of history and his means of representation. He could not avoid constantly looking to Herodotus, where he found virtually 'all the insightful ideas of Thucydides' but 'less clearly or fully worked out'.[119] Herodotus seemed to him to anticipate in an unreflective manner what Thucydides then developed consciously and thus transformed into a new quality. He considered this succession necessary, and could therefore only 'praise the decision of divine wisdom that Thucydides had to be preceded by a Herodotus, and Herodotus had to be followed by a Thucydides'.[120]

It is difficult to say why Roscher abandoned his grand project after the first volume, why after Thucydides neither Herodotus nor the other ancient historians were accorded a monograph. Perhaps he had the impression that the main work was already done. Why should he have continued the project, after the ancient historian who was by far the most important for the present had been depicted in the most extensive manner! Another reason may have been more important, namely that in the course of working on the Thucydides book his actual theme became more and more obscured. For what he produced was no 'highest model', but historical knowledge which reconstructed an entirely individual phenomenon. Even the title, looking away from the present, was suggestive. *Leben, Werk und Zeitalter des Thukydides*; that promised a book which focused on the specified author in his individual context. The development of this theme was entirely suited to fulfil this expectation. Not only that Roscher, before embarking on his analysis, described 'Thucydides' external circumstances' and thus set his reader within the historical horizon of a singularity; the analysis too, although formally ordered according to the precepts from the 'Prolegomena', proved, in its subject matter, concrete observations and material results, to be historical through and through. Finally, Roscher had already, while working on Thucydides, developed an interest in the historical grounding of 'state economy' which set him on a quite different path of research.[121] However, it is noticeable that from the start he wanted to investigate 'laws of development' which are reminiscent of the 'stages of development of the historical art'. The 'aesthetics of historical art in general' here become the logic of 'state-economic' processes. In this respect the 'artistic historian' Thucydides is one of the founders of the older German Historical School of National Economy.

It is necessary to go back one or even two generations to encounter a judgement on Herodotus and Thucydides diametrically opposed to the

[119] Ibid. 286.   [120] Ibid. 289–90.   [121] Ibid. vii.

traditional aesthetic–classicising mode of thought and based solely on the
genuine principles and postulates of modern historical science; namely,
that of Arnold Herrmann Ludwig Heeren. He was the youngest and most
important representative of the renowned Göttingen Historical school;
a political–cultural historian of antiquity and the modern era, who had
a clear notion of historical research and detested all forms of rhetorical
history-writing, something which separated him utterly from an older
Göttingen historian like Gatterer. Born in the mid-eighteenth century, he
lived until 1842, by which point he had long appeared to have outlived his
era and become untimely. There were many among the younger German
historians who sought to enhance their reputations by setting themselves
against Heeren. One of these was Gervinus,[122] who also acted in the name
of his teacher Schlosser. The chief instruments of his criticism were the
Historische Briefe of 1832. The common reproach was that Heeren led a
purely scholarly existence, instead of taking part in public life as was the
duty of the historian. He belonged to a sphere 'where the breath of free
public life dissipates into oil lamps and writing'.[123] There is in him 'not
a trace of the spirit which infuses the whole generation'; 'alongside his
contemporaries he seems like a stranger'.[124] Gervinus thus argued that
Heeren was not the right sort of political historian, unlike himself, and he
sought through his critique to expel him altogether from his time. Even
his remarks about the 'political' Thucydides and the 'scholarly' Herodotus
were essentially directed against Heeren. They were intended to contradict
Heeren's remarks on the subject, and once again to distinguish the 'political'
Gervinus from the 'scholarly' Heeren. However, Gervinus was so caught up
in his polemic that he was entirely unaware of the implications of Heeren's
incriminating remarks. He read and cited him,[125] without recognising the
consequences.

There were only a couple of lines, from Heeren's *Ideen über die Politik,
den Verkehr und den Handel der vornehmsten Völker der alten Welt*, in
the volume about the Greeks.[126] The *Ideen*, one of Heeren's two chief
historiographical works, were intended to cover the history of the ancient
world up to the fourth century BCE; they remained uncompleted. They
presented constitutional history in connection with the history of trade, but
also included science and art: political–cultural history in Heeren's sense,
built on a vast study of the sources and written in language concerned with
'the greatest lucidity and clarity'.[127] Heeren was interested throughout in
political knowledge, even if political engagement in Gervinus' style was

---

[122] Cf. Hübinger 1984: 73ff.   [123] Gervinus 1838: 92.   [124] Ibid. 132–3.
[125] Ibid. 110–11 and 113.   [126] Heeren 1826.   [127] Heeren 1824: viii.

and had to be far from his mind. He found in this period a 'multiplicity of state forms', 'independence' of peoples, 'peaceful intercourse between ancient peoples' and 'social intercourse',[128] all of which he set in parallel to the modern European state system, the theme of his second main work.[129] He had no direct practical application in mind: engagement with the ancient world should rather sharpen one's gaze for the past situation and thereby also for the uniqueness of the present. Antiquity was thus ascribed a significance for the present without altering its specific historical physiognomy: an example of its new valuation within modern historical science.

Heeren discussed Herodotus and Thucydides in one of the final chapters in the Greek volume, entitled 'Science in relation to the state', which supplemented his characterisation of Greek state relations in accordance with the general theme of the *Ideen*. Having considered philosophy, Heeren turned to historiography. Their relationships to the state were quite different: 'If the relationship of philosophy to the state must be determined by its repercussions, with history it is the opposite case. It stands in a relation to the state which emerges from its changes and destinies.'[130] From this perspective Heeren considered Greek historiography from its origins to Xenophon. Herodotus and Thucydides appear here solely as objects of historical contemplation. Nevertheless it was clear that at the same time they were established in a whole new relationship to the present. Heeren wholly disregarded the aesthetic–literary tradition of the genre, which had previously determined the interpretation of these authors, but ascribed to them an achievement which until then had been discussed only in passing: the foundation of modern historical science.

Herodotus began the process. Before him history had existed merely in conjunction with poetry. He was 'the first who undertook to deal with purely historical material; and thereby the decisive step occurred of giving history its independence'.[131] He could do this because the 'material' had accrued through an unprecedented event of the most recent past. The 'storm of the Persian war'[132] had confronted the Greeks for the first time with historical reality at a scale for which the categories of poetry were no longer sufficient and which required a whole new approach in order to deal with it: history. 'What material for history!' and 'this material of its nature belonged completely to it'.[133] Herodotus took up the challenge and created 'a historical work which for the first time showed what history is; and which was capable of awakening the sense for it'.[134]

---

[128] Ibid. 40–1.   [129] Heeren 1830.   [130] Heeren 1826: 376.   [131] Ibid. 386.   [132] Ibid. 389.
[133] Ibid. 384.   [134] Ibid. 388.

It is obvious that Heeren was not simply describing the transition from 'historical poetry' to 'history', from 'fable to truth'; that was familiar enough from the earlier literature. The discovery of the historical world in the 'storm of the Persian war' and with it the development of an independent historiography: that was for Heeren the discovery of the 'world as history' in the emphatic sense of the emerging historicism and the development of history as science. He had experienced the emergence of modern historical thought out of the dynamic spirit of the French Revolution, and transferred this experience onto the situation of Herodotus; or rather he reached from a new development of the present to a new understanding of the Greek historian.

With Herodotus 'the first great step was taken'.[135] Thucydides followed: he took the 'giant step' to historical criticism,[136] which completed the foundation work. He could do this because, from the experience of a period of 'wars' and 'state revolutions',[137] he became 'the historian of his time'.[138] Because he could not build on anything handed down but 'had to research everything through his own enquiries', he required the highest possible source-critical precision: 'his material must have made him into a critic',[139] but in such a way that he thereby established standards which were valid for all historical writing. Thucydides had thus 'for the first time revealed the heart of the nature' of history: from that developed the 'whole historical culture' of the west.[140]

With this judgement, Heeren exploded traditional assumptions. It was nothing new to emphasise Thucydides' exorbitant critical ability. With Heeren, however, this was an achievement to be measured against the criteria of modern historical science. The 'world as history' required a huge intensification of source criticism, because historical truth could not otherwise be obtained. After Herodotus had discovered the 'world as history', Thucydides initiated this intensification; this was his basic contribution to the development of a historical-critical methodology, in which modern historical science could recognise itself.

Heeren's view gained acceptance among German historians in the same degree as the revolutionary transformation of historical studies through modern historical thought came to consciousness. This process was concluded with Johann Gustav Droysen and Leopold Ranke; they established for their time the standing of Herodotus and Thucydides, if measured against the principles of modern historical science.

---

[135] Ibid.   [136] Ibid. 393.   [137] Ibid. 390.   [138] Ibid. 389.   [139] Ibid. 389 and 391.
[140] Ibid. 392.

In Droysen, almost half a century younger than Heeren, different tendencies came together. He began like Creuzer with the study of Greek and Roman antiquity, in Berlin between 1826 and 1829 under Boeckh. Later he turned to history in general, starting with the most recent period. This led him into the ranks of the political historians and united him with his near contemporary Gervinus; both stood together in 1848 in the national–liberal camp, before Gervinus took a left-republican turn. What drove Droysen even during his ancient historical studies was the question of the philosophical-theoretical foundations of the subject. This interest had been awoken by his second great teacher Hegel, who taught him epistemology and the philosophy of history of German idealism down to Kant. When Droysen gave lectures on *Historik* in Jena in 1857, he had in mind a kind of 'critique of historical reason'. In these lectures he returned several times to Herodotus and Thucydides.

Droysen pursued in his *Historik* a goal which was directly opposed to the *Historik* of Gervinus. He explained unambiguously: 'Because the *Grundzüge der Historik* of Gervinus considers throughout only the art of historical writing, it undertakes to be for history what in Gervinus' view Aristotle's *Poetics* was for poetry. There is not the slightest notion that history must find a place in the great system of human knowledge and establish its relationship to the other sciences, still less any idea of how it achieves its results, on what foundation it stands.'[141] Droysen intended to present not artistic but rather scientific rules for history: it was a branch of knowledge, not of literature; it should be defined in terms of other branches of knowledge, not other literary genres; it was founded on logic, not aesthetics. His *Historik* was to specify its purpose, definition and logic. This was a rejection not only of Gervinus but of the whole tradition of the historiographical genre reaching back into antiquity. Droysen was so certain of his own view that he did not make this rejection the centre of his account. It occurred in passing; what really interested him was the definition of history in relation to 'the other sciences', especially natural science, which was then being widely promoted as a model for historiography. Droysen's *Historik* was actually directed against this 'positivistic' challenge; he wanted in contrast to this, to give a 'scientific justification of our studies'.[142]

Droysen first dealt with 'Methodology', which was identical with the rules of procedure of historical research. These led from the gathering of sources via source criticism to the interpretation of the material extracted; at the end of the process stood 'Apodeixis', the historiographical

---

[141] Droysen 1977: 51. Cf. Gervinus 1962: 49.   [142] Droysen 1977: 44.

representation of the results of interpretation: not a literary–aesthetic act, but a 'logical work of art'.[143] In the second part Droysen set out the 'System' of history: the contents or field of objects of historical science. These unfolded a grand theme: 'the emergent *humanitas*, the emergent education (*Bildung*)', that is the historicity of humanity, the 'world as history'.[144] Historical research was fulfilled in the historicity of its objects and therefore disregarded the barriers previously erected for it.

Droysen did not refer to Herodotus and Thucydides very frequently in his lectures; they were simply part of the general historiographical tradition at his disposal. However, he did ascribe to them a quality which awarded them an eminent rank.

The form of reference varied. Sometimes they were introduced as sources: Droysen took from them certain factual information or simply used them to exemplify the process of source criticism. In the latter case, though, the boundary with a fundamental appreciation of them could be fluid. Thucydides, named as an example of a reliable 'historian of his time' was in the same breath referred to as 'the greatest historian of all time';[145] Roscher's *Thukydides* seemed 'exemplary' to Droysen, because one became 'fully familiar' with the author and his time.[146] In Herodotus, labelled 'the foremost source for the Persian wars', Droysen identified, entirely in the spirit of Heeren, the birth of history out of the experiences and problems of the present.[147] On the other hand Thucydides was again recommended as a model, this time in clear contrast to Herodotus, when Droysen discussed what he called 'catastrophic' representation, i.e. striving for a dramatic high-point or turning-point.[148] In general it was important to him to show clearly in Herodotus and Thucydides that historiographical representation does not exist in its own right but is determined by the results of research: ἱστορίης ἀπόδειξις, as Herodotus describes his work in the first line' is 'a label which contains more than our word "representation" (*Darstellung*)',[149] and 'when Thucydides wrote κτῆμα ἐς ἀεί, is he supposed to have meant with this proud word the artistic form in which he wrote and not the historical drama of which he wrote?'[150] All these judgements allow a basic idea to be recognised: Herodotus and Thucydides – the one as precursor, the other bringing the process to completion – were the first to practise historical science in the modern or at least in a comparable sense.

---

[143] Ibid. 228.   [144] Ibid. 14.   [145] Ibid. 96.   [146] Ibid. 153.   [147] Ibid. 148.
[148] Ibid. 246–7.   [149] Ibid. 57.   [150] Ibid. 459.

Droysen integrated Thucydides onto still another line of development, which related directly to the theme of his lectures. Before embarking on his *Historik*, understood as the scientific rules of history, he asked about 'previous attempts'.[151] The answer was mixed. On the one hand there had always been a significant level of practice of historical science; on the other hand there had previously been only a few attempts at setting this practice within a set of scientific rules. The rules of historiography remained incomplete, followed irregularly on one another, were not made proof against relapses or relativisation, at any rate did not result in a path of unilinear progress; the first to tackle this task, after the entirely unsuccessful efforts of Wilhelm von Humboldt, was Droysen himself. The history of *Historik* appeared, rather in the manner of Hegel, as a process in which history achieved, via arduous paths, consciousness of the principles which determined it, until finally Droysen attained the decisive insight which qualified him to reconstruct this process. Thucydides had a key role in this. Certainly the Greeks had 'not arrived at any theory or definitive knowledge', but 'its premises were there . . . in the great historiography of Athens' maturity', which, even if limited to 'merely political history', 'in Thucydides achieved a model of representation that has never again been reached'.[152] Right at the beginning of the process stood a first-class scientific performance that has been unsurpassed since and is basically unsurpassable, but only at its endpoint, in the present, was the possibility created through Droysen of adequately conceptualising 'this unsurpassed model'. The genius of the ancient historian came to fruition in the modern historian. Thucydides compared with Droysen was like scientific instinct compared to scientific reflection or self-reflection.

It was not unusual for many of these authors to draw comparisons between Leopold Ranke and Thucydides. Roscher, who had studied with Ranke for a period, dedicated his Thucydides book to him and to the philosopher Heinrich Ritter; when he asked for Ranke's permission for this, he pulled out all the stops: 'In you I honour not just the leading living historian but also, along with Niebuhr, the leading historian of our people: one of the very few moderns who have successfully contended with the greats of antiquity.'[153] In the course of the book he made the idea more concrete, repeatedly comparing Ranke to Thucydides: he presented Ranke along with Winckelmann and Niebuhr as belonging to the ranks of the 'real historical artists', and thus on the same level as Thucydides,[154] or

---

[151] Ibid. 44ff.   [152] Ibid. 46.   [153] Roscher 1908: 383.   [154] Roscher 1842: 57–8.

he compared the Sophists' critique of Thucydides with the neo-Hegelian one of Ranke, each of which he described as *pseudogeistreich*, 'pseudo-intelligent'.[155] Droysen, in contrast, although he named both historians in his discussion of 'catastrophic' representation and introduced Ranke as 'the greatest historian of our century', clearly ranked him lower than Thucydides. Ranke surpassed Thucydides 'in fineness of formation and wealth of knowledge', but fell short in 'ethical strength and rigour'.[156] This corresponded to the typical critique offered by political historians of Ranke's demand for impartiality; Roscher, in contrast, enlisted Thucydides for precisely this agenda,[157] without questioning 'his political, his practical party-ability'.[158]

Both these comparisons reveal more about their authors than they do about Ranke. However, they hit the mark to some extent since Ranke himself not only studied Thucydides throughout his scholarly life but thought of himself in a definite relationship to his predecessor which he felt to be quite exclusive.

Ranke encountered Thucydides during his studies at Leipzig from 1814 to 1817; his doctoral disputation dealt with him. He got to know Herodotus while working as a teacher in Frankfurt an der Oder from 1818 to 1825. Both accompanied his further scientific development. Thucydides remained the one with whom he felt the greatest affinity. Ranke's respect for him knew no bounds: no one could have 'the pretention to be a greater historian than Thucydides';[159] Thucydides was 'the father of all true history'.[160] In his last work, the *Weltgeschichte*, he found an opportunity for a wide-ranging characterisation of the two Greek historians, in which he also made explicit the basis of his judgement.[161]

Ranke's *Weltgeschichte* encompasses the history of ancient oriental – Mediterranean – Western 'humankind' up to the end of the fifteenth century. It was a history of 'prevailing (*vorwaltenden*) nations', which won through the ongoing 'antagonism of nations' and established themselves as 'historical world powers' of universal importance: a political history, which however always incorporated religion, law, society, literature, science and art, the totality of 'cultural endeavours' – in other words a 'total history' integrated around political history.[162] The work further set out the basis of

---

[155] Ibid. 185–6.   [156] Droysen 1977: 247.
[157] Roscher 1842: 230–1; he refers here to a comment in Droysen's translation of Aristophanes (vol. II, Berlin, 1837, 298ff.).
[158] Roscher 1841: 251.   [159] Ranke 1971: 82.   [160] Ranke 1888a: 574.   [161] Ranke 1881: 1.2, 37ff.
[162] Ranke 1881: 1.1, iiiff.

his previous oeuvre, his history, developed through many monographs, of the early modern European state system.

Between the sections on the history of archaic and classical Greece up to the end of the Peloponnesian war and on the background and history of Philip and Alexander, a chapter was inserted on the 'internal history of the Greek spirit' from the end of the sixth to the second half of the fourth century, offering a parade of poets, philosophers, artists and also Herodotus and Thucydides, coming between the three great tragedians and a general account of intellectual conditions in fifth-century Athens. Ranke emphasised the close connection between this 'internal' history and political developments, but also gave it an autonomous dynamic: 'For therein lies the nature of the developments of the spirit, that it cannot emerge without the influence of historical life in general, but at the same time is independent of it;'[163] Ranke here described equally his attitude towards the 'life in general' of his own time. All the thinkers, poets and artists gathered together in this chapter had a common motive: 'they sought to solve the most difficult problems which concerned the relationship between the divine and the human . . . so that their work as a whole presents a conclusion which has an inestimable value for humanity'.[164] Ranke added that this 'value' lay not in 'rules and dogma' but in the 'imagining of the great thoughts, out of which the internal life of the spiritual world springs'.[165] The Greek 'spirit' managed a double achievement for humanity: it wrestled with a world problem, and it left it up to future times to solve this problem in their own way; one learnt from it at the same time as one reflected on one's own situation.

Herodotus and Thucydides participated in this 'internal history' in their own manner. They turned the underlying motivation of the Greek 'spirit' towards the historical world and thereby achieved an increased clarification of the problem. Herodotus accepted 'a divine element, which exerted an always intervening influence on human affairs'.[166] Thucydides likewise accepted 'a divine element in human affairs', but rejected the view 'that the gods intervene directly in human affairs' and explained everything on the basis of 'the qualities of human nature'.[167] The succession from Herodotus to Thucydides represents a progression from a transcendental to an immanent conception of history. It also represented a change in truth-claims. While Herodotus still knew of much that was 'miraculous', Thucydides 'placed value on the fact that he tried to investigate events as

---

[163] Ranke 1881, 1.2, 3. [164] Ibid. [165] Ibid. [166] Ibid. 44. [167] Ibid. 45–6.

they occurred';[168] for 'history' delimited 'in human terms' had as one of its 'immanent conditions . . . that it seeks to seize, to understand and to make comprehensible human affairs as they are' and 'sticks to the simple facts';[169] the researcher's impartiality found in Thucydides thus became possible. In this sense Herodotus and Thucydides were for Ranke the 'two founders of all historical science and art'.[170]

Ranke thus described the core of his own turn to history as science.[171] This began through a religious impulse: repelled by Lutheran orthodoxy, which he had encountered during his Leipzig studies, he set out to seek the workings of God in history, and to do God's work in historical research. Ranke's conception of objectivity, his radical source criticism, his strictly empirical approach: all these derived from this decisive foundation. What Ranke intended was nothing other than a religious justification of modern historical science. As far as metaphysics were concerned, they were wrapped up with the new logic of research to which Ranke was committed. It is clear that the Thucydides of the *Weltgeschichte* took a turn comparable to that of Ranke. It would be too simple to suggest that Ranke simply transferred his concerns onto Thucydides. One may rather suspect that to a certain degree the opposite holds true: that the young Ranke learnt from the Greek historian, who was present to him as no other ancient or modern author. It has long been recognised that one of Ranke's best-known methodological statements – 'say, how it actually was'[172] – was borrowed directly from Thucydides;[173] the quotations from the *Weltgeschichte* above also suggests this connection.

In the *Weltgeschichte* Ranke acknowledged the human significance of the Greek 'spirit' from a further perspective: that it dealt not with 'rules and dogma' but with problems which time and again had to be solved anew. The same applied to the 'two founders of all historical science and art'. In the movement from Herodotus to Thucydides a transformation from ahistorical transcendence to historical immanence had taken place, but entirely under its own conditions and in its own specific form. Ranke endeavoured to describe this specific situation precisely, as well as the strangeness which one must sense in it in the present. This strangeness related especially to the speeches in Thucydides, which presented 'the internal differences' of the Greek world 'with a reasonable degree of truth' but nevertheless were far 'from the ground of exact truth'; Ranke made a connection

---

[168] Ibid. 47–8.   [169] Ibid.   [170] Ibid. 37.
[171] Cf. Muhlack 2006b: 34ff. Ranke's autobiographical writings in Ranke 1890: 3ff.; cf. also Ranke 1888b: 585ff. The correspondence of the young Ranke can now be found in Ranke 2007.
[172] Ranke 1824: vi.   [173] Thucydides 2.48.3; see Repgen 1988.

to rhetoric which also made it comprehensible for him that exactly this aspect 'constituted the character of ancient historiography'.[174] So it related to the special nature of the Thucydidean situation that it encouraged the 'literarisation' of historical writing, which went against the scientific bent of history. In any case other approaches and means were required in the completely different present in order to bring about historical immanence.

Here too Ranke's background supplied a motive. Along with Lutheran orthodoxy, the emerging historian with typical intensity opposed the unbroken classicising veneration of antiquity. The historicisation of antiquity which was one of the consequences of modern historical thought became for him the prime example for the 'world as history', and he tested it initially in the context of the ancient authors with which he was familiar. In a letter of May 1823 he set out a formal programme for the correct reading of ancient writers: one must 'read the ancients in such a way as they read one another'; one should never see 'a work as a genre', 'to which we could attach our own battalion, but as a true individual with its own roots, breath, nature, its own existence'.[175] Such a work then loses 'its apparent instructiveness', 'for it no longer teaches how one should tackle a thing', 'but it gains a true spiritual educational value'. [176] The Greek and Roman authors were here no longer 'exempla' for literary genres which served as models for later writers, but offered instead individual products which should spur later writers to further individual production. On what classical writer could Ranke form such insights other than Thucydides, with whom he had been familiar for so long? At any rate it sounds plausible, when in an autobiographical text of 1863 he describes his Leipzig reading of Thucydides from this perspective: 'a great, powerful spirit, before whom I bowed, without coming close to him through attempts at translation . . . The impression of the original, the greatest possible understanding of it was everything that I desired'.[177] Thucydides had a direct effect on Ranke through his originality, which could be grasped only through historical interpretation; one could not imitate it, but must train oneself in one's own originality. Similarly Ranke commented in an autobiographical text of 1869 about his first encounter with Herodotus: a 'textbook of historical knowledge' which at the same time was not to be removed from its historical context.[178]

[174] Ranke 1881.1.2, 51–2.   [175] Cf. Muhlack 2006b: 34ff.   [176] Ranke 2007: 356.
[177] Ranke 1890: 30–1.   [178] Ibid. 39.

Ranke formulated this view in its sharpest form in the lectures which he gave in the autumn of 1854 in Berchtesgarden before King Maximilian II of Bavaria, published posthumously under the title *Ueber die Epochen der neueren Geschichte*.[179] Remarks on the concept of historical progress gave him the opportunity. He denied the teleological concept of progress of idealistic philosophy of history; progress in history was only conceivable as a 'sequence' of different epochs, never attaining an external goal, each of which was 'immediate to God';[180] 'absolute progress' in the old sense seemed to him acceptable only 'in the area of material interest'.[181] As evidence against the idealistic conception of progress he cited ancient historians: 'The real greats are unsurpassable, and people like Thucydides and Tacitus are unsurpassable;' 'our ambition can only go so far as to develop independently something similar, but never to surpass them'.[182] 'People like Thucydides and Tacitus' could not be surpassed because they belonged to a specific context which was now gone for ever; but one could in the present through a new achievement, appropriate to the time, become unsurpassable in turn. Ranke was sufficiently self-confident to claim such an achievement for himself. Only a few pages later he added: 'No one can have the pretention to be a greater historian than Thucydides. However, I have the pretention to achieve in history something different from the ancients.'[183] The greatest historian of antiquity inspired the greatest historian of the present: that was the comparison which Ranke drew between Thucydides and himself.

With this full-blown historicisation of the two Greek historians Ranke introduced an unprecedented element into the discussion. All the authors considered above had, however much they understood Herodotus and Thucydides as historical figures, still retained some spark of normative valuation. Anyone who, like Creuzer, Niebuhr, Gervinus and Roscher, held fast to the standards of 'history as art' remained wedded to long-revered generic rules which prescribed how history was to be written. Not even Heeren, who measured both authors only by the criteria of modern historical science, was free from normative implications; he saw in Herodotus, Thucydides and Xenophon 'all the main forms of history... developed', and thereby gave these authors a paradigmatic significance.[184] The same is true of Droysen, who repeatedly cited Herodotus and Thucydides as examples for the epistemological procedures of modern historical science and distinguished himself from the great Greek historians solely on the

---

[179] See n.1.   [180] Ranke 1971: 60 and 62.   [181] Ibid. 68.   [182] Ibid. 69.
[183] Ibid. 82.   [184] Heeren 1826: 393.

basis of a higher level of consciousness or reflexivity. Ranke took the final step. The 'two founders of all historical science and art' became for him the protagonists of a problem which they had solved for their time in an inimitable manner, and each new era had to solve in its own manner. Normative and historical judgements here collapsed completely. The debate amongst German historians of the nineteenth century over Herodotus and Thucydides thus came to its logical conclusion.

Translated by Neville Morley

CHAPTER 9

Monumentality and the meaning of the past in ancient and modern historiography

Neville Morley

THEORIES OF THE MONUMENTAL[1]

History belongs to the living man in three respects; it belongs to him as one who acts and strives, as one who preserves and honours, and as one who suffers and needs liberation. This trinity of relationships corresponds to a trinity of kinds of history.[2]

Friedrich Nietzsche's essay 'On the uses and disadvantages of history for life' is one of the few extended discussions of the nature and significance of a desire for the past and of the motives that drive the production and consumption of history.[3] In contrast to the prevailing mid-nineteenth-century German view, which saw the acquisition of historical knowledge as an end in itself, he focused on the psychology of the individual historian and of the whole modern age in which 'we all suffer from a consuming historical fever'.[4] In place of a simplistic and self-aggrandising distinction between the misconceived or inadequate historiography of the past and the increasing perfection and objectivity of modern scientific history, he outlined at the beginning of the essay three different species of history, in which, in different ways, the pursuit of the past served other needs than the search for pure knowledge – whether or not this was acknowledged by the historian or the reader. The first of these is the 'monumental'.

History belongs above all to the man of deeds and power, to the man who fights a great fight, who needs models, teachers, comforters and cannot find them among his contemporaries or in the present.[5]

Consciousness of and concern with the past is, Nietzsche argued, an integral part of being human: having some sense of living in the present,

---

[1] I am especially grateful to Aleka Lianeri for her perceptive and helpful comments on an earlier draft of this paper.
[2] Nietzsche 1874: 258.
[3] For general introductions to Nietzsche's account of historiography see Stern 1983 and Breazeale 1997; and Strong 2000: 31–5.
[4] Nietzsche 1874: 246.   [5] Ibid. 258.

distinguished from the past and future, rather than in the endless 'now' of the animal. As a consequence, all three of his species of history derive directly from the particular relation of an individual to his or her present. The turn to a monumental history is inspired by a sense of the deficiencies of the present and its inhabitants, its lack of inspirational models or heroic deeds. Nietzsche wrote sympathetically of the desire to look backwards in order to move forwards, to avoid resignation to the apparent limitations and trivialities of the present by drawing upon the examples of the past.

That the great moments in the struggle of the individual form a chain, that in it a mountain-range of humanity is bound together through the millennia, that for me the highest point of one of those long-past moments may be still living, light and great – that is the basic thought in the belief in humanity which pronounces itself in the demand for a *monumental* history.[6]

Throughout the essay, Nietzsche's concern is not only with the motives that drive the creation of a particular conception of the past but with the efficacy of that conception, its capacity for serving the cause of life – in the case of monumental history, its ability to innoculate the reader against despair and resignation and keep him on towards his goal, even if there is little hope of reward.

Of what use to the man of the present is the monumental contemplation of the past, the preoccupation with the classics and the rarities of earlier times? He takes from it that the greatness which once existed was at any rate once *possible* and therefore will certainly be possible once again; he goes on his way with greater courage, for now the doubt which attacked him in his weaker moments, whether he was not perhaps wishing for the impossible, is driven from the field.[7]

Monumental history thus serves life, and expands the sense of what humans are capable of – even in the face of the apparently implacable and inescapable present, dominated by mediocrity and frustration.[8]

Characteristically, however, Nietzsche was equally alive to the less positive qualities of such a history, not least the way that a fragmented, inconsistent and frequently unheroic past must be made tractable and rewritten in order to serve a monumental function.

How much difference must, if the past is to have that strengthening effect, be overlooked, how violently must the individuality of the past be forced into a common mould and all its sharp corners and outlines broken into pieces in favour of conformity![9]

[6] Ibid. 259.   [7] Ibid.   [8] Cf. Morley 2009: 74–8.   [9] 1874: 261.

Where it suited him, Nietzsche was happy to offer the same sort of critique of a monumental approach as might be presented by a more conventional historian: it is clear that the past can be presented in monumental terms only through a mighty work of selection, distortion and omission.

As long as the soul of historical writing lies in the great *impetus* which a powerful man takes out of it, as long as the past must be described as worthy of imitation, as imitable and possible for a second time, it is in danger of becoming somewhat changed, turned into something beautiful and thereby brought near to free invention... If the monumental conception to the past rules over the other kinds of conception, I mean the antiquarian and the critical, then the past itself suffers *damage*: whole great parts of it are forgotten, held in contempt and flow away like a grey uninterrupted flood.[10]

However, unlike contemporary historians, Nietzsche did not believe in the possibility of establishing a single objective account of the past; the choice, in his view, is not between a partial account driven and distorted by present concerns and desires and a true history, but only ever between equally partial accounts, each one driven and distorted in different ways.[11] His critique of monumental history is therefore founded not on its departures from scholarly accuracy and the presence of distortions and omissions, but on the particular nature of those distortions and their consequences.

Always it will approximate, generalise and endlessly treat the dissimilar as similar, always it will diminish the differences of motives and causes, in order at the expense of the *causae* to establish the monumental *effectus* – that is to say exemplary and worthy of imitation.[12]

This misconception of the past can lead individuals into foolish actions, deceived by apparent analogies between past and present: 'it stimulates with seductive similarities the courageous to foolhardiness, the inspired to fanaticism'.[13] It can lead people to pursue the wrong goals, concentrating too much on past greatness and losing sight of the present needs which the turn to the past was supposed to meet: 'Their path will be lost, their air will be darkened, if one dances around a half-understood monument of some great past like an obsequious idol-worshipper.'[14] Above all, monumental history obscures the differences between past and present, whereas for Nietzsche it is precisely the otherness of the past that gives it efficacy as a counterweight to the present.[15]

---

[10] Ibid. 262.   [11] Porter 2000: 225–88.   [12] 1874: 262.   [13] Ibid.   [14] Ibid. 263.
[15] Morley 2009: 131–4, 144–5.

For I do not know what meaning classical studies would have in our time if not that of working in their untimeliness – that is to say, against our time and thereby on our time and, let us hope, for the benefit of a time to come.[16]

The whole of Nietzsche's essay has a complicated and problematic relationship to the actual practice of historiography. The discussion, as well as moving – without always clearly signalling the shifts – between *Geschichte* (history) and *Vergangenheit* (past), shifts between more or less universalising statements (human beings' relation to the past, present and future) and the specific diagnosis of nineteenth-century culture. The analysis of the different complexes of desire for the past is equally relevant to understanding the production of historiography and its consumption, and does not make any distinction between them – even when this might have been helpful. It does not offer detailed discussions of individual works of history – the only writers considered at any length are a philospher, Hartmann, and a dramatist, Grillparzer – but seems rather to work on the principle of *de te fabula narratur*; Nietzsche made bold assertions about the nature and failings of historiography in the confident expectation that readers would recognise these tendencies from historical works with which they were already familiar and carry out their own critiques using the same categories of analysis. This indirect approach makes it hard to be certain whether we should expect always to be able to classify an individual historical work or historian as monumental, antiquarian or critical, as implied by phrases like 'a trinity of kinds of history',[17] or whether these different kinds of knowledge about the past, corresponding to different needs and desires, may be found combined in different quantities in the same individual or the same work – that is, whether we should direct our attention towards 'monumental history' as a distinct sub-genre, or rather towards 'the monumental theme within historiography'.

If Nietzsche intended the former, then his choice of category seems distinctly untimely. His other two labels are less clearly problematic. By the middle of the nineteenth century, 'antiquarian' was increasingly deployed by historians as an insult, denoting the wrong sort of history, that which favoured the accumulation and cataloguing of data as end in itself. Nietzsche's use of the term was unusual for the time because he emphasised the positive aspects of antiquarianism, if not taken to excess, but it worked as a label because there continued to be works that might, fairly or unfairly, be labelled antiquarian. Conversely, the label of 'critical history' would be

---

[16] Nietzsche 1874: 247.   [17] Ibid. 258.

widely accepted as approbation by most if not all contemporary practitioners – if not in the form of Nietzsche's provocative interpretation of it as a
call for moral judgement in opposition to the 'wie es eigentlich gewesen'
of the historicists – and certainly, along with 'antiquarian', it offered a
workable tool for categorising historical works. The term 'monumental',
however, seems to have only limited purchase on contemporary historiography, referring instead to the works of earlier eras – the heroic histories
of the rise of the Roman people, for example, or the already discredited
philosophical history of Hegel – or, perhaps, to less scholarly and more
popular endeavours.

   By the date of Nietzsche's essay, the word 'Denkmal' and its cognates,
like 'monument' in English, were increasingly applied only to physical
objects of an imposing size and symbolic resonance – tombs, statues,
buildings and the like – whereas in earlier usage the terms could be used for
surviving written texts, including historical accounts.[18] Latin phrases like
'monumenta rerum gestarum' (Cic. Or. 1.46.201) were echoed in the titles
of collections of source material like the Monumenta Germaniae Historica,
begun in 1826; the dictionary of the brothers Grimm, the first volume of
which appeared in 1854, quotes Kant on 'die Denkmalen der Geschichte'
to demonstrate the validity of this usage. The progressive restriction of
the term, its displacement in historiographical discourse by the idea of
the 'document' and the implications of this change of terminology for
historical practice, a process studied by Jacques Le Goff among others, is
of great interest in itself.[19] It does tend to reinforce the impression that
Nietzsche was, in his choice of term, 'untimely', or at any rate belated –
intentionally or not. From this point on, references to a work of history
as a 'monument' were usually metaphorical – and what was seen to be
commemorated was most often the historian's own labours.

   By the turn of the century, Alois Riegl's classic study of Der Moderne
Denkmalkultus, the founding text for twentieth-century understanding
of monuments, shows no awareness that Denkmal might refer to anything other than imposing physical objects.[20] Riegl's analysis exhibits no
obvious debt to Nietzsche's essay, although they had a common concern
with the psychological foundations of the turn to the past. While Riegl
distinguished between 'deliberate' and 'unintentional' monuments, those
constructed with the express aim 'of keeping single human deeds or events
(or a combination thereof) alive in the minds of future generations' and
those objects which are ascribed such a role by posterity, he emphasised

---

[18] Le Goff 1978.   [19] Ibid.   [20] Riegl 1982; discussed by Choay 2001.

that in both cases the judgement and the need for the past of the modern viewer is paramount in giving the monument a living power.[21] He went on to discuss the changing bases of the valuation of monuments, from the sense of a direct political or genetic connection prevalent in pre-industrial societies (so that a monument survived only as long as those for whom it was erected retained an interest in its preservation) to the 'historical value' of the nineteenth century (valuing objects because of their place in a narrative of historical development) and then what he predicted as the dominant approach of the twentieth century, age-value, the monument as the marker of the past, entirely separate from the present. Like Nietzsche, he sought to understand the source of modernity's obsessive concern with (certain aspects of) the past in terms of ideas of value, need and desire, and to consider it in a broader context of conceptions of time, change and history.

A third theoretical engagement with the idea of the monument came another sixty years later in Michel Foucault's *The Archaeology of Knowledge*, where he sought to characterise shifts in the practice of historiography, and above all the rise of the *Annales* school and his own approach, through the contrast between 'document' and 'monument'.

> Let us say that history, in its traditional form, undertook to 'memorize' the *monuments* of the past, transform them into *documents*, and lend speech to those traces which, in themselves, are often not verbal, or which say in silence something other than what they actually say; in our time, history is that which transforms *documents* into *monuments*.[22]

Foucault's focus, like that of commentators on his work, was on the changing status and valuation of the document; the monument features in the discussion as a foil, as in his characterisation of archaeology as a non-interpretative discipline because of its concentration on discourse not as document but as monument.[23] The document is a sign of something else; the monument speaks for and of itself, or simply *is* without speaking. The shift which Foucault identified in modern historiography is partly a matter of a change in the historian's choice of materials, from canonical literary texts and imposing buildings to archives, fragments and material evidence. More importantly, however, it represents a change in the valuation and conception of those materials and the idea of the historian's task: from the reconstruction of a chronological narrative on the basis of surviving histories and other texts – monuments into documents – to the reconstruction of the structures, both physical and mental, that shaped the life of the past.

[21] Riegl 1982: 21–3.   [22] Foucault 1989: 7–8.   [23] Ibid. 155.

Discourse, for Foucault, is a monument, to be treated in its own terms rather than as a sign for something else; the document, meanwhile, is no longer a mere vehicle for history as a kind of memory, a retelling of the heroic deeds of the past, but is important in itself as a means to establishing a critical and self-conscious perspective on historical change.

Foucault's characterisation is applied to historiography as a whole, distinguishing simply (if not crudely) between the various strands of French structuralism since the 1930s and everything else; it contrasts with Nietzsche's wish to identify different tendencies within the historiography of any era. Although Nietzsche is cited in general terms in *The Archaeology of Knowledge*, there is no obvious sign that Foucault engaged directly with his concept of the monumental in this discussion. As with Riegl, we seem to be dealing with an entirely self-contained discourse, which overlaps with other theoretical approaches only because they are drawing on the same general concept and its common range of reference within similar cultural contexts. Foucault defined the monument against the document, Riegl against other sorts of constructions and objects, Nietzsche against other approaches to the past; they offered quite different chronological frameworks for understanding the process of change relevant to their object of study. However, their arguments have a common concern with temporality, the nature of the relation between past, present and future, and the potential meanings of the past for the present; they all, with varying degrees of explicitness, relate these issues to broader questions of power. It may then be no coincidence that each chose to address these issues through the powerful but problematic concept of monumentality, as the, or a, characteristic modern form of interaction with and complex of desire for the past.

What constitutes monumentality in historiography? I want to suggest, on the basis of the ideas developed by these three writers, that it consists of three separate but interdependent aspects. (i) The past is conceived in terms of greatness; or rather, what is considered important and worthy of the historian's attention in the past are the great events and, commonly, great individuals. (ii) This great past is conceived as having a direct relevance to the present and for the future; the proper task of the historian is thus to ensure that it is not forgotten but brought to the attention and kept in the mind of the present. (iii) This commemoration is carried out not as an end in itself but in order to have an effect on the present and future. These three aspects influence and reinforce one another; thus the need for inspiration and heroic *exempla* shapes the view of the past (compare debates about what sort of history should be taught in schools to inculcate a proper sense of national identity), while a historical account organised around great deeds gives rise to the sense that these ought to be emulated, both of these lines of thought resting on an assumed connection between past and present.

Monumentality in these terms is always a possibility within historiography. Books can be and have been written with the more or less explicit intention of monumentalising the past, usually the national past, but more commonly the monumental is a tendency that can be identified within a historical work of broader scope, and the issues it raises – the selection of material, the relation between past and present, the purpose of historiography – have to be addressed by anyone venturing to write history. Each of its three aspects, however banal they may seem when stated in this manner, can be seen as problematic, but it is their combination that arouses the greatest anxiety. Monumental history is invariably engaged in a struggle over the past and its influence on the present and future: what is monumentalised, for whose benefit and with what consequences?

THE MONUMENTAL IN ANCIENT AND MODERN HISTORIOGRAPHY

Monumentality may be encountered in the historiography of any era, but it is interpreted and valued differently at different periods; sometimes taken more or less for granted as the proper task of all historiography, sometimes fervently condemned as the mythologising antithesis of true, scientific, history. The dominant tone in classical antiquity regarding the proper subject matter of history was set by Herodotus; echoing the Homeric emphasis on *kleos*, fame or renown, he described his task as ensuring that events might not be forgotten and that the great and wonderful deeds (*erga*) of both Greeks and barbarians might not become unrenowned (1.1).[24] This matches exactly the first aspect of monumentality described above. His successor Thucydides emphasised his intention to establish and investigate the facts of events, rather than to praise men's deeds, and it must certainly be conceded that his account includes numerous incidents which would not be considered worthy of imitation; nevertheless, 'greatness' defines his choice of subject matter – the belief that the Peloponnesian war would be *megan* and *axiologōtaton*, great and most worthy of notice (1.1) – and he expended considerable effort at the beginning of his first book in showing how previous events paled in comparison to those he was about to describe. As the genres of classical historiography developed, 'history' was explicitly conceived as the narration of deeds, *praxeis* or *res*

---

[24] See generally Immerwahr 1960.

gestae, whether of individual wars or of the political and military life of a region.[25] This was the model taken up by the Roman annalists and their successors, as the history of a single city increasingly became the history of the whole (Mediterranean) world.[26] Other forms of 'historical writing' dealt with different subject material like local tradition or ethnography; 'history', when defined strictly, was directly concerned with the actions of individuals – inevitably in most cases the leading individuals of the time – in politics, diplomacy, war and law.[27] As Livy put it in his preface, 'it will be a satisfaction to me to have done as much as lies within me to commemorate the deeds of the foremost people of the world' (*Pr.* 3).

It is only comparatively recently that this conception of the historian's task has been challenged. In the eighteenth and nineteenth centuries there was some dispute, organised around the comparison of Herodotus and Thucydides as possible models, as to whether historiography should aspire to encompass all aspects of life, including subjects that might be labelled 'geography' or 'ethnography', or should focus on the traditional subject matter of war and politics.[28] This debate was decided for at least several generations in favour of the latter approach as a result of the preference for Thucydides amongst both the German historicists and the British historians; at the same time, the study of economy, society, ethnography and geography developed in different directions, and increasingly became institutionalised in separate disciplines.[29] It was only from the beginning of the twentieth century in Britain and elsewhere that proponents of economic and social history were able effectively to question the way that history's remit was conceived, followed by the *Annales* school's polemic against the traditional fixation of historians on the deeds of the mighty.[30] One key criticism of traditional monumental history is that its view of what is significant in the past is narrow and politically suspect. Arguably, of course, these new approaches simply set up an alternative conception of what is *axiologon* and so should command the historian's attention. It is perfectly possible to imagine a history of, say, the relationship between humanity and its environment that is analogous, in its underlying assumptions about the proper relation between past and present, to a more traditional account of the activities of 'world-historical' individuals.[31] Such a history would

---

[25] Fornara 1983: 1–2, 29–46.   [26] Wiseman 1994.   [27] Fornara 1983: 2–3.
[28] Burke 1988; Muhlack (this volume).
[29] Hodgson 2001. Compare the fate of the 'German Historical School' of economics, marginalised by both economics and history: Grimmer-Solem 2003.
[30] Kadish 1989; Burke 1990.
[31] Indeed, Hughes 1994 comes close to such an approach.

engage with quite different subject matter, in support of an entirely different political agenda, it would need to establish its own criteria of significance rather than being able to draw upon a shared conception of the national past, but nevertheless it could fairly be said to be pursuing the same task of monumentalising certain aspects of the past. Monumental history is not defined solely through its principles of selection of material but also through its purpose and its conception of historical change.

The task of monumental history is to bring the past into the present for the sake of the future; it depends on the assumption that there is a direct connection of some kind between these different temporalities. This was taken almost entirely for granted in antiquity; Thucydides' explanation of the usefulness of the understanding to be gained from reading his history, that, human nature being what it is, the events he describes will recur in a similar form in the future (1.22), is paradigmatic. Most histories directly addressed the past of the society of their audience, or developments that impinged on the course of that past (such as Herodotus' account of Persia or Polybius' of the rise of Rome). In so far as any fundamental discontinuity is identified in the past, it is between those periods which are accessible to proper historical knowledge and interpretation and those which might, arguably, be consigned instead to the world of myth – not necessarily less relevant or qualitatively different in themselves, but less knowable.[32] What is missing is any sense that parts of the known past of a society might somehow be separated from the present by more than the passage of time, that the past might become 'other' as a result of historical change. On the contrary, the attraction of historical *exempla* for Augustan Rome was that they tied a society that had indeed undergone dramatic political and social changes back into a longer tradition, simultaneously drawing upon and restoring a sense of continuity.[33] This can be interpreted sceptically, as the cynical attempt of a revolutionary regime to establish its legitimacy through the manipulation of the past, but such an attempt could scarcely have succeeded if there had not been a general belief in the continuing relevance and likeness of the past to the present and future.[34] Even if not all the historiography of classical antiquity was monumental, therefore, it had the capacity to be so. This attitude continued into the Renaissance; Machiavelli mocked those who claimed it was impossible to draw useful lessons from Livy 'as if the sky, the sun, the elements, men, were changed in motion, arrangement and power from what they were in antiquity'.[35]

---

[32] Cartledge 2002: 18–35.   [33] Chaplin 2000: 202.   [34] Gowing 2005: 22–3.
[35] Machiavelli 1989: 191.

The emergence of modernity as a way of conceiving of the present brought about a fundamental break in this tradition, with the development of a sense of a rupture between past and present: while the natural world was assumed to remain essentially unalterable, both humans and their social institutions were seen to be radically different at different periods. The nature of the difference between past and present, and its causes, were conceived in many different ways, depending on whether one turned one's attention to politics, society, the economy, culture, morality or value; however, what all theories of modernity have in common is the conviction that modernity exists and that this explains our present state, not least our estrangement from the past.[36] The *Manifesto of the Communist Party* offers the most eloquent evocation of modernity's unprecedented power:

[The bourgeoisie] has been the first to show what man's activity can bring about. It has accomplished marvels wholly different from Egyptian pyramids, Roman aqueducts and Gothic cathedrals . . . The ongoing revolutionising of production, the constant unsettling of all social conditions, the eternal uncertainty and agitation mark out the epoch of the bourgeoisie from all earlier ones. All firm, rusted-shut relations with their entourage of time-honoured ideas and opinions are dissolved, all new-formed ones become antiquated before they can ossify. Everything solid and permanent evaporates, everything holy is desecrated, and men's eyes are finally opened to the conditions in which they live and their relations with one another.[37]

Marx's account emphasises both modernity's casual surpassing of the great monuments of the past in terms of scale and spectacle, and its complete failure to do so in terms of longevity and significance – modernity's monuments are ephemeral and basically vulgar, and their promise of a better future remains unfulfilled.[38] The contrast between past and present is not always in modernity's favour, with many commentators experiencing a deep nostalgia for what has been lost in the transition; but the sense of the past as different and distant, and the conception of historical development in terms of a fundamental discontinuity, is common to the cheerleaders and critics of modernity alike. As Reinhard Koselleck has put it, the ever-widening gap between the space of experience and the horizon of expectation, the sense that the present is unlike the past and the future will be unlike the present, spelt the death of exemplarity and *historia magistra vitae*.[39]

The advent of a sense of modernity did not, however, automatically bring an end to the possibility of monumental history; it simply increased

---

[36] Morley 2009.   [37] Marx and Engels 1964: 465.   [38] Berman 1983.
[39] Koselleck 2004c: 26–42.

the work involved in constructing an effective one, in order to demonstrate what could previously be taken for granted, the relevance of the past (or certain aspects of it) to the present. In the face of the economic, political and social transformation perceived to have divided modernity from all that went before, it was necessary to identify higher, deeper or more abstract continuities. One might, for example, posit the existence of a national identity or spirit that transcends historical change, so that the struggles of Arminius (or Hermann) against the Romans or of Arthur against the Saxons can be claimed as the birth of German or British nationhood and hence of enduring relevance to those nations.[40] One might alternatively identify an aesthetic principle such as the 'classical' as the source of all true artistic production; the study of its origins, in the period which had also produced its finest examples, then becomes a vital task in order to rescue the moribund art of the present or to diagnose its deficiencies.[41] It scarcely needs to be noted that such procedures involved quite as much imaginative projection of anachronistic assumptions into the past as Livy's interpretation of early Rome or Machiavelli's readings of Livy. Both Marx, especially in the essay *The 18th Brumaire of Louis Bonaparte*, and Nietzsche offered searching critiques of modern self-serving historical narratives which enshrined the present as the culmination of world-historical development and which 'deceived through analogies'. However, both were also conscious of the desperate need for roots and precedents in a society that appeared to have severed all links with the past. Modernity becomes the era of the historical monument, as Riegl argued, not in spite of the new sense of difference between past and present, but precisely in response to it.[42]

This brings us to the third aspect of monumentality, which is suggested by the range of meanings of the verb *moneo*: to bring to mind, to admonish, advise, warn, instruct and teach. The monument is not intended to be a merely passive memorial; it seeks 'to preserve a moment in the consciousness of later generations', proclaiming its immortality and eternal relevance, in order to influence those generations.[43] Monumental history does not seek to recover and preserve the past as an end in itself – that, in Nietzsche's terms, is antiquarianism – but in order to have an effect on the present and hence the future. The monumental should inspire, overawe, encourage; arouse emotion, even change people. The contemplation of the monumental history of classical art, for example, is intended to spark inspiration in the present:

---

[40] Cf. Todd 1992: 256–68; Cantor 1993: 79–117; Bryden 2005.
[41] Cf. Müller 1972; Nisbet 1985; Potts 1994.   [42] Riegl 1982: 28–9.   [43] Riegl 1982: 38.

May some charitable deity snatch the infant from his mother's breast, nourish him
with the milk of a better age and let him ripen to maturity under a distant Grecian
sky. When he has then become a man, he returns, an alien figure, to his own
century; but not to gladden it by its appearance, but, terrifying as Agamemnon's
son, to cleanse it. He will indeed take his material from the present, but borrow
his artistic forms from a nobler time, indeed from beyond all time . . . [44]

The monumental history of the nation, like the historical monument or the
war memorial, is intended to establish a template for future action, inspiring
emulation of the heroes of the mother country in deeds or demeanour. By
evoking (or creating) a living memory, it aims not merely to inform but to
mobilise, arouse and engage.[45]

   This is the stated intention of much classical historiography, especially
in the Roman tradition: the past is preserved and represented precisely
in order to affect the present through the reactions of the audience. The
Roman view of *historia* is that it is the author's task to give the past meaning:
not only what should be remembered but how it should be remembered.[46]

What chiefly makes the study of history wholesome and profitable is this, that
you behold the lessons of every kind of experience set forth as on a conspicuous
monument; from this you may choose for yourself and for your own state what
to imitate, from this mark for avoidance what is shameful in the conception or
shameful in the result.[47]

Literary records are often explicitly compared with physical monuments,
with the claim that they will have greater longevity – Horace claimed that
poetry was a far better monument than bronze or the pyramids (*Odes*
3.30.1–2) – but a similar effect, preserving the memory and maintaining
its efficacy.[48] Monuments, whether physical or textual, serve as a prompt
for the collective memory of the community, which should then be acted
upon; Livy presents his work as a contribution to the healing of the state
by reconnecting Augustan Rome with the traditions that used to inspire
the actions of its citizens.[49] However, this is not simply a matter of providing useful lessons; the historian was expected to exert an influence on
the audience's emotions.[50] Cicero, for example, remarked approvingly that
a history focused on the actions of leading individuals could produce sus-
pense, delight, annoyance, fear and hope.[51] Dionysius of Halicarnassus
criticised early historians who lacked the rhetorical skill to produce 'emotion arousing the mind', and praised Thucydides for his ability to disturb,

[44] Schiller 1965: Letter 9.4.   [45] Cf. Choay 2001: 6–8.   [46] Gowing 2005: 10.
[47] Livy, Preface 10.   [48] Habinek 1998: 10–11; Fowler 2000.   [49] Feldherr 1998: 7–12.
[50] Woodman 1988.   [51] *Fam.* 5.12.5.

terrify and arouse emotion.[52] Obviously this was not done gratuitously, for merely literary effect, but precisely in order to convey a sense of past events and, as Diodorus Siculus put it, to ensure their 'eternal transmission to posterity' (2.5) and their continuing power – in other words, to serve as a monument to the past.

There was, however, also a dissenting tradition in antiquity. Thucydides expressly contrasted his own enterprise with accounts that were constructed primarily to produce an immediate effect on their audience; his version of events may be less easy to read, but it offers an accurate account of events that will be more useful in the future (1.21–2). This argument extends into a critique of the power of monuments to create false impressions of the past and hence give rise to wrong decisions and actions. Whereas Herodotus had taken physical remains such as the tomb of Alyattes at face value as a reliable measure of the greatness of their builders (1.93), Thucydides emphasised the unreliability of ruins in the case of Mycenae, whose great fame seemed to be put in question by its insignificance in the present, by imagining how the ruins of Sparta and Athens might be interpreted in future: the one would appear far inferior to its actual power, the other much greater than it actually was (1.10).[53] Individuals and states seek to manipulate their own reputations for posterity; their successors are always in danger of being misled by appearances and accepting at face value the image of greatness which the monument was intended to convey.

'People are inclined to accept all stories of the past in an uncritical way – even when those stories concern their own native land' (1.20). In questioning the story of the Athenian tyrannicides and replacing an account of heroic resistance to oppression with one of dubious motivation and accident – 'the wounded feeling of a lover . . . a momentary failure of nerve' (6.59) – Thucydides is not simply putting right a misapprehension about the past but undermining precisely the sort of monumental history that sustained the Athenian sense of identity.[54] It was, he suggests, their false 'memory' of these events that fostered the atmosphere of anger and suspicion in Athens after the mutilation of the Hermae, and led to the recall of Alcibiades from Sicily (6.60). Thucydides' approach to the past, based on autopsy and the critical interrogation of the most reliable evidence available, offered the only sure basis for decision-making; the task of the historian is then not to excite or manipulate his readers but simply to set out the events which occurred. Polybius followed in this anti-monumental tradition: the historian should record what really happened, however commonplace.

---

[52] *Thuc.* 23–4. [53] Immerwahr 1960; Marincola 1997: 101. [54] Cf. Loraux 1986a: 287–8.

While the tragedian should thrill and charm his audience, the historian should instruct and convince by the truth of the facts; his readers may be stirred by pity or anger, if he has properly examined the causes of events – but this is to be prompted by the events themselves, faithfully transmitted and explained, not by a history that uses the past as a means of arousing and manipulating emotion (2.56.10).

Thucydides' approach was not typical of classical historiography; his work became a 'classic' for reasons other than those he intended, simply slotted into the succession of historical narratives between Herodotus and Xenophon, and his methodological precepts were not widely adopted.[55] The perception of him as the most important classical historian is a modern invention, the product of debates about the historian's proper task that in part drew directly from his example and certainly cited him regularly as an inspiration. The rise of historicism and 'history as science' can be seen as a reaction against the more troubling aspects of monumental history along the lines that Thucydides identified. The antiquarian tradition, as Momigliano has argued, began with the sense that ancient accounts, shaped by the prejudices and biases of their authors, were not to be trusted unless corroborated by physical remains; bronze and marble were less subject to passion.[56] The *Aufklärers* and the historicists were still more suspicious of the way that the past sought to influence later judgements, and increasingly concentrated their attention on 'inadvertant' testimonies, above all archives, that offered (apparently) unmediated access to past events.[57] As Schlözer argued, 'I readily concede that many ideas about what constitutes great and noble have been created by the notion which the ancients had of their contemporaries and ancestors, but is not that very notion demonstrably illusory, deceptive and unhistorical?'[58] This sense of the power of a mythologising, monumental history to impose its version of the contested past onto the present, most often in the service of the most reactionary causes, gave urgency to the development of a scientific historiography that should persuade solely through the truth of its interpretation.

CONCLUSION

It was precisely at this moment that the 'monument' came to be associated solely with physical objects expressly designed to influence posterity, and thus pushed to the margin of the historian's interests. Such objects inspire

---

[55] Gabba 1981.   [56] Momigliano 1955c: 79–94.
[57] Reill 1975; Bödecker *et al.* 1986; Ricoeur 1988: 116–26.   [58] 1979: 41.

feelings of 'wonder and mystery', as Ranke suggested, but history begins only when credible written records exist to make monuments properly comprehensible.[59] Thucydides' accounts of the ruins of Mycenae and the Athenian tyrannicides, and above all his methodological statements at the beginning of Book 1, were cited regularly in support of this narrower, more rigorous approach to different kinds of evidence; so too his view of the usefulness of history, not as a source of *exempla* intended to inspire emulation but as a means to understanding the dynamics of politics and international relations.[60] Indeed, Thucydides' work became itself a monument of historiography, with its admirers insisting on its greatness, on its direct relevance to the present and on the need to revere and emulate its example. Wilhelm Roscher insisted on the transformative effect of reading the work in the correct spirit: 'someone whose reading of Thucydides has not charged his resolutions with new life – who looks to learn nothing more than so many grammatical rules or historical facts – he has read Thucydides in vain'.[61]

Ranke and his followers also echoed Thucydides in their disavowal of emotional or rhetorical effects; history was to be a science, persuading through the presentation of the facts, not a literary genre.[62] This led to precisely the sort of misreading of the past in order that it might serve present needs that Nietzsche had warned against. Ranke claimed of Thucydides, entirely without irony, that 'his account is free of all rhetoric; this alone may be the great triumph of the speeches'.[63] History dealt with the most pressing issues of human life – 'everything that concerns, threatens and inspires us seeks to be expressed in the study of history'[64] – but in a sober, considered manner; in a diary entry following a visit to Mme Tussaud's, Ranke noted that, compared with his own approach, 'for most of my colleagues history is also a chamber, not always of horrors but of stupidity and crime'.[65] Suspicion of the power of the monumental to naturalise subjective judgements and manipulate emotions led to an insistence on the need to exclude all modern influences on historical judgement and all rhetorical effects in the representation of the past; and it was from Thucydides, once again, that Ranke drew his oft-cited maxim to this effect, that the task of the historian was simply to show 'wie es eigentlich gewesen', how it really was.[66]

---

[59] Ranke 1881: iii–iv; generally, Le Goff 1978.
[60] Roscher 1842; generally, Muhlack, this volume.
[61] 1842: x–xi.   [62] Cf. Muhlack, this volume.   [63] Ranke 1881: 52.
[64] Quoted by Krieger 1977: 349.   [65] Quoted by Angermeier 1987: 409.
[66] Blanke 1991: 266; Ranke is drawing on Thucydides 2.48.

The continuing debate over this pronouncement – monumental in its wish to establish a subjective judgement as having eternal significance – shows how many questions remain.[67] The overtly monumental historiography of Hegel has long been discredited, even if, as Ricoeur has argued, we no longer recognise our reasons for not being Hegelian in the arguments of those who overthrew him.[68] However, a historiography that entirely lacked the qualities of the monumental – the sense of some connection between past and present, the sense that it is necessary to recollect the past in order to act for the future – would be entirely senseless. This is Nietzsche's argument, that humanity needs different kinds of knowledge of the past at different times; the risks inherent in a monumental approach are not grounds for rejecting it altogether, just as the risks of an excessively critical historiography are not grounds for abandoning all criticism. In any case, just as the disavowal of rhetoric is not the same as the absence of rhetoric – least of all in Thucydides – so the disavowal of effect in historiography does not produce an absence of effect. Even as monumental history is explicitly rejected in the name of objective science or a more radical political agenda, monumentality remains a constant possibility in all historiography; we need to recognise this tendency in ourselves as much as in the work of others. Historians need to accept responsibility for their role in the construction and reconstruction of monuments, for the political, ethical and psychological consequences of bringing the past into the present, and for their own desire for the past, as much as for their treatment of evidence.

[67] See e.g. Novick 1988.   [68] Cf. Ricoeur 1988: 202–3.

*Unfounding Time in and through
Ancient Historical Thought*

CHAPTER 10

Thucydides and social change:
Between akribeia and universality

Rosalind Thomas

When Aristotle in the *Poetics* tried to compare poetry and history, he famously declared that poetry was 'more philosophical and more serious than history' (φιλοσοφώτερον καὶ σπουδαιότερον ποίησις ἱστορίας ἐστίν), for poetry deals with the universal (τὰ καθόλου), history with the particular; and as he elaborated, universal means 'the kind of thing it suits someone to say or do κατὰ τὸ εἰκὸς ἢ τὸ ἀναγκαῖον (according to likelihood or necessity), the particular, what Alcibiades did or suffered' (*Poetics* 1451b3ff.).[1] Thucydides might have been surprised or disappointed by this. His hopes for the usefulness of his *History* and the degree of universality it would have, given human nature, imply a seriousness of purpose that goes far beyond merely relating what had happened. As M. Węcowski has recently noted, Thucydides' successors seemed unable to grasp his synthesis of 'wisdom' and 'history' for which Herodotus paved the way,[2] and Aristotle's reaction may not be untypical of later Greek readers of the fifth-century historians. By contrast his readers of the Renaissance and early modern period, most notably Thomas Hobbes, took Thucydides as a source of wisdom in politics, a crucial tool for the developing study of political science,[3] seizing upon the universality (to put it another way) of Thucydides' *History*.

What I would like to concentrate upon here is one aspect of Thucydides' 'universal history' (to misuse and re-apply the term universal history deliberately), and examine his universalising and almost theoretical treatment of certain key moments relating to social breakdown in the period covered by his *History*. A volume devoted to different conceptions of time,

---

[1] This paper has benefited a great deal from the comments of Kinch Hoekstra, Tim Rood and Michael Drolet, and the audience of the Swiss Classical Association to which a version was delivered in April 2008.

[2] Węcowski 2004: 162. See also Geuss 2005, ch. 13 on Bernard Williams and Thucydides.

[3] See, for instance, Kinch Hoekstra: paper given to Workshop on Thucydides and his Influence, November 2007, Oxford.

the construction of history and non-modern historicities is an appropriate opportunity to re-examine the way this master of the detailed, factual
and accurate political-military narrative produced virtuoso descriptions of
certain changes during the Peloponnesian war which seem to stand for all
time. His method is well recognised: that of taking one great moment or
period of transition and making it stand either for later similar examples
during the war, or for a process of change meant to apply throughout the
later periods covered by the *History*. This creates a type of 'exemplar' or
paradigm, a description which stands for other examples of similar events
or processes.[4] Thus many of the speeches have claims as 'possessions for
ever' (1.22.4), the antithetical Mytilenean debate or the Melian Dialogue
most obviously. This also raises the question of how Thucydides made
sense of his world and events within it in order to present a picture of what
he evidently thought was the clear truth to his audience.

There is a particularly powerful air of universality in the descriptions of
the Plague at Athens (2.47–54) and the stasis at Corcyra. As is well known,
the Plague account gives a devastating description of the physical symptoms
so that if it strikes again, 'one might, by having some advance knowledge,
not fail to recognize it' (2.48.3; trans. W. R. Connor), but ends with the
terrifying social effects, the breakdown of social mores that occurred in
Athens and that Thucydides claimed had long-lasting effects at Athens
(2.53.1).[5] The stasis episode in Corcyra (3.69ff.)[6] has a peculiar status: it is
'the first' episode of *stasis*[7] (factional strife), in the war, and it also serves as
the prototype, to use a modern expression, of all the ensuing episodes of
stasis during the war. Because it is the first it is in fact comparatively mild and
Thucydides gives us to understand that as competition and inventiveness
spread, later examples were still more extreme (3.82.1, 85.1). Yet with the
exception of the Athenian *stasis* in Book 8, the later *staseis* merit relatively
brief descriptions, for Corcyra stands for them all. The great universalising
analysis of the breakdown of social values and the change in men's mentality
that he gives for the Corcyrean participants of the fighting (particularly
3.81, and then 3.82–3) is meant to cover all *staseis* and the whole of the war.

---

[4] On this penchant for the virtuoso and paradigmatic piece, see trenchant remarks of Connor 1984:
149–51; de Romilly 1956.
[5] 2.53.1: πρῶτόν τε ἦρξε καὶ ἐς τἆλλα τῇ πόλει ἐπὶ πλέον ἀνομίας τὸ νόσημα ('Nor was this the
only form of lawless extravagance which owed its origin to the plague' (trans. Crawley)); lit. 'the
plague introduced'. Hornblower 1991–1996, 1: ad loc., 326 suggests tentatively that this is ambiguous
and not expressing absolute causation, but I am less sure.
[6] Note also the final phase at 4.47–8.
[7] 3.82.1, 'the first' rather than one of the first: as Hornblower 1991–1996, vol. 1, ad loc. translates, 'and
this seemed to be the worst of revolutions because it was the first'. Yet later ones were still worse, in
fact.

We note how the text slips seamlessly from the participants in Corcyra to the generalisations of the *stasis* model. We are supposed to think that the social and moral effects of the Plague were lasting and continuous at Athens, even though the ensuing narrative hardly shows a lasting neglect of the religious and social bases of Athenian society (nor does other Athenian evidence). Do we think that the Athenians really continued to disregard proper burial customs? Hardly, but the ensuing *anomia* or lawlessness Thucydides claims (2.53.1) is left ominously wide open. When Thucydides has reason to describe the occurrence of later *staseis* in the Peloponnesian war, he does not emphasise, or indeed even mention, the general social dislocation and alienation from customary and traditional values that he outlined with such magnificence in Book 3. Though there are dislocations of values in Thucydides' account of the rest of the Peloponnesian war, as Jonathan Price has recently emphasised,[8] nevertheless, the one *stasis* stands for all, and, one imagines, for all time.

It is instructive to reflect briefly just how far this lies in method and style from the ideal practices of modern historians, the accurate and impartial observation and interpretation of modern professional historiography. While the practice of using an exemplar is obviously not modern practice, Thucydides' text is so firmly a part of the classical tradition that classicists can have difficulty achieving distance, and consider it from the point of view of a historian trying to isolate, understand and describe profound and important social change. First, he treats *intense human suffering* in one large and single description and then says similar episodes occur repeatedly: for the Plague there is the main highly detailed description of the disease and its effect on Athenian society, but no similar treatment of its outbreaks elsewhere (as it did spread) nor of the further flare-ups in Athens. There is no quantification of each outbreak, no social analysis of where and how it progressed, just one superb description once and for all.[9]

Similarly with *stasis*, one might expect each outbreak to be fully chronicled; the fact that cruelty, brutality, cynicism, suffering and death on a large scale were to recur throughout the Greek world would hardly exempt the modern social historian from examining each example. There would be local variants to examine, prominent and lesser individuals, innumerable

---

[8] Price 2001, an excellent sustained treatment of Thucydides' view of *stasis*, which also argued that the whole Peloponnesian war is conceived as *stasis* by Thucydides. Other main treatments of the *stasis* section to which I am indebted include the important and extensive commentary in Gomme 1945–81: ad loc., Hornblower 1991–1996, I: 316ff.; Wassermann 1954; Loraux 1986b; Macleod 1983; Orwin 1988; Orwin 1994: 172–84.

[9] Further outbreaks: 3.87.

details, analyses of the social or political factors for each city or region with
the minutiae of political demands and disagreements.[10] Yet socio-economic
analysis is significantly absent in Thucydides.[11] To take one of the more
detailed examples of later *stasis* in Thucydides, that of Argos in 417, we are
briefly told that the people's party fell on the oligarchs; there is nothing on
local interests or conditions, but much on the involvement of the outside
powers of Sparta and Athens, the building of the long walls. Killings are
mentioned, but there is remarkably little on the internal Argive situation.[12]
For the *stasis* in Amphipolis which was to lead to Thucydides' disgrace as
a general, most attention is given to the mechanisms and ruse used by the
Spartan Brasidas, the betrayers in the city, and Thucydides' own status in
the region. For Corcyra, in contrast, which serves as the great paradigm,
we learned of the complicated details of the initial outbreak of revolution
(3.69), and the details of how it continued with impressive specificity and
detail for both sides, and the way the external powers interfered or affected
the revolution (70ff.); then the indiscriminate slaughter now conducted for
seven days by the Corcyreans, some to save the democracy, some merely
in pursuit of private hatreds (81.4). Then it becomes increasingly general,
culminating in the large-scale changes in mentality and behaviour across
the Greek world:

Death thus raged in every shape (πᾶσα τε ἰδέα κατέστη θανάτου); and, as usually
happens at such times, there was no length to which violence did not go; sons
were killed by their fathers, and suppliants dragged from the altar or slain upon it;
while some were even walled up in the temple of Dionysus and died there.

So bloody was the march of the revolution, and the impression which it made
was the greater as it was one of the first to occur. Later on, one may say, the
whole Hellenic world was convulsed; struggles being everywhere made by the
popular chiefs to bring in the Athenians, and by the oligarchs to introduce the
Lacedaimonians.(3.81.5–82.1, trans. R. Crawley)

There follows the general description of *stasis* (the so-called '*stasis* model'),
the analysis of the reasons for increasingly bloody *stasis*, the terrible sufferings of the whole of the Greek world (82.2: 'The sufferings which revolution
entailed upon the cities were many and terrible, such as have occurred and

---

[10] Price 2001, esp. ch. 1 notes Thucydides' neglect of the relationship of different parties, and local
factors in each city. I would differ from him in seeing this not so much as an erasing of the polis
context – surely Thucydides took this for granted – but more in terms of what Thucydides took to
be common ground and generalisable.

[11] I should stress that I will not be treating the actual socio-economic background to Greek *stasis*
(either).

[12] Thuc. 5.82–4, 6.61.3.

always will occur, as long as the nature of mankind remains the same; though in a severer or milder form and varying in their symptoms, according to the variety of the particular cases', trans. Crawley), culminating in the famous section on the erosion of all forms of moderation, the cruelty, brutality and every form of iniquity, and the changes of values and the connotations of words: 'And they exchanged their usual verbal evaluations of actions for new ones, in the light of what they thought justified; thus irrational daring was considered courage and loyalty to one's party' (82.4).[13] The neuter plurals give universality and perhaps an almost impersonal character to the process: καὶ ἐπέπεσε πολλὰ καὶ χαλεπὰ κατὰ στάσιν ταῖς πόλεσι, γιγνόμενα μὲν καὶ αἰεὶ ἐσόμενα, ἕως ἂν ἡ αὐτὴ φύσις ἀνθρώπων ᾖ.

The opening of the sentence quoted above, is more literally translated, 'And there fell upon the cities many and terrible things . . . such as occur and always will occur as long as human nature remains the same' (82.2).[14] As Macleod has noted on these neuters,[15] the merging of human beings and cities thus achieved gives the impression of all caught up in an impersonal and inevitable cycle of destruction. Similarly, 'Every kind of death' (81.5), 'Every kind of iniquity' (83.1).[16] The specific is drowned in the general and universalising truth, its pace not held up or interrupted by any explicit comparisons or examples. The terrifying picture may lead the reader to forget how often the bloodshed was caused more simply by Athenian imperial power (for even though the *stasis* was supposed to be triggered by the war, and indeed made worse, the universalising both of war and the *stasis* model may obscure the fact that the Athenian Empire had a hand). Indeed in this typically Thucydidean selection of Corcyra to stand for all *stasis* which is then generalised, it forces the reader to a picture of terrifyingly repeated devastation which, because it is presented without individual instances, implied a kind of blanket *stasis* over the whole Greek world (τὸ ἑλληνικόν, another neuter at 82.1, and again at 83.1). It is unclear whether neuter plurals might imply a law of nature or some kind of scientific accuracy. This practice seems quite the opposite of 'tragic *akribeia*', 'tragic

---

[13] Rather than 'the customary meanings of words changed': see Wilson 1982; Worthington 1982; also Hogan 1980. It's not that a phrase like 'irrational daring' came to mean something else entirely; rather, actions that used to be described as 'irrational daring' now became described as courageous and loyal. See Loraux 1986b, esp. 113–20 for a still more profound analysis – Thucydides had 'laid a trap' for the reader (113).

[14] Note also 3.82.3, 'ἐστασίαζέ τε οὖν τὰ τῶν πόλεων, καὶ τὰ ἐφυστερίζοντά που πύστει τῶν προγενομένων . . . ' (lit. 'the affairs of the cities were in stasis, and those that came later . . . ').

[15] Macleod 1983: 131–2. Note also, perhaps, the generalizing singular of 81.5, 'father killed son'.

[16] This seems to be a favourite phrase in Book 3. Note also 3.98.3, 'every form of flight and destruction'. See excellent comment on this phrase in Hornblower 1991–1996, vol. i: 173–5 on 1.109.1.

accuracy or precision', the phrase coined by Hornblower to express the way tiny and apparently passionless details might speak eloquently and tragically in the narrative.[17] Rather, alongside this *akribeia*, is a tragic universalism: no need to detail the kinds of death, just every kind of death.

We have no reason to question that Thucydides thought this general picture was a true one, but we may well wonder whether it was all based on the painstaking examination of witnesses and cross-checking of accounts that he claimed for his *History* (1.20–2), generally accepted as his distinctive method.[18] The corruption of morals, of values and the transvaluation of words as a result of *stasis* with which he ends (82–3) can hardly be the product of careful comparative research across the cities and revolutions of Greece, as J. Price has thought – but that, of course, is not the point. They are the writer's personal views on the effect of war and *stasis* and his powerful vision of the collapse of polis society. In some respects they are, to use Aristotle's phrase, 'the kind of things that would occur', the universals.

MODELS FOR UNDERSTANDING SOCIAL CHANGE

If we approach Thucydides' historical method from another perspective, we may ask how a historian in the fifth century might find it possible to master, describe or analyse large scale change in the societies he dealt with. What models were available? How far did Thucydides carve out a method for himself? Are some of the peculiarities in his claim for large scale social change a sign of influence or of methods of constructing change from other writers not concerned with the past? Thucydides offers a reading of the past here through the lens of other ideas about the development of society.

Here we should mention Edmunds' thesis that Thucydides was being surprisingly Hesiodic in offering a schema of change (and decline) that could be compared to Hesiod's scheme of the Ages of Man. Loraux, how-ever, complicated 'the lines of reference', and one can go still further by pointing out the anthropological tendencies of late fifth-century thought which could add considerably to the traditional ideas of decline available.[19]

One possibility is virtually certain, that Thucydides was influenced in his presentation of *stasis* (as well as the Plague) by certain medical methods of

---

[17] Hornblower 1987: 34–5.
[18] Here I differ from Price 2001: 11–22, who seems to assume accurate careful research for the *stasis* model. As Price admits (77) Thucydides' claim that *stasis* became more violent as the war progressed is not really clear from the individual events as given in the text later in the *History*.
[19] Edmunds 1975b; Loraux 1986b: 107–8. Cf. also Solon fr. 4W which, however, is replete with both religious terms and claims of socio-economic interest.

analysing illness. There are several aspects to this, and it is useful to separate the larger picture of change created from the details of analysis.[20] First, the larger picture: Thucydides used evocative verbs appropriate for illness for the 'onset' and 'progression' of the *stasis* (note esp. 3.82.1, προυχώρησε, the *stasis* 'progressed', and the use of ἐπιπίπτω, as at 82.2, καὶ ἐπέπεσε πολλὰ καὶ χαλεπά, literally, 'many terrible things fell upon' the cities). As widely noted, these are expressions suitable for the visitation and ravages of illness.[21] The connotations of illness are not in themselves signs of medical methods (see below for other signs), and could be metaphors expressive of the horror of disease; after all, Herodotus had used the metaphor of illness for *stasis* in Miletus (5.28, νοσήσασα), and the idea of illness in the body politic was also current.[22] It is perhaps less often emphasised that the very use of the disease metaphor implies a striking and unusual way of conceptualising and isolating social change: revolutions start and spread in Greece and the disease metaphor not only enhances the horror but it thereby categorises large scale social change of this kind as a kind of contagion coming from outside and eating into the body of the polis.[23] Moreover it is partially implied that factional strife is abnormal,[24] perhaps even unnatural. Serious disease may be normal in the sense of being part of the natural world and at the same time abnormal in that it is a violent interruption to normal life.

Another aspect concerns the central 'model' of *stasis* of 3.82–3 and all the later manifestations of *stasis*, which were different but related. As Thucydides puts it, the other disasters that befell the Greek cities through *stasis* varied in form (τοῖς εἴδεσι): 'There fell many terrible disasters on the cities because of *stasis*, such as have happened and always will happen while human nature remains the same, but which are more or less severe and

---

[20] For Thucydides and medical methods, see especially Weidauer 1954; Hornblower 1987, ch. 5, esp. 131 ff.; Swain 1994, though note that he implies at times a more solid and coherent body of medical theory in the fifth century than is perhaps plausible, and presses similarities too far (note Lloyd 1979, e.g. for the blurred boundaries of the discipline). Cochrane 1929 is extreme; Price 2001: 14–17 gives a balanced view. Also for Plague: Page 1953; Parry 1969; Hornblower 1991–1996, 1: 316ff.; Thomas 2006. Much of contemporary medicine was highly theoretical.

[21] See esp. Hornblower 1991–1996, 1: ad loc., 480–1 (esp. *prouchōrēse*); Swain 1994, esp. 306–7 (*epipiptein* for unexpected visitation – but also for simple brutality of war, 7.29, three times).

[22] Swain 1994: 305 cites *Prt.* 322d, Protagoras' view that someone not sharing in *dikē* and *aidōs* is ὡς νόσον πόλεως (as a plague to the city) – though this could conceivably be Platonic.

[23] Lest this sounds too modern, the Plague was explicitly described as coming from outside, from Ethiopia via Egypt and Libya (2.48.1). The *stasis*–disease metaphor continues in fourth-century writing: see Kalimtzis 2000.

[24] Loraux 1986b: 97–8, argued that *stasis* here was both a disease and an inherent feature of human existence like other evils. Yet whether or not *stasis* is like a plague, natural but evil, the very use of the metaphor here seems to deflect the reader from social or political analysis.

differ in form with every new combination of circumstances' (Hornblower's trans., ad loc.), μᾶλλον δὲ καὶ ἡσυχαίτερα καὶ τοῖς εἴδεσι διηλλαγμένα, ὡς ἂν ἕκασται αἱ μεταβολαὶ τῶν ξυντυχιῶν ἐφιστῶνται (82.2).

This concentration on the central phenomenon with its fundamental manifestations (which he then describes) while differing circumstances may cause alterations and variations, is reminiscent of the way medical writers tried to isolate the primary illness and the different forms it would take depending on the individual constitutions of each human being.[25] Hippocratic texts tend to consider human nature in general and the particular character of each person. Thus for instance, *Epidemics* I ch. 23 talks of the circumstances surrounding the disease, and of learning from the common nature of all (ἐκ τῆς κοινῆς φύσιος) and the particular nature of the individual, from the disease, the patient, the regimen prescribed and the prescriber. In the more sophistic work *On Breaths* (ch. 6), the author considers different reactions to the same illness, 'one differing from another'; arguing that the cause of plague, a form of fever, was air, he imagines the potential objection that it attacks only one species, and counters this by explaining that the same things are not well-adapted or ill-adapted to all species, or *ethnē*, of animal.[26] In Thucydides' own account of the Plague he emphasised that every case was slightly different, that a single remedy helped some and harmed others (2.51.2), but also that strong and weak constitutions faltered alike. So even behind the veil of intense pessimism here about any rational analysis of the Plague, we can see a similar conception of a basic form of the disease with variations in symptoms and in the effects of different remedies on different human constitutions. Thucydides' idea of human nature as a constant may also have been helped by medical theory; yet we should be careful not to exaggerate,[27] for the astute political observer in the sophistic period might well have conceived of human nature as a constant and a moral or immoral agent quite independently of any doctors. Thucydides' vision of human nature in 3.82 is that it is a grim, threatening agent quite distant from the medical or biological constant of the Hippocratic works.[28]

---

[25] Hornblower 1991–1996, I: ad loc., 481 comments, 'an important sentence for the understanding of Thucydides' method, and a pioneering scientific statement in itself, with its clear recognition of the importance of differing combinations of circumstances'. For the closely related *eidos* and *idea* in Thucydides and Hippocratics, see Hornblower 1991–1996, I: 173–5 and refs there; Swain 1994: 312–14, 316–17.

[26] *Breaths* ch. 6.2]: ἀλλ᾽ ἕτερα ἑτέροισι σύμφορα καὶ ἕτερα ἑτέροισιν ἀσύμφορα.

[27] E.g. Swain 1994: 314 ff., 318: it is unclear why he thinks the *stasis* description is then charting the external signs of human nature as a doctor looks for signs of illness.

[28] Cf. Connor's (1984) conclusions on Thucydides' pessimism (below p. 243 and n. 43).

It seems then, that Thucydides may well have been helped in his concep-
tualisation of *stasis* as susceptible to a single description by these medical
methods of approaching disease, though the theoretical and abstract tendencies of so much thought of the time warns us not to privilege this too
much. His abstract *stasis* model gives the basic phenomenon, as it were,
as a central fact (like a disease), alongside which all manifestations of *stasis* are simply variations depending on local circumstances[29] – though it
must be added that Thucydides in 3.82 is actually rather dismissive of local
variations. The interest of examining the relation to medical theory should
not, however, distract us from the fact that this is, by modern historical
standards, an odd way to approach social change on a large scale and across
large stretches of the Aegean. This may help explain why he could therefore
treat *stasis* and its effects on behaviour as universals, while other phenomena
of human history required particular and detailed descriptions (to which
we return).

But alongside the medical *technē*, there was also an intense interest in
the second half of the fifth century in the development of human civilisation and society. Greek ideas of progress and the development of human
society have been much discussed, and Thucydides' *archaeologia* shows
that his historical approach was well 'integrated' with such discussion. I
would like to revisit the question of whether (or how far) Thucydides' con-
ceptualisation of disastrous social change was formed on the model or in
the same mould as other contemporary speculations about human society.
The question is most easily approached via Greek ideas of progress. As de
Romilly showed in 1966 in a long and subtle discussion, fifth-century texts
of all kinds (tragedy, comedy, philosophy, medicine) were intensely preoccupied with human progress; Hesiod's vision of present-day decline from
a golden age was reversed, and the well-known fifth-century optimism in
human development and improvement through discoveries and inventions
is to be found everywhere.[30] Certain features of human life in their early
miserable existence recur, as do certain purported causes of improvement
(mainly 'necessity'), and it is likely that there were one or more highly
influential core theories. Thucydides described the collapse of society in
both the Plague description and the *stasis* episode, and de Romilly argues
convincingly that Thucydides' presentation was an attack on the theories
of progress, a critique of theories of progress which takes up many of the

[29] See Price 2001, esp. ch. 6.
[30] See de Romilly 1966; also Dodds 1973; note also that Guthrie 1971: 79ff. has an appendix of passages
on human progress. Macleod's article (1983) appears to be much influenced by her idea that the very
elements of progress themselves impede progress (i.e. in *stasis*): see further below.

same elements isolated by the theories and describes their collapse: thus a crisis in the fifth-century theory of progress.

I would like to develop this still further, but pressing the question of how a historian in the late fifth century might conceptualise and describe widespread social change rather than 'progress'; I suggest that Thucydides was able to see and describe both Plague and *stasis* in terms of total social collapse in part precisely because of contemporary abstract theories of the development of human civilisation. These gave him the conceptual framework, as it were, and the building bocks with which to describe the opposite process. This would help explain some of the disjuncture between the description of the social effects of the plague on Athens: after all, Thucydides states that this was the start of the '*anomia*' or lawlessness in Athens, as traditional customs of religious respect and ritual and traditional values broke down (2.53.1), and yet even in his own narrative and even in conditions of the strain of war, this is a large exaggeration. The norms of everyday life and religious observance (which themselves would be called *nomoi*) do continue, and there is little plausible trace of such dereliction of traditional customs in any of the rest of late fifth-century literature (above all, Aristophanes).[31] Some state laws (also *nomoi*) might be disregarded, but others are made, and no general *anomia* is visible even to the most jaundiced observer.

It would also clarify why his emphasis in the *stasis* account is in some respects disappointing as socio-political history, an oddity that Jonathan Price has recently emphasised.[32] Thus there is little on social class, conflicts between different groups of citizens, differing political aims, local quarrels, beyond the main categories of leaders of the demos and the oligarchs.[33] In the Corcyrean *stasis* account we do hear of the actions of the demos' leaders, and their opponents, but only Peithias is named; in Athens' *stasis* the aims of the Athenian oligarchs are somewhat more detailed (and contradictory) but in both *staseis* the attempt to bring in external powers or change the external relations of the city receives more emphasis than internal politics.

In Corcyra, moving from analysis of local factors, we move to the general horrors and savagery, fathers killing sons, suppliants dragged from altars

---

[31] Cf. Price 2001: 217–36, however, on the violations of temples in Thucydides' later narrative.

[32] Price makes much of this (ch. 1), suggesting that *stasis* is defined not politically but by behavioural change: I remain unconvinced that we are being given a 'definition' as such; Thucydides may stress behavioural change because that interested him and fundamentals of human nature taught him to be cynical about the rest. It is problematic to see a definition in a passage describing *stasis*' effects.

[33] Cf. Fuks 1971 who analyses this absence in Thucydides' main description well, though concentrating on the suspect chapter 3.84, which is exceptional in introducing socio-economic factors; on the use of this criterion for judging ch. 84, see trenchant remarks by Hornblower, comm. ad loc.

(81.5, still on Corcyra: a vision, incidentally, combining many elements separately familiar from Greek tragedy).[34] Then in the general *stasis* model, to pick out the main elements which concern us, loyalty to political party overrode duties to family: every side in *stasis* sought to bring in external powers and the wider Greek war meant factional strife could flourish by bringing in troops from outside (82.1). Terrible things happened because of human nature (82.2); greed and ambition for power, brought in later, are evidently a main part of this (82.6). To single out some elements from this famous passage, when everyday comfort (*euporia*) is gone the needs of the present seem more urgent, judgements are worse; the accustomed *axiosis* of words are exchanged so that qualities or behaviour that used to be condemned are now looked on favourably (82.4). Family ties become weakened through this change, moderate and sensible virtues are derided, oaths of reconciliation no longer have value, rogues (κακοῦργοι) are admired. Laws are not sought out by associations of men (συνοδοί), but they are forced to act against the established laws by πλεονεξία (greed, 82.6). Divine law is disregarded: 'the confidence of their members in each other rested less on religious sanctions (τῷ θέῳ νόμῳ) than upon complicity in crime' (τῷ κοινῇ τι παρανομῆσαι, lit. acting unlawfully in common, 82.6). The leaders use fine words but the root of everything is *pleonexia* and *philotimia* (82.8: πάντων δ᾽ αὐτῶν αἴτιον ἀρχὴ ἡ διὰ πλεονεξίαν καὶ φιλοτιμίαν). No one observes piety (82.8). Every form of *kakotropia*/iniquity was visible in Greece because of the *staseis* (83.1).

It is certainly true that these elements of decline can sometimes be traced in the full narrative of events later in the war, but there is still a tension between the general theory and the particular real-life examples later in the *History*. Words and values have already been corrupted in the Mytilenean debate between Cleon and Diodotus; actions of needless and probably increasing brutality in the rest of the war abound; Alcibiades provides an excellent example of the new contortions of word and motives even before *stasis* occurs in Athens; and the prominent members of the oligarchic coup in Athens are conspicuously lacking in coherent and consistent vision and aims, the main players like Phrynichus and Alcibiades notable for their baffling change of tack for totally personal and private gain.[35] Yet despite these correspondences, we recall that many of the later brutalities, disregard for conventional diplomatic and religious sanctions, and contortions of language, are taking place in Thucydides' narrative in the course of the war

[34] I owe this point to Pierre Bouvier.
[35] Cf. Loraux 1986b: 121–3 on the 'language of sedition' in Book 8.

itself, rather than in a specific example of *stasis*. The misuse of language and moral values progresses in Thucydides' narrative within Athenian politics and as part of Athenian imperialism quite without the help (or excuse) of *stasis*.[36] In other words the *stasis* description stands somewhat apart from the main flow of the narrative of events. Indeed the use of nouns rather than verbs to describe the 'Newspeak' may serve still further to remove it from any temporal dimension.[37] Devastating and memorable, it leaves something of a gap between its grand generalising and the details of the course of the war. As Loraux puts it (1986: 110–11), he ceases to recount and starts to generalise and while clothed in the garb of the impartial observer (also without first persons), the historian really begins to judge.

On the other hand it is not difficult to see that the *stasis* model contains in a reverse scheme of development many of the elements isolated and discussed by fifth-century thinkers as part of the development of human civilisation and political society. Since these theories have been excellently discussed,[38] I need only single out Protagoras' theory in Plato's dialogue by which human society developed for mutual protection and benefits as men and women came together from their scattered existence; how once they had the basics that raised them above animals, the beginnings of political society were made possible by the gifts of justice (*dikē*) and *aidōs*; political *aretē* developed and the polis guided its citizens through its laws (*Prt.* 322c–323c). The obvious casualties of the plague and *stasis* were *dikē* – this is assumed throughout the *stasis* model – and *aidōs*, for respect and reverence are destroyed by both plague and *stasis*. The polis laws are disregarded in the *stasis* model as are divine laws, and the wider *nomoi* in the sense of inherited mores are disregarded in both plague and *stasis*. For Protagoras *nomoi* gave guidance to men and formed the basis of a social agreement about what was acceptable, an early Greek equivalent of the 'social contract'. Scholars differ about when and where an idea of the social contract may have originated in Greek thought,[39] and perhaps Democritus should be added, but there is general agreement that such an idea was around by the end of the fifth century, perhaps among several writers. Reading the account of the effects of *stasis* on the societies of different Greek poleis in Thucydides, one could hardly say that the basic foundations for a social contract were able to

---

[36] Price 2001 would say this is because the wider war is conceived of as stasis too. But this is the problem: virtually any conflict could be so defined. See the review by Taylor 2003.

[37] Loraux 1986b: 119.

[38] De Romilly 1966; Guthrie 1971; also Kerferd 1981. Nestle 1914: 674 for comparison with the extreme Sophists' reversal of values.

[39] See e.g. Kahn 1981.

survive once *nomoi*, oaths, religious observances are set aside in favour of ambition and greed; in addition values and even the language which expressed them were distorted.

Interesting passages in the late fifth-century *Anonymus Iamblichi*, an anonymous sophistic work, also have much that is related: the anonymous writer states that obeying the laws was necessary to enable men to maintain communal life (3.6), 'This is what brings and holds together men and cities', and he continues (chs. 6–7) to the importance for humans of avoiding lawlessness (*anomia*, 6.1); humans are incapable of living alone, and pressured by necessity (*anankē*) they have developed the whole way of life (ἡ ζωή) and necessary skills (τὰ τεχνήματα) for this end, living together. Ch. 7 on the importance of lawfulness (*eunomia*) and evils of *anomia* could almost be a crude abstraction from Thucydides' account (though *anomia* here, deriving from the absence of law and justice, then gives rise to tyranny or monarchy, as well as *stasis*).[40] As de Romilly showed, this text can be seen in close proximity to the other fifth-century discussions of the development of human society under the force of necessity visible in other texts like *Ancient Medicine* on the painful, often fatal, process of discovering edible food that is suitable for humans (ch. 3). The religious pressure of fear of the gods put upon humans to maintain morality is of course treated in the fragment of *Sisyphus* attributed to Critias (DK 88 B25, but possibly Euripidean). Fear of religious sanctions is another element which disappears in Thucydides' scheme of the effects of *stasis* (3.82.8, *eusebeia*).

Thucydides' scheme does not involve the practical basics of human life that bulk large in the evolutionary theories, the discovery or invention of clothes, food and housing. The basic *technai* do not disappear, though *euporia* is lacking. Strikingly it is the second order elements of Protagoras' scheme which give way, the elements so important in social and political cohesion and in short in civilised society in the polis: *dikē, aidōs, nomos* (esp. 82.6 for polis laws) and belief in divine sanctions. So far as one can see, the idea of language, the very basis of human communication, being misused in a transvaluation of words is a Thucydidean creation.[41] It is understandable that the upbeat and optimistic theories of progress traditionally get more scholarly attention, but the dark image in Thucydides is effectively that of the collapse of society and should surely be seen more firmly as part of

---

[40] Ch. 7.12–14; *stasis* at 7.10.

[41] De Romilly finds little on language in this sense in theories of progress; sophistic debates about the correctness of names seem engaged in different questions, though one side of the debate treats language as mere convention. Note also Loraux 1986b: 113–16 and her stress on ἐνομίσθη – implying language as *nomos* for the conspirators.

Greek thought on the nature of human society, the polis and the 'social contract'.[42] The way Thucydides formulated this vision of profound decline owes much to the opposite theories of progress. The difference is that he presents it as drawn from actual experience, the Greeks' own history.

The contrast with the earlier historian Herodotus is instructive. Herodotus had noted large-scale and profound social change, either pacific or accompanied by violent revolution. While his ethnography is, it is true, often static, he also attempted to describe fundamental change in a city-state or an ethnos. It is interesting that it is often couched in terms of changing *nomoi* or learning new *nomoi*. The Lydians become less impressive in war because they take on new customs and effeminising pastimes such as playing musical instruments and shop-keeping (on the defeated Croesus' advice to Cyrus: 1.155). The Spartans suffered from δυσνομία, bad government, until wholesale reforms gained them *eunomia*, good government or good order (1.65). Profound change in social practice is conceived as being caused by changing *nomoi* or having a reformer. A powerful moral charge often hangs over long-term social change: decline in manly courage, punishment for hubris, citizens of a polis becoming braver and more successful. After the Athenian revolution of the late sixth century and the Cleisthenic reforms which brought Athens democracy, Herodotus remarks famously that *isēgoriē* brought Athenians success in war, for they were now fighting for themselves (5.78). Yet this psychological explanation for large-scale social change is hardly profound analysis of long-term social change, though such social change is evidently being noted. It seems to be conceived, almost pigeon-holed, as a matter of *nomoi* and change of *nomoi* – and this in itself may help us see how far Thucydides had to work to create a picture of collapse. Herodotus' treatment on the other hand seems to be more akin to the optimistic manner of Greek writers who see development in terms of a series of discoveries, inventions and 'first discoverers'. Herodotus' ethnographic slant adds the very frequent idea that one people learn customs from another.

Herodotus was far less governed by the demands of narrative history than Thucydides. Thucydides' self-imposed plan to follow the events of the war by winter and summer of each year may have constrained him in his treatment of slow social (and mental) change: such analysis of change of mentality perhaps had to be placed in a single section. Or did the conventions of narrative polis history make it inconceivable to do a synchronic treatment of a polis? That seems unlikely, and Herodotus'

---

[42] Thucydides is not mentioned in Kahn 1981 for example, nor Kerferd 1981, chapter on theories of society.

method of treating the customs of a given people in a single description provides a perfectly good model. Or perhaps the problem would be bridging the chronological narrative and the 'ethnographic'. It is important to recall that Herodotus had treated *stasis* in the *Histories*, though very differently. *Stasis* is certainly regarded as a horror (*stasis emphylos*, the same phrase used by Democritus (B249), is worse than united war, 8.3.1); it is clearly violent, the naked pursuit of power or hegemony are indeed present. But for the main examples, Athens in the mid sixth century and Miletus' two generation *stasis* which left ruin and deserted countryside, the narrative is on the surface. Miletus' troubles were neatly wrapped up by the Parians (5.28–9), Athens' *stasis* is in form like a military narrative. There is no inner analysis of social change during the *stasis*, inner motives, contorted values, nor does the *stasis* provoke fundamental changes to the citizens' behaviour or their leaders, except in so far as democratic Athenians become more courageous.

Thucydides' analysis of the inner psychological changes and changes in behaviour and values produced a powerful picture of *stasis* like no other. The collapse attendant on the Plague and then all over Greece with the spread of *stasis* stand paradigmatically for the decline of Greek society as a result of the war. Experience of these events and the sheer horror of demoralisation and defeat surely helped paint this picture, yet to analyse so innovatively in just these terms via the systematic breakdown of the building blocks of human society, he seems to have been helped by the framework of philosophical ideas about human life and human society. Thucydides' vision may seem inevitable. But we only need to contrast possible alternative ways of explaining decline in Greek thought which are absent here: for instance, excessive attention to women, sexual mores, or luxury, visible in Greek criticisms of the Persians; or hubris and *atē* as in Solon's delineation of *stasis* (fr. 4W). The fact that Thucydides does not paint decline in these terms draws us close to the conclusion that he is 'unravelling' current theories of human development. Seeing this in terms of the total breakdown of social norms, decent behaviour, linguistic stability and the elements necessary to civil society offers a picture which, as Connor has pointed out,[43] is far more inexorably pessimistic than 'archaic pessimism'.

A key word here is ἀνομία, inadequately translated as lawlessness because *nomos* denotes customs as well as law, and for reasons of space I will concentrate on this as symbolic of the whole. Considering the intense

---

[43] Connor 1984: 104–5. Note that in the Plague all *technē* is useless, though 2.50.2 admits that 'no single remedy established itself' (Hornblower 1991–1996, I: ad loc., 324; cf. Thomas 2006). Cf. also remarks of Geuss 2005.

interest in *nomos* in late fifth-century thought, the quality of *anomia* is rather rare, though the spectre of *anomia* may hover over all discussions of the importance of *nomos* itself. It occurs in Critias' *Sisyphus* fragment, Thucydides' Plague, in Herodotus in an interestingly theoretical account of the setting up of absolute monarchy in Media where the would-be king first produces a state of *anomia* (1.96–8; cf. also III.82.3); and it recurs in *Anonymus Iamblichi* coupled with thoughts about *stasis*. It is here that we are getting closer to thoughts on how *anomia* might arise and once it exists, what effects it might generate. In the anonymous writer's assertions about the importance of *nomos* to stable society and what he calls *eunomia*, which seems here to be a state of law-abidingness in society, ch. 6 produced his version of the familiar fifth-century theory of the necessity of *nomos* and justice for communal life in the first place. Then he asserts that *anomia* brings on external war and *stasis*, and tyranny or monarchy arise from *anomia*. Implying that there were alternative theories, he reveals that it was under debate:

The vicissitudes of good and bad fortune have the opposite result in a state of *anomia*; good fortune is not secure but is under attack by others; misfortune, on the other hand, cannot be dispelled but grows stronger for lack of trust or association . . . (10) Foreign war and internal strife (*oikeia stasis*) are brought on more frequently for the same reason, and if these did not exist earlier, they now occur. One is continually involved in public affairs because of mutual plotting . . . (12) Tyranny too, that huge and horrible evil, arises from no other sources than *anomia*. Some people who reason incorrectly, think that the installation of a tyrant has some other cause, and that when men are deprived of their freedom, they are not themselves to blame but are overpowered by the established tyrant . . . (13) Whoever thinks a king or tyrant arises from any other cause than *anomia* and *pleonexia* (greed) is a fool. This happens only when everyone turns to evil; for people cannot live without laws (*nomoi*) and justice (*dikē*).(Ch. 7.9, trans. Gagarin and Woodruff, adapted)

For the anonymous writer, *anomia* will give rise to *stasis* or to tyranny and monarchy (he leaves open how *anomia* starts in the first place, and seems to see it simply as an evil which needs to be avoided in itself). Thucydides is more interested in how *anomia* itself might arise, but there is a similar group of preoccupations. Not only does Thuycydides' analysis of the collapse of society have *nomos* and *anomia* as the focal points, though taking it still further with the abuse of language, but he is clear that the cause of this breakdown is first the Plague, then *stasis* itself, exacerbated by the wider Greek war ('*anomia*' as such is not explicitly mentioned in the *stasis* description but is clearly present). There is a rash of *staseis* with each side turning to Spartans or Athenians, for in peace there would be less excuse or opportunity to appeal to an outside power (3.82.1); in time of peace both cities and individuals have better judgement because not pressed by necessity. 'But the war removed the day-to-day well-being (*euporia*), a *biaios didaskalos*, a violent teacher'[44] (82.2). Thus the war makes *stasis* more possible, providing extra opportunities and external powers ready to help with internal revolution for their own expediency. The distortion of values and language ensue. Human nature is the constant (82.2), ready with its (apparent) tendency to brutality as well as greed and ambition, for as he continues, 'The initial cause of all these things [contortion of values etc.] was *pleonexia* and *philotimia*' (82.8), that is, greed and love of honour or ambition. It is for this reason that I am not convinced by the interesting suggestion of Macleod and de Romilly that it is the *technai*, and progress themselves, which are destroying society in Thucydides' mind.[45] The *Anonymus Iamblichi* connected *stasis*, *pleonexia* and tyranny with *anomia*, and it is attractive to think that experience of the Peloponnesian war gave ample opportunity to ponder *war's* effects on civilised polis life (rather than the effects of progress). Indeed Thucydides' grim formulation that war is a violent teacher may be echoing in order to improve upon the many contemporary claims about various agents of education, including, of course, teachers themselves.[46] He implies that it is not the Sophists who distorted values, as their critics claimed, but war itself.

Greek writers and thinkers did not, so far as one can tell, devote much attention to the collapse of society,[47] yet Thucydides did try to do just that, seeing it as happening in his own times. The theories of progress and social cohesion helped him delineate the reverse. They may also help explain why Thucydides' description is so general, so universalising, standing at

---

[44] Connor suggests that Thucydides intended both 'violent teacher' and 'teacher of violence'. Connor 1984: 102, n. 57.

[45] Briefly in Macleod 1983: 125–6, apparently following de Romilly 1966. It is true there is some invention of techniques in the *stasis* description (82.3) but *technai* themselves get little emphasis from Thucydides. De Romilly's argument that Thucydides implies that progress 'se retourne contre l'homme' (178) seems to go as follows: there is progress in military *technē* and political groups which affects the war; war affects men and cities, therefore progress eventually turns against man. But what about *stasis* itself, or the dictates of the Athenian expansion which we might not want to see merely as a subset of progress (as she does, p. 174).

[46] Cf. Macleod 1983: 125 – war is the teacher, not people; de Romilly (1966) gives some examples of alternatives: fr. 509 N (time is a discoverer); Eurip. 715 N (χρεία διδάσκει); cf. *Anc.Med.* 3.2 J, necessity (*anankē*) made men discover medicine; Thuc. 3.42.2, debate/*logos* the teacher; and Democritus DK 68 B76 (with thanks to Sandra Rocha for this reference).

[47] Before Plato and Aristotle, that is; a further implication is that their interest may have been stimulated by Thucydides'.

one remove from the main narrative of events.[48] After the description of *anomia* as the result of the Plague, and then the great further stages of disintegration delineated by the *stasis* description, the reader might justifiably think that Greek society could not carry on, yet it continues to do just that. The paradigmatic descriptions of *anomia* from Plague and *stasis* carry on in readers' minds to colour their view of the war even when the ensuing narrative reveals polis society continuing.

A further question remains: why did Thucydides choose to delineate *stasis* in terms of a model, Corcyra the paradigm, and the *stasis* model to stand for them all, while the Peloponnesian war itself deserved a full and detailed narrative? (and related, *stasis* as the great agent of destruction rather than war itself?). Why are all *staseis* more or less the same, as he implies, whereas the Peloponnesian war deserves the fullest blow-by-blow account? It is a difficult, tantalising question probably with multiple answers. But at least one guess would be that it is partly to do with the devastating nature of internal division which rent communities and families apart, the basics of Greek life – whereas war, as Democritus could cheerfully say, could be a uniter of communities and bringer of concord (DK 68 B250). In Greek society for most periods war against external enemies was a source of fame and glory. Another guess is that he implies that the basics of human nature tending towards greed, self-interest and naked ambition for power, are enough, universals which render the *stasis* model sufficient. But narrative of war was the great narrative of Greek culture from Homer to Herodotus and Thucydides; Thucydides' rivalry with his predecessors is displayed from the beginning; war was the stuff of great narrative. It is ironic that it is his compressed and abstracted studies of plague and *stasis*, internal matters, that do so much to raise his narrative to the level of greatness. While war itself formed the great narrative, the social and class conflicts within the cities were moulded into a stylised form that was indeed more akin to universalising theory than social history. We are back to the universals Aristotle attributed to poetry.

---

[48] Price (2001) sees a different form of universalising, claiming esp. (ch. 1) that the *stasis* model is not inevitably tied to the polis. But Thucydides assumes like any Greek that the entity concerned was the polis; moreover the polis is explicitly mentioned in the *stasis* description (e.g. 3.82.2, 82.3). This doesn't detract from Price's fascinating analysis of the *History* in terms of a more general internal war within Greece.

CHAPTER 11

Historia magistra vitae *in Herodotus and Thucydides? The exemplary use of the past and ancient and modern temporalities*

Jonas Grethlein

THE EXEMPLARY USE OF THE PAST IN ANTIQUITY
AND THE MODERN AGE

Reinhart Koselleck starts his book *Futures Past* with a discussion of Albrecht Altdorfer's painting 'Die Alexanderschlacht'.[1] Altdorfer seems to have taken pains to be as exact as possible. His painting shows in much detail the different sections of the battlefields. On the flags, we even find inscribed the number of troops as listed by Curtius Rufus. And yet, strikingly, the Persians look more or less like the Turks who besieged Vienna when the picture was painted in 1529 CE. On the other hand, three hundred years later, Friedrich Schlegel described the painting as an expression of old knighthood, thereby distinguishing both antiquity and the sixteenth century CE from his own time:

> Formulated schematically, there was for Schlegel, in the three hundred years separating him from Altdorfer, more time (or perhaps a different mode of time) than appeared to have passed for Altdorfer in the eighteen hundred years or so that lay between the Battle of Issus and his painting.[2]

As Koselleck points out, the 'temporalization of history' created an awareness of the specific features of times and thereby led to an emphasis on the individuality or even autonomy of epochs. One of the consequences of this is the questioning of the topos of 'historia magistra vitae'. While the exemplary use of the past has not completely vanished in the modern age,[3] the uniqueness of epochs makes direct juxtapositions of different events rather problematic and if such juxtapositions want to claim some

---

[1] Koselleck 2004c: 9–11.   [2] Koselleck 2004c: 10.

[3] For a recent discussion of the topos *historia magistra vitae*, see the contributions to a special issue of *Österreichische Zeitschrift für Geschichtswissenschaften* 16/2: 2005. While the growing scepticism towards exempla is owed to an emphasis on differences between past and present, Vlassopoulos, in this volume, alerts us to a variety of modes of linking the past with the present in the eighteenth and nineteenth centuries. Focusing on the construction of the dichotomy 'antiquity–modernity', he distinguishes between alterity, proximity, polarity and immanency.

plausibility, they have to take into account and carefully weigh the cultural settings of the events that are compared with one another.

If we raise the question of how the past is related to the present for ancient Greece, we find an attitude that is rather similar to the use of the past in the Middle Ages. To start with art, there seem to be no significant differences between representations of contemporary events and the heroic past.[4] That is why scholars can still indulge in discussions of whether, for example, the frieze of the temple of Athena Nike represented mythical or recent events.[5] While Altdorfer casts the ancient battle in a contemporary mould, ancient artists rather put the present into a heroic frame or used at least the same typology for both recent and archaic past.[6] Nonetheless, both are different from most modern representations in that neither sharply distinguishes between past and present. The same difference between modern and ancient perceptions of the past is borne out by the attitude towards old buildings. While the modern Western world is obsessed with preserving historical objects, there are only a few signs of deliberate restoration in the time before the Hellenistic Age and even then it was not the preservation of buildings because they were seen as testimonies to the past, but rather the future fame of prominent individuals that was at the core of the efforts.[7] Restoration programmes require that specific features of the past are recognised and deemed worthy of being preserved.

Further evidence that qualitative differences between past and present did not figure prominently can be found in inscriptions and in literary texts. Only a few years after the battle of Plataea, Cimon was allowed to put up three herms with inscriptions in the Athenian agora.[8] The first inscription

---

[4] Cf. Boardman 2002: 157–82. See also Lissarrague 1984. On the representation of historical events in general, see Hölscher 1973.

[5] Traditionally, the south frieze has been taken to present the Greeks against Persians, while the west and north friezes have been interpreted as battles between Athenians and other Greeks; cf. Hölscher 1973: 91–8; Stewart 1985. However, Felten 1984: 123–4 and Knell 1990: 148 argue that battles from the Trojan War are depicted. Against this thesis see Hölscher 1997: 146 and Thöne 1999: 62–3. A comparable example from vase painting is a cup in Oxford by the Brygus painter, augmented by fragments from New York (Beazley 1963: 399: Oxford, Ashmolean Museum 1911.615 from Cervetri and fr. New York, Metropolitan Museum of Art 1973, 175.2). Herford 1914 argues that either an attack on the Persian camp at Plataea or an episode from the seizure of the Palladion by Odysseus and Diomedes is represented. For another interpretation, however, see Kron 1997: 65–6.

[6] Hölscher 1973: 44–5 argues that the similar representation of contemporary events does not indicate a mythicisation, but is due to the 'typisierende Darstellungsweise'.

[7] This is argued in a chapter entitled Vorstufen der 'Denkmalpflege' in a forthcoming book by Dally. On restoration in ancient Greece, see also Buchert 2000.

[8] On the date, see the literature in Erskine 2001: 69 n. 35 who argues for the late 470s BCE. Furthermore see the discussion by Jacoby 1945: 185–211; Hölscher 1998: 165–6.

invokes the achievements of the Athenians in the Trojan war as a foil for their deeds in the battle at Eion which are praised in the second and third inscriptions.[9] Thus, the recent past is directly juxtaposed with the heroic past. In our fragments of the Plataea-elegy, Simonides mentions Achilles (1–8) and the fame that the Muses have bestowed on him and on the other Greeks (15–18).[10] He goes on to implore the Muses to preserve the praise for the dead warriors at Plataea (20–8). Epic glory is used as a model for the fame spread by elegy. Again, the recent past is seen in the light of the heroic age – fifth-century soldiers are compared to epic heroes.[11] Aeschylus' *Persae* presents a slightly different case. Here, the recent past is not juxtaposed with the heroic past, but is itself fashioned as a heroic event.[12] The direct juxtaposition and the blurring of the borderlines between different epochs leave aside the qualitative difference that has become prominent in modern perceptions of the past.

In the main bulk of this chapter, I will explore the exemplary use of the past in the first Greek historians. Both Herodotus and Thucydides, as we shall see in the next section, use the past in an exemplary way. However, upon closer inspection, the *Histories* and the *Peloponnesian War* also reveal the intricacies of exempla (section 3). The way of relating the past to the present distinguishes Herodotus and Thucydides from other contemporary media of memory, while at the same time striking a different chord from the modern scepticism towards the topos *historia magistra vitae*. In his influential work, Momigliano argued that the ancient historians laid the foundation on which modern historiography was built.[13] My argument, on the other hand, draws attention not only to the complexity of Herodotus' and Thucydides' use of the exemplary mode of memory, but also to the underlying temporality that is different from the temporality at the core of modern historical thinking (section 4).[14]

---

[9] Simon. 40 (a) *FGE* = Aeschin. *In Ctes.* 183ff. See also Plut. *Cim.* 7.6 and Dem. 20.112 on the herms and the inscriptions. Cf. the literature in Hölkeskamp 2001: 348 n. 104. See also Boedeker 2001: 126.

[10] I follow the reconstruction by West. On the Plataea-elegy, cf. the contributions in Boedeker and Sider 2001; Kowerski 2005.

[11] In another paper, Grethlein 2007a, I argue for a similar interpretation of Mimnermus fr. 14W².

[12] The heroic shaping of the recent past in Aeschylus' *Persians* is examined for example by Barrett 1995, who argues that the messenger stylises himself as an epic bard. On the Persians as a reflection on memory, see Grethlein 2007b.

[13] See, for example, Momigliano 1990.

[14] For a collection of papers on constructions of time in Greek antiquity, see Darbo-Peschanski 2000; for philosophical, historical, sociological and anthropological approaches, see Bender and Wellbery 1991.

THE EXEMPLARY USE OF THE PAST IN HERODOTUS
AND THUCYDIDES

In order to grasp Herodotus' and Thucydides' exemplary view of history
in its complexity, I will focus not only on the use they explicitly or implicitly ascribe to their own works, but I will also take into account acts of
exemplary memory at the level of the action. Embedded in the historians'
account of the past, there is a previous past, events that are already past
for the characters – a 'plupast'. The characters' references to their own past
are of course different from the historians' written history, but nonetheless
both characters and historians engage in acts of memory and seen from this
perspective the characters' 'plupast' can either mirror or throw into relief
the historians' account of the past. I therefore suggest reading the characters' use of the past as meta-historical. Meta-history, as used by Hayden
White, and others, signifies theoretical reflections on memory and history.
Needless to say, the characters' references to the past do not provide such
treatises, but I suggest enlarging the concept of meta-history in analogy to
meta-poetics which embraces explicit as well as implicit reflections of texts
on themselves. The 'plupast' illustrates how (not) to remember and use
the past and thereby provides an implicit commentary on the historian's
account of the past.

The exemplary use of the past figures prominently in Herodotus. In
trying to come to grips with the *Histories'* complex structure, scholars
have elaborated on a dense net of patterns such as the crossing of straits,[15]
the figure of the wise advisor[16] or the hybristic laughter[17] on which the
overarching pattern of the rise and fall of rulers rests.[18] These patterns are
not only a literary device, but also establish an exemplary view of history.
The recurring features juxtapose the various military expeditions and make
them mirror one another. What is more, the exemplary view of history does
not end with the defeat of the Persians in Greece, but extends to 'futures
past', events that are still to come at the level of the action, but already lie
in the past for the readers, and perhaps also to the future in general. At
the end of the *Histories*, an increasing number of prolepseis adumbrate the
future history of Athens.[19] While it is not legitimate to see a warning to
Athens as the major goal of Herodotus, it is difficult to deny that the fate of
the Eastern empires sheds light on the Athenians' struggle for hegemony.

---

[15] Immerwahr 1954: 28 with n. 22; Konstan 1983; Lateiner 1989: 129–30.
[16] Bischoff 1932; Lattimore 1939.   [17] Lateiner 1977; Flory 1978.
[18] Cf., above all, Immerwahr 1966.
[19] See, e.g., Fornara 1971; Stadter 1992; Moles 2002: 48–52. On the importance of analogy in the
Histories, see Corcella 1984.

In projecting the frame of his narrative beyond the defeat of Xerxes in Greece, Herodotus indicates an instructional function for his work that goes beyond the explicitly proclaimed preservation of the past.

While Herodotus does not elaborate on the pragmatic goals of his *Histories*, Thucydides uses his methodological reflections to point out that his records may be 'the less enjoyable for listening', but that they will be 'judged useful by any who wish to look at the plain truth about both past events and those that at some future time, in accordance with human nature, will recur in similar or comparable ways' (1.22.4). Thus, the *History* claims not only to present a clear account of the past, but also to provide its readers with an insight into human nature that will help them better assess the future.[20] This, however, does not imply that history simply repeats itself. At the beginning of the Corcyrean *stasis*, Thucydides states (3.82.2): 'And during the civil wars the cities suffered many cruelties that occur as long as men have the same nature, sometimes more terribly and sometimes less, varying in their forms as each change of fortune dictates.'

And yet, despite such variations the assumption of a human nature makes past, present and future comparable with one another. This is nicely illustrated by the reconstruction of the archaic history in the archaeology. Thucydides' account of the Trojan War deviates from the Homeric account in significant aspects (1.9–11). It was not so much the Tyndarids' oath as the fear of mighty Mycenae that prompted the Achaeans to join the expedition. Moreover, the army was rather small and the siege took so long because parts of the army had to be sent out to provide food. As Lisa Kallet shows, the motivation of the allies, the size of the army and the insufficiency of funding are modelled on the template of the Sicilian expedition.[21] The archaeology relies on the assumption that the dynamics of power politics and the features of military expeditions are the same as in the Mycenaean Age. The very assumption that enables Thucydides to come up with an alternative reconstruction of the distant past on the basis of more recent events allows him to claim that his *History* will be useful for better assessing the future. History may not repeat itself, but the constants of human nature allow Thucydides and his readers to draw conclusions about the future from parallel situations in the past.

---

[20] Some scholars argue that all that Thucydides offers is a better understanding of the past: Kapp 1930: 92–4; Gomme 1945–1981, I: 149–50; de Romilly 1956; Edmunds 1975a: 149–55; Stahl 2003: 15–17. However, the text of 1.22.4 also implies a better understanding of the future, cf. Classen and Steup *ad* 1.22.4; von Fritz 1967, I: 530–3; II: 247–50 (n. 15); de Ste. Croix 1972: 29–33; Connor 1984: 242–8; Erbse 1987: 340–6; Farrar 1988: 131–7.

[21] Kallet 2001: 97–112.

Herodotus' and Thucydides' willingness to juxtapose different times with one another is particularly striking in passages in which the past of their account is juxtaposed both with a previous past and the future. An interesting case in point is Herodotus' praise for Sophanes, the Athenian who excelled at Plataea (9.73).[22] His origin from Deceleia brings Herodotus to the mythic past. After Theseus had raped Helen and hidden her somewhere, her brothers, the Tyndarids, invaded Attica and threatened to destroy everything on their search. Either Decelon himself or other Deceleians, angry about Theseus' hybris and concerned about Attica's fate, revealed to them the place, Aphidna, where Theseus had put Helen. For this, the Deceleians were awarded privileges from Sparta, 9.73.3:

This deed earned the people of Decelea the right to be exempt from tax in Sparta and to occupy the front seats at festivals there – rights which they have continued to hold all the way down to today. Even during the war which was fought many years later between the Athenians and the Peloponnesians, although the Lacedaemonians devastated the rest of Attica, they left Decelea alone.[23]

In a zigzag course, Herodotus uses the affiliation of Sophanes to turn to the mythic past from where he jumps right to the recent past. A far reaching analepsis leads to a prolepsis that comes close to the narrator's present. In their commentary, Flower and Marincola suggest that the Theseus story serves not only as an *aition* for the saving of Deceleia, but also as a mirror for the Peloponnesian war:

The hybris of Theseus here in provoking a Spartan invasion may allude to Athens' (or Pericles'?) role in the outbreak of the Peloponnesian War. Decelus, we are next told, revealed Helen's whereabouts because 'he feared for the whole land of Attica'. In Alcman's version of this myth (Paus. 1.41.4 = *PMG* 21) the Dioscuri actually captured Athens; by not accepting that version H. is perhaps providing contemporary Athenians with a mythic paradigm for preserving their city in the current war: by following the example of Decelus and coming to terms with Sparta, they could still save themselves from destruction.[24]

If this interpretation is correct, then Herodotus uses Sophanes to set up a panopticon in which three different time levels, the heroic past, the past of his account and the rather recent future shed light on one another.

As Koselleck and others have noted, around 1800 CE the use of exempla was called into question. Since then, particularly professional historians

---

[22] The translations of Herodotus and Thucydides are based on Waterfield 1998 and Lattimore 1998.

[23] For later ancient testimonies, see Macan 1908: *ad* 9.73.2. See also Mills 1997: 7–10.

[24] Flower and Marincola 2002: *ad* 9.73.2.

have been aware of the individuality of epochs and therefore very careful with direct juxtapositions of different events. Herodotus and Thucydides may be hailed as the founding fathers of historiography, but the exemplary use of the past figures prominently in their accounts. In this regard, Herodotus and Thucydides are closer to other commemorative genres of their time than to their modern successors. However, upon closer inspection, if we take into account the characters' uses of the past and read them as meta-historical, the exemplary use of the past in Herodotus and Thucydides turns out to be more complex.

THE INTRICACIES OF EXEMPLA IN HERODOTUS AND THUCYDIDES

I

It is noteworthy that time and again in both Herodotus and Thucydides the narrative demonstrates the limits of *historia magistra vitae* or characters even fail to learn from the past. Let me give two examples from each historian respectively: Croesus first dismisses Solon's emphasis on human fragility, but on the pyre, after losing his son and being defeated by Cyrus, he recalls Solon. Cyrus is touched and saves him. In response, Croesus promises that, building on his experiences, he will serve him as an advisor. However, Croesus does not prevent Cyrus from disaster. When Cyrus marches against the Massagetae, their queen offers him to battle either on her or on his own territory. Croesus convinces Cyrus to fight in the Massagetae's land. His strategy – to leave the weakest part of the army with alcohol and to abandon them to the Massagetae (1.207) – works out and it does not take the Persians much to overcome the enemies in their drunken stupor. Finally, however, the Persians are devastatingly defeated in an open battle and Cyrus dies.

Croesus' advice is sound and I do not think that he can be blamed for losing 'that deep sense of humanity'.[25] At the same time, Croesus' pointed reference to his role as wise advisor when he proposes his stratagem (1.207.1) alerts the readers that he fails to live up to his claim to protect Cyrus from disaster. Such a reading is reinforced by a later comment of Cambyses. Rejecting Croesus' advice not to kill his brother (beyond

---

[25] Stahl 1975: 24. He presses the case too hard that Croesus is responsible for the death and defeat of Cyrus. Shapiro 1994, on the other hand, argues that Croesus gives sound advice and cannot be held responsible for Cyrus' disaster (see already Aly 1969: 58; Flory 1987: 95–6). I think this interpretation falls short too, since Cyrus' death does question Croesus' role as a wise advisor.

doubt wise advice!), he reminds him of his failures as ruler of Lydia and as counsellor of Cyrus (3.36.3). Again, it may not be justified to blame Croesus for Cyrus' disaster, but nevertheless his case indicates the limits to history's instructional function. Learning from the past does not necessarily protect against disaster.

Another interesting passage in which the role of history as *magistra vitae* is ambiguous is Xerxes' consultations on whether or not to invade Greece. In the council scene, both Mardonius (7.9) and Artabanus (7.10) draw on the past to buttress their arguments. While Mardonius claims that he did not experience any notable resistance when he attacked the Greeks in Asia, Artabanus adduces the expedition against the Scythians as illustrating the dangers that will await the Persians in Greece. Later, he also mentions Cyrus' war against the Massagetae and Cambyses' expedition to the Ethiopians (7.18.2).[26] Both Mardonius' and Artabanus' references to the past parallel the preceding narrative. Through their internal analepseis, Mardonius and Artabanus become interpreters of the past parallel to Herodotus. Mardonius' take on the past strikingly contradicts the Herodotean narrative in which his expedition ends rather in a disaster after a storm at Mount Athos.[27] Artabanus' retrospective, on the other hand, not only repeats important aspects of Herodotus' account, but also anticipates the numerous parallels through which Xerxes' expedition will insert itself into the series of failed enterprises in the *Histories*.[28]

Nonetheless, Xerxes first rejects Artabanus' objections. Only after some further reflections does he cancel the expedition. Finally, however, his dreams are haunted by an apparition that appeals to him to attack Greece, presaging a sudden downfall in case he does not obey this command. Confused and bewildered, Xerxes turns to Artabanus for advice. After the famous discussion about dreams, Artabanus puts on Xerxes' clothes and sleeps on his throne. He, too, is haunted by the same apparition that points out that what is fated has to happen, threatening him with blindness if he does not yield (7.17). Under the impression of this dream, Artabanus recommends the invasion of Greece. Thus, even the wise advisor who first draws the right lessons from the past in the end encourages Xerxes to go on the expedition that will turn out to be a failure (cf. 7.18.4). While Xerxes' first decision reveals how easy it is to discard the lessons from the past, the

---

[26] The juxtaposition of the wars (7.18.2) is similar to the enumeration of wars by Herodotus not much later in 7.20.2.

[27] Cf. Solmsen 1982: 84.

[28] On Artabanus as wise adviser, see Immerwahr 1954: 37–40. Regenbogen 1930: 234 and Solmsen 1982: 85 rightly compare him to Solon.

supernatural apparition indicates the limits that are set to following the right lessons.

In Thucydides too, characters fail to learn from the past.[29] Two cases are particularly interesting as they reveal that historical ignorance can have detrimental consequences. When Thucydides starts his account of the Sicilian expedition, he gives no explicit prolepseis that anticipate the final disaster. However, he illuminates the Athenian miscalculation through an analepsis. The Sicilian archaeology (6.1.2–6.5) which outlines the past and the current situation of Sicily is introduced by the statement that the Athenians went on the expedition without knowing what Thucydides is about to present in the following digression.[30] Thus, it is implied that a better knowledge of Sicily and its past, just as it is unfolded by Thucydides, could have prevented a big disaster.

Another digression, namely the account of the tyrannicide, serves a similar function in the narrative (6.54–9). Thucydides presents a rather lengthy account discussing different kinds of evidence, but there are basically three points in which he corrects the Athenians' assumptions: Hippias, not Hipparchus was the tyrant of Athens. The assassination of Hipparchus was not so much a political act, but rather the result of a love affair. Only after the assassination did the Peisistratids' reign become violent. There are striking similarities between the digression on the tyrannicide and the main plot of the narrative,[31] but the link that Thucydides points out explicitly is that the deficient knowledge of the end of the tyranny made the Athenians over anxious about anything possibly related to an oligarchic or tyrannical revolution (6.60.1). A wrong idea of the past led to the witch-hunt that culminated in the recalling of Alcibiades from Sicily and thereby seriously harmed Athens (6.15.4).[32]

Herodotus develops a panopticon in which different times shed light on one another, most strikingly the Persian wars serve as a foil to later intra-Hellenic conflicts, and Thucydides explicitly propagates an exemplary use of his work. However, as the passages discussed in this section reveal, the narratives of both illustrate how complex the employment of exempla from

---

[29] Hunter 1973 offers a fascinating examination of patterns and the ways that characters learn from the past in the *History*. However, many of her cases are rather weak and the failures to learn from the past are more striking than passages in which somebody benefits from the lessons of the past.

[30] Cf. Ober 1998: 105–6; Kallet 2001: 31. On 'Sicilian archaeology', see also Rawlings 1981: 65–70, who draws attention to the similarities to the archaeology in Book 1, and Tsakmakis 1995: 167–75.

[31] See particularly Rawlings 1981: 101–12. See also Schadewaldt 1929: 84–94; Connor 1984: 178–9; Farrar 1988: 148.

[32] Cf. Stahl 2003: 8; Kallet 2006. Stahl 2003: 6 argues against Rawlings' interpretation, but I do not think that the function of the digression as a mirror and as an explanation for the Athenians' exaggerated anxiety are mutually exclusive.

history can be. It is easy to argue that the Athenians' failures to learn from the past underline the relevance of historical research and thereby reinforce Thucydides' claim to usefulness *via negationis* – after all, Thucydides presents evidence that would have made the Athenians act differently. The cases of Croesus and Xerxes, on the other hand, undermine the possibility to learn from the past at a more general level. Even solid knowledge of the past is not able to cancel out the unpredictability of the future and can be made useless by forces beyond man's control.

II

Exemplary uses of the past are further challenged by the characters' rejections of historical arguments some of which resonate in authorial statements. To start with Herodotus, at Plataea the Athenians and Tegeans have a fierce argument about who is to be given the honour of holding the second wing (the first being taken by the Spartans).[33] The Tegeans insist that they have always enjoyed a privileged position (9.26.2–7). Their main argument is the duel between Heracles' son, Hyllus and their king Echemus which was to decide whether or not the Heracleidae would be allowed to settle in the Peloponnese within the next hundred years. The victory of Echemus, the Tegeans claim, entitles them to special honours. Echemus not only serves as evidence for the Tegeans' excellence, he also offers a parallel to the present situation. In their attempt to conquer Greece, the Persians resemble the Heracleidae who tried to push into the Peloponnese. Similarly to the ancient Peloponnesians facing the sons of Heracles, the present residents of the peninsula gather at the Isthmus. Thus, the Tegeans adduce an ancient parallel to strengthen their claim in the present.

In their rejoinder (9.27), the Athenians first question the whole discussion by juxtaposing mere words to deeds, but nevertheless come up with a catalogue of achievements themselves: they defended the rights of the Heracleidae, helped the Argives to bury their dead, fought off the Amazons and were not outshone by anybody at Troy.[34] However, the Athenians continue, these ancient events should not count for too much – who was strong in the past can now be weak and vice versa. They therefore refer to their victory at Marathon, a recent display of virtue.

---

[33] On the speech duel, see Solmsen 1944; Pallantza 2005: 167–8.

[34] Scholars have not failed to notice the similarity with the catalogue of deeds in the funeral speeches, cf. Meyer 1899: 219–21; Jacoby 1913: 491; Schmitz-Kahlmann 1939: 63–5; Solmsen 1944: 249; Loraux 1986a: 65.

At first glance, the Athenians' rejection of ancient deeds is only a rhetorical strategy that throws into relief their strongest point, Marathon.[35] After all, despite their criticism, the Athenians do mention a series of ancient achievements. At the same time, the Athenians' argument, even if only used as a rhetorical device, is likely to prompt the readers to reflect on the use of mythical exempla in speeches. The Athenians' point recalls the *Histories'* proem (1.5.3–4):

I will cover minor and major human settlements equally, because most of those which were important in the past have diminished in significance by now, and those which were great in my own time were small in times past. I will mention both equally because I know that human happiness never remains long in the same place.

The echo of this central narratorial statement gives the point weight beyond its rhetorical function within the Athenians' speech and draws the reader's attention to a general flaw of exemplary uses of the past: any exemplum presupposes that the present resembles the past. This assumption of regularity squares badly with the changeability that comes to the fore in the *Histories.*

In Thucydides, the use of the past in diplomatic negotiations is subject to a different kind of criticism. In their speech in Sparta, the Athenian envoys say (1.73.2):

Now as for the remote past, what need is there to speak when the audience would have the evidence of hearsay accounts rather than their personal experience? As for the Persian War, however, and all events of which you have knowledge of your own, even if it is rather tiresome for us to bring them up constantly, we are forced to speak.

The Athenians' rejection of archaic history is strongly reminiscent of Thucydides' methodological reflections. Thucydides has them share his own scepticism towards the possibility of reconstructing the archaic past. Later, at the beginning of the Melian dialogue, the Athenians' critique of historical arguments reaches further (5.89):

In that case, we will neither use noble phrases to furnish a lengthy and unconvincing speech ourselves, about having the right to rule because we put down the Mede or attacking now because we were wronged, nor expect you to think that you can convince us by saying that you are colonists of the Lacedaemonians and did not

---

[35] Cf. Pallantza 2005: 167–8, who criticises Cartledge 1993: 28–9 (see rev. edn Cartledge 2002: 29–30) for seeing a distinction between *spatium mythicum* and *spatium historicum*, and herself emphasises the 'okkasionelle Element dieser Aufwertung der Gegenwart'. On the central role of Marathon in the Athenians' speech, see Solmsen 1944: 249.

campaign with them, or that you have done us no injury, but to deal with the possibilities defined by what both parties really believe, understanding as well as we do that in human considerations justice is what is decided when all equal forces are opposed, while possibilities are what superiors impose and the weak acquiesce to.

The Athenians unveil the rhetorical character of historical arguments in general, no matter if they refer to more recent or archaic events. Not reflections on the past, but considerations of expediency are what counts in power politics. The same point is borne out by the Plataean debate (3.53–67).[36] When the Plataeans have to hand over their city in 427, they are asked what good they have done to Sparta during the present war. In their lengthy speech, the Plataeans mainly dwell on their merits from the Persian wars and argue that they ought to be saved on account of their stand against the Persians. The Plataeans' speech prompts the Thebans to a rejoinder with an alternative account of the past. However, neither of the speeches has an impact on the Spartans' decision (3.68.4): 'In virtually every respect, it was on account of the Thebans that the Lacedaemonians were as unfeeling as they were about the Plataeans, since they thought the Thebans were useful to them in the war which had recently broken out.' This brief narratorial statement forcefully marks the futility of the lengthy historical arguments presented by Plataeans and Thebans. The Spartans do not take into account the past at all, but they are guided in their decision only by what is most conducive to their present interests.[37]

To sum up, Herodotus' *Histories* as well as Thucydides' *History* reveal the intricacies of the exemplary use of the past. In Herodotus, Croesus tries to learn from his own downfall, but fails to prevent Cyrus from the same fate. It first seems that the lessons of the past will save Xerxes from the hybristic invasion of Greece; an apparition in his dreams, however, prompts him to repeat the mistakes of previous oriental monarchs. Thucydides uses the digressions on the archaeology of Sicily and on the tyrannicide to drive home the message that in ignoring the past the Athenians inflict serious harm on themselves. Moreover, both historians have characters explicitly challenge the exemplary use of the past. The Athenians at Plataea refer to the changeability, a central creed of Herodotus, to question the exemplary use of the archaic past by the Tegeans. In Thucydides, the Athenians call into doubt the possibility of a solid knowledge of the ancient past and

[36] For a detailed examination of the uses of the past in the Plataean debate, see Grethlein 2010: 228–40.
[37] Cf. Connor 1984: 93–4; Hornblower 1991–6, 1: 462.

unveil the rhetorical character of historical arguments which are ultimately powerless against considerations of expediency. How far, we must now ask, does the rejection of historical arguments at the level of the action undermine the instructional goals of the historical accounts? This question will help us to locate Herodotus and Thucydides in relation to other ancient commemorative genres and to the modern scepticism towards exempla.

ANCIENT AND MODERN TEMPORALITIES

While the Athenians' critique of arguments from ancient history (1.73.2) parallels Thucydides' own stance, the juxtaposition of expediency with history, explicit in the Melian dialogue and implicit in the Plataean debate, obviously contrasts with the usefulness that Thucydides ascribes to his own act of memory. The critique addresses a specific use of the past and thereby alerts us to a crucial difference between Herodotus and Thucydides on the one hand, and other contemporary media of memory on the other. The Plataeans' and the Thebans' arguments illustrate a legitimising use of the past. While the Plataeans ask to be spared, the Thebans want them to be annihilated. In a similar vein, pieces as different as the Stoa Poikile, the Eion-epigrams and the new Simonides juxtapose the recent with the heroic past in order to glorify it. While in these cases there is no specific assertion to be backed up by the past exemplum, the tendency to shed positive light on the present is parallel to historical arguments in speeches.

Herodotus and Thucydides, on the other hand, use the past rather for critical purposes. Of course, Herodotus' openly proclaimed goal is the preservation of great deeds and he gives praise for remarkable achievements. At the same time, however, the pattern of the rise and fall of empires that emerges in the *Histories* has a rather critical thrust. The prolepseis at the end of the *Histories* shed light on the struggle for hegemony which would prove disastrous after the Persian wars. A strong case in point is the Syracusan embassy scene which reveals both the abuse of the past for legitimising purposes in speeches and the critical use of the past by Herodotus himself. In another paper, I argue that while the Spartan ambassador tries to buttress his claims through an epic quote, the very Homeric passage that he evokes rather undermines his argument and alerts the readers to the detrimental consequences of the fights for hegemony.[38]

---

[38] Grethlein 2006a.

Likewise, in his account of the Peloponnesian War Thucydides eluci-
dates rather problematic aspects such as the cruelties of civil strife that
are mentioned at the beginning of the Corcyrean *stasis*. The insight into
anthropological constants, e.g. the role of fear or the dynamics of power,
enables his readers to engage critically with their own time. The difference
between using the past for critical and for legitimising or glorifying purposes comes with a set of other differences. Speeches or poems that draw
on the past to buttress present claims or foster identities are intended for
oral delivery to a particular audience in a particular situation. Herodotus
and perhaps also Thucydides may have presented part of their works orally,
but they both composed written works that are independent of a particular
context.[39] Moreover, neither Herodotus nor Thucydides writes from the
perspective of a single polis, but both follow Homer in taking a panhellenic
stance.

Let us turn to the rejection of exempla that we have encountered in
Herodotus. At first glance, the argument that the changeability of human
life undermines conclusions drawn from the past to the present may remind
us of the modern scepticism towards exempla. In both cases, time challenges
the juxtaposition of different events. However, there is a crucial difference.
As Koselleck points out, the modern critique of the exemplary use of the
past hinges on the experience of 'temporalisation'. Herodotus' emphasis
on changeability ought not to be mixed up with the modern idea that the
present is qualitatively different from the past and that the future will bring
something new and unseen. Herodotus emphasises the role of chance, but
all the changes that he takes into account remain within the framework of
what is already known. While Herodotus does not advocate the regularity
that inheres in a circular view of history – there is no regularity in when
and how rulers rise and fall – the very pattern of rise and fall stays the
same. Similarly, Thucydides can reconstruct the Trojan War in a frame
that he derives from the Sicilian expedition, because he assumes that the
basic features of politics and war are stable. When he argues that the
Peloponnesian War supersedes all previous wars, he is only concerned with
size; qualitatively all has stayed the same.

The exemplary use of the past by Herodotus and Thucydides may
be complex; as we have seen, the action and the characters' reflections
challenge exemplary uses of the past, and, unlike other contemporary

[39] On the written nature of Herodotus' *Histories*, see Rösler 1991; 2002; on Thucydides and writing,
see Loraux 1986c; Edmunds 1993; Morrison 2004.

genres of memory, the two historians rely on exempla for critical rather than legitimising or glorifying purposes, but nonetheless their exemplary use of the past is not affected by the 'temporalisation' which started to chip away at exempla in the eighteenth century CE. Thus, while offering a use of the past that is different from other commemorative genres, the rise of Greek historiography is firmly embedded in the horizon of its time. In many aspects, Herodotus and Thucydides may be viewed as the 'classical founders of modern historiography';[40] but the temporality underlying their works is different from the one that led to the rise of historicism.

It would be wrong to claim that the Greeks had not yet discovered the idea of development. Various 'Kulturentstehungslehren' as in the *Prometheus Bound* are evidence for an evolutionist view of history. In some tragedies such as Sophocles' *Philoctetes* and *Ajax* and Euripides' *Heracles* and *Orestes*, heroic values have ceased to be an unquestioned normative model;[41] the strong dissonances that emerge between the heroic frame and the contemporary world testify to an awareness of the gap that separates the past from the present. However, this awareness was not so strong that it would seriously challenge exemplary uses of the past. What Rüsen calls the genetic mode of memory, i.e. viewing history as a unified process and development leading to the present, did not have the prominence it would gain in the nineteenth century CE.[42] This difference is borne out by the 'Begriffsgeschichte': While the focus on developments led to the coinage of the singular terms *Geschichte / histoire / storia*,[43] there is no Greek word for history as a process with its own dynamic.

Instead of the genetic mode, the exemplary and traditional modes of memory dominated. Besides the tendency to directly juxtapose different times and events with one another that I have elaborated on in this paper, past and present were often linked by the idea of continuity. For example, the *epitaphioi logoi* present Athenian history as an unbroken sequence of great deeds.[44] This sequence does not form a development but rather establishes timelessness. The idea of a *patrios politeia* which was so popular at the end of the fifth century BCE also relies on the continuum between past and present.[45] Exemplary and traditional uses of the past often reinforce

---

[40] Cf. Momigliano 1990.
[41] On Sophocles, see Altmeyer 2001; on Euripides, see Neumann 1995.
[42] Rüsen 1982 proposes an agenda of four different modes of memory (traditional, exemplary, critical, genetic). For a critique and further development of Rüsen's functionalist approach from a phenomenological perspective, see Grethlein 2006b: 20–41.
[43] Cf. Koselleck 1975: 647–58.   [44] Cf. Loraux 1986a.
[45] Cf. Fuks 1953; Cecchini 1975; Finley 1975: 34–59.

one another. The direct juxtaposition of times ultimately hinges on the assumption of a continuum; traditions, on the other hand, gain poignancy through specific parallels.

Thus, the different attitudes to exempla alert us to different temporalities in the first Greek historians and modern historiography. Exempla and traditions have not disappeared, but the modern master narratives, first of progress, then of development, undermine notions of regularity and continuity.[46] In classical Greece, on the other hand, developmental schemes were not unknown, but exemplary and traditional approaches to the past were more influential. The crucial difference is, I suggest, different constructions of contingency.[47] Building on Aristotle, Bubner points out that contingency is the frame for both action and chance.[48] Where things are 'neither impossible nor necessary', man can act, but his plans can also be crossed by chance. Both aspects, which can be termed 'Beliebigkeitskontingenz' and 'Schicksalskontingenz',[49] depend on one another and are both present all the time; however, their prominence varies from culture to culture.[50]

In ancient Greece, chance or forces beyond man's control are very prominent. Various genres such as epic, epinicean poetry, tragedy, but also historiography, emphasise the fragility of human life.[51] The arbitrariness of chance impedes the construction of developments. At the same time, exempla and traditions are the attempt to create the stability that is necessary for action by balancing chance through regularity and continuity.

The axial age around 1800 CE,[52] on the other hand, is carried by the feeling that the future is open and can be shaped. Here, contingency is experienced not so much as chance but rather as the freedom to act. The past is seen as a development with a direction, leading to the present. In most modern historiography, chance plays only a minor role.[53] Even though the belief in progress has lost much of its plausibility since the age of Enlightenment, even though the end of history has been proclaimed, and even though a new régime d'historicité has entered the stage of

---

[46] On the idea of development as replacing the idea of progress, see, for example, Jaeger and Rüsen 1992.
[47] For a fuller argument, see Grethlein 2006b: 97–105.   [48] Bubner 1984.
[49] These terms were coined by Marquard 1986; von Graevenitz and Marquard 1998. For more on this, see Grethlein 2006b: 28–31.
[50] Makropoulos 1997: 16–18 stresses that contingency is seen differently in different cultures.
[51] See, e.g., for the epics, Grethlein 2006b; for epinicean poetry, Theunissen 2000; for Herodotus, Harrison 2000; for Thucydides, Stahl 2003.
[52] For new non-essentialist takes on the concept of axial ages, see Arnason 2005.
[53] This is emphasised by Ferguson 1997 in his plea for the use of counterfactuals by historians.

scholarship, the notion that epochs are individual and ought to be carefully distinguished from one another has not faded and this volume testifies to its unbroken plausibility.[54] Herodotus and Thucydides, it seems, thought differently.

[54] On the end of history, see, most prominently, Fukuyama 1992; on a new *régime d'historicité*, see Hartog 2003. I rather side with Oexle 1996, who argues that our thinking is still heavily indebted to historicism. See also Steenblock 1991.

CHAPTER 12

Repetition and exemplarity in historical thought: Ancient Rome and the ghosts of modernity

Ellen O'Gorman

> Inheritance is never a *given*, it is always a task.
> Jacques Derrida, *Specters of Marx*

In this chapter I explore some of the various ways in which modernity configures repetition as an improper relation to the past. This exploration mediates the wider question of what modernity wants to do with the past, whether it is to break with it, to sublimate it, or to form a new kind of relation altogether. This leads us to consider the tropes of repetition and of exemplarity as the grounds for an engagement with the past. That is to say, modernity does not merely employ these tropes in configuring a relation with the past; rather modernity's relation with the past is marked by the difference between ancient and modern uses of these tropes. Therefore, in the middle section of this chapter I turn to the theory and practice of exemplary thinking in ancient Rome, as a mode of thinking which infuses the present with the complex temporalities of subjective pasts and futures. Framing this discussion is a consideration of some ways in which Marx, in particular, characterised repetition and engaged with exemplarity in his attempt to create a new modernity.

In the *Eighteenth Brumaire* Marx presented, in the form of a political commentary on the revolutionary events in France between 1848 and 1851, a historical meditation on what it was to be modern, differentiating nineteenth-century forms of repetition – and of revolution – from what had gone before. Famously he described the past as 'a nightmare' which 'weighed upon the brain of the living'. Terrell Carver, the most recent translator of Marx, comments on the 'shock for the contemporary reader . . . finding out that this nightmare world of tradition is, in Marx's view, *politically productive*'.[1] The reason why this might be a shock for the *contemporary* reader is not spelt out, but Carver's later emphasis on the emotional and psychological conceptualising of revolutionary processes

---

[1] Carver 2002: 121, his emphases.

suggests that our supposed shock here must derive from our Freudian inheritance. Freud's thinking on repetition, which intersects but does not fully overlap with Marx's, sees the repeated past as not only sterile, but even unhealthy and damaging. Despite the nightmare imagery, repetition for Marx operates differently, as even the illusion of repetition serves some political purpose. The new theory of history he proposes in this text, more-over, itself enters the structure of repetition when it is presented to us in the opening sentences as a supplement:

Hegel observes somewhere that all great events and characters of world history occur twice, so to speak. *He forgot to add*: the first time as high tragedy, the second time as low farce.[2]

What Hegel forgot, but already knew, is 'repeated' by Marx's supplementary text[3] in the service of a new understanding of a new type of revolution; thus Marx initiates a consideration of the various modes of engagement with the past, and the various ways in which forgetting may look towards the future. These work up to his manifesto for a modernity which stands independent of the past:

The social revolution of the nineteenth century cannot create its poetry from the past but only from the future. It cannot begin till it has stripped off all superstition from the past. Previous revolutions required recollections of world history in order to dull themselves to their own content. The revolution of the nineteenth century must let the dead bury the dead in order to realise its own content.[4]

Here too Marx's language intersects with Freud's, evoking the process of mourning through which an individual decouples all affective links with the loved one who is lost, as opposed to the disavowal of the reality of death inherent in the superstitious invention of ghosts.[5] Yet, ghosts proliferate in the pages of Marx's text and haunt the present in many guises. Jacques Derrida, tracing the exemplary status of Marx[6] and his texts in *Specters of Marx*, takes up an explicitly Freudian position of reading, and thereby opens up the difference between the two thinkers on precisely this issue. Derrida asks,

What does Marx mean, the dead Marx? He knew very well that the dead have never buried anyone. Nor have the living who were not also *mortals*, that is, who

---

[2] Marx 2002: 19, my emphases.   [3] Harries 1995: 38.   [4] Marx 2002: 22.
[5] Freud 2005: 203–18. Though, as Maud Ellmann points out, 'it is only through the invention of the ghost that the reality of death can be acknowledged. By getting rid of ghosts, "civilized man" has lost his grasp of the reality they represent,' 2005: xxiii–xxiv.
[6] See especially Derrida 1994: 41. Leonard 2005: 135–47 examines Derrida's thinking on exemplarity in a wider context.

properly bear within themselves, that is, outside themselves, and before themselves, the impossible possibility of their death. It will always be necessary that still living mortals bury the already dead living.[7]

What Derrida focuses on here – and considers so important that he returns to it at the end of his work – is the profound break with the past proposed (but not actualised) by Marx. By calling on the revolution of the nineteenth century to 'let the dead bury the dead', Marx suggests that even the process of mourning is irrelevant to modernity, and sets up a double barrier between past and present.

The significance of mourning reaches beyond the individual's or community's coming to terms with a particular loss, for the ritual of burying the dead has from antiquity been bound up with memory, memorialisation and historical consciousness. We will return to the funerals of ancient Rome in the next section and consider how they too bear the Derridean description of the 'already dead living'. What Derrida evokes here is the *continuing effective presence* of the dead throughout our lives, in a space which he identifies with the process of 'learning to live'.[8] Thus he resists the Marxian decoupling of modernity from mourning, situating himself instead in the historical tradition where learning from and honouring the dead are joint activities.

It is in the context of this tradition, as well as of the Freudian and Derridean responses, that we can see the full force of Marx's stark separation of the nineteenth century from what went before. Indeed, we can also see this tradition challenged by Marx's complex and often contradictory account of the processes of repetition, recollection and forgetting in the revolutions of the past. By troping repetition as low farce, caricature and parody, Marx effectively empties the present of meaning in so far as it depends upon the past.[9] Modernity breaks, therefore, with two forms of past: with the (recent) past rendered meaningless by its false historical consciousness; and with antiquity, whose historical consciousness is not visible in this text. Nevertheless, the Marxian view of repetition as parody itself operates as a parody of ancient modes of historical thinking which involve conjuring up the past to explain, understand, and act in the present.[10] Thucydides'

---

[7] Derrida 1994: 143.

[8] See esp. Derrida 1994: xvii: 'To live, by definition, is not something one learns. Not from oneself, it is not learned from life, taught by life. Only from the other and by death. In any case from the other at the edge of life. At the internal border or the external border, it is a heterodidactics between life and death.'

[9] See also Mehlman (1977) on the parasitism and Rabelaisian excess of Bonapartism in Marx's text.

[10] On Marxian parody as a critique of ideology, see LaCapra 1983: 281–4.

famous claim that his work is to be a 'possession for all time' is predicated precisely on such a seamless transition from representation to action and from past to present, as well as upon a fundamental, trans-historical human nature, which makes the repetition of events across time both inevitable and natural.

It will be enough that these books are judged useful by those who want to see clearly things that have happened and that will happen again sometime, being much the same on account of the human element. So this has been composed as a possession for all time rather than as a recitation to be heard in the present.[11]

Thucydides' words echo ironically throughout the *Eighteenth Brumaire*,[12] not least in the image of the past weighing upon the present 'like a nightmare on the brain of the living'. Here and elsewhere Marx seems to suggest that a break with the past is not simply a matter for modernity, that the past appears sometimes as an active and sometimes vengeful entity, in whose ongoing potency the living agents of the present are perhaps only partly complicit.

The concept of haunting, however, takes on a particular charge in the mid-nineteenth century; modern man no longer passively endures nightmares, but becomes active in the summoning of and inquiry into ghosts. The activity of the séance – a counterpart to burial – is evoked by Marx immediately after his deployment of nightmare imagery.

Tradition from all the dead generations weighs like a nightmare on the brain of the living. And just when they appear to be revolutionising themselves and their circumstances, in creating something unprecedented, in just such epochs of revolutionary crisis, that is when they nervously summon up the spirits of the past, borrowing from them their names, marching orders, uniforms in order to enact new scenes in world history, but in this time-honoured guise and with this borrowed language.[13]

What Marx delineates here is the double movement of revolution. This involves on the one hand the creation of something new (revolutionary desires in ancient Rome were designated *res novae*), and on the other hand a repetition, a return to the past.[14] Crucially, for Marx's revolutionary necromancers as for the ancient Romans, a new state of affairs evokes anxiety, confronting them with the challenge of taking responsibility for 'creating something unprecedented'. The return to the past is a response

[11] Thuc. 1.22.4.   [12] On ancient parody of Thucydides' claim, see O'Gorman 2007: 237–8.
[13] Marx 2002: 19–20.
[14] Koselleck 2004b: 45 characterises the early nineteenth century as a time which had 'forgotten' the meaning of revolution as repetition. See also Mehlman 1977.

to that anxiety, but the past is also itself a source of anxiety. The past appears as potential judge of new events, events which will not be 'time-honoured' because they have never yet existed; but these new events would escape not only the honour of time, but the very judgement itself, and here the anxiety lies. So the past is evoked as a mode of representation, 'to present the new' – but to whom? Marx's later arguments suggest that this is about revolutionaries' understanding of their own actions,[15] but the degree of agency afforded to the ghosts of the past throughout the *Eighteenth Brumaire* could lead us to consider whether the past here can be seen as the audience towards which the representation of the new as repetition is anxiously addressed.

The issue of representation in both a mimetic and a political sense is central to the *Eighteenth Brumaire*. In both senses of representation, repetition has a disruptive effect on meaningful action. Repetition threatens the true representation of revolutionary action, inhibits the revolutionaries' proper understanding of the process and thereby infects the revolution itself with the falsity of representation: it becomes a simulacrum of revolution. In two places, however, Marx imagines how repetition might be redeemed by certain forms of forgetting; the first occurs after he has imagined the new scene of world history presented 'in this time-honoured guise and with this borrowed language':

Likewise a beginner studying a new language always translates it back into his mother tongue; but only when he can use it without referring back, and thus forsake his native language for the new, only then has he entered into the spirit of the new language, and gained the ability to speak it fluently.[16]

The speaker begins with a meaningless and dependent repetition, words which cannot stand by themselves but which originate from and are rendered back into another tongue. Yet repetition in the context of language learning does not impede understanding but provides a structure within which the learner may progress towards full independent discourse. This analogy concludes the famous paragraph which begins 'Men make their own history, but they do not make it just as they please', but just as the analogy talks about translation, so it translates the terms of the foregoing discussion. The 'borrowed language' of the past, which was used to misrepresent the truth of the new, has become a 'mother tongue'; the 'spirits of the past' are forgotten as the speaker assimilates 'the spirit of the new language'.

---

[15] See in particular his comments on the French and English Revolutions examined later in this chapter.
[16] Marx 2002: 20.

The repetition here translates 'spirit' from the underworld to the realm of living speech – a new form of resurrection. Thereby spirit and speaker are redeemed from the dead weight of the past.[17] In fact, what is striking about this analogy is its disavowal of death even at a metaphorical level; what is discarded and forgotten is a 'mother tongue', a 'native tongue', but not a dead language.

Ghosts are more easily exorcised from the historical discourse of repetition with which Marx continues, as he delineates the French and then the English revolutions of the eighteenth and seventeenth centuries in terms of their resurrection and subsequent disavowal of ancient Rome and the Old Testament. What facilitates this exorcism is the slippage of translation between 'spirit' and 'ghost' which his language analogy has set to work:

Thus the resurrection of the dead in those revolutions served to glorify new struggles, not to parody the old; to magnify fantastically the given task, not to evade a real resolution; to recover the spirit of revolution, not to relaunch its spectre.[18]

Here Marx enacts the exorcism by using *Geist* for the resurrected and living spirit, not for the haunting ghost: 'den *Geist* der Revolution wiederzufinden, nicht ihr *Gespenst* wieder umgehen zu machen'.[19] The discursive and affective engagements with the past, with its 'speech, passions, and illusions', enables effective and fully self-conscious action in the present. In this evocative account particularly of the French Revolution's re-enactment of ancient Rome, Marx gives depth to the distinction he will draw between these earlier revolutions and those of the nineteenth century. But what he does not draw attention to here is how difference within antiquity itself is flattened out in the service of the eighteenth century. So, for the French Revolution, ancient Rome is institutionalised as 'the Brutuses, the Gracchuses, the Publicolas, the tribunes, the senators and Caesar himself', collapsing the political heterogeneity of the various Roman revolutions over 600 years into one 'exemplary' past as it is seen by the (eighteenth century) present: the dead of world history.

What is significant about this institutionalising of 'the resurrected Romans' is that it repeats among the 'strict classical traditions of the Roman republic' precisely the mode of historical thinking we have already observed, exemplified by Thucydides and parodied by Marx. In this process of exemplarity, repetition and representation are central and justify the

[17] Harries 1995: 47 observes that Marx's use of *Geist* underwrites his 'campaign to reverse Hegel and his master trope'.
[18] Marx 2002: 21.   [19] See also Derrida 1994: 134–41 on *Geist* versus *Gespenst*.

practice of history itself. By the time we reach the historical writings of
late Republican/early Imperial Rome, Thucydides' fundamental principles
have become formalised as explicit lessons for the reader, as articulated by
Livy.

And this is an especially healthy and fruitful aspect to historical understanding, that
you look on the evidence of every exemplum as if placed on a notable monument;
and from this you can take examples of what you should imitate – for your own
sake and for that of your state – and what you should avoid, shameful in its
inception and shameful in its outcome.[20]

Juxtaposing these comments with Marx's thoughts on repetition, as we
have seen, appears to deepen the gulf between antiquity and modernity.

Men make their own history, but they do not make it just as they please in circumstances they choose for themselves; rather they make it in present circumstances,
given and inherited.[21]

Carver's up-to-date translation emphasises the 'presentness' of the past; the
final phrase has more traditionally been rendered as 'circumstances directly
encountered, given, and *transmitted from the past*'. These circumstances,
inherited in part from the ancient historians, include the very practice of
presenting the new in the guise of the old. But what also emerges is a difference between antiquity and modernity in the *experience* of exemplarity;
even the revolutionaries of 1789, as we have seen, experience a 'healthy
and fruitful' aspect to repetition, 'to *recover* the spirit of the revolution'. By
contrast, people of the nineteenth century begin to experience repetition as
something which happens to them, rather than something actively picked
out in the process of historical understanding.

The nation is like the mad Englishman in Bedlam who thinks he is living in
the time of the pharaohs and complains every day how hard it is to work in the
Ethiopian gold mines, immured in a subterranean prison, a flickering lamp fixed
to his head, behind him the overseer with his long whip, and at the exits a mass
of barbarian mercenaries, who can understand neither the slave labourers in the
mines nor one another, since they have no common language.[22]

The past here becomes a 'possession for all time' in a more nightmarish
sense. Spirits are no longer anxiously conjured up, but walk about, and
'translate' the streets of Paris and the walls of Bedlam with their inhabitants
to other, more ancient locations. The subjects of the nineteenth century
are thus denied 'authentic' historical experience, since they do not know

---

[20] Livy, *Pref.* 6.   [21] Marx 2002: 19, my emphases.
[22] Marx 2002: 21; cf. his comments on 'parliamentary cretinism', 75.

where they belong in time. By contrast, the process of exemplarity as it is theorised by the historians of antiquity seems to involve a conflation of times which does not overwhelm the historical subject, but rather enhances their experience of both past and present, and enables their movement towards the future.

ROMAN EXEMPLARITY

It is perhaps no coincidence that one of the most frequently cited cultural practices which encourages exemplarity for the ancient Romans is the funeral procession; this dramatises an engagement with the past as simultaneously dead and living in terms which directly intersect with the nightmarish imagery of Marx, and with Derrida's formulation of burial as performed by 'still living mortals' for the 'already dead living'.

An important factor to bear in mind when considering the significance of the Roman funeral procession for our understanding of ancient repetition and exemplarity is the usual practice of aristocratic Roman nomenclature, where we see an extraordinary tendency to situate the individual in a genealogical context which is figured as repetitive continuity. The fact that a Roman aristocrat would emerge into public life bearing exactly the same name as his father or uncle, his grandfather, great-grandfather and any other number of male relatives/ancestors attests to what R. H. Martin and A. J. Woodman have called 'the remarkable Roman capacity for seeing one individual in terms of another'.[23] Again, this may be contrasted with Marx's analysis of the French peasantry and their misunderstanding of Louis Napoleon's political significance, where the repetition of names triggers a confusion of times, with consequences analogous to the madness in Bedlam:

> Through historical tradition it has come to pass that the French peasantry believed in a miracle, that a man of the name of Napoleon would bring them back to their former glory. And there came an individual who presented himself as such a man because he bore the name Napoleon, in accordance with the Napoleonic Code which stipulates: 'All inquiry into paternity is forbidden.' . . . the prophecy was fulfilled and the man became emperor of the French.[24]

By contrast, Roman political culture, faced with another Q. Fabius Maximus or M. Aemilius Lepidus, holds past and present in tension, seeing the present Lepidus simultaneously in the modes of repetition and of difference. In similar ways, the practice of ancestor cult focused on funeral masks

---

[23] Martin and Woodman 1989: 85.   [24] Marx 2002: 101; cf. Watkins 2002.

representing the dead, yet the association of mask with representation or with pretence is played down in favour of the mask as 'making present' the past. Polybius' well-known account of Roman funeral practices draws on this peculiar presence and its effects.[25] After describing the construction of the ancestral mask in the likeness of the dead ancestor, and the display of all the ancestral masks, worn by individuals of similar build, Polybius remarks,

There cannot be a finer spectacle for a young man to look on, one who is a lover of glory and nobility; for who would not be inspired by looking on the images of men glorified for their virtue, all in the same place as if living and breathing? What spectacle would seem finer than this?[26]

First, we may note the celebration of mimesis in this passage, which enables the past to come alive at the funeral ceremony, a moment where we moderns would expect the past to be laid to rest. Significantly, the function of experienced present is here more important than 'letting the dead bury the dead'. Instead, *all* the ancestors are revived, as if living and breathing, as the 'already dead living'. A ceremony that appeared alien even to the Greek historian who recorded it,[27] the Roman funeral ceremony demonstrates the gulf between ancient and modern senses of the past's presence and its potency. The young Roman at the funeral is not haunted by the past, nor does he experience a confusion of times, rather he engages competitively with figures from the past just as he would with contemporary rivals. The competitiveness of the Roman character contributes, in Polybius' account, to this suspension of temporal difference; it is because the young man desires glory that he 'takes on' his ancestors in this way. In Sallust's account of the same process of emulation we see how the very competitiveness and drive for glory which inspires Romans to imitation is itself an inherited characteristic.

For I have often heard Q. Maximus, P. Scipio and other eminent men of our city say that when they look on their ancestors' masks, their spirits are fired to pursue virtue with the utmost energy. But really the wax itself and the form of the mask does not possess such force; rather, the memory of ancestral deeds arouses that flame in the hearts of exceptional men, and it will not be extinguished before their virtue matches their ancestors' fame and glory.[28]

Sallust's opposition of the visual appearance of the masks to the memory of the ancestor's deeds suggests that he too is evoking the funeral ceremony,

---

[25] For further discussion of the historical effects of the funeral mask, see O'Gorman 2000: 56–69.
[26] Pol. 6.53.10.   [27] As rightly emphasised by Chaplin 2000.   [28] Sall. *Iug.* 4.5–6.

where the display is accompanied by a narrative account of the dead man's achievements. This emulation of the past, at the very moment when the ancestors appear as if living and breathing, also represents a refusal to allow the present to be entirely subsumed by the past. The young Romans of both passages are inspired by the desire to glorify themselves and perpetuate their 'own' names (in so far as their names can stand for themselves and not for their *gens*); their engagement with the past is of a provisional nature, in that it looks to the future when they too will 'haunt' their descendants. Sallust's choice of Q. Fabius Maximus and P. Cornelius Scipio as exemplary figures instantiates this aim, by citing two of the most illustrious statesmen of the previous generation. But they do not appear here as examples of virtuous action, but as examples of Romans inspired to virtue by the deeds of their ancestors. By retrospectively looking back on their fame as provisional, Sallust valorises the moment of inspiration to glory over the moment of achievement of that glory. Indeed, his account implicitly points up how the experienced temporalities of glory and fame are always retrospective (as others remember Fabius' glorious deeds) or prospective (as Fabius anticipates achieving glory). And these temporalities, in the accounts of the funeral ceremonies, are inextricably intertwined, as the anticipation of glory is triggered by and mediated through the retrospective act of remembrance.

These idealised accounts of exemplarity in Roman culture (an idealism with which I am temporarily complicit) should be tempered by accounts from the same historians of how the past is evoked in practice, where the question of which past to evoke, and how to use the lessons of the past, is much more prominent, and much less easily settled. What these debates illuminate is a greater degree of self-consciousness about the process of thinking about the present by way of the past, and considerably less sense of continuity across the ages. In situating these debates alongside the modalities of repetition traced in the *Eighteenth Brumaire* we should also recall that Marx explicitly situates his discussion of repetition and historical thought in epochs of revolutionary crisis. Conversely, the ancient theoretical discussions of exemplarity are quoted in contemporary scholarship in order to present exemplary thinking in the context of education and everyday cultural practice, and thereby create the illusion of a mode of thought which is characteristic of a stable state. In fact, if we look more closely at the ancient texts from which these accounts are taken, we find exemplarity evoked at different sorts of crisis points in Roman history. Not all of these can be termed 'revolutionary crisis' in Marxian terms, though many can be described as the emergence of *res novae*. Livy's exhortation to his reader to

follow the 'healthy and fruitful' practice of exemplary thought comes in the
wake of his remarks about the present state of Rome, 'where we can endure
neither our ills nor their remedies'. As Jane Chaplin comments, '*exempla*
have a special value for a generation whose past had collapsed and whose
future was uncertain'.[29] More than this, *exempla* became, for the Romans of
the Augustan period and beyond, what Marx calls 'the self-deceptions that
they needed, in order to hide from themselves the constrained . . . character
of their struggles'.[30] What we find in the ancient historians of the period,
however, is an analysis of these self-deceptions and their consequences,
whether productive, illusory, or both at the same time.

   To examine the use of exemplarity in strategic thinking, and its implication in historical thought, we turn to a later book of Livy, and the debate in
senate over whether the consul P. Cornelius Scipio should be sent to Africa
to end the war with Carthage. As Chaplin points out, this is one of the
sets of paired speeches in Livy's history which pits an elder statesman with
considerable authority (in this case Q. Fabius Maximus) against a younger
speaker (Scipio, who has already declared his populist tactics), thereby
dramatising a conflict between past and present, or rather, we should say,
between different perspectives on the past.[31] Since the theoretical accounts
of exemplarity explicitly focus on young men as the target of *exempla*,
these speeches constitute a particularly charged demonstration of whether
and how exemplarity works – whether (as we would say in contemporary
educational discourse) the learning outcomes of exemplarity have been
achieved.[32] In the speech of Fabius the *exempla* chosen illustrate how cam-
paigns overseas can end disastrously; Fabius, moreover, self-consciously
moves from one *exemplum* to another by drawing attention to his mode of
selection.

The Athenians, a very cautious state, left war behind them at home, and sent a
huge fleet over to Sicily under the guidance of a young man as active as he was
noble, and in one naval battle they inflicted a permanent injury on their flourishing
state. But I repeat examples which are foreign and too out-of-date. Let Africa itself
and M. Atilius Regulus stand as evidence for us, an exceptional example of both
extremes of fortune.[33]

---

[29] Chaplin 2000: 31. Since Ronald Syme's study of 1939 Livy's age has been known to us as the period
of 'The Roman Revolution'.

[30] Marx 2002: 20–1.   [31] Chaplin 2000: 120 ff.

[32] It is important, however, to acknowledge that there is no clear winner in the debate; Scipio gets his
wished-for command more through negotiations behind the scenes, as well as the threat of popular
support.

[33] Livy 28.41.17–42.1.

Fabius moves from an *exemplum* which operates very neatly at the level of similarity (Athens–Rome; Sparta–Hannibal; Alcibiades–Scipio; Sicily–Carthage) to one which is internally ambiguous (Regulus serves as *exemplum* for both good fortune and bad), but which he deems more effective because it is both Roman and more recent.[34] His 'rejection' of the Athenian example, incidentally, presents a sidelong challenge to Thucydides' claim that all events in his narrative will repeat at some time or another, since the Sicilian expedition is one of the great set pieces of Thucydides' history. But more importantly, Fabius' turn to Regulus represents a valorisation of temporal proximity and Roman tradition over similarity of events. Fabius does not go on to outline in detail the ways in which Regulus' situation is in parallel with Scipio's. Though there are some implicit parallels there are also many divergences, and Scipio's refutation of this *exemplum* goes into considerably more detail about the story of Regulus precisely in order to point up its inapplicability in this context.

Fabius recalls that M. Atilius was captured in Africa, as if M. Atilius was defeated on first arriving in Africa, nor does Fabius seem to remember that even for this unfortunate general the ports of Africa were open, and that in his first year he waged war with success, and remained to the end unbeaten at least by any Carthaginian leader. Therefore in no way can you frighten me with this exemplum.[35]

Scipio's display of detailed historical knowledge is significant given that he is, as I remarked earlier, the younger man; his probing of the applicability of the *exemplum* serves not only to argue against Fabius but also to demonstrate his own command of exemplary thinking.[36] Chaplin argues that, while Fabius sees the past as essentially fixed, Scipio considers, and demonstrates, that historical examples change their meaning over time and according to their usage.[37] But what is problematic about this is that Fabius appears to hand Scipio the perfect examples for illustrating this view of history; he himself acknowledges that Regulus can be used to illustrate good fortune and bad. He also seems to reject the example of the Sicilian expedition because it is too old, that is to say, it has become overshadowed by more recent events; it has changed in meaning over time. What the exchange illustrates, in contrast to the theoretical accounts, therefore, is not merely the living engaging with the dead, but the living evaluating the terms on which the dead should be engaged. The shifting significance

---

[34] Fabius later picks an even more recent *exemplum* with which to argue his case (28.42.17). On the general arguments for recent *exempla*, see Chaplin 2000: 123–5.

[35] Livy 28.43.17.

[36] Scipio, in fact, goes on to attack this *exemplum* too as out of date. See Chaplin 2000: 95 for the potential weakness of Scipio's use of *exempla*.

[37] Chaplin 2000: 130.

of the exemplary past, moreover, breaks down the universalising tendency which we see both in the theoretical accounts of exemplarity and in Marx's description of 'resurrected Romans' in the eighteenth century.

If there is any anxiety to be detected in the practice of exemplarity as it appears in this exchange, it is perhaps to be located in the specific fear of repetition which the *exemplum* of Regulus' capture indirectly expresses. This conjuring up of the dead, which Scipio suggests is done to *terrify* him, serves as a warning of possible failure, and demonstrates the way the past threatens to return in the present. This represents a more Freudian than a Marxian view of repetition; whereas for Marx the present becomes emptied of significance, becomes a parody, when it repeats the past, Freud is more concerned with the way in which past traumas, improperly processed through memory, lock an individual – and we might say a culture[38] – into endlessly repeating destructive behavioural patterns. Here repetition occurs as a symptom of the failure of historical thinking, and a concomitant failure to distinguish between remembrance/representation on the one hand, and reality/lived experience on the other. For Freud's patients, as for Marx's revolutionaries, the past truly weighs like a nightmare, while it is experienced as waking life. As Freud remarks in *Beyond the Pleasure Principle*,

None of these things [which patients repeat in analysis] can have produced pleasure in the past, and it might be supposed that they would cause less unpleasure today if they emerged as memories or dreams instead of taking the form of fresh experiences. They are of course the activities of instincts intended to lead to satisfaction; but no lesson has been learnt from the old experience of these activities having led instead only to unpleasure.[39]

At first glance, Freud's professed therapy for such a condition appears to create a sharp distinction between real/lived present and remembered/represented past, as the patient is encouraged to understand that what they experience is not real, not in the here and now, but can safely be consigned to the past, to memory and to discourse.

He [the analyst] must get him [the patient] to re-experience some portion of his forgotten life, but must see to it, on the other hand, that the patient retains some degree of aloofness, which will enable him, in spite of everything, to recognize that what appears to be reality is in fact only a reflection of a forgotten past.[40]

---

[38] For a discussion of how Freud's theories translate to analysis of groups in history, see Roth 1995: 137–99; Lear 2005: 119–20 discusses how the psychoanalytic treatment includes the 'social world' of both analyst and analysand.

[39] Freud 1991: 292.

[40] Freud 1991: 289.

We can see how exemplarity, and the evocation of figures such as Regulus, cut across these distinctions; exemplarity, as a form of historical thought, works as a cultural memory process, and *at the same time* as a mode of pragmatic deliberation. Regulus in particular, moreover, does not belong to a forgotten past, but is remembered, represented and 'exemplarised' to excess.[41] Indeed, the very excess of remembrance in this instance, as well as the considerable ambiguities around the question of what it is Regulus is supposed to exemplify, may represent a different kind of haunting. Whereas for Freud trauma escapes the memory process, the *exemplum* of Regulus appears within, but is not fully comprehended by the memory system itself. Hence its continual reworking testifies to the difficulty with its assimilation.[42] In that sense the debate between Fabius and Scipio over Regulus' exemplarity suggests that here 'no lesson has been learnt'.

While the theoretical analyses of exemplarity concentrate on the different temporalities of the individual who thinks with *exempla* – the young man at the Roman funeral, for instance – such accounts as Livy's of exemplarity in practice enmesh speakers like Fabius and Scipio in further temporal inter-actions, not least in their debates about how 'past' any event from the past might be. This self-consciousness about temporalities affects the reader of Livy's text too, who observes the characters in their own past, present and future, on which is superimposed a simultaneous vision of these presents and futures as themselves past. The *exemplum*, which occupies different forms of past for both characters and readers, serves as a sort of 'shared past', by means of which the reader can experience the modalities of hope, fear, desire, and decision through which the characters live their present and move towards their future. We can see, for example, how Fabius' fear and suspicion of Scipio is modulated through figures from the past, Regulus and Alcibiades. We can see at the same time how Scipio's future, which we experience in this passage as a sort of 'anticipated past', will set to rest the terrors of the Regulus *exemplum* by reversing his fate, but will to an extent fulfil the suspicions aroused by the name of Alcibiades. This reminds us, of course, that the *exempla* express something about Scipio in Livy's retro-spective view as well as in Fabius' prospective view, and that what we read in this text is simultaneously a representation of exemplarity in deliberative practice and a mobilisation of *exempla* for implicit historical analysis.

---

[41] Polybius initiates the presentation of Regulus as an *exemplum* at 1.35, discussed by Walbank 1970: 92–4, who cites the many variants of this story. See also Mix 1970.

[42] Goldhill 1994: 70 argues that such excess is an effect of narrativisation: 'The example's narrative form always threatens to produce an excess of signification beyond the controlling lines of the case it is designed to illustrate.'

NO TIME LIKE THE PRESENT

To break out of the repetitions and create something entirely new, to leave the dead to bury their dead, must surely entail exorcising the ghost of exemplarity. This would be unthinkable for ancient Rome, but it appears to be Marx's aim: in Reinhardt Koselleck's words, to 'found the singularity of the coming revolution'.[43] Derrida, in his conclusion to *Specters of Marx*, resists this proposed break as unethical even if it is possible, and indeed, when we examine Marx's characterisation of this redemptive modernity, we find new structures of repetition, paradoxical allusions to the past, and a primordial vision of the dead who will not die.

[P]roletarian revolutions, such as those of the nineteenth century, *engage in perpetual self-criticism*, always *stopping* in their own tracks; they *return* to what is apparently complete in order to begin it anew, and *deride* with savage brutality the inadequacies, weak points and pitiful aspects of their first attempts; *they seem to strike down their adversary, only to have him draw new powers from the earth and rise against them once more with the strength of a giant*; again and again they *draw back* from the prodigious scope of their own aims, until a situation is created which *makes impossible any reversion*, and circumstances themselves cry out:

  Hic Rhodus, hic salta!

  Hier ist die Rose, hier tanze![44]

Despite the insistent present tense of this passage, Marx is describing an ideal but impending future. In place of the repetitions of the past which blind us to the content of our actions, he proposes a self-critical process of interrupted and repeated action. Instead of parody, future revolutions savagely deride their own immediate past. Marx traces a gradual and difficult approach to the revelatory moment, when circumstances themselves cry for an intervention grounded in full knowledge. Again, this account intersects with Freudian descriptions of the analytic procedure, where the unhealthy repetitions of the patient's life are replaced with the repetition in analysis which moves the patient to a new understanding of the present. But the Freudian context might lead us to consider whether Marx's imagined revolutionaries are engaged in analysis terminable or interminable, whether they can respond when circumstances call out to them. Two features of this passage contribute to this sense of doubt: first, the way that Marx turns away from the future immediately after the call, back to the present inadequacies of the Bonapartist *coup*; secondly, the obscurity of

---

[43] Koselleck 2004b: 54.   [44] Marx 2002: 22–3, my emphases.

the call itself, which problematises the moment of historical revelation. Much scholarly attention has been devoted both to the meaning of the Latin tag and to Hegel's quasi-mystical translation.[45] Terrell Carver renders it idiomatically as 'There's no time like the present!', and thus effects precisely the break with the past which Marx seems to aim at. This translation, however, bypasses what Martin Harries has observed, that '[a]gain, a passage in which Marx describes the process of revolution ends in an allusion'.[46] Here circumstances themselves, asserting the immediacy of the moment, speak with the (difficult) language of the past.

But, in moving too quickly to the end of the proletarian revolution, readers recapitulate the movement of the earlier, unsuccessful revolutions, which attain their zenith too soon. In the middle of the process of self-interruption and recapitulation which characterises this new modernity, Marx presents us with the exemplary figures of the future, not from history but from myth. Antaeus, the giant born of the earth who drew continual strength from contact with his mother,[47] appears as a potent figure in socialist ideology, often symbolising the working class in its resilient struggle against oppression. What is striking in Marx's formulation is that he presents the proletarian revolutionaries not with Antaeus but with his opponent Hercules as their exemplar. What is also striking is how this myth of resurrection forecloses on the possibility of spectres or haunting: Antaeus as an earth-born giant and Hercules as a semi-divine hero are not subject to the laws of mortality. Derrida, as we have seen, resists this move away from a position which takes account of our being between life and death. These non-human exemplary figures, then, present not so much a break with the past as a new kind of relation with the past, and repetition differently manifested as self-analysis. In choosing Hercules and Antaeus, Marx, like Fabius and Scipio, perhaps demonstrates the problematics, even the excesses, of exemplarity in action. But it may be that in this almost perverse choice of an *exemplum* which does not quite fit its application Marx situates the conditions for redeeming the future of modernity.[48]

---

[45] Carver 2002: 128 n. 17 offers a succinct explanation.   [46] Harries 1995: 57.

[47] An account of the downfall of Antaeus at the hands of Hercules can be found in Lucan *Pharsalia* 4.587–655.

[48] I am grateful to Terrell Carver, Miriam Leonard and Aleka Lianeri for reading and commenting on drafts of this chapter.

CHAPTER 13

Time and authority in the Chronicle of Sulpicius Severus

Michael Stuart Williams

'Christianity,' wrote a young Alasdair MacIntyre, 'cannot dispense with the notion of men having parts in a cosmic drama.'[1] This was a drama that played out on the level of history – for it was a defining feature of Christianity that the claims it made were not only transcendental but also, importantly, historical.[2] It mattered for Christianity that Christ had been born at a specific historical moment, just as it mattered for Judaism – and ultimately for Christianity too – that the Jewish patriarchs had historically encountered and made covenants with their God. The structure of the Christian Bible itself makes this aspect plain: by taking over much of the Jewish tradition, the Christians were able to begin their authoritative account of the world with its creation, and to follow a privileged strand of history through the successes and travails of the Jews, so that even the books of the laws and the prophets, and of proverbs and psalms, were placed in a thoroughly historical context. The New Testament was bound equally tightly into this tradition, not only by an explicit grounding in a particular historical moment – as when Luke relates the birth of Christ to the reigns of Augustus and Herod – but also in the efforts of the New Testament writers to identify Jesus of Nazareth as the anticipated subject of Jewish messianic prophecies, not least by making him a descendant of the House of David.[3] This kind of interpretation may be labelled 'historical typology': it was a method of identifying the significant correspondences between distinct historical events.[4] History, for Christians, was therefore more than a narrative, more than a mere sequence of unconnected events. As in any good drama, these events possessed a deeper significance: they formed part of an underlying plot.

---

[1] MacIntyre 1971: 68.   [2] Croke 2001: 263: 'Christianity was essentially a historical religion.'
[3] Luke 1.5, 2:1–4; Matthew 1:1–17. For the rhetorical relationship between the Old and New Testaments, see Kermode 1968, Mortley 1996: 120 ff. and Kofsky 2000: 100 ff.
[4] Williams 2008, with compatible definitions at Auerbach 1959; Charity 1966: 1–9 and Hollander 1977.

Thus it was the events of history, and the actions of individuals within that history, which above all justified the claims of Christianity.[5] With such historical relationships at the heart of its understanding of the world, it should be no surprise that the advent of Christianity as a dominant force in the Roman Empire has been credited with prompting a reassessment of the classical approach to historiography. This was not, however, primarily evident in those historians (such as Ammianus Marcellinus) who continued to write in an avowedly classical tradition. Indeed, Arnaldo Momigliano found it remarkable that the same historians whose work – in his view – could be characterised as part of 'the classical historiography of change' nevertheless failed for the most part 'to register the particular change represented by Christianity'.[6] Yet as part of the same discussion he provided the beginnings of an answer: that 'it was the violent, rather than the slow, change that the [classical] historian presented to his readers'.[7] The emphasis was on immediate political upheavals – and where Christianity was implicated in these, it was indeed brought into such histories. Any broader, more gradual change in the progression of human history was overlooked, or even deliberately ignored. The Greeks and Romans, of course, were well aware of the passage of time and its effects; and antecedent events could be divided into 'history' (which stretched back as far as could be known) and 'myth' (which covered all that happened before that).[8] Classical and classicising historians thus focused their attention on the events of the recent past, and placed the highest value on autopsy and on personal experience.

Christianity, by contrast, followed Judaism in making little or no distinction between knowable recent historical events and unknowable myth. As Momigliano points out, the Hebrew authors of Genesis 'did not think it necessary to explain how they came to know the conversation between Eve and the serpent'.[9] In broader terms, the Christian understanding of time focused less on understanding the contingent events of history than on its overall design: on the larger story which revealed 'the continuous intervention of God in the world he had created'.[10] With the rise of Christianity in the Roman Empire, then, it might well be imagined that a new understanding of time came to the fore. Any such transition, however, was far from immediate. Certainly the earliest Christian histories – and, above all, the Ecclesiastical History of Eusebius of Caesarea – were innovative in a

---

[5] As argued in Ricoeur 1952: 246–50.   [6] Momigliano 1977a: 167, 165.
[7] Momigliano 1977a: 173.
[8] For this view of time in classical historiography – opposed to the idea that the Greeks conceived of time as a cycle – see Momigliano 1977b: 185–93.
[9] Momigliano 1977b: 194.   [10] Momigliano 1977b: 194.

great number of areas: for example, Eusebius challenged some of the most important conventions of classical historiography by transferring attention from the political manoeuvrings of the recent past to the development over the long term of a single institution, and in the process replaced the classical commitment to autopsy and to independent interpretation with an emphasis on quotations from authorities and 'the lavish use of documents'.[11] On this basis, Momigliano offered the *Ecclesiastical History* as a formative influence on modern, footnoted, non-contemporary history.[12] Nevertheless, in this work Eusebius continued to follow the lead of the classical tradition, if only because this particular story took place almost entirely within the world of the Roman Empire. The *Ecclesiastical History* reached back only into the relatively recent past. It recorded events that could equally have featured in any classical history, and merely refocused attention from the political centre to the formerly marginal Christian story. Here at least, Christian time did not replace classical time but was instead subsumed within it.

A more substantial challenge to classical conventions was issued in another of Eusebius' works: his *Chronicle*.[13] There he dispensed with narrative altogether and presented a 'universal history' in tabular form, with events from classical history and from Scripture offered side by side for the sake of chronological comparison. The apologetic aim was to prove the antiquity – and indeed the priority – of the Christian and Jewish traditions. The two timescales were therefore ostensibly in competition; and yet by incorporating the two of them into a single representation Eusebius in fact brought them together. Thus the alternative classical and Christian models of time could be maintained in a permanent tension and could be seen simultaneously, with neither necessarily privileged over the other. Once again the classical model was not replaced but only supplemented; and conversely, in its juxtaposition with the Greek and Roman past Christianity was somewhat classicised. This useful compromise was not invented solely by Eusebius – for there were precedents in the works of Clement of Alexandria, Julius Africanus and Hippolytus of Rome – but it was Eusebius' system which would become the point of departure for subsequent authors, especially in the Latin West.[14] Within fifty years, Jerome had translated the *Chronicle* and continued it down to 378 CE; later continuators of the same tradition include Prosper of Aquitaine, Hydatius and the anonymous Gallic chronicler of 452, along with the Byzantine Latin chronicle

---

[11] Momigliano 1963: 83, 85, 90–1.   [12] Momigliano 1963: 92.
[13] Specifically, the second book of his *Chronicle*: see the comprehensive account in Burgess 1999.
[14] Momigliano 1963: 83–7.

of Marcellinus.[15] It would prove an acceptable model for representing the past at least until the Renaissance; and in recent years such chronicles have begun to be taken more seriously as interesting historiographical enterprises in their own right.[16]

Yet standing somewhat apart from this tradition is the so-called *Chronicle* (or *Sacred History*) written at the turn of the fifth century CE by the Gallic aristocrat and ascetic Sulpicius Severus.[17] Although he quite clearly engages with the chronographical tradition of Eusebius and Jerome, Sulpicius offers in place of a table of dates and events a connected (if rather condensed) narrative account. He thus followed the earlier chronographers in bringing together the classical and Christian pasts; but instead of preserving them independent and intact, in splendid isolation from each other, he set out to integrate them into a single story. This then was far from a claim for the essential priority of one tradition over another – for although Christianity filled gaps in the classical past, so too could the classical tradition be used to supplement, or even correct, Christian history. What Sulpicius produced, then, was something of a hybrid: a work which in some ways resembled contemporary epitomes and *breviaria* and which made some attempt to conform to the literary and historical approaches of Tacitus and Sallust, but in which the presentation of the past is firmly Christian and is founded above all on the Christian scriptures.[18]

This might be recognised as a brave and deliberate attempt to resolve the incompatibility between the classical and Christian understandings of the past – to resolve, that is, the tensions preserved in the unwieldy tabular chronologies in which they were presently combined. In the process, however, Sulpicius drew attention to a problem inherent in the very idea of a Christian historiography. For Christians already possessed an authoritative – and indeed, unchallengeable – account of the past in the Bible itself. Moreover, the authority of the biblical account did not rest only in the events it recorded, but also in the very words that were used to

---

[15] Muhlberger 1990; Croke 2001.

[16] Aside from studies of individual chronicles, see Johnson 1962; von den Brincken 1969; Croke 1983; Burgess 1990 and Zecchini 2003.

[17] Latin text (with new paragraphing, followed below) in de Senneville-Grave 1999, with an explanation of the naming issue at 11–12. All translations are my own except where noted.

[18] For the connection with contemporary histories in general see Prete 1955: 9; the connection is noted but not explored in Momigliano 1963: 86–7. For the link to epitomes, see Costanza 1980; the introduction to the *Chronicle* is compared with that of Eutropius' *Breviarium* at Stancliffe 1983: 178–9; Zecchini 2003: 336 calls the work 'a cross between chronicle and compendium'. For Sulpicius as a 'Christian Sallust' or 'Christian Tacitus', see especially Fontaine 1975 and Tanner 1989, with additional references at Murru 1979: 962–3 and de Senneville-Grave 1999: 40–3. Jerome draws attention to his own use of Suetonius in the preface to his *Chronicle*.

record them. By taking on the attitude of a classical historian, and by seeking not only to incorporate secular history into the biblical story but to retell that story in his own words, Sulpicius was trespassing on territory that Christianity had conceded to the inspired authors of Scripture. In seeking to establish its own narrative authority, therefore, the *Chronicle* of Sulpicius Severus risked calling into question the authority of the Bible itself.

THE NATURE OF THE *CHRONICLE*

The innovative – indeed, experimental – nature of the *Chronicle* has frequently prevented it from being understood as a unified work. It does not fit easily into any familiar historiographical category, being 'partly an epitome of the Old Testament, partly a chronicle in the tradition of Eusebius, and partly a more or less independent form of historiography based on individual use of sources'.[19] In fact, the balance of the text throws by far the most weight on the Old Testament narrative, which takes up more than three-quarters of the work; then, following a sketch of events since the conclusion of the New Testament, a final section is devoted to an account of the Arian and Priscillianist controversies of the fourth century.[20] The awkward yoking together of these seemingly disparate elements has led a number of historians to separate them out, and to deal with a single aspect of the *Chronicle* in isolation from its context in the work as a whole. It has proved especially popular with those historians interested in the late-antique controversies to which Sulpicius was a contemporary witness, and the short final section has often been treated with little regard to the rest of the work (and very often as an adjunct instead to the author's *Life of Martin*).[21] Yet any attempt to understand the purpose and function of the *Chronicle* must look beyond these final few chapters, and recognise that they were deliberately placed in the shadow of a reconstruction of biblical history which starts at the very beginning.[22]

Similarly, although the *Chronicle* is divided into two books, the fact that the division comes with the epitome of the Old Testament in full flow must frustrate any attempt to make that part of the project merely a preliminary to Sulpicius' contemporary concerns. Nor can the work be divided into

---

[19] Van Andel 1976: 7.   [20] de Senneville-Grave 1999: 20; Van Andel 1976: 3.
[21] See for example Burrus 1995: 134–8; Stancliffe 1983 is mainly interested in the relationship between Sulpicius and Martin, but provides a valuable (if brief) discussion of the *Chronicle* at 174–82.
[22] Thus Bertrand 2001: 467; Sulpicius differs from Eusebius in beginning with the Creation rather than with Abraham.

two sections, with one devoted to a kind of 'sacred history' and the other not.[23] Instead, the narrative of the Old Testament is continued through the use of secular historians down to the time of Christ, with the reader referred elsewhere for the events of his life and the acts of the apostles; and the history resumes with Herod's successors and without even a paragraph break.[24] There is no significant difference stated or implied between biblical events and those of the postbiblical era: indeed, an opportunity has surely been missed to draw a pointed contrast between Jewish and Christian histories, or between biblical and postbiblical history.[25] Sulpicius' model of history did not depend on any temporal rupture, dividing historical time irrevocably at the Incarnation or at the end of the canonical scriptures. There is no sense that the advent of Christianity 'inaugurated a whole new epoch of divine-human interaction'.[26] Rather, Sulpicius seems entirely unperturbed by the passing of the biblical age. He persists throughout with his stated intention, simply 'to provide the sequence of events'.[27] The challenge must therefore be to approach the *Chronicle* on its own terms, as precisely what it seems to be: a single, connected narrative from the beginning of the world to the present day.[28]

This is entirely in keeping with the breezy unconcern with which he describes this project in the preface to the work: 'it seemed to me not out of place that, after I had run through the sacred history down to the crucifixion of Christ, and the doings of the Apostles, I should add an account of events which subsequently took place'.[29] He does take care to acknowledge that he has used secular sources to establish precise dates for the events of the Old Testament and, where necessary, to correct errors on these matters in the text.[30] This, however, was to do little more than to follow the example of Eusebius and Jerome: Eusebius had referred in his own preface to the variant chronologies that arose in the biblical texts, and Jerome was careful to blame potential disagreements on the negligence of copyists rather than authors.[31] Sulpicius, indeed, brings very little in the way of secular history

---

[23] Murru 1979: 972.   [24] *Chron.* 2.27.

[25] Murru 1979: 973; Van Andel 1976: 55 refers to 'the division of the Chronicle' into the history of Israel and the history of the church, but this does not accord with any textual divide, and arguably not with Sulpicius' references to 'historia sacra' and subsequent 'gesta' in *Chron.* pref.2.

[26] Robbins 2007: 11, based on Hooker 1986 and Badiou 2003.   [27] *Chron.* 2.7.3.

[28] An alternative approach to the *Chronicle* has frequently been to see it in terms of an eschatological claim: thus Prete 1958; Vaesen 1988; Weber 1997: 30–41 and de Senneville-Grave 1999: 51–4. My intention here is not to dismiss these arguments, but merely to focus attention on a different aspect of the *Chronicle*.

[29] *Chron.* pref.2, trans. A. Roberts 1894.   [30] *Chron.* pref.2.

[31] Jerome, *Chronicle* pref.; Sulpicius similarly blames copyists for an error in biblical chronology at *Chron.* 1.39.1.

into his summary of the Old Testament, limiting himself to lists of kings and to occasional dates, such as that of the Battle of Marathon.[32] That event is used to locate the biblical history being recounted in its proper relation to Herodotus, and also both to the foundation of Rome and to Sulpicius' end-point in the consulship of Stilicho of 400 CE.[33] Aside from these few interventions intended to fix the chronological frame, however, Sulpicius departs only rarely from the events of the Old Testament and hardly ever from the history of Israel.[34] His universal history of the biblical age is not a parallel history of multiple civilisations: it is a single thread picked out and shown in relief against a broader historical background.[35]

The fact that Sulpicius set out to provide a single narrative thus meant that – up to the end of the New Testament, at least – secular sources were required only for dating and, occasionally, for historical context.[36] Even this minimal recourse to secular history, however, seems to have caused Sulpicius some concern. At one point, confronted with a particularly knotty problem of biblical chronology, he even seems to comment on the absurdity of his self-imposed task. The difficulty is identifying the Persian king under whom the biblical Judith lived.[37] Sulpicius offers his own explanation – that the king impossibly called 'Nebuchadnezzar' was in fact the Persian king Artaxerxes III Ochus – and he credits his knowledge to his research in secular histories.[38] That these secular writers (*scriptores saecularium litterarum*) should have failed to record the story of Judith, or certain other stories from the holy books (*sacris uoluminibus*), should not be surprising:

[for] the spirit of God veiled that history so that, untainted by any corrupt mouth or by any mingling of falsehood with truth, it might be confined wholly within its own mysteries (*mysteria*). Kept apart from worldly concerns and revealed only by sacred voices (*sacris . . . uocibus*), it was right that it should not be mingled with the rest as if on an equal footing. Indeed it would have been most improper for it to be mixed up with other histories dealing with different subjects or having different aims.[39]

Sulpicius thus defends the separation of sacred and secular histories in a way that must cast doubt upon his own project. His own practice is, if not to reintegrate the two traditions, then at least to bring them into close

[32] Van Andel 1976: 60; Bertrand 2001: 464; Zecchini 2003: 336; *Chron.* 2.9.3.

[33] *Chron.* 2.9.3; Bertrand 2001: 464–5.   [34] Zecchini 2003: 336.

[35] Zecchini 2003: 336, drawing a contrast with the work of Orosius.

[36] The relatively rare authorial interventions in which Sulpicius deals with these matters are tabulated at Murru 1979: 968–71.

[37] *Chron.* 2.14.1–2. Similar problems continued to vex chronographers down to early modern times: see for example Grafton 1975: 160–1.

[38] Prete 1955: 57–8; de Senneville-Grave 1999: 407.   [39] *Chron.* 2.14.3.

collaboration – and not always to the detriment of the secular account. He is quite prepared to jettison the biblical tradition when he considers it unreliable.[40]

For some this is evidence that Sulpicius adopted a 'praiseworthy' attitude to the writing of history that was owed to classical historiography.[41] His willingness to disregard the Bible has been taken to demonstrate his 'open-mindedness', and to reveal a 'limited, but real, historical ability' not apparent in some of his other writings.[42] On this reading, Sulpicius would emerge as an author for whom 'the historical value of the Old Testament remains unimpaired' despite his determination to provide the occasional important correction.[43] He was explicitly committed to the historicity of the scriptures, but approached them from a 'literary-historical' viewpoint which acknowledged that errors could arise in recording or transmission and required emendation by an appropriate expert.[44] Such apparent praise of Sulpicius, however, can shade too easily into a dismissal of his work as betraying an unsophisticated understanding of history and of the Bible – as if, deliberately or otherwise, he were setting out to reduce the richness of the scriptures to a flat and excessively reasonable account of the past as just one damn thing after another.[45]

There is a real distinction at stake here, and one that Sulpicius does seem to countenance. In the preface and elsewhere in the *Chronicle*, he allows for a distinction between the *gesta* (or *rerum ordo*) which he intends to narrate and the *diuinarum rerum mysteria* which are to be sought elsewhere.[46] His understanding of the Bible can therefore be seen to involve at least two levels: a *historia simplex* which consists of only the recounting of *res gestae* – although neither phrase appears in the *Chronicle* itself – and the frequent appearance of *mysteria* with meanings which 'were only discernible to the wise'.[47] Sulpicius claims to aspire only to the first. That *historia* for him was indeed frequently a matter of classical *res gestae* is clear from his tendentious comment on the reigns of two kings from the book of Judges: 'it being a time of peace, they did nothing that history records'.[48] Similarly, he goes on to note the existence of *mysteria* at certain moments in his narrative – in

[40] Stancliffe 1983: 175–7, 181.   [41] Stancliffe 1983: 177.
[42] Stancliffe 1983: 181; Murru 1979: 971 also notes that Sulpicius gives the impression of 'objectivity'.
[43] Van Andel 1976: 61.   [44] Stancliffe 1983: 41; cf. Prete 1955: 58–61.
[45] Stancliffe 1983: 180: 'Everything that is frightening and irrational is softened, if not ironed out altogether. And he will give a *reason* for why the raven sent out by Noah did not return to the Ark...'
[46] Van Andel 1976: 8; *Chron.* pref.2 (*gesta*), pref.3 (*mysteria*) and 2.7.3 (*rerum tantum ordinem*).
[47] Sulpicius occasionally uses the word *historia* without qualification (e.g. at *Chron.* 1.19.1 and 1.25.3); the terms given here are proposed by Van Andel 1976: 68, and followed by Stancliffe 1983: 41 (quoted).
[48] *Chron.* 1.25.7; Stancliffe 1983: 179; a fuller account of the reigns is given in Judges 12:11–15.

the very first chapter he identifies the murder of an anonymous young man as 'a fact which is thought by the wise to have presaged a future mystery', and a few chapters later mentions the *mysterium* involved in the renaming of Abraham and Sarah – but adds that these are matters which 'it is not for this work to explain'.[49] Sulpicius might therefore seem to conform to the stereotype of the chronographer: wholly uninterested in speculating about meanings, and 'less concerned with the sense of his facts than he was with their existence'.[50]

The distinction that Sulpicius outlined between sacred and secular history might then be taken at face value. Given his prominent use of secular authors – and the apparently seamless transition between the Bible and the postbiblical world in the second book of his *Chronicle* – he would seem to be condemned by his own proscriptions. If supplementing the scriptures with such non-Biblical material was indeed to compromise the unique character of the sacred writings, it would follow that the *Chronicle* as a whole was irredeemably secular. It could have value in the same way as any other secular history – so that, for example, it might continue to serve as a source of moral exempla – but it could never aspire to the status of sacred history.[51] At first sight this seems to be accepted by Sulpicius: certainly in his preface he is careful to acknowledge the importance of the biblical text, and to express the hope that the work will not tempt his readers to neglect the holy scriptures.[52] His *Chronicle* is presented as a reminder and not a replacement – as Sulpicius confirms elsewhere, referring readers to the book of Daniel or to the New Testament for the authoritative account he does not claim to provide.[53] Biblical history was the domain of the *sacrae uoces*, the inspired authors of Scripture, among whom Sulpicius does not number himself: for 'concerning those things that I have summarised from the holy books, I do not wish to appear before my readers as their author'.[54] Instead, it seems, he restricts himself to that *historia simplex* which invites and requires no deeper interpretation.

THE PROBLEM OF AUTHORITY

Yet authority – and interpretative authority in particular – is not to be disposed of so easily. That Sulpicius felt it necessary to raise the point in the preface suggests that he was conscious of the risk he was taking: that his work might establish him as a rival to the scriptural authors. And arguably

---

[49] *Chron.* 1.1.1, 1.5.1; Van Andel 1976: 62.   [50] Johnson 1962: 125.
[51] Thus Van Andel 1976: 68–9; Prete 1955: 119–21.   [52] *Chron.* pref.3.
[53] *Chron.* pref.3; *Chron.* 2.7.3, 2.27.2.   [54] *Chron.* pref.3; cf. Weber 1997: 104–5.

it was a problem inherent in the very nature of his project. Thus although he refused to provide an exegesis of the names of Abraham and Sarah, for example, this served to exclude only one of the various approaches to the interpretation of Scripture. Sulpicius is denying any place in his work to allegorical interpretation: and indeed, the one exception to this is his comment on the dream of Nebuchadnezzar, where the interpretation is not his own but the (historical) explanation provided by the prophet Daniel.[55] Sulpicius, admittedly, makes use of his own chronographical knowledge to confirm the truth of the interpretation – identifying the empires whose rise and fall the prophet had correctly predicted.[56] Nevertheless, if this kind of allegorical interpretation is otherwise foreign to the *Chronicle*, this is not to say that the history recorded by Sulpicius was confined to the literal meaning. For the Bible was understood to be bound together not only by the allegorical and prophetic relationship between the Old and New Testaments, but also by that 'historical typology' which operated almost entirely on the level of narrative.[57] This was not a relationship between historical events and the timeless truths they symbolised; nor was it a matter of words and images that could be given historical significance. Rather, it was the belief that 'something real and historical' could correspond to something else equally 'real and historical': that meaning could be found in the recognisable relationship between distinct historical events.[58]

Thus although in his *Chronicle* he restricted himself to the narration of historical events, Sulpicius nevertheless left room for *mysteria* – and their implications – to emerge. The selection and arrangement of events is of course an inescapable part of any historical account, but Sulpicius was clearly aware of the meanings that could be derived from the correspondences that emerged: he had evidently read the work of Hilary of Poitiers on the subject, for instance, and can be found alluding to certain of his interpretations.[59] Similarly, there are a number of occasions on which Sulpicius selected and presented historical events in the light of their typological significance. He narrates Old Testament stories in the light of their future fulfilment in the New, as when Moses in killing an Egyptian is said to have 'delivered his brother from injury', using terms derived from

---

[55] *Chron.* 2.2–3; Daniel 2:31–45.
[56] *Chron.* 2.3.1. Nebuchadnezzar's dream would become a central image for chronographers, at least as late as the Reformation: see Grafton 2003: 222.
[57] The terminology used here is thus different from that employed at Van Andel 1976: 62 and at Bertrand 2001: 458; my distinction between allegory and typology is founded on the discussions in Auerbach 1959; Charity 1966 and Fabiny 1992.
[58] Auerbach 1959: 29; cf. Hollander 1977: 6ff.
[59] Thus Van Andel 1976: 62ff.; see also de Senneville-Grave 1999: 54–6.

Stephen's association of Moses and Christ as spurned prophets in the Acts of the Apostles.[60] In much the same way, David's evasion of any punishment for his numbering of the tribes is narrated by Sulpicius in terms which give disproportionate credit to David's apparent willingness to die for his people – a departure from the Old Testament version – and which borrows a phrase from 2 Corinthians in order to highlight the typological parallel with Christ.[61] His account of the intervention of Deborah makes this mode of interpretation more explicit, with Sulpicius directly admitting that she 'was sent forth as a type of the church'; in addition she evidently anticipates the gospels, representing another instrument of divine salvation rejected (initially, at least) by the people of Israel.[62] This, then, is biblical typology in its most traditional form: the demonstration through the scriptural narrative of 'history's relation to its fulfilment in Christ'.[63]

Yet for Sulpicius this typological approach was not limited to the Bible – for it has already been noted that he refused to draw any firm line between the end of the biblical account and the subsequent history of the postbiblical world. Precisely the same kind of connections are made between situations in the scriptures and in the Roman Empire. On a broad level, parallels have been recognised between Sulpicius' portrayal of the predicament of the Jews under foreign potentates and his account of the persecution of the Christians under the Roman Empire.[64] But as with the scriptures, these connections are frequently confirmed on the level of historical and linguistic detail. The biblical narrative is remodelled to bring it in line with the conventions of postbiblical history: as when the virtues and vices of biblical kings are related in terms borrowed from Sallust, who also provides the prevailing moral attitude.[65] Moreover, it is suggested that certain postbiblical events were re-enactments of their biblical predecessors. Thus in the story of Esther, her opponent Haman excoriates the Jews in words directly taken from Tacitus; and in the same phrase he applies to them Pliny's dismissal of the persecuted Christians as followers of a 'depraved superstition'.[66] These allusions have a point, in that they emphasise the historical relationship that underlay the two persecutions. That it was

[60] *Chron.* 1.12.2; Acts 7:24; Van Andel 1976: 19.
[61] *Chron.* I.37.3; 2 Samuel 24:16–17; Van Andel 1976: 21; de Senneville-Grave 1999: 378. The phrase *unum pro omnibus* is borrowed by Sulpicius from 2 Corinthians 5:14.
[62] Judges 4; *Chron.* 1.23.3; see Van Andel 1976: 64–5. This is the only appearance of the word *typus* in the *Chronicle*, although the term *figura* is also used twice: see Van Andel 1976: 63ff.
[63] Charity 1966: 5.   [64] Murru 1979: 973; Van Andel 1976: 76ff.
[65] *Chron.* 1.23.1: 'ut semper fieri rebus secundis solet, morum disciplinaeque immemor'. For more on these reminiscences of Sallust, see Van Andel 1976: 69–74, and de Senneville-Grave 1999: 40.
[66] *Chron.* 2.13.2; Tacitus, *Historiae* 5.3–4; Pliny, *Epistulae* 10.96.8. Van Andel 1976: 57, followed by de Senneville-Grave 1999: 406, also suggests a connection with Tacitus, *Annales* 15.44 on the Christians.

possible to recognise such a pattern in history implied the presence of a divine Author – and one present not only in the authoritative past recorded in the scriptures. Rather, the characteristic patterning of the Bible was extended to the secular tradition, incorporating them both within the 'unified network of narrative and imagery' that best expressed the unity of sacred history.[67]

The presence of historical typology in the *Chronicle* can therefore hardly be dismissed as incidental, or as something included by Sulpicius 'almost against his will'.[68] It is certainly clear that Sulpicius was willing to see even his own time in terms of the authoritative past, as when he models his portrait of the heretic Priscillian on Sallust's description of Catiline.[69] Perhaps more revealing, however, is the apparent parallel between Martin of Tours and the prophet Jeremiah. The imprisonment of Jeremiah has long been suggested as a model for the treatment of Martin, who in a like manner offered unwelcome advice to his king, the Emperor Maximus.[70] Certainly it is possible to see a connection between the bishops advising Maximus (in the trial of Priscillian) and the priests (*sacerdotes*) who act as Zedekiah's advisers.[71] Sulpicius, however, seems to have in mind a more complex association of figures: for there is a more general resemblance between Jeremiah and Martin in the image of a prophet rejected by ecclesiastical and secular authorities; and this model applies not only to these two but also, of course, to Christ. Such an association seems particularly strong in the account of Jeremiah, thrown into prison by the king:

Before long he [Zedekiah] regretted this cruel action; but being opposed by the leaders of the Jews (whose custom it had been from the beginning to persecute the righteous), he did not dare to release the innocent man.[72]

Such a description may also have applied to Maximus, but it clearly applied to Pontius Pilate; and Sulpicius in his aside draws attention to a familiar course that events were taking. This same impression is furthered as Sulpicius goes beyond the biblical account to explain that Jeremiah was subsequently cast into an empty cistern 'so that he might not die an ordinary death'.[73] If Jeremiah is the model for Martin, then both men are also to be connected with Christ.[74] The Old Testament here is united with

---

[67] Frye 1982: xvii.   [68] Van Andel 1976: 68.

[69] *Chron.* 2.46.2; Sallust, *Bellum Catilinae* 5.1–5. For details, see Fontaine 1975; Van Andel 1976: 72–4; Burrus 1995: 135–7.

[70] *Chron.* 1.53; Jeremiah 37–8; *Chron.* 2.50: references at Van Andel 1976: 107–8.

[71] Prete 1955: 65; Van Andel 1976: 108.   [72] *Chron.* 1.53.2; Van Andel 1976: 138.

[73] *Chron.* 1.53.2; cf. Jeremiah 38:6.   [74] Bertrand 2001: 464.

contemporary secular history in terms of their common relationship with the all-important New Testament narrative.

The very importance of the New Testament might therefore provide an explanation of its omission from the *Chronicle*. It was not the point at which Sulpicius chose to divide the work; but the structural parallels might allow us to recognise its place in the design. For the story of the imprisonment of Jeremiah, with its foreshadowing of the gospel story, is narrated in the final chapter of the first book of the *Chronicle*. The first mention of Martin, introduced by Sulpicius as 'a man plainly worthy to be ranked with the apostles', appears in the penultimate chapter of the second book, with the death of Priscillian concluding the work.[75] Each of the two sections, that is, culminates in an allusion to the events of the New Testament – which remains, if not the literal centre of the book, then the axis on which its history turns. Thus when Sulpicius arrives in his chronological sequence at the birth of Christ and the acts of the apostles, he is careful to place the moment in relation to both Jewish history (through Herod) and Roman history (through Stilicho); but he excuses the lack of a narrative by his reluctance to detract from the dignity of events.[76] That he was rather less scrupulous with regard to the Old Testament only emphasises the extent to which the New Testament is a special case. It was not that the New Testament authors were more inspired than their Old Testament counterparts, but that the events related in the New Testament were not strictly historical but transcended history. The Incarnation and the events surrounding it could not be given any further meaning: rather, they were themselves the meaning that underlay all of the significant events recorded in the *Chronicle*.

This might allow a more positive reading of Sulpicius' statement in his preface, that he wishes the *Chronicle* to serve as nothing more than a reminder of things already familiar.[77] This can be seen as more than self-deprecation, and as pointing instead to the apologetic purpose of the work. Sulpicius was not setting out simply to summarise the scriptures; nor did he understand the Incarnation as the final act of a story of spiritual progress, or as a definitive moment of transition which marked off an obsolete past from an enlightened present.[78] Similarly, that he confined himself to what he considered the facts is not to say that he stripped his history of meaning

---

[75] *Chron.* 2.50.1; other such biblical images of Martin in the works of Sulpicius are discussed at Stancliffe 1983: 187–8.

[76] *Chron.* 2.27.1; see also the remarks of Prete 1955: 55–6 and Zecchini 2003: 336 on the implications of the dating methods here.

[77] *Chron.* 2.27.2; pref.3.   [78] Cf. Stancliffe 1983: 180; Murru 1979: 973.

and *mysteria*.[79] Rather, Sulpicius sought to demonstrate how all Jewish and Christian history could be related to its fulfilment in the New Testament. The events recounted in the *Chronicle* were arranged by their author to form an 'intelligible pattern' in which 'the historical life of Christ' represented 'one of the chief preordained features'.[80] This was precisely the message of historical typology, which looked for meaning in events as well as in words, and which allowed history to be understood as 'the theatre of God's hidden purposes'.[81] Sulpicius had merely extended this argument to include non-biblical history – all of which was to be situated, in time and in meaning, in relation to New Testament events. Thus despite his acknowledgement of the lasting authority of the biblical account, the inclusion of postbiblical history in the *Chronicle* did not necessarily render the whole narrative meaningless. Rather, it took seriously the Christian claim regarding the historicity of the Incarnation, placing it firmly in ordinary historical time; and implicitly making the grander claim that 'all history . . . is sacred once God acts within it'.[82]

Sulpicius thus proposed an essential unity not only between the Old and New Testaments, but also between biblical history and the history of his own day. This was perhaps an important implication of the chronicle form itself, which through the influence of Jerome in particular had already 'made it possible to fit local history into the context of God's time'.[83] The consequences for Sulpicius, however, were more obvious than for a chronographer such as Eusebius or Jerome, who were content to record discrete events without placing them in a narrative frame. In departing from that tradition by offering his readers a narrative account instead of a tabular chronology, Sulpicius provided his own grand Christian narrative, taking his lead from the scriptures not only in content but also in form. Thus the *Chronicle*, like the Bible, offered a guide to 'the unmistakable pattern of divine intervention in history'.[84] These 'supernatural interventions' are often related in 'a very matter-of-fact way'; but the aim for Sulpicius was not to dazzle his readers with miracles, but to demonstrate how these interventions combined to reveal a meaningful pattern in history.[85] He set out to present the essential events in the history and prehistory of Christianity, and to demonstrate the interconnectedness of all these events whether before or after the key historical moment of the Incarnation. His

---

[79] Cf. Van Andel 1976: 68ff., followed by Stancliffe 1983: 43, 180.
[80] Collingwood 1946: 50, on this as a general characteristic of Christian chronicles.
[81] Markus 1986: 40; for this as a theme of the *Chronicle*, see Weber 1997: 44ff.
[82] Charity 1966: 164.   [83] Croke 1983: 126; cf. Collingwood 1946: 50–1.
[84] Momigliano 1963: 82.   [85] Stancliffe 1983: 181; cf. Prete 1955: 74–5.

universal history was therefore unavoidably a new sacred history.[86] Rather than dividing history at the Incarnation, Sulpicius united history around it. Similarly, 'secular' and Christian events were no longer presented along parallel timelines, but were all encompassed within a single, unified model of Christian time.

The recombination of biblical and secular events into a single historical narrative, however, inevitably raised the problem of Sulpicius' own authority. In yoking together the two traditions, he could easily be accused of reducing the events of the Bible to the level of mere chronology; alternatively, his *Chronicle* might seem to be usurping the place of the scriptures.[87] Either way, he was implicitly establishing himself as an authority on the canonical Christian past – and so risked setting himself up in competition with the authorised version. The outstanding authority of the scriptures, after all, lay in the fact that their authors had been inspired: not only in regard to the accuracy of their account, but more importantly in their selection and presentation of the most significant events. Augustine understood the biblical author to be distinguished in precisely this way: he was set apart by 'his judgement, his interpretation of [events] in terms of the pattern of redemptive history into which divine inspiration vouchsafes him insight'.[88] In offering his own account of the pattern of biblical and Christian history, Sulpicius thus found himself trespassing on the domain of the *sacrae uoces*. It is clear enough that he resisted this interpretation: he insists that his abridgement – as is said of every abridgement – was meant to supplement and not replace its original. All the same, his readers were here offered a pocket handbook which could tell them more conveniently what they needed to know. Indeed, for all his modesty, Sulpicius might with justice be credited with an even grander achievement: for by cutting away the extraneous detail, Sulpicius was able to reveal more clearly the overarching pattern of sacred history.[89] Interested readers are referred to the Bible for more detail on individual events: but what Sulpicius preserves is the essential narrative of Christian history. For if Scripture remained the 'key to all mysteries', Sulpicius had nevertheless exposed its underlying plan.[90]

---

[86] McKitterick 2006: 13, attributing the point to Dorothea von den Brincken. Cf. also Ricoeur 1952: 251: 'The Christian interpretation of history is . . . a hope that profane history is also part of that meaning which is revealed in sacred history, that in the final analysis there is only one history, that all history is sacred.'

[87] Bertrand 2001: 462.   [88] Markus 1996: 14.

[89] Thus Momigliano 1963: 85: Christian chronicles 'showed concern with the pattern of history rather than with the detail'.

[90] *Chron.* pref.3: 'uniuersa diuinarum rerum mysteria non nisi ex ipsis fontibus hauriri querent'.

THE *CHRONICLE* AND CHRISTIAN HISTORIOGRAPHY

In this sense, the *Chronicle* of Sulpicius Severus paved the way for medieval historiography, which set for itself 'the task of discovering and expounding [the] objective or divine plan' in history.[91] Sulpicius brought secular history into agreement with the scriptures not only on the level of chronological detail, but also with regard to its theological purpose and meaning. The result – though no doubt unintentional – was to undermine the status of the Bible as sufficient in itself. This was a problem for Augustine, who essentially wanted interpretation to look like interpretation, and who sought to keep a clear distinction between what could be known for certain and what was merely an educated guess.[92] In the *City of God* he thus distinguished ordinary historical writing from the 'immediate divine authority' inherent in:

that Scripture which, not by the chance impulses of mortal minds but manifestly by the guiding power of supreme providence, stands above the literature of all peoples and, excelling in divine authority, has subordinated to itself every kind of human ingenuity.[93]

Augustine's view would come to be the orthodox understanding of the status of Scripture in the west. It was highly visible, for example, in the works of Cassiodorus, for whom the style, form and content of the scriptures were to be considered 'precise and wholly without fault', and could not be transferred or summarised into an alternative secular account: for 'what is in the scriptures unshakeably true often becomes uncertain elsewhere'.[94] Indeed, 'his preferred term' for the canonical scriptures as a whole acknowledged their unique and separate nature: they were 'the divine authority' (*auctoritas diuina*).[95]

The preservation of this distinction in the medieval west might go to show 'that even more necessary than the prophets – true and false – who would claim to discern God's hand in events . . . is the prophet who will remind his Church that outside the narrow bounds of the scriptures no one is authorised to proclaim what God is up to'.[96] And yet these prophets – and this reminder – were needed because the claim would continue to be made: for Christian authors before and after Augustine were consistently willing

---

[91] Collingwood 1946: 53; see also the remarks of Croke 2001: 166–9.
[92] For a more thorough account of the views of Augustine with regard to sacred history, see Markus 1988: ch. 1 and appendix A, with a brief summary at Markus 1990: 87–9.
[93] Augustine, *De ciuitate Dei* 11.1, quoted in Vessey and Pollmann 1999: 8.
[94] Cassiodorus, *Explanatio in Psalmos* pref.15 (tr. Walsh), quoted at Vessey 2004: 31.
[95] Vessey 2004: 45; an example at Cassiodorus, *Instituta* 12.   [96] Markus 1990: 88.

to elide this distinction. Simply by writing a new history of the biblical and Christian era, contemporary authors were able to set themselves up as authorities on the Christian past. They were able not only to redescribe the facts but also, as part of the process, to divine and thus define their proper significance. The effect was to place contemporary historians in the tradition of the Old Testament authors or the evangelists; and to claim for themselves something of the authority of a prophet or an apostle.[97] If Christian history did then represent a shift from the conventions of classical historiography, it was in many cases only at the level of rhetoric. The obtrusive authorial persona of a Sallust or a Tacitus was replaced by a modesty which attributed the arrangement of events to divine agency, and which affected to reduce the historian to the level of a scribe or mere chronographer.[98] At the same time, however, the credibility of Christian historians continued to depend on their skill in discerning the proper interpretations of events. Their histories could only be a success if they were able to show that they had got it *right*. Their own narrative authority continued to matter.

In his *Chronicle*, therefore, Sulpicius resolved one difficulty at the cost of creating another. By writing a Christian history which engaged directly with classical models, but which required him, in effect, to rewrite long sections of the Bible in his own words, he necessarily drew attention to the conflict between his own narrative voice and the authoritative voice of Scripture. Sulpicius may have claimed in his preface to be deferring to the authority of the biblical authors, but his actual practice makes clear that he took final responsibility for the disposition of events in his history – that it was, in the end, his own account. His apparent acknowledgement of the authority of Scripture amounted to the significantly different claim that, with the biblical authors as his guide, his own authority could be similarly trusted. He was neither seeking to replace the inspired authors of Scripture nor leaving the field to them alone: rather, he was associating himself in their enterprise.

For all his modesty, and for all his apparent objectivity, Sulpicius remains a conspicuous presence in the text.[99] He is explicitly engaged in the task of making a story out of a 'mere chronicle'; and indeed, it is possible to doubt

---

[97] For this argument in more detail, see Krueger 2004: 15–32 and Williams 2008.

[98] Murru 1979: 976–7 thus defines Sulpicius' approach in the *Chronicle* in terms of *humilitas*; for this modesty as primarily a rhetorical stance, see Prete 1955: 19–20. See also Richardson 1965: 65 for a medieval rhetoric in which history was only 'something to be received' and 'not something to be enquired into by curious minds'.

[99] Prete 1955: 124.

whether any such category of mere chronicle could exist without implying a narrative framework or some kind of recognisable 'emplotment'.[100] This is largely to reiterate a point already well made by Moses Finley, who in reducing historical narrative to its essential components might almost have been thinking of Sulpicius and his *Chronicle*:

> The barest bones of any historical narrative, the events selected and arranged in a temporal sequence, imply a value judgment (or judgments). The study and writing of history, in short, is a form of ideology.[101]

Sulpicius was well aware that his account of events might be taken as a challenge to the authority of the scriptures: but his bravura display of modesty and deference failed to disguise that he had gone ahead all the same. A similar contradiction would bedevil Christian historiography long after its understanding of time had triumphed in the later medieval west; and it was perhaps never adequately resolved. A belief in the absolute authority of the Bible had to be balanced against the authority and the critical independence of the individual historian; and a safe course therefore had to be steered between excessive credulity and an unacceptable *lèse-majesté*. The *Chronicle* of Sulpicius Severus was a rare attempt in antiquity to combine orthodox Christian belief with a firm commitment to the historian's task. It may be no surprise that it found few imitators.

---

[100] White 1978: 83; see also his discussion of possible categories of 'naïve' and 'sentimental' chronicles at 90–3. For even the simplest chronicle form imposing its own narratives and interpretations, see especially Croke 2001: 3–5 and McKitterick 2006: 18–19.
[101] Finley 1985: 4.

Afterword

CHAPTER 14

Ancient history in the eighteenth century

Oswyn Murray

As imperceptibly one approaches ripe old age, time becomes an ever more problematic concept. One's relationship to events changes, for they lie in the past rather than the future: so time past overtakes time future, as one becomes truly an ancient historian. As a result I begin to feel more at home in the twentieth century, which is supposed to have passed away, than in either antiquity or the present. Does this mean that I can stand outside the relationship between these two polarities that we are considering? Certainly new ideas seem more and more to reflect old ones – and I mean reflect rather than repeat; for it is no criticism to see the renewal of past ideas in a modern guise.

My situation is of course the inverse of the theory proposed by François Hartog. For him the regimes of historicity move from the dominance of the past until the nineteenth century to the dominance of the future in the post-Darwinian age, and now to a form of presentism that, since the collapse of Marxism, sees all history as meaningless except in relation to the present, and therefore as relative to our current issues in a post-modern sense. This movement is the opposite of natural human experience, which progresses from a situation where the future is all that holds meaning, to a form of activity that embraces presentism in adult life, and finally to Shakespeare's sixth age of 'the lean and slipper'd pantaloon', where meaning is created by memories of the past, and where old friends, old books and old wine are better than new. Literature perhaps encapsulates this temporal movement better than history: none of our contributors mentions the greatest of all writers on this age of memory, Marcel Proust, *À la recherche du temps perdu*; and that is a pity, for he has much to teach us.

Above all this book celebrates the revival of eighteenth-century studies in classical history that was pioneered fifty years ago by Arnaldo Momigliano, who rightly saw that the foundations of modern historiography were established in this period. The same period is now acquiring a prominence that directs us away from the easy assumption that we are the heirs of a nineteenth-century political and critical historiography. Indeed the eighteenth century is becoming an ever more complex area of research, as is shown by another contemporary book, *Reinventing History: The Enlightenment Origins of Ancient History*.[1] Among young historians it seems that a movement is being formed that will transform our understanding of the eighteenth century and the *Sattelzeit* that leads on to the nineteenth and the twentieth centuries.

But not all the cards are yet on the table. To take one example, Giovanna Ceserani draws a complex picture of eighteenth-century histories of Greece; in the time since the Craven seminar, from which this book originated, was held, I can already add a new discovery: the earliest critical histories of Greece were written not at the end of the century by William Mitford and John Gillies, but by the Irishman John Gast of Dublin, whose writing career began as early as 1753. Greek history turns out to be in advance of the mainstream of eighteenth-century historians, William Robertson, David Hume and Edward Gibbon. In the 1780s Gast was even set up by his publisher John Murray in a vain attempt to wrest the title of the historian of decline and fall from Edward Gibbon. This example shows how incomplete our picture of the eighteenth century is; but it also demonstrates the importance of Montesquieu, and especially his *Considérations sur les causes de la grandeur des Romains et de leur décadence* (1734) – not just for Roman but also for Greek history: Gast, a Huguenot refugee, was a close relative of Montesquieu, and it was Montesquieu who inspired both his positive conception of Athenian democracy and his vision of the decline and fall of Greece.[2]

Exemplarity is not of course a situation from which we can escape: every generation of historians is bound to pursue the myth of abstract historical truth with the tools of the modern age, and only present experience can illuminate the distant past. That is the ultimate revenge of contemporaneity, the fact that we are caught in a world where *vita historiae magistra est*: thus it needed Karl Marx to discover the ancient economy, and Jacob Burckhardt to see the centrality of the polis in Greek culture. All we can try to do, as we hunt the Snark of history with our modern tools, is to hope that it will not turn out to be a Boojum after all:

> For then
> You will softly and suddenly vanish away
> And never be met with again!

[1] Moore, Macgregor Morris and Bayliss 2008.   [2] See Murray forthcoming.

Hartog focuses our attention on periodisation. Here I have two problems. The first is that in the chapters in this book, notwithstanding Lianeri's brave attempt to evoke comparative studies in her introduction, most of our contributors prefer an immanentist or internal focus, resolutely based on the Western historical experience: in order to understand the various forms of periodisation we need to juxtapose Western and non-Western heritages, to set out in Marcel Detienne's words 'a comparison of the incomparables'. Despite all his wisdom, so well recalled by many of our contributors, and despite his attempt to include Jewish and Persian history in the Western tradition, Momigliano's vision was perhaps limited by his insistence that the purpose of the study of historiography was methodological, to reveal the sources of our modern Western preconceptions. The historical world surely looks very different from an Indian, an Egyptian or a Chinese perspective. I recall a remark of the nonagenarian Chinese historian Lin Zhi-Chun at the First International Conference of Ancient World Historians in Tianjin in 1993: he said that he could not see what Western historians had to teach China, for they are continually losing their civilisations and having to reinvent them by means of Renaissances, while Chinese civilisation has been continuous for five thousand years. At the time, with typical Western arrogance, I thought that forgetting civilisations from time to time was perhaps an advantage, in that it allowed new forms to develop; but now I am not so sure. As Plato's Egyptian priests said: 'You Greeks are never anything but children, and there is not an old man among you.'

A second problem emerges from Giuseppe Cambiano's demonstration that the history of philosophy requires a quite different rhythm of periodisation from that of the common history of events – an observation that could indeed be repeated in relation to the history of many other forms of human thought, like medicine, art or science. Periodisation is relative to the phenomenon studied. As Hegel and most of his contemporaries and successors saw, as far at least as Nietzsche, the death of Socrates was the most important event in world history – a fact that Jacob Burckhardt missed completely.[3] And as Hartog sees clearly the history of religion offers many similar religious temporalities which cut across the history of events, from BCE/CE to pagan and Christian Roman empires. But I have always regarded periods like Burckhardt, as simply useful tools for the analysis of clusters of events: I once overheard two colleagues, one of whom was asked a historical question: he threw up his hands and replied, 'Not my period.'

---

[3] Murray 2002.

The eminent medievalist A. B. Emden, a venerable bachelor, rebuked him, saying, 'George, at your age you should have stopped having periods.'

In response to the chapters of this book and the discussions they provoked, let me outline what I believe to be the development of the historiography of the ancient world in the period from the late seventeenth century to the mid-nineteenth century.

The antiquarian interest in both Greek and Roman history that had been an important feature of the previous two centuries began to be more systematic with the foundation of the post-Renaissance learned academies in France and Italy, leading to a proliferation of antiquarian treatises on individual topics and the extension of the conception of the past into the study of ancient customs and material objects. It was Montesquieu who stimulated the idea of a more general narrative centred on the conception of 'grandeur et décadence'; and the French *philosophes* insisted that behind the individual epiphenomena must lie a general structure of society that could be elucidated by some form of narrative history. But it was in the British Isles that the conception of critical narrative history first emerged, beginning around the 1750s. The reasons I believe lie in the development of an educational system and a set of values that was both based on study of the ancient world, and also expected it to explain the problems of the modern. There is no one author who can be held responsible for this breakthrough, and it seems to have occurred almost simultaneously in both Roman and Greek history. Nor is it confined to ancient history. From the 1750s onwards there begins the great age of historical narrative that is associated with William Robertson, David Hume and Edward Gibbon. This form of narrative history rested on the assumption of a shared set of values in all periods and the notion of *historia magistra vitae*. The only element of doubt allowed to intrude is the conception of decline and fall: there must be reasons for the collapse of the Greek and Roman worlds, and these events might have a relevance to modern problems. Liberty was the highest value, and justified imperialism, because only the free and virtuous had a right to rule over others; free trade was an essential value of this historical universe, which explained the prosperity of the modern age, and perhaps distinguished it from the ancient world. In the final words of John Gast's *Rudiments of Grecian History in Thirteen Dialogues* of 1753:

Such are the Effects of *Upright* and of *Degenerate* Manners; the latter always ending in *Weakness* and *Servitude*; the former productive of *Liberty*, *Wealth* and *Empire*. Never, my *Eudoxus*, never my *Cleanthes*, may ye forget the instructive Lesson; *The*

Ways of Virtue are the Ways of Happiness. Have it in rememberance. Make the trial. And certainly shall ye find the one, if ye sincerely pursue the other.[4]

Is it significant that attention appears to move towards the end of the eighteenth century from Roman to Greek history? Is it even true? Despite the thesis of *Athens on Trial,*[5] there were plenty of supporters of Athenian democracy in the eighteenth century; and the Roman Republic was a supreme example of the decline and fall of liberty into tyranny from Montesquieu's *Considérations* onwards.

The vision of Athens was that of a prosperous, liberal, imperial, naval power capable of offering examples to the growing power of Britain in the years of prosperity after the Glorious Revolution. This began to be questioned with the American War of Independence, which revealed a split between traditional values and modern progressive thought: what was liberty to some was anarchy and the dissolution of empire to others. In Britain an age of reaction set in with the French Revolution. This is the period of reactionary historians like John Gillies and William Mitford; Athens was a dangerous model, and the counter-example of Sparta came into greater prominence. Gillies has had a undeservedly high reputation, because of his interest in the history of Prussia and its relationship to the rise of Philip of Macedon; but his history is in fact rather pedestrian and unoriginal. In contrast Mitford is a highly original historian with a fully developed and wide-ranging comparativist approach; he has suffered unfairly from the ridicule of his style by Byron and his content by Macaulay, and from the attacks mounted on him for his anti-democratic views by the Radical historians Bulwer Lytton and George Grote, and by the scorn of their philosophical mentors, James and John Stuart Mill.

Romantic history begins with the example of Sir Walter Scott, as both Macaulay and Carlyle noted,

whose Historical Novels have taught all men this truth, which looks like a truism, and yet was as good as unknown to writers of history and others, till so taught: that the bygone ages of the world were actually filled by living men, not by protocols, state-papers, controversies and abstractions of men. Not abstractions were they, not diagrams and theorems; but men, in buff or other coats and breeches, with colour in their cheeks, with passions in their stomach, and the idioms, features and vitalities of very men. It is a little word this; inclusive of great meaning! History will henceforth have to take thought of it.[6]

---

[4] Gast 1753: 647 and 1793, I: 537–8. [5] Roberts 1994.
[6] Carlyle 1869 [1838]: 71f.; Macaulay 1913 [1828]: 217. For France see especially Augustin Thierry's praise of Scott written in 1834, reprinted in Gauchet 2002: 53.

Scott's influence on French historical writing was enormous, and in Germany Hegel in his early drafts of the lectures on the philosophy of history in 1822 and 1828 regards him as an important if unsatisfactory influence on modern 'reflective history'.

B. G. Niebuhr's combination of romantic and imaginative history with an apparently scientific scholarship in the form of source criticism represents the transition from Romantic to Positivist history; in the next generation the reaction to Hegel's philosophical history of the liberty of the human spirit produced the school of C. O. Müller and August Boeckh. This strange and heady combination of 'scientific' history with Romantic narrative created the *Roman History* of Theodor Mommsen; and from the same source the German tradition of national history developed with the later positivist historians, whose vision of the ancient world, as Kostas Vlassopoulos has pointed out, represents the triumph of Nationalism in world history. The result was two 'World Wars' (in fact of course European wars) and a dark century of nationalism and ideological conflict, that is perhaps the worst age of intolerance since the seventeenth-century wars of religion. From this legacy we have plunged into an unnecessary and unwinnable 'War on Terror'. From such nightmares we are only slowly and painfully liberating ourselves in the early twenty-first century.

In this perspective it has to be admitted that history since 1750 has continually served the function of modern myth. Throughout the eighteenth century myth was indeed a significant part of history, in the sense that the truth or falsity of myth remained problematical, with many theories designed to reduce myth to history, or at least reduce its uncertainties. It is perhaps the most significant contribution of the nineteenth century that first Niebuhr for Roman history and then Grote for Greek history managed to separate out clearly *spatium mythicum* from *spatium historicum*. But their victories were only temporary, and myth soon returned as the truth that lies behind history. Today we have come to recognise that all history is indeed myth designed to validate the present, and we are not happy bunnies; for we object to national history as much as to Marxist history, and to the relativisation that is implied in the post-modern discourse of history. We still feel a desperate need for a philosophy of history to replace Marxism and the Whig interpretation of history, not just in their claims to determine the future, but also in their contributions to our ability to understand the past.

CHAPTER 15

Seeing in and through time

John Dunn

What has history to do with me? Mine is the first and only world.

Ludwig Wittgenstein

Once they choose to reflect on their lives at all, human beings have no alternative but to conceive and imagine them in the dimension of time. Time is the frame of all agency and the shifting horizon of hope and fear through which every conscious being moves. The most dramatic projects for escaping its sway organise themselves by necessity through attempts to negate it or defy its implications, and re-enact its relentless authority as they do so. As a literary genre, in all its heterogeneity, history sets itself to present consequential aspects of the past as they were, and capture and convey their significance to an audience in the present and future. Within the intellectual tradition of the west two canonical renderings of history, classical and Christian, have furnished the principal paradigms for identifying and conveying that significance, effectively obliterating all those that preceded them, and framing much of the imaginative history of Europe as they passed along their way. It has been the cumulative experience of reflecting on each of them which has done most to define the sense of history within which Europeans have lived for well over a millennium.[1] As Alexandra Lianeri's rich collection shows, intellectual resources generated elsewhere, whether earlier or in more recent times, have still done remarkably little to shake the intellectual hegemony of visions of time and its meaning for human life which emerged from and continue to centre on these two great domains of experience. Many certainly were absorbed

---

[1] The most relentlessly reflexive historiography of the last half century in the anglophone world, that of J. G. A. Pocock (see DeLuna 2006) has moved inexorably from a narrowly English screen (Pocock 1957), through a broader Atlantic framework (Pocock 1971 and 1975a), back to a classic moment in the European registration of the encounter of Rome with Christianity (Pocock 1999–2005 and onwards), and back to a still earlier antipodean perspective (Pocock 2005), interrogating its mode of travel throughout (Pocock 1971 and 2009).

into each from the beginning. But even its most drastic challengers – Islam and more recently China – have still made very little dent in its sense of imaginative integrity. Long after it has ceased to dominate the world, many now suspect, it dreams on in its own private world.

Within the British academic milieu, over the last century, the two most powerful presences in the interrogation of historiography and the recovery of its history, R. G. Collingwood and Arnaldo Momigliano, were both historians of aspects of the ancient world, the latter every inch a professional ancient historian in the grand style, and the former a most singular amateur who focused on one of the empire's drabber provinces. Momigliano is in many ways the hero of this volume, but Collingwood, significantly, barely surfaces within it. All the great issues of the meaning of time in human collective life come into focus at intervals over the preceding pages and anyone who reads through them with minimal intellectual attention will see again and again, and from an impressive variety of angles, just why the effort to orientate or steady ourselves in response to those issues, for any current vector of this intellectual tradition, still has to set out from that mandatory starting point. More disquietingly, in the enforced intimacy of the third millennium, even those whose encounter with the intellectual traditions of the west has been relatively recent, and who have always had and emphatically retain countervailing and often fiercely resistant orientations of their own, now have to assess seriously how far, if at all, to deflect those orientations to take account of the traditions whose trajectory is explored here.[2]

For a British child growing up in the 1940s and 1950s, it is hard to exaggerate the fustiness and apparent irrelevance of initial encounter with the relics of that very distant world. At that point, whatever may be true now, the educational mission to vindicate its continuing relevance must often have seemed as futile and dismaying as the Jesuit encounter with Tokugawa Japan.[3] But even for unresisting denizens of François Hartog's third regime of historicity,[4] the obsessive presentism of the epoch in which we now recognisably live, both the fustiness and the futility come through here as largely illusory; and the sense that this still remains the mandatory starting point for any possibility of steady orientation or stable apprehension of our situation in time reasserts itself peremptorily.

---

[2] The most momentous of these encounters is currently being enacted in China, continuing centuries of earlier preoccupation (see notably in recent years the strikingly ambitious reading of Metzger 2005 and his pupil Huang 2008).

[3] Elison 1988. Or in the unforgettable fictional depiction of Shusaku Endo published in 1978.

[4] Hartog 2003.

Between them, these essays touch, and cast light upon, an astonishing range of themes across two and a half millennia. The meaning of lived time and its sustained pressure on continuing agency, the struggle to achieve and sustain critical distance from the present and the more or less gleeful capitulation to its complacencies and presumptions, the iteration of myth and shared delusion, the re-enactment of complicity in ancient and not so ancient wrongs and mendacities, all pass to and fro across these pages, and show themselves trapped in a single bewildering medium: a repertoire of ancient intellectual projects and its long slow journey towards the banalities of contemporary academic life.

The most important conclusion enforced by the collection as a whole (for all its unforensic tone and editorial address) should come as no surprise. It is a truth, above all, about the inescapable necessity of the academic endeavour to reach decisively beyond parochialism and ideology, and the inherent futility of that endeavour. The most resolute straining for critical distance, the most disciplined efforts to explain dispassionately, can never escape the elemental site of human life. Every historian, whose subject begins and ends with that setting, enacts their values, if with varying ingenuousness, as soon they begin to tell their story. As Michael Williams calls Moses Finley to witness in the concluding chapter, the barest bones of any historical narrative express its author's values.[5] If all translation is in some measure betrayal all history likewise is in some measure ideology. Most of Lianeri's contributors are highly attuned to ideology, and surely more so than a counterpart assembly fifty years ago would have shown themselves to be. But their common preoccupation has comprehensively failed to generate a common framework for professional understanding, or even a shared strategy for keeping ideology in its place (containing its ravages, demarcating its potential authority from its impermissible intrusions). The triumphs of historicism over exemplarity, and of professional over amateur, have certainly generated an ample repertoire of shared practices and paradigms. But historicism is no escape from ideology; and the lure of exemplarity remains at least as potent for ancient historians as it does in the most belligerently nationalist purlieus of modern history. As the ancient world recedes ever further, it shows disconcertingly little trace of any intention to lie down and die. The analytic poise of historicising, and the conscientious impulse to reflexivity embodied in historicising their long line of predecessors, provide a rich harvest of heterogeneous insight. They singularly fail to compose into any single common and explicit project

[5] Finley 1985: 4.

of understanding or explanation, or any shared method for apprehending what has been taking place over this lengthy journey.

Discomfiting though this may be, it could scarcely have proved otherwise. In the historicising impulse to recognise the distance and otherness of the human past in all its heterogeneity (our past, yet never fully ours[6]), there is still insistently present the personal disposition and imaginative horizons of everyone who reaches out towards it. Only erasing the impress of the mental from the human record could leave a subject matter impervious to the idiosyncrasies of would be interpreters (and probably not even that). Even with the record of human thinking and its products in the past[7] any project of capture requires a closure of context on the part of the historian.[8] That closure can be made interrogatively and with a measure of self-conscious awareness, or inadvertently and by sheer obtuseness. But every act of recuperation which goes beyond a simple reproduction of text is marked by the mind of the historian who performs it: by the movement of their consciousness and the contours of their sensibility. The existential appeal of historicism lies in its promise to elude parochialism, and to disinfect the past of the historian's unruly subjectivity. But that appeal is always a trifle forlorn – best seen as a summons to an endless project of self-discipline which could never wholly succeed: an ascetic spiritual aspiration, not a serviceable epistemic procedure.

Exemplarity, in all its reckless vulnerability, addresses directly the question of how to live. Historicity contents itself with the effort to recognise and record what has been. It has no intrinsic propensity to presume one way of living better than another, or that life has any firm goals beyond those we choose to assign to it. But the most strenuous induction into the density and determinacy of historicity does not still the question of how to live; and the awkward squirmings which that induction leaves behind it, like the long drawn out death throes of a wounded animal, still attest to the force of that question. The most academic of professionalisms, however powerfully organising a format they may furnish for labour and self-advancement, cannot eliminate the question of how to live or serve as reasons for bothering to do so. We may no longer believe that it is history which does or could hold authority over our lives. But we have not come instead to the blithe conclusion that nothing holds authority within or for those lives,[9] or that the sole site of authority towards them must be our passing whims, or some automatised pseudo-scientific metric like

---

[6] Dunn 1980b.   [7] Dunn 1996: 10–38.   [8] Dunn 1980a, esp. 27–8.
[9] Taylor 1989, 1991 and 1995.

utilitarianism. It is easier to see François Hartog's third regime of historicity less as a historical site than as just one imaginative frame amongst a handful of others. Within that regime we are certainly no longer positioned within a long and presumptively directive past, or facing an inspirational and equally brusquely directive future. We are merely adrift, in a consciously disorientated manner, within a very short past indeed, and groping for intimations, prudential or vitalising, from a future we have no obvious competence to imagine. Opportunists without conviction, and with little sense of when or where to display alacrity.

Seen over its entire course, as Lianeri's volume comes surprisingly close to enabling us to see it, these two epic strands of the Western intellectual experience, the search for orientation, and the deepening will to understand undeceptively what our past has been, and how much of what is and has been true in our current habitats genuinely belongs to our own past, still dominate the intellectual landscape of the west centuries after the birth of modern natural science.

The less ambitious of these two themes, converging on the genealogy of the modern profession of ancient history, makes a tidier tale and offers better prospects for cumulating intellectual assent. Much of the volume duly tells parts of this tale; but its overall weight falls more towards the more ambitious and intractable (and older) alternative.

Exemplarity presumes the possibility of identification and raises simultaneously the issues of validity and propriety within each individual act of identification. The issues of validity are epistemic, and perhaps even ontological. They place in question the lucidity, honesty, or even sanity, of any or all such identifications. They interrogate the imagined self as a shaky edifice, part voluntarily erected, part opportunistically appropriated, part passively bestowed from the outside: an edifice of partial intimations and self-deceptions, but also potentially of all but comprehensive delusion. The puzzle they promise to aid us to answer is what within ourselves we have good reason to believe, and to trust in because we can and should believe it, and what that merited trust should prompt and enable us to do. The issues of propriety, by contrast, are above all ethical. Within the imagined self, they question which aspects it is good or right to affirm, and which it is edifying or imperative to reject or struggle to eliminate. They challenge us to judge the balance of pride or shame or even guilt which we should feel and try to respond to in what we seem to be. The past (our past) as they construe it is an arena of exploration and a framework for thinking about what to do and what to try to become. In the west, for better or worse (it barely makes sense to ask which on balance), the issue of propriety is still dominated by the intrusion of Christianity, an impact duly registered in Lianeri's volume but scarcely explored with any amplitude in its own terms. The attempt to offset that impact, long after the eleventh hour, by reverting to a defiantly Greek heritage,[10] however powerful the intelligence or steady the personal assurance which went into it, was breasting a torrent it never had much chance of stemming.

A relaxed historicism dissipates such issues without residue, but does so largely by averting its eyes from the questions which raise them. Since it holds no resources for addressing them, and furnishes no imaginative aid in stilling them, its most expansive assertions leave them necessarily untouched. The most powerful interrogations of these issues in the west over the last half century have come less from historians than from philosophers, whether practising or renegade, most notably in Britain Bernard Williams[11] and in France Michel Foucault. Each deployed history as an epistemic check, not merely on what there are grounds to believe, but also on what there is good reason to feel: and not least on the lingering shadows cast by what David Hume called 'the monkish virtues'. Neither Williams nor Foucault intrude much into this volume; but the basis and bearing of their very different oeuvres, taken as a whole, assuredly form an indispensable complement to it.

The judgement that in philosophy (the generalised interrogation of authority claims) Greek precedent remains exemplary across all subsequent critical interrogation, for all the bitter challenges it has faced over the last century, still dominates the academic philosophy of the Anglophone world. ('The legacy of Greece to Western philosophy is Western philosophy.'[12]) It is intriguing that its most brilliant recent Anglophone defender should have come so late in life to place such weight both on the grandest Greek recognition of the epistemic authority of history,[13] and on the force of Collingwood's conception of history's philosophical bearing.[14] In gauging its residual capacity for exemplarity and its continuing epistemic force, the legacy of the ancient historians is as much a matter for philosophers to assess as it is for the modern sub-profession of historiography.

What is striking, in face of Lianeri's volume, is how little consecutive effort recent philosophers or historians have chosen to make to clarify and justify the role of conceptions of time itself in organising and vindicating their strategies for grasping either experience or agency in time. There

[10] Williams 1985 and 1993.   [11] Williams 2006a and 2006b.   [12] Williams 2006a: 3.
[13] Williams 2006a: 341–58 and cf. Williams 2006b, esp. 210–13.   [14] Williams 2006a.

have certainly been protracted squabbles, on the Lilliputian scale of the modern academy, between partisans of continuity and those of disjunction. Because exemplarity presupposes continuity, the price of repudiating the former has seemed (and will no doubt continue to seem) prohibitively high to all who see the possibility of coherent political life[15] or moral experience[16] as radically dependent on tradition and practice. Because historicism asserts radical discontinuity, it is necessarily flippant in such address as it chooses to offer towards the question of what to strive to do and what at all costs to insist on avoiding. The stand off between the two leaves unresolved the choice between viewing time as a field of unfettered imaginative discretion, limitlessly open to fictive reconfiguration, or conceiving it instead as an iron cage of fatality impervious to the interpreting imagination on pain of delusion. The odyssey of ancient Greece assuredly left behind it, above all in the pages of Thucydides, better reason to presume the second. But it did not still the impulse to dally with the first. In its reckless promethean *fuite en avant*, in so many different ways, our species has bet all but blindly on the viability of the first.

The conversation which Homer and Hesiod and Herodotus and Thucydides began for us, and so many others have begun for so many other human communities all across the world, is still audibly going on. We cannot hope (and should not wish) to narrow it decisively or bring it under steady personal intellectual control by poring over, as Lianeri contrives to do, the historiographical trajectory from Homer to Simon Schama. But we also cannot hope to comprehend our own speeches or the speeches which others make to us from within this still astonishingly continuous space without taking the trouble to grasp where so many elements of those speeches have come from.

In the long run we are assuredly all dead (a secular conviction). But in the meantime, however long it proves to be for each and all of us, to understand ourselves and our lives must be to see ourselves and them in time. Time remains by turns a mystery, an idyll, an enigma, a tragedy, a farce, a horizon of diffuse hope, a terminal nightmare. None of its guises is reliably irrelevant for a historian. Whether they care to recognise it or not, every historian has taken on a lot. The presence and weight of time in human life thus far is theirs to register and explicate as best they can. All of this, after their own fashion, a number of those distant Greek figures saw coming very long

---

[15] Oakeshott 1962 and 1975.
[16] MacIntyre 1981, 1988 and 1990; and more diffusely Taylor 1989, 1991 and 1995.

ago. The fragmented memory of their recognitions, endlessly recomposed, has passed by now through many acutely disconcerting adventures, from projects of world domination and would be global spiritual adventure to more parochial bloodlettings or exercises in narrowly domestic spite. We can try to retrace their steps as soberly as we can; but we cannot take the chaos out of their erratic journey or absorb most of the weight of the life which has passed through them. Because history can never fully grasp life, it was never a plausible claimant to authority over it.

Bibliography

Agamben, G. (1993) [1978] *Infancy and History: The Destruction of Experience*, trans. L. Heron. London.

(2007) *Il Regno a la Gloria: Per una genealogia teologica dell'economia e del governo*. Vicenza.

Allen, M. J. B. (1998) *Synoptic Art. Marsilio Ficino on the History of Platonic Interpretation*. Florence.

Allonnes, M. Revault d' (2006) *Le pouvoir des commencements. Essai sur l'autorité*. Paris.

Altmeyer, M. (2001) *Unzeitgemäßes Denken bei Sophokles*. Stuttgart.

Aly, W. (1969) *Volksmärchen, Sage und Novelle bei Herodot und seinen Zeitgenossen. Eine Untersuchung über die volkstümlichen Elemente der altgriechischen Prosaerzählung*, 2nd edn. Göttingen.

Ampolo, C. (1997) *Storie greche. La formazione della moderna storiografia sugli antichi Greci*. Turin.

Angermeier, H. (1987) 'Ranke und Burckhardt', *Archiv für Kulturgeschichte* 69: 407–52.

Arendt, H. (1972) *La crise de la culture*, trans. M.-C. Brosselet and H. Pons. Paris.

Armstrong, A. H. (1987) 'Iamblichus and Egypt', *Les études philosophiques* 2–3: 179–88.

Arnason, J. P. *et al.* (eds.) (2005) *Axial Civilizations and World History*. Leiden.

Ash, M. G. (ed.) (1999) *Mythos Humboldt. Vergangenheit und Zukunft der deutschen Universitäten*. Vienna.

Ataç, A. (2006) 'Imperial lessons from Athens and Sparta: Eighteenth-century British histories of ancient Greece', *History of Political Thought* 27: 642–60.

Athanassiadi, P. (1999) 'The Chaldaean Oracles. Theology and theurgy', in *Pagan Monotheism in Late Antiquity*, eds. P. Athanassiadi and M. Frede. Oxford: 41–67.

Auerbach, E. (1959) 'Figura', in *Scenes From the Drama of European Literature: Six Essays*, trans. R. Manheim. Gloucester, MA: 11–71.

Avlami, Ch. (ed.) (2000) *L'antiquité grecque au XIXe siècle: un exemplum contesté?* Paris.

(2001) 'Libertà liberale contro libertà antica', in *I Greci. Storia, cultura, arte, società. Vol. III: I Greci oltre la Grecia*, ed. S. Settis. Turin: 1311–50.

Badiou, A. (2003) *Saint Paul: The Foundation of Universalism*, trans. R. Brassier. Stanford, CA.

Baker, K. M. (2001) 'Transformations of classical republicanism in eighteenth-century France', *Journal of Modern History* 73: 32–53.

Bakker, B. (2000) *The Exemplary Society*. Oxford.

Baltes, M. (1999) 'Der Platonismus und die Weisheit der Barbaren', in *Traditions of Platonism. Essays in Honour of John Dillon*, ed. J. J. Cleary. Aldershot: 115–38.

Barnes, J. (2002) 'Ancient philosophers', in *Philosophy and Power in the Graeco-Roman World: Essays in Honour of Miriam Griffin*, eds. G. Clark and T. Rajak. Oxford: 295–306.

Barnes, J. and Griffin, M. (eds.) (1997) *Philosophia togata II. Plato and Aristotle at Rome*. Oxford.

Barrett, J. (1995) 'Narrative and the messenger in Aeschylus' *Persians*', *American Journal of Philology* 116: 539–57.

Battisti, D. (1990) 'Συνετός as aristocratic self-description', *Greek, Roman and Byzantine Studies* 31: 5–26.

Baudelaire, Ch. (1964) *The Painter of Modern Life and Other Essays*, trans. and ed. J. Mayne. London.

Bayly, C. A. (2004) *The Birth of the Modern World, 1780–1914: Global Connections and Comparisons*. London.

Beazley, J. D. (1963) *Attic Red-Figure Vase-Painters*, 2nd edn. Oxford.

Bender, J. and Wellbery, D. E. (eds.) (1991) *Chronotypes. The Construction of Time*. Stanford, CA.

Benjamin, W. (2003) [1928] *The Origin of German Tragic Drama*, trans. J. Osborne. London.

Benner, D. (1995) *Wilhelm von Humboldts Bildungstheorie. Eine prob-lemgeschichtliche Studie zum Begründungszusammenhang neuzeitlicher Bil-dungsreform*, 2nd edn. Weinheim–Munich.

Berglar, P. (ed.) (2003) *Wilhelm von Humboldt. In Selbstzeugnissen und Bilddoku-menten*, 9th edn. Reinbek near Hamburg.

Berlin, I. (1977) *Vico and Herder: Two Studies in the History of Ideas*. New York.
   (1979) 'The counter-Enlightenment', in *Against the Current. Studies in the His-tory of Ideas*, ed. Henry Hardy. Oxford: 1–24.

Berman, M. (1983) *All that is Solid Melts into the Air: The Experience of Modernity*. London.

Bernal, M. (1987) *Black Athena. The Afroasiatic Roots of Classical Civilization. Volume I: The Fabrication of Ancient Greece, 1785–1985*. London.

Bertrand, D. (2001) 'Chronologie et exégèse chez Sulpice Sévère', in *L'Historiographie de l'Eglise des Premiers Siècles*, eds. B. Pouderon and Y.-M. Duval. Paris: 451–67.

Bett, R. (2002) 'Is there a sophistic ethics?', *Ancient Philosophy* 22: 235–62.

Bichler, R. (1983) '*Hellenismus*'. *Geschichte und Problematik eines Epochenbegriffs*. Darmstadt.

Bidez, J. (1945) *Eos ou Platon et l' Orient*. Brussels.

Bidez, J. and Cumont, F. (1973) *Les mages héllénisés. Zoroastre, Ostanès et Hystaspe dans la tradition grecque*, 2nd edn. (2 vols.). Paris.

Bischoff, H. (1932) *Der Warner bei Herodot*. Marburg.

Blanke, H. W. (1991) *Historiographiegeschichte als Historik*. Stuttgart and Bad Cannstatt.

Blanke, H. W. and Rüsen, J. (eds.) (1984) *Von der Aufklärung zum Historismus. Zum Strukturwandel des historischen Denkens*. Munich.

Blaut, J. M. (1993) *The Colonizer's Model of the World: Geographical Diffusionism and Eurocentric History*. New York.

Blumenberg, H. (1999) *La légitimité des temps modernes*, trans. M. Sagnol, J. L. Schlegel and D. Trierweiler. Paris.

Boardman, J. (2002) *The Archaeology of Nostalgia. How the Greeks Re-created their Mythical Past*. London.

Bödeker, H. E., G. G. Iggers, J. B. Knudsen and P. H. Reill (eds.) (1986) *Aufklärung und Geschichte. Studien zur deutschen Geschichtswissenschaft im 18. Jahrhundert*. Göttingen.

Bodin, J. (1967) [1650] *Methodus ad facilem historiarum cognitionem*. Aalen.

Boeckh, A. (1877) *Encyklopädie und Methodologie der philologischen Wissenschaften*, ed. E. Bratuscheck. Leipzig.

Boedeker, D. (2001) 'Heroic historiography. Simonides and Herodotus on Plataea', in Boedeker and Sider 2001: 120–34.

Boedeker, D. and Sider, D. (eds.) (2001) *The New Simonides. Contexts of Praise and Desire*. Oxford.

Boer, P. den (1998) *History as a Profession: The Study of History in France, 1818–1914*, trans. A. J. Pomerans. Princeton.

Bolgar, R. R. (1954) *The Classical Heritage and its Beneficiaries*. Cambridge.

Bollenbeck, G. (1996) *Bildung und Kultur. Glanz und Elend eines deutschen Deutungsmusters*. Frankfurt am Main.

Borges, L. J. (1989) *Obras Completas* (2 vols.). Buenos Aires.

Bossuet, J-B. (1976) [1679] *Discourse on Universal History*. Chicago, IL.

Boys-Stones, G. R. (2001) *Post-Hellenistic Philosophy*. Oxford.

Bravo, B. (1968) *Philologie, histoire, philosophie de l'histoire: étude sur J. G. Droysen, historien de l'antiquité*. Breslau–Warsaw.

Breazeale, D. (1997) 'Introduction', in F. Nietzsche, *Untimely Meditations*, trans. R. J. Hollingdale. Cambridge: vii–xxxiii.

Brisson, L. (1987) 'Proclus et l' orphisme', in *Proclus lecteur et interprète des Anciens*, eds. J. Pépin and H. D. Saffrey. Paris: 43–104.

Brown, T. S. (1949) *Onesicritus. A Study in Hellenistic Historiography*. Berkeley, CA and Los Angeles.

Bruch, R. vom (1999) 'Langsamer Abschied von Humboldt? Etappen deutscher Universitätsgeschichte 1810–1945', in Ash 1999: 29–57.

(2001) 'Zur Gründung der Berliner Universität im Kontext der deutschen Universitätslandschaft um 1800', in Müller, Ries and Ziche 2001: 63–77.

Bruford, W. H. (1975) *The German Tradition of Self-Cultivation. 'Bildung' from Humboldt to Thomas Mann*. Cambridge.

Bryden, I. (2005) *Reinventing King Arthur: The Arthurian Legends in Victorian Culture*. Aldershot.

Bubner, R. (1984) *Geschichtsprozesse und Handlungsnormen. Untersuchungen zur praktischen Philosophie*. Frankfurt.

Buchert, U. (2000) *Denkmalpflege im antiken Griechenland. Maßnahmen zur Bewahrung historischer Bausubstanz*. Frankfurt.

Bulwer Lytton, E. (2004) [1837] *Athens: Its Rise and Fall, with Views of the Literature, Philosophy, and Social Life of the Athenian People*, ed. O. Murray. London.

Burgess, R. W. (1990) 'History vs historiography in late antiquity', *Ancient History Bulletin* 4: 116–24.

(1999) *Studies in Eusebian and Post-Eusebian Chronography*. Stuttgart.

Burke, P. (1966) 'The popularity of ancient historians 1450–1700', *History and Theory* 5: 135–52.

(1969a) *The Renaissance Sense of the Past*. London.

(1969b) 'Tacitism', in *Tacitus*, ed. T. A. Dorey. London: 149–71.

(1980) 'Did Europe exist before 1700?', *History of European Ideas* 1:21–9

(1988) 'Ranke als Gegenrevolutionär', in *Leopold von Ranke und die moderne Geschichtswissenschaft*, ed. W. J. Mommsen. Stuttgart: 189–200.

(1990) *The French Historical Revolution: The Annales School, 1929–89*. Cambridge.

(2001) 'The sense of anachronism from Petrarch to Poussin', in *Time in the Medieval World*, eds. C. Humphrey and W. M. Ormrod. York: 157–73.

Burkert, W. (1972) *Lore and Science in Ancient Pythagoreanism*, trans. Edwin L. Minar, Jr. Cambridge, MA.

(1992) *The Orientalizing Revolution. Near Eastern Influences on Greek Culture in the Early Archaic Age*, trans. M. Pinder. Cambridge, MA.

Burkhardt, J. (1971) *Die Entstehung der modernen Jahrhundertrechnung. Ursprung und Ausbildung einer historiographischen Technik von Flacius bis Ranke*. Göppingen.

Burrow, J. W. (1967) *Evolution and Society: A Study in Victorian Social Theory*. Cambridge.

(2007) *A History of Histories: Epics, Chronicles, Romances and Inquiries from Herodotus and Thucydides to the Twentieth Century*. London.

Burrus, V. (1995) *The Making of a Heretic: Gender, Authority, and the Priscillianist Controversy*. Berkeley–Los Angeles–London.

Butler, E. M. (1935) *The Tyranny of Greece over Germany. A Study of the Influence Exercised by Greek Art and Poetry over the Great German Writers of the Eighteenth, Nineteenth and Twentieth Centuries* (rpt Boston 1958; abridged German translation *Deutsche im Banne Griechenlands*, Berlin 1948). Cambridge.

Butterfield, H. (1955) *Man on his Past. The Study of the History of Historical Scholarship*. Cambridge.

Cambiano, G. (1974) 'Montesquieu e le antiche repubbliche greche', *Rivista di filosofia* 65: 93–144.

(1983) *La filosofia in Grecia e a Roma*. Rome–Bari.

(1984) 'La Grecia antica era molto popolata? Un dibattito nel xvIII secolo', *Quaderni di Storia* 20: 3–42.

(1988) *Il ritorno degli antichi*. Rome–Bari (French trans. *Le retour des anciens*, Paris 1994).

(2000) *Polis. Un modello per la cultura Europea*. Bari.

Canfora, L. (1987) *Ellenismo*. Rome–Bari.

Cantor, N.F. (1993) *Inventing the Middle Ages*. London.

Carlyle, T. (1869) [1838] 'Sir Walter Scott', in *Critical and Miscellaneous Essays*. vol. vI. London.

Cartledge, P. (1996) 'Classical studies', in *Encyclopedia of Social and Cultural Anthropology*, eds. A. Barnard and J. Spencer. London–New York: 100–2.

(2001) 'Introduction', in G. Grote, *A History of Greece: From the Time of Solon to 403 B.C.*, eds. J. M. Mitchell and M. O. B. Caspari. London: ix–xx.

(2002) *The Greeks: A Portrait of Self and Others*, rev. edn. Oxford.

Carver, T. (2002) 'Imagery/writing, imagination/politics: Reading Marx through the *Eighteenth Brumaire*', in Cowling and Martin 2002: 113–28.

Cecchini, S. (1975) *Patrios politeia. Uno tentativo propagandistico durante la Guerra del Peloponneso*. Turin.

Certeau, M. de (1986) *Heterologies. Discourse on the Other*, trans. Brian Massumi. Minneapolis, MN.

Chakrabarty, D. (2000) *Provincialising Europe. Postcolonial Thought and Historical Difference*. Princeton, NJ.

Chaplin, J. D. (2000) *Livy's Exemplary History*. Oxford.

Charity, A. C. (1966) *Events and their Afterlife: The Dialectics of Christian Typology in the Bible and Dante*. Cambridge.

Choay, F. (2001) *The Invention of the Historical Monument*, trans. L. M. O'Connell. Cambridge.

Christ, K. and Momigliano, A. (eds.) (1988) *L'Antichità nell'Ottocento in Italia e Germania – Die Antike im 19. Jahrhundert in Italien und Deutschland*. Bologna–Berlin.

Clark, G. (1999) 'Translate into Greek. Porphyry of Tyre on the New Barbarians', in *Constructing Identities in Late Antiquity*, ed. R. Miles. London–New York: 112–32.

Clarke, K. (2008) *Making Time for the Past: Local History and the Polis*. Oxford.

Classen, J. and Steup, J. (eds.) (1862–1922) *Thukydides* (8 vols.). Berlin.

Clay, D. (1983) *Lucretius and Epicurus*. Ithaca, NY–London.

Cochrane, C. (1929) *Thucydides and the Science of History*. London.

Cochrane E. (1981) *Historians and Historiography in the Italian Renaissance*. Chicago, IL.

Cohn, N. (1970) *Pursuit of the Millennium*, rev. edn. Oxford.

Collingwood, R. G. (1946) *The Idea of History*. Oxford.

Collini, S., D. Winch, and J. Burrow (1983) *That Noble Science of Politics. A Study in Nineteenth-Century Intellectual History*. Cambridge.

Connor, W. R. (1984) *Thucydides*. Princeton, NJ.
  (1985) 'Narrative discourse in Thucydides', in *The Greek Historians. Literature and History. Papers Presented to A. E. Raubitschek*, ed. M. H. Jameson. Saratoga: 1–17.
Conze, W., J. Kocka, R. Koselleck *et al.* (eds.) (1985–92) *Bildungsbürgertum im 19. Jahrhundert* (4 vols.). Stuttgart.
Corcella, A. (1984) *Erodoto e l'analogia*. Palermo.
  (2006) 'The new genre and its boundaries: poets and logographers', in Rengakos and Tsakmakis 2006: 33–56.
Costanza, S. (1980) 'I "Chronica" di Sulpicio Severo e le historiae di Trogo-Giustino', in *La storiografia ecclesiastica nella tarda antichità*, ed. S. Calderone. Messina: 275–312.
Cowling, M. and Martin, J. (eds.) (2002) *Marx's 'Eighteenth Brumaire'. (Post)modern Interpretations*. London.
Cozzi, G. (1958) *Il Doge Niccolò Contarini*. Venice.
Creuzer, G. F. (1798) *Herodot und Thucydides. Versuch einer nähern Würdigung einiger ihrer historischen Grundsätze mit Rücksicht auf Lucians Schrift: Wie man Geschichte schreiben müsse*. Leipzig.
  (1803) *Die historische Kunst der Griechen in ihrer Entstehung und Fortbildung*. Leipzig.
Croke, B. (1983) 'The origins of the Christian world chronicle', in *History and Historians in Late Antiquity*, eds. B. Croke and A. Emmett. Toronto: 116–31, reprinted in B. Croke, *Christian Chronicles and Byzantine History, 5th–6th Centuries*. London, 1992.
  (2001) *Count Marcellinus and his Chronicle*. Oxford.
Crossley, C. (1993) *French Historians and Romanticism. Thierry, Guizot, the Saint-Simonians, Quinet, Michelet*. London.
Crouzel, H. (1962) *Origène et la philosophie*. Paris.
Dally, O. (forthcoming) 'Rückblick und Gegenwart. Vergleichende Untersuchungen zur Visualisierung von Vergangenheitsvorstellungen in der Antike', in *Ergänzungshefte. Jahrbuch des Deutschen Archäologischen Instituts*.
Darbo-Peschanski, C. (ed.) (2000) *Construction du temps dans le monde grec ancien*. Paris.
Deissler, J. (2000) *Antike Sklaverei und deutsche Aufklärung: im Spiegel von Johann Friedrich Reitemeiers 'Geschichte und Zustand der Sklaverey und Leibeigenschaft in Griechenland' (1789)*. Stuttgart.
DeLuna, D.N. (ed.) (2006) *The Political Imagination in History: Essays Concerning J. G. A. Pocock*. Baltimore, MD.
Demetriou, K. N. (1999) *George Grote on Plato and Athenian Democracy. A Study in Classical Reception*. Frankfurt am Main.
Den Brincken, A.-D. von (1969) 'Die lateinische Weltchronistik', in *Mensch und Weltgeschichte: zur Geschichte der Universalgeschichtsschreibung*, ed. A. Randa. Salzburg–Munich: 43–86.
Derrida, J. (1994) *Specters of Marx. The State of the Debt, the Work of Mourning and the New International*, trans. P. Kamuf. London.

(2002) 'The right to philosophy from a cosmopolitan point of view', in *Negotiations: Interventions and Interviews*, ed. and trans. E. Rottenberg. Stanford, CA: 329–42.

Descartes, R. (1963) *Oeuvres Philosophiques*, ed. F. Alquié. Paris.

Detienne, Marcel (2008) [2000] *Comparing the Incomparable*, trans. J. Lloyd. Stanford, CA.

Dodds, E. R. (1973) 'The ancient concept of progress', in *The Ancient Concept of Progress and Other Essays on Greek Literature and Belief.* Oxford: 1–25.

Donato, R. Di (1990) *Per un'antropologia storica del mondo antico*. Florence.

(2007) 'Arnaldo Momigliano from antiquarianism to cultural history: Some reasons for a quest', in Miller 2007a: 66–96.

Dorandi, T. (ed.) (1991) *Filodemo, Storia dei filosofi. Platone e l' Accademia (Pherc. 1021 e 164).* Naples.

Douhain, G. (1910) *Jaques de Tourreil traducteur de Démosthène (1656–1714).* Paris.

Dover, K. J. (ed.) (1992) *Perceptions of the Ancient Greeks.* Oxford.

Droysen, J. G. (1977) *Historik. Historisch-kritische Ausgabe, vol. I: Rekonstruktion der ersten vollständigen Fassung der Vorlesungen (1857); Grundriß der Historik in der ersten handschriftlichen (1857/1858); und in der letzten gedruckten Fassung (1882)*, ed. P. Leyh. Stuttgart–Bad Cannstatt.

Dunn, J. (1980a) 'The identity of the history of ideas', in *Political Obligation in its Historical Context.* Cambridge: 13–28.

(1980b) 'Practising history and social science on "realist" assumptions', in *Political Obligation in its Historical Context.* Cambridge: 81–111.

(1996) *The History of Political Theory.* Cambridge.

Edelstein, L. (1940) 'Primum Graius homo (Lucretius I 66)', *Transactions and Proceedings of the American Philological Association* 71: 78–90

Edmunds, L. (1975a) *Chance and Intelligence in Thucydides.* Cambridge, MA.

(1975b) 'Thucydides' ethics as reflected in the description of stasis', *Harvard Studies in Classical Philology* 79: 73–92.

(1993) 'Thucydides in the act of writing', in *Tradizione e Innovazione nella cultura Greca da Omero all' età Ellenistica. Scritti in onore di Bruno Gentili*, vol. II, ed. Roberto Pretagostini. Rome: 831–52.

Eissfeldt, O. (1974) *The Old Testament: An Introduction*, trans. P. R. B. Ackroyd. Oxford.

Elison, G. (1988) *Deus Destroyed: The Image of Christianity in Early Modern Japan.* Cambridge, MA.

Elliott, J. H. (1984) *Richelieu and Olivares.* Cambridge.

Ellman, M. (2005) 'Introduction: bad timing', in *On Murder, Mourning and Melancholia*, ed. S. Freud. Harmondsworth: vii–xxvii.

Endo, S. (1978) *Silence*, trans. W. Johnston. London.

Engelhardt, U. (1986) *'Bildungsbürgertum.' Begriffs– und Dogmengeschichte eines Etiketts.* Stuttgart.

Erbse, H. (1987) 'Zwei Fragen zur Geschichtsbetrachtung des Thukydides', in *Agora. Zu Ehren von Rudolph Berlinger (Perspektiven der Philosophie. Neues Jahrbuch 13).* Amsterdam: 331–46.

Ermarco (1988) *Frammenti*, ed. and trans. F. L. Auricchio. Naples.

Erskine, A. (2001) *Troy between Greece and Rome. Local Tradition and Imperial Power*. Oxford.

Eucken, C. (1983) *Isokrates. Seine Auseinandersetzung mit dem zeitgenössischen Philosophie*. Berlin–New York.

Fabbrini, F. (1983) *Translatio imperii. L'impero universale da Ciro ad Augusto*. Rome.

Fabiny, T. (1992) *The Lion and the Lamb: Figuralism and Fulfilment in the Bible, Art and Literature*. London.

Fahrmeir A. (2005a) 'Bürgerlichkeit', *Enzyklopädie der Neuzeit* 2: 567–71.

(2005b) 'Bürgertum', *Enzyklopädie der Neuzeit* 2: 583–94.

(2005c) 'Bildungsbürgertum', in *Enzyklopädie der Neuzeit* 2: 242–6.

Farrar, C. (1988) *The Origins of Democratic Thinking. The Invention of Politics in Classical Athens*. Cambridge.

Fedi, L. (2000) 'La contestation du miracle grec chez Auguste Comte', in Avlami 2000: 157–92.

Feldherr, A. (1998) *Spectacle and Society in Livy's History*. Berkeley–Los Angeles–London.

Felten, F. (1984) *Griechische tektonische Friese archaischer und klassischer Zeit*. Waldsassen.

Ferguson, N. (1997) 'Introduction. Virtual history: towards a "chaotic" theory of the past', in *Virtual History. Alternatives and Counterfactuals*, ed. N. Fergusson. London: 1–90.

Ferrary, J.-L. (1988) *Philhellénisme et impérialisme. Aspects idéologiques de la conquête romaine du monde hellénistique, de la seconde guerre de Macédoine à la guerre contre Mithridate*. Rome.

Festugière, A.-J. (1950) *La révélation d' Hermès Trismégiste. 1. L' astrologie et les sciences occultes*, 2nd edn. Paris.

(1971) *Etudes de philosophie grecque*. Paris.

Finley, M. I. (1975) *The Use and Abuse of History*. London.

(1985) *Ancient History: Evidence and Models*. London.

Flashar, H. (1986) 'Wilhelm von Humboldt und die griechische Literatur', in *Wilhelm von Humboldt. Vortragszyklus zum 150. Todestag*, ed. B. Schlerath. Berlin–New York: 82–100.

Flory, S. (1978) 'Laughter, tears and wisdom in Herodotus', *American Journal of Philology* 99: 145–53.

(1987) *The Archaic Smile of Herodotus*. Detroit.

Flower, M. A. and J. Marincola (2002) *Herodotus. Histories Book IX*. Cambridge.

Fontaine, J. (1975) 'L'affaire Priscillien ou l'ère des nouveaux Catilina. Observations sur le "sallustianisme" de Sulpice Sévère', in *Classica et Iberica: A Festschrift in Honor of the Rev. Joseph M.-F. Marique, S. J.*, ed. P. T. Brannan, S. J. Worcester, MA: 355–92.

Forbes, D. (1952) *The Liberal Anglican Idea of History*. Cambridge.

Fornara, C. W. (1971) 'Evidence for the date of Herodotus' publication', *Journal of Hellenic Studies* 91: 25–34.

(1983) *The Nature of History in Ancient Greece and Rome*. Berkeley–Los Angeles–London.

Foucault, D. and Payen, P. (eds.) (2007) *Les Autorités: Dynamiques et mutations d'une figure de référence à l'Antiquité*. Grenoble.

Foucault, M. (1989) *The Archaeology of Knowledge*, trans. A. M. S. Smith. London–New York.

Fowden, G. (1986) *The Egyptian Hermes. A Historical Approach to the Late Pagan Mind*. Cambridge.

Fowler, D. (2000) 'The ruin of time: monuments and survival at Rome', in *idem, Roman Constructions: Readings in Postmodern Latin*. Oxford: 193–217.

Frede, M. (1997) 'Celsus' attack on Christians', in Barnes and Griffin 1977: 218–40.

(1999) 'Origen's Treatise against Celsus', in *Apologetics in the Roman Empire. Pagan, Jews, and Christians*, eds. M. Edwards, M. Goodman, S. Price, and C. Rowland. Oxford: 131–55.

Freeman, E. A. (1873) 'Ancient Greece and medieval Italy', in *idem, Historical Essays, Second Series*. London: 1–51.

Freud, S. (1958) 'Remembering, repeating and working through', *Freud: Standard Edition*, vol. XII. London: 147–56.

(1991) 'Beyond the Pleasure Principle', in *On Metapsychology*. Harmondsworth: 275–338. Originally translated by J.Strachey (1920) for the Standard Edition 18: 7–64.

(2005) 'Mourning and melancholia', in *On Murder, Mourning and Melancholia*, trans. S. Whiteside. Harmondsworth: 203–18.

Friedman, A. (ed.) (1966) *Collected Works of Oliver Goldsmith*. Oxford.

Fritz, K. von (1967) *Die griechische Geschichtsschreibung* (2 vols.). Berlin.

Frye, N. (1982) *The Great Code: The Bible and Literature*. London.

Fuhrmann, M. (1979) 'Die "Querelle des anciens et des modernes", der Nationalismus und die deutsche Klassik', in *Classical Influences on Western Thought, A.D. 1650–1870*, ed. R. R. Bolgar. Cambridge: 107–29.

Fuks, A. (1953) *The Ancestral Constitution*. London.

(1971) 'Thucydides and the stasis in Corcyra: Thuc. III 82–3 versus [Thuc.] III 84', *American Journal of Philology* 92: 48–55.

Fukuyama, F. (1992) *The End of History and the Last Man*. New York.

Fumaroli, M. (2007) 'Arnaldo Momigliano et la réhabilitation des "antiquaires": Le comte de Caylus et le "retour à l'antique" au XVIIIe siècle', in Miller 2007a: 154–83.

Furley, D. (1978) 'Lucretius the Epicurean' in *Lucrèce*, ed. O. Gigon. Vandoeuvres–Geneva: 1–27.

Gabba, E. (1981) 'True history and false history in classical antiquity', *Journal of Roman Studies* 71: 50–62.

Gaeta, F. (1955) *Lorenzo Valla: Filologia e storia nell'umanesimo italiano*. Naples.

Garbarino, G. (1973) *Roma e la filosofia greca dalle origini alla fine del II secolo a.C.* (2 vols.). Turin.

Garin, E. (1961) *La cultura filosofica del Rinascimento italiano*. 2nd edn. Florence.

(2006) *Ermetismo del Rinascimento*, 2nd edn. Pisa.

Garlan, Y. (2000) 'La démocratie grecque vue par Condorcet', in Avlami 2000: 55–69.

Gascoigne, J. (1991) 'The wisdom of the Egyptians and the secularization of history in the age of Newton', in *The Uses of Antiquity: The Scientific Revolution and the Classical Tradition*, ed. S. Gaukroger. Dordrecht: 171–212.

Gast, J. (1753) *Rudiments of the Grecian History: From the First Establishment of the States of Greece to the Overthrow of their Liberties in the Days of Philip the Macedonian. In Thirteen Dialogues.* London.

(1793) *The History of Greece* (2 vols.). Dublin.

Gatterer, J. C. (1767) 'Vom dem Plan des Herodots', in *Allgemeine historische Bibliothek*, 2: 46–123.

(1990) [1767] 'Vom historischen Plan und der daraus sich gründenden Zusammenfügung der Erzählungen', in *Theoretiker der deutschen Aufklärungshistorie*, eds. H. W. Blanke and D. Fleischer, vol. ɪɪ (*Fundamenta historica*, vol. 1.2). Stuttgart–Bad Cannstatt: 621–62.

Gauchet, M. (1985) *Le désenchantement du monde: Une histoire politique de la religion.* Paris.

(2002) *Philosophie des sciences historiques. Le moment romantique.* Paris.

(2003) 'Visages de l'autre. La trajectoire de la conscience utopique', *Le Débat* 125: 112–20.

Gawantka, W. (1985) *Die sogenannte Polis: Entstehung, Geschichte und Kritik der modernen althistorischen Grundbegriffe der griechische Staat, die griechische Staatsidee, die Polis.* Stuttgart.

(1990) '"Die Monumente reden". Realien, reales Leben, Wirklichkeit in der deutschen Alten Geschichte und Altertumskunde des neunzehnten Jahrhunderts', in *Heinrich Schliemann nach hundert Jahren*, eds. W. M. Calder III and J. Cobet. Frankfurt: 56–117.

Gernet, L. (1981) [1968] *The Anthropology of Ancient Greece*, trans. J. Hamilton and B. Nagy. Baltimore, MD.

Gervinus, G. G. (1838) [1832] *Historische Briefe. Veranlaßt durch Heeren und das Archiv von Schlosser und Bercht*, in *Gesammelte kleine historische Schriften* (*Historische Schriften*, vol. 7). Karlsruhe: 1–134.

(1962) *Grundzüge der Historik*, in *Schriften zur Literatur*, ed. G. Erler. Berlin.

Geuss, R. (2005) 'Thucydides, Nietzsche and Williams', in *idem*, *Outside Ethics*. Princeton, NJ: 219–32.

Ghisalberti, G. (1997) 'Tragedy and repetition in Marx's *The Eighteenth Brumaire of Louis Bonaparte*', *Clio* 26: 411–25.

Gillies, J. (1778) *The Orations of Lysias and Isocrates.* London.

Goldhill, S. (1994) 'The failure of exemplarity', in *Modern Critical Theory and Classical Literature*, eds. I. J. F. De Jong and J. P. Sullivan. Leiden: 51–73.

Goldsmith, M. M. (1987) 'Liberty, luxury and the pursuit of happiness', in Pagden 1987: 225–51.

Gomme, A. W. (1945–81) *An Historical Commentary on Thucydides.* 5 vols.; vol. ɪv and v completed by A. Andrewes and K. J. Dover. Oxford.

(1962) 'Thucydides and fourth-century political thought', in *idem, More Essays in Greek History and Literature*. Oxford: 122–38.

Gossman, L. (1968) *Medievalism and the Ideologies of the Enlightenment: The World and Work of La Curne de Sainte-Palaye*. Baltimore, MD.

(1983) *Orpheus Philologus. Bachofen versus Mommsen on the Study of Antiquity*. Philadelphia, PA.

(1990) *Between History and Literature*. Cambridge, MA–London.

Gottschalk, H.B. (1980) *Heraclides of Pontus*. Oxford.

Goulemot, J.-M. (1996) *Le règne de l'histoire: Discours historiques et révolutions, XVIIe–XVIIIe siècle*. Paris.

Gowing, A. M. (2005) *Empire and Memory: The Representation of the Roman Republic in Imperial Culture*. Cambridge.

Graevenitz, G. von and Marquard, O. (1998) 'Vorwort', in *Kontingenz*, eds. G. v. Graevenitz and O. Marquard. Munich: xi–xvi.

Grafton, A. (1975) 'Joseph Scaliger and historical chronology: The rise and fall of a discipline', *History and Theory* 14: 156–85.

(1981) 'Prolegomena to Friedrich August Wolf', reprinted in Grafton 1991: 214–43.

(1983a) *Joseph Scaliger. A Study in the History of Classical Scholarship. I. Textual Criticism and Exegesis*. Oxford.

(1983b) 'Polyhistor into Philolog: Notes on the transformation of German classical scholarship, 1780–1850', *History of Universities* 3: 159–92.

(1987) 'Portrait of Justus Lipsius', reprinted in Grafton 2001: 227–43.

(1991) *Defenders of the Text. The Traditions of Scholarship in an Age of Science, 1450–1800*. Cambridge, MA–London.

(1992) *New Worlds, Ancient Texts. The Power of Tradition and the Shock of Discovery*. Cambridge, MA.

(1997) *Commerce with the Classics: Ancient Books and Renaissance Readers*. Ann Arbor.

(1999) 'Introduction', in *The New Science* of Giambattista Vico, trans. D. Marsh. London, xi–xxxiii. Reprinted in Grafton 2001: 259–78.

(2001) *Bring Out Your Dead. The Past as Revelation*. Cambridge, MA–London.

(2003) 'Some uses of eclipses in early modern chronology', *Journal of the History of Ideas* 64: 213–29.

(2007a) 'Momigliano's method and the Warburg Institute: Studies in his middle period', in Miller 2007a: 97–126.

(2007b) *What Was History? The Art of History in Early Modern Europe*. Cambridge.

Grell, C. (1993) *L'histoire entre érudition et philosophie: étude sur la connaissance historique à l'âge des Lumières*. Paris.

(1995) *Le Dix-huitième siècle et l'antiquité en France 1680–1789* (2 vols.). Oxford.

Grethlein, J. (2006a) 'The manifold uses of the epic past. The embassy scene in Hdt. 7.153–163', *American Journal of Philology* 127: 485–509.

(2006b) *Das Geschichtsbild der Ilias. Eine Untersuchung aus phänomenologischer und narratologischer Perspektive*. Göttingen.

(2007a) 'Diomedes redivivus. A new reading of Mimnermus fr. 14 W²', *Mnemosyne* 60: 102–11.

(2007b) 'The hermeneutics and poetics of memory in Aeschylus' *Persae*', *Arethusa* 40.3: 363–96.

(2010) *The Greeks and their Past. Poetry, Oratory and History in the Fifth Century BCE.* Cambridge.

Gribbin, W. (1972) 'Rollin's histories and American republicanism', *William and Mary Quarterly* 29: 611–22.

Griggs, T. (2007) 'Universal history from Counter-Reformation to Enlightenment', *Modern Intellectual History* 4: 219–47.

Grimmer-Solem, E. (2003) *The Rise of Historical Economics and Social Reform in Germany. 1864–1894.* Oxford.

Grote, G. (1826) 'Fasti Hellenici by H. F. Clinton', *The Westminster Review*: 269–331.

Gruen, E.S. (2001) 'Jewish perspectives on Greek culture and ethnicity', in Malkin 2001: 347–73.

Guerci, L. (1979) *Libertà degli Antichi e libertà dei moderni. Sparta, Atene e i 'philosophes' nella Francia del 700.* Naples.

Guicciardini, F. (1933) *Considerazioni intorno ai Discorsi del Machiavelli*, ed. Roberto Palmarocchi. Bari.

Guthrie, W. K. C. (1971) *The Sophists.* Cambridge, first published as part 1 of *A History of Greek Philosophy*, vol. III. Cambridge 1969.

Habinek, T. N. (1998) *The Politics of Latin Literature: Writing, Identity and Empire in Ancient Rome.* Princeton, NJ.

Hadot, P. (1995) *Qu' est-ce que la philosophie antique?* Paris.

Hahn, H.-W. and Hein, D. (eds.) (2005) *Bürgerliche Werte um 1800. Entwurf – Vermittlung – Rezeption.* Cologne.

Hall, J. M. (2002) *Hellenicity. Between Ethnicity and Culture.* Chicago–London.

Hampton, T. (1990) *Writing from History: The Rhetoric of Exemplarity in Renaissance Literature.* Ithaca, NY.

Hankins, J. (1990) *Plato in the Italian Renaissance* (2 vols.). Leiden–New York.

Harries, M. (1995) 'Homo Alludens: Marx's Eighteenth Brumaire', *New German Critique* 66: 35–64.

Harrison, T. (2000) *Divinity and History. The Religion of Herodotus.* Oxford.

Hartog, F. (1980) *Le miroir d' Hérodote. Essai sur la représentation de l' autre.* Paris.

(2000) 'La Révolution française et l'Antiquité. Avenir d'une illusion ou cheminement d'un quiproquo?', in Avlami 2000: 7–46.

(2002) *Memoria di Ulisse. Racconti sulla frontiera nell' antica Grecia*, trans. A. Tadini Perazzoli. Turin.

(2003) *Régimes d'historicité. Présentisme et expériences du temps.* Paris.

(2005) *Anciens, modernes, sauvages.* Paris.

(2007) 'Ouverture – Autorités et temps', in Foucault and Payen 2007: 23–33.

Haskell, F. (1991) 'Winckelmann et son influence sur les historiens', in *Winckelmann: la naissance de l'histoire de l'art à l'époque des Lumières*, ed. E. Pommier. Paris: 85–99.

Haym, R. (ed.) (1859) *Wilhelm von Humboldts Briefe an Friedrich Gottlieb Welcker.* Berlin.

Hazard, P. (1953) *The European Mind (1680–1715),* trans. J. Lewis May. London.

Heeren, A. H. L. (1821–6) *Historische Werke* (15 vols.). Göttingen.

(1824) [1796] *Ideen über die Politik, den Verkehr und den Handel der vornehmsten Völker der alten Welt. 1. Asiatische Völker, 1. Einleitung, Perser,* in Heeren (1821–6) v. 10, 4th edn. Göttingen.

(1826) [1812] *Ideen über die Politik, den Verkehr und den Handel der vornehmsten Völker der alten Welt. 3. Europäische Völker. 1. Griechen,* 4th edn. Göttingen.

(1830) [1809] *Handbuch der Geschichte des europäischen Staatensystems und seiner Colonien.* Vol. 1 (2 vols.), 5th edn. Göttingen.

Heilbron, J. (1995) *The Rise of Social Theory,* trans. S. Gogol. Cambridge.

Heilman J. D. (1760) *Thucydides. Geschichte des Peloponnesischen Krieges aus dem griechischen übersetzt und mit kritischen Anmerkungen erläutert von D. Johan David Heilman.* Lemgo.

Hein, D. and Schulz, A. (eds.) (1996) *Bürgerkultur im 19. Jahrhundert. Bildung, Kunst und Lebenswelt.* Munich.

Henze, C. (1966) *Wilhelm von Humboldt und Christian Gottlob Heyne.* Ratingen.

Herder, J. G. (1991) *Briefe zu Beförderung der Humanität,* ed. H. D. Irmscher. Frankfurt am Main.

Herford, M. A. B. (1914) 'A cup by Brygos at Oxford', *Journal of Hellenic Studies* 34: 106–13.

Heuß, A. (1981) *Barthold Georg Niebuhrs wissenschaftliche Anfänge. Untersuchungen und Mitteilungen über die Kopenhagener Manuscripte und zur europäischen Tradition der lex agraria (loi agraire) (Abhandlungen der Akademie der Wissenschaften in Göttingen, Philologisch-Historische Klasse,* 3rd series, vol. 114). Göttingen.

Hicks, P. S. (1996) *Neo-Classical History and English Culture: From Clarendon to Hume.* New York.

Highet, G. (1949) *The Classical Tradition: Greek and Roman Influences on Western Literature.* London–New York.

Hobbes, T. (1966) [1843] *The History of the Grecian War Written by Thucydides,* translated by Thomas Hobbes of Malmesbury, vol. 1 (*The English Works of Thomas Hobbes of Malmesbury,* vol. VIII), Aalen.

Hobsbawm, E. (1962) *The Age of Revolution: Europe, 1789–1848.* London.

Hodgson, G. M. (2001) *How Economics Forgot History: The Problem of Historical Specificity in Social Science.* London–New York.

Hogan, J. T. (1980) 'The ἀξίωσις of words at Thuc. 3.82.4', *Greek, Roman and Byzantine Studies* 21: 139–49.

Hölkeskamp, K.-J. (2001) 'Marathon – vom Monument zum Mythos', in *Gab es das Griechische Wunder? Griechenland zwischen dem Ende des 6. und der Mitte des 5. Jahrhunderts v. Chr.* eds. D. Papenfuß and V. M. Strocka. Mainz: 329–53.

Hollander, R. (1977) 'Typology and secular literature: Some medieval problems and examples', in *Literary Uses of Typology from the Late Middle Ages to the Present,* ed. E. Miner. Princeton, NJ.

Hölscher, T. (1973) *Griechische Historienbilder des 5. und 4. Jahrhunderts v. Chr.* Würzburg.

    (1997) 'Ritual und Bildsprache. Zur Deutung der Reliefs an der Brüstung um das Heiligtum der Athena Nike in Athen', *Mitteilungen des Deutschen Archäologischen Instituts (Athen. Abt)* 112: 143–66.

    (1998) 'Images and political identity. The case of Athens', in *Democracy, Empire, and the Arts in Fifth-Century Athens*, eds. D. Boedeker and K. Raaflaub. Cambridge, MA: 153–83.

Hont, I. and Ignatieff, M. (eds.) (1983) *Wealth and Virtue. The Shaping of Political Economy in the Scottish Enlightenment.* Cambridge.

Hooker, M. D. (1986) *Continuity and Discontinuity: Early Christianity in its Jewish Setting.* London.

Hornblower, S. (1987) *Thucydides.* London.

    (1991–6) *A Commentary on Thucydides, Books I–V* (2 vols.). Oxford.

    (1995) 'The fourth-century and Hellenistic reception of Thucydides', *Journal of Hellenic Studies* 115: 47–68.

Huang, M. K. (2008) *The Meaning of Freedom: Yan Fu and the Origins of Liberalism in China.* Hong Kong.

Hübinger, G. (1984) *Georg Gottfried Gervinus. Historisches Urteil und politische Kritik (Schriftenreihe der Historischen Kommission bei der Bayerischen Akademie der Wissenschaften*, vol. 23). Göttingen.

Hughes, J. D. (1994) *Pan's Travail: Environmental Problems of the Greeks and Romans.* Baltimore, MD.

Humboldt, W. von (1903–36) *Gesammelte Schriften*, vols. 1–17. Berlin.

    (1960–81) *Werke in fünf Bänden*, eds. A. Flitner and K. Giel. Darmstadt.

Hume, D. (1759a) 'Letter 27 to Robertson of February 8, 1759', in *New Letters of David Hume*, eds. R. Klibansky and E. C. Mossner [1954]. Oxford: 47.

    (1759b) 'Letter 28 to Robertson of April 7, 1759', in *New Letters of David Hume*, eds. R. Klibansky and E. C. Mossner [1954]. Oxford: 48.

    (1963) 'On the populousness of ancient nations', in *Essays: Moral, Political and Literary.* Edinburgh: 381–451.

Hunter, V. (1973) *Thucydides the Artful Reporter.* Toronto.

Huppert, G. (1970) *The Idea of Perfect History. Historical Erudition and Historical Philosophy in Renaissance France.* Urbana, IL.

Iggers, G. G. (1968) *The German Conception of History. The National Tradition of Historical Thought from Herder to the Present.* Middletown, CT.

Immerwahr, H. R. (1954) 'Historical action in Herodotus', *Transactions and Proceedings of the American Philological Association* 85: 16–45.

    (1960) '*Ergon*: History as a monument in Herodotus and Thucydides', *American Journal of Philology* 61: 261–90.

    (1966) *Form and Thought in Herodotus.* Cleveland.

Jacoby, F. (1913) 'Herodotus', *RE, Supplement-Band II*: 205–520.

    (1945) 'Some Athenian epigrams from the Persian wars', *Hesperia* 14: 157–211.

Jaeger, F. (1994) *Bürgerliche Modernisierungskrise und historische Sinnbildung. Kulturgeschichte bei Droysen, Burckhardt und Max Weber.* Göttingen.

Jaeger, F. and Rüsen, J. (1992) *Geschichte des Historismus. Eine Einführung*. Munich.

Jameson, F. (2002) *A Singular Modernity. Essay on the Ontology of the Present*. London–New York.

Jauss, H. R. (1982) [1969] 'Literary history as a challenge to literary theory', in *Toward an Aesthetic of Reception*, trans. T. Bahti Minneapolis, MN: 3–45.

(2005) 'Modernity and literary tradition', trans. C. Thorne, in *Critical Inquiry* 31: 329–64.

Jeanneret, M. (1998) 'The vagaries of exemplarity', *Journal of the History of Ideas* 59: 565–80.

Jecht, D. (2003) *Die Aporie Wilhelm von Humboldts. Sein Studien- und Sprachprojekt zwischen Empirie und Reflexion*. Hildesheim.

Jeismann, K.-E. (1996) *Das preußische Gymnasium in Staat und Gesellschaft*, vol. I: *Die Entstehung des Gymnasiums als Schule des Staates und der Gebildeten, 1787 – 1817*; vol. II: *Höhere Bildung zwischen Reform und Reaktion, 1817–1859*, 2nd edn. Stuttgart.

Jeismann, K.-E. and Lundgreen, P. (eds.) (1987) *Handbuch der deutschen Bildungsgeschichte vol. 3: 1800 – 1870. Von der Neuordnung Deutschlands bis zur Gründung des Deutschen Reiches*. Munich.

Jenkyns, R. (1980) *The Victorians and Ancient Greece*. London.

Johnson, J. W. (1962) 'Chronological writing: its concepts and development', *History and Theory* 2: 124–45.

Kadish, A. (1989) *Historians, Economists and Economic History*. London–New York.

Kaehler, S. A. (1927) *Wilhelm von Humboldt und der Staat. Ein Beitrag zur Geschichte deutscher Lebensgestaltung um 1800*. Munich–Berlin.

Kahn, C. H. (1981) 'The origins of social contract theory in the 5th c. B.C.', in *The Sophists and their Legacy*, ed. G. B. Kerferd. Wiesbaden: 92–108.

Kalimtzis, K. (2000) *Aristotle on Political Enmity and Disease. An Inquiry into Stasis*. New York.

Kallet, L. (2001) *Money and the Corrosion of Power in Thucydides. The Sicilian Expedition and its Aftermath*. Berkeley, CA.

(2006) 'Thucydides' workshop of history and utility outside the text', in *Brill's Companion to Thucydides*, eds. A. Rengakos and A. Tsakmakis. Leiden: 335–68.

Kant, I. (1985) [1784] 'Ideen zu einer allgemeinen Geschichte in weltbürgerlicher Absicht', in *Schriften zur Geschichtsphilosophie*, ed. M. Riedel. Stuttgart: 29–39.

(1998) [1784] 'Idea for a universal history from a cosmopolitan point of view', trans. L. W. Beck in *Classical Readings in Culture and Civilization*, eds. J. Rundell and S. Mennell. London: 39–47.

Kantorowicz E. (1928) *Kaiser Friedrich der Zweite*. Berlin.

(1957) *The King's Two Bodies: A Study in Medieval Political Theology*. Princeton, NJ.

Kapp, E. (1930) 'Review of W. Schadewaldt, Die Geschichtsschreibung des Thukydides', *Gnomon* 6: 76–100.

Kelley, D. R. (1970) *Foundations of Modern Historical Scholarship. Language, Law and History in the French Renaissance.* New York–London.

(1998) *Faces of History: From Herodotus to Herder.* New Haven–London.

Kerferd, G. B. (1981) *The Sophistic Movement.* Cambridge.

Kermode, F. (1968) *The Sense of an Ending: Studies in the Theory of Fiction.* Oxford.

Kernan, A. (1987) *Printing Technology, Letters and Samuel Johnson.* Princeton, NJ.

Kerschensteiner, J. (1945) *Platon und das Orient.* Stuttgart.

Keßler, E. (1982) 'Das rhetorische Modell der Historiographie', in *Formen der Geschichtsschreibung* (*Theorie der Geschichte. Beiträge zur Historik*, vol. IV), eds. R. Koselleck, H. Lutz. and J. Rüsen. Munich: 37–85.

Kienle, W. von (1961) *Die Berichte über die Sukzessionen der Philosophen in der hellenistischen und spätantiken Literatur.* Berlin.

Klempt, A. (1960) *Die Säkularisierung der universalhistorischen Auffaschung. Zum Wandel des Geschichtsdenkens im 16. und 17. Jahrhundert.* Göttingen, Berlin–Frankfurt am Main.

Kloft, H. (1994) 'Antikenrezeption und Klassizismus. Ästhetische und politische Überlegungen', *Klassizismus in Bremen. Formen bürgerlicher Kultur, Jahrbuch 1993/94 der Wittheit zu Bremen*, ed. M. Rudloff. Bremen: 17–23.

Knell, H. (1990) *Mythos und Polis. Bildprogramme griechischer Bauskulptur.* Darmstadt.

Kocka J. (ed.) (1987) *Bürger und Bürgerlichkeit im 19. Jh.* Göttingen.

(ed.) (1995) *Bürgertum im 19. Jahrhundert* (3 vols.). Göttingen.

Kofsky, A. (2000) *Eusebius of Caesarea against Paganism.* Leiden–Boston–Cologne.

Konstan, D. (1983) 'The stories in Herodotus' Histories. Book I', *Helios* 10: 1–22.

(2001) 'To Hellenikon Ethnos: Ethnicity and the Construction of Ancient Greek Identity', in Malkin 2001: 29–50.

Koselleck, R. (1972) 'Einleitung', in *Geschichtliche Grundbegriffe. Historisches Lexikon zur politisch-sozialen Sprache in Deutschland*, v.1, ed. O. Brunner, W. Conze and R. Koselleck Stuttgart: xiii–xxiii.

(1975) 'Geschichte, Historie', in *Geschichtliche Grundbegriffe. Historisches Lexikon zur politisch-sozialen Sprache in Deutschland*, eds. O. Brunner, W. Conze, and R. Koselleck, v. 2, Stuttgart: 593–717.

(1988) *Critique and Crisis. Enlightenment and the Pathogenesis of Modern Society.* Cambridge MA.

(1997) [1975] *L'expérience de l'histoire*, ed. M. Werner, trans. A. Escudier *et al.* Paris.

(1998) 'Social history and *Begriffsgeschichte*', in *History of Concepts. A Comparative Perspective*, eds. I. Hampsher-Monk, K. Tilmans and F. Vree. Amsterdam: 23–35.

(2004a) [1967] 'Historia Magistra Vitae', in *Futures Past. On the Semantics of Historical Time*, trans. K. Tribe. New York: 26–42.

(2004b) [1969] 'Historical criteria of the modern concept of revolution', in *Futures Past. On the Semantics of Historical Time*, trans. K. Tribe. New York: 43–57.

(2004c) [1979] *Futures Past. On the Semantics of Historical Time*, trans. K. Tribe. New York.

(2006) *Begriffsgeschichten. Studien zur Semantik und Pragmatik der politischen und sozialen Sprache*. Frankfurt.

Kost, J. (2004) *Wilhelm von Humboldt – Weimarer Klassik – Bürgerliches Bewußtsein. Kulturelle Entwürfe in Deutschland um 1800*. Würzburg.

Kowerski, L. (2005) *Simonides on the Persian War. A Study of the Elegiac Verses of the 'New Simonides'*. New York.

Kraus, H.-C. (2008) *Kultur, Bildung und Wissenschaft im 19. Jahrhundert*. EDG 82. Munich.

Krieger, L. (1977) *Ranke: The Meaning of History*. Chicago, IL.

Kristeller, P.O. (1937) *Supplementum Ficinianum* (2 vols.). Florence.

(1956) *Studies in Renaissance Thought and Letters*. Rome.

Kron, U. (1997) 'Patriotic heroes', in *Ancient Greek Hero Cult*, ed. R. Hägg. Stockholm: 61–83.

Krueger, D. (2004) *Writing and Holiness: the Practice of Authorship in the Early Christian East*. Philadelphia, PA.

Kyrtatas, D. I. (2002) Κατακτώντας την Αρχαιότητα. Ιστοριογραφικές Διαδρομές *[Kataktôntas tên archaiotêta: Istoriografikes Diadromes]*. Athens.

La Noue, F. (1967) [1587] *Discours politiques et militaires*, ed. F. E. Sutcliffe. Geneva.

LaCapra, D. (1983) 'Reading Marx: the case of *The Eighteenth Brumaire*', in *idem, Rethinking Intellectual History. Texts, Contexts, Language*. Ithaca, NY: 268–90.

Landfester, M. (1988) *Humanismus und Gesellschaft. Untersuchungen zur politischen und gesellschaftlichen Bedeutung der humanistischen Bildung in Deutschland*. Darmstadt.

(1996) 'Griechen und Deutsche: Der Mythos einer "Wahlverwandtschaft"', in *Mythos und Nation. Studien zur Entwicklung des kollektiven Bewußtseins in der Neuzeit*, ed. H. Berding, vol. III. Frankfurt am Main: 198–219.

(2001) 'Die neuhumanistische Begründung der Allgemeinbildung in Deutschland', in *Humanismus und Menschenbildung. Zu Geschichte, Gegenwart und Zukunft der bildenden Begegnung der Europäer mit der Kultur der Griechen und Römer*, ed. E. Wiersing. Essen: 205–23.

Landfester, R. (1972) *Historia Magistra Vitae: Untersuchungen zur humanistischen Geschichtstheorie des 14. bis 16 Jahrhunderts*. Geneva.

Larsen, M. T. (1989) 'Orientalism and Near Eastern archaeology', in *Domination and Resistance*, eds. D. Miller, M. J. Rowlands and C. Tilley. London: 229–239.

Lateiner, D. (1977) 'No laughing matter. A literary tactic in Herodotus', *Transactions and Proceedings of the American Philological Association* 107: 173–82.

(1989) *The Historical Method of Herodotus*. Toronto.

Lattimore, R. (1939) 'The wise advisor in Herodotus', *Classical Philology* 34: 24–35.

Lattimore, S. (1998) *Thucydides. The Peloponnesian War*. Indianapolis, IN.

Le Goff, J. (1978) 'Documento/monumento', in *Enciclopedia Einaudi*, Vol. V. Turin: 38–48.

Lear, J. (2005) *Freud*. London.

Lefort, C. (1986) 'Marx: From one vision of history to another', trans. T. Karten, in *idem, The Political Forms of Modern Society. Bureaucracy, Democracy, Totalitarianism.* Cambridge: 139–80.

Leitzmann, A. (ed.) (1934) *Wilhelm von Humboldts Briefe an Johann Gottfried Schweighäuser.* Jena.

Lekas, P. (1988) *Marx on Classical Antiquity. Problems of Historical Methodology.* Brighton.

Lemay, E. (1976) 'Histoire de l'antiquité et découverte du nouveau monde chez deux auteurs du XVIIIe siècle', *Studies on Voltaire and the Eighteenth Century* 153: 1313–28.

Leonard, M. (2005) *Athens in Paris. Ancient Greece and the Political in Post-War French Thought.* Oxford

Lepsius M. R. (1987) 'Zur Soziologie des Bürgertums und der Bürgerlichkeit', in *Bürger und Bürgerlichkeit im 19. Jh.*, ed. J. Kocka. Göttingen: 79–100.

Levine, J. M. (1991) *The Battle of the Books: History and Literature in the Augustan Age.* Ithaca, NJ–London.

   (1995) 'Deists and Anglicans: the ancient wisdom and the idea of progress', in *The Margins of Orthodoxy: Heterodox Writing and Cultural Response, 1660–1750*, ed. R. D. Lund. Cambridge: 219–39.

Lewy, H. (1978) *Chaldean Oracles and Theurgy*, 2nd edn. Paris.

Lianeri, A. and Zajko, V. (eds.) (2008) 'Introduction: Still being read after so many years: Rethinking the classic through translation', in *Translation and the Classic: Identity as Change in the History of Culture.* Oxford: 1–23.

Liddel, P. (ed.) (2007) *Bishop Thirlwall's History of Greece: A Selection.* Exeter.

Lintott, A. (1982) *Violence, Civil Strife and Revolution in the Classical City.* London.

Lissarrague, F. (1984) 'Autour du guerrier', in *La cité des images. Religion et société en Grèce antique*, eds. C. Bérard *et al.* Paris: 35–48.

Liu, L. (1995) *Translingual Practice. Literature, National Culture and Translated Modernity. China 1900–1937.* Stanford, CA.

Livesey, J. (2001) *Making Democracy in the French Revolution.* Cambridge, MA–London.

Livingstone, N. (2001) *A Commentary on Isocrates' Busiris.* Leiden–Boston–Cologne.

Lloyd, G. E. R. (1979) *Magic, Reason and Experience. Studies in the Origin and Development of Greek Science.* Cambridge.

   (2004) *Ancient Worlds, Modern Reflections. Philosophical Perspectives on Greek and Chinese Science and Culture.* Oxford.

   (2005) *The Delusions of Invulnerability. Wisdom and Morality in Ancient Greece, China and Today.* London.

Lohse, G. (1997) 'Die Homerrezeption im "Sturm und Drang" und deutscher Nationalismus im 18. Jahrhundert', *International Journal of the Classical Tradition*, 4.2, Fall: 195–231.

Lombard, J. (1998) 'Introduction', in *Discours préliminaire du traité des études*, ed. Ch. Rollin. Paris.

Loraux, N. (1980) 'Thucydide n'est pas un collègue', *Quaderni di Storia* 12: 55–81.

(1986a) *The Invention of Athens: The Funeral Oration in the Classical City*, trans. A. Sheridan. Cambridge MA.

(1986b) 'Thucydide et la sédition dans les mots', *Quad. di Storia* 23: 95–134.

(1986c) 'Thucydide a écrit la Guerre du Péloponnèse', *Metis* 1: 139–61.

(2001) *The Divided City. On Memory and Forgetting in Ancient Athens*, trans. Corinne Pache with Jeff Fort. New York.

Löwith, K. (2002) *Histoire et Salut, Les présupposés théologiques de la philosophie de l'histoire*, trans. M.-C. Challiol-Gillet, S. Hurstel and J.-F. Kervégan. Paris.

Luce, T. J. and Woodman, A. J. (eds.) (1993) *Tacitus and the Tacitean Tradition*. Princeton, NJ.

Lundgreen, P. (ed.) (2000) *Sozial- und Kulturgeschichte des Bürgertums. Eine Bilanz des Bielefelder Sonderforschungsbereichs (1986–1997)*. Göttingen.

Lyons, J. D. (1990) *Exemplum. The Rhetoric of Example in Early Modern France and Italy*. Princeton, NJ.

Macan, R. W. (1908) *Herodotus. The Histories. The Seventh, Eighth, and Ninth Books*, i–ii. London.

Macaulay, T. B. (1913) [1828] 'History' (1828), in *Complete Works. Vol. 7 Essays and Biographies. Vol. 1*. London.

Machiavelli, N. (1952) *Discours sur la première décade de Tite-Live*. Oeuvres complètes de la Pléiade. Paris.

(1989) 'Discourses on the first decade of Titus Livius', in *ibid. The Chief Works and Others, Volume I*, trans. A. Gubert. Durham, NC.

MacIntyre, A. (1971) *Marxism and Christianity*. Harmondsworth.

(1981) *After Virtue*. London.

(1988) *Whose Justice? Which Rationality?* London.

(1990) *Three Rival Versions of Moral Enquiry*. London.

Macleod, C. (1983) *Collected Essays*, ed. O. Taplin. Oxford.

Makropoulos, M. (1997) *Modernität und Kontingenz*. Munich.

Malingrey, A. M. (1961) *'Philosophia'. Etude d'un groupe de mots dans la littérature grecque, des présocratiques au IVe siècle après J.-C.* Paris.

Malkin, I. (ed.) (2001) *Ancient Perceptions of Greek Ethnicity*. Cambridge, MA.

Mandelbaum, M. (1971) *History, Man and Reason. A Study in Nineteenth-Century Thought*. Baltimore, MD–London.

Mansfeld, J. (1992) *Heresiography in Context. Hippolytus' Elenchos as a Source for Greek Philosophy*. Leiden–Utrecht–Cologne.

Manuel, F. E. (1959) *The Eighteenth Century Confronts the Gods*. Cambridge, MA.

Marchand, S. L. (1996) *Down from Olympus. Archaeology and Philhellenism in Germany, 1750–1970*. Princeton, NJ.

Marincola, J. (1997) *Authority and Tradition in Ancient Historiography*. Cambridge.

Markus, R. A. (1986) 'Chronicle and theology: Prosper of Aquitaine', in *The Inheritance of Historiography, 350–900*, eds. C. Holdsworth and T. P. Wiseman. Exeter: 31–43.

(1988) *Saeculum: History and Society in the Theology of St Augustine*. Cambridge.

(1990) *The End of Ancient Christianity*. Cambridge.

(1996) *Signs and Meanings: World and Text in Ancient Christianity*. Liverpool.

Marquard, O. (1986) 'Apologie des Zufälligen. Philosophische Überlegungen zum Menschen', in *idem, Apologie des Zufälligen. Philosophische Studien*. Stuttgart: 117–39.

Martin, R. H. and Woodman, A. J. (1989) *Tacitus Annals Book IV*. Cambridge

Marx, K. (2002) 'The Eighteenth Brumaire of Louis Napoleon', trans. T. Carver, in Cowling and Martin 2002: 19–109.

Marx, K. and Engels, F. (1964) [1848] *Manifest der Kommunistischen Partei*, in *Marx-Engels Werke* IV. Berlin: 459–93.

Matthiessen, K. (2003) 'Wilhelm von Humboldt und das Studium des Altertums', in *Aktualisierung von Antike und Epochenbewußtsein. Erstes Bruno Snell-Symposion der Universität Hamburg am Europa-Kolleg*, ed. G. Gerhard Lohse. Leipzig: 179–97.

Mattson, P. (ed.) (1990) *Wilhelm von Humboldt. Briefe an Friedrich August Wolf.* Berlin.

Maurer, M. (1996) *Die Biographie des Bürgers. Lebensformen und Denkweisen in der formativen Phase des deutschen Bürgertums (1680–1815)*. Göttingen.

McKitterick, R.M. (2006) *Perceptions of the Past in the Early Middle Ages*. Notre Dame, IN.

Meek, R. L. (1976) *Social Science and the Ignoble Savage*. Cambridge.

Mehlman, J. (1977) *Revolution and Repetition. Marx/Hugo/Balzac*. Berkeley, CA.

Meier, C. and Rüsen, J. (eds.) (1988) *Historische Methode*. Munich.

Meinecke, F. (1972) [1936] *Historism. The Rise of a New Historical Outlook*, trans. J. E. Anderson. London.

Meineke, S. (2003) 'Thukydidismus', *Der Neue Pauly*, vol. 15. Stuttgart and Weimar: 480–94.

Meister, K. (1990) *Die griechische Geschichtsschreibung. Von den Anfängen bis zum Ende des Hellenismus*. Stuttgart–Berlin–Cologne.

Menze, C. (1975) *Die Bildungsreform Wilhelm von Humboldts*. Hanover.

(1992) 'Das griechische Altertum und die deutsche Bildung aus der Sicht Wilhelm von Humboldts', in *Aspects of Antiquity in the History of Education*, eds. F.-P. Hager *et al.* Hildesheim: 45–60.

Mercier, L.-S. (1971) [1771, 1786] *L'an deux mille quatre cent quarante, Rêve s'il en fut jamais*, ed. R. Trousson. Bordeaux.

Messling, M. (2008) *Pariser Orientlektüren. Zu Wilhelm von Humboldts Theorie der Schriften*. Paderborn.

Metzger, T. A. (2005) *A Cloud across the Pacific: Essays on the Clash between Chinese and Western Political Theories Today*. Hong Kong.

Meyer, E. (1899) *Forschungen zur Alten Geschichte II*. Halle.

Meyer-Zwiffelhoffer, E. (1995) 'Alte Geschichte in der Universalgeschichtsschreibung der Frühen Neuzeit', *Saeculum* 46: 249–73.

Miles, G. B. (1995) *Livy: Reconstructing Early Rome*. Ithaca, NY–London.

Miliori, M. (2000) 'Ἀρχαῖος ελληνισμός και φιλελληνισμός στη βρετανική ιστοριογραφία του 19ου αιώνα. Οι πολιτικές και εθνικές διαστάσεις του 'εθνικού' και οι ευρύτερες σημασιοδοτήσεις της ελληνικής ιστορίας' ['Archaios Ellênismos kai Philellênismos stê Bretanikê istoriografia tou 19ou aiôna. Oi politikes kai êthikes diastaseis tou 'ethnikou' kai oi eyryteres sêmasiodotêseis tês ellênikês istorias'], *Mnêmôn* 20: 69–104.

Millar, F. (1997) 'Porphyry: ethnicity, language, and alien wisdom', in Barnes and Griffin 1997: 241–62.

Miller, P. (ed.) (2007a) *Momigliano and Antiquarianism. Foundations of the Modern Cultural Sciences*. Los Angeles.

(2007b) 'Introduction: Momigliano, antiquarianism and the cultural sciences', in Miller 2007a: 3–65.

(2007c) 'Momigliano, Benjamin, and antiquarianism after the crisis of historicism', in Miller 2007a: 334–78.

Mills, S. (1997) *Theseus, Tragedy, and the Athenian Empire*. Oxford.

Mitford, W. (1797) *The History of Greece*, vol. III. London.

Mix, E. R. (1970) *Marcus Atilius Regulus. Exemplum Historicum*. Paris.

Moatti, C. (1997) *La raison de Rome: La naissance de l'esprit critique à la fin de la République*. Paris.

Moles, J. (2002) 'Herodotus and Athens', in *Brill's Companion to Herodotus*, eds. E. J. Bakker *et al.* Leiden: 33–52.

Momigliano, A. (1955a) 'George Grote and the study of Greek history', in Momigliano 1955c: 213–31.

(1955b) 'Ancient history and the antiquarian', in Momigliano 1955c: 67–106.

(1955c) *Contributo alla Storia degli Studi Classici*. Rome.

(1963) 'Pagan and Christian historiography in the fourth century A.D.', in *idem, The Conflict Between Paganism and Christianity in the Fourth Century*. Oxford: 79–99.

(1966a) 'Ancient history and the antiquarian', reprinted in Momigliano 1966b: 1–39.

(1966b) *Studies in Historiography*. London.

(1970) 'La città antica di Fustel de Coulanges', trans. in Momigliano 1977a: 325–43.

(1975a) *Quinto contributo alla storia degli studi classici e del mondo antico*, vol. 1. Rome.

(1975b) *Alien Wisdom: The Limits of Hellenization*. Cambridge.

(1977a) 'Tradition and the classical historian', in Momigliano, 1977d: 161–77.

(1977b) 'Time in ancient historiography', in Momigliano 1977d: 179–204.

(1977c) 'Eighteenth-century prelude to Mr. Gibbon', reprinted in Momigliano 1980c: 249–63.

(1977d) *Essays in Ancient and Modern Historiography*. Oxford.

(1978) 'Greek historiography', *History and Theory*, 17.1: 1–28.

(1980a) 'Eighteenth-century prelude to Mr. Gibbon', in Momigliano 1980c: 249–63.

(1980b) 'The place of ancient historiography in modern historiography', reprinted in Momigliano 1984: 13–36.

(1980c) *Sesto contributo alla storia degli studi classici e del mondo antico*. Rome.

(1982) 'New paths of classicism in the nineteenth century', reprinted in Momigliano 1994: 223–85.

(1984) *Settimo contributo alla storia degli studi classici e del mondo antico*. Rome.

(1987a) *On Pagans, Jews and Christians*. Middletown, CT.

(1987b) 'A note on Max Weber's definition of Judaism as a pariah religion', in Momigliano 1987a: 231–7.

(1987c) 'Some preliminary remarks on the "religious opposition" to the Roman Empire', in Momigliano 1987a: 120–41.

(1987d) 'The disadvantages of monotheism for a universal state', in Momigliano 1987a: 142–58 (first published in 1986 in *Classical Philology* 81: 285–97).

(1987e) 'Biblical studies and classical studies: simple reflections upon historical method', in Momigliano 1987a: 3–10.

(1987f) 'The origins of universal history', in Momigliano 1987a: 31–57.

(1987g) 'What Josephus did not see', in Momigliano 1987a: 108–19.

(1987h) *Pagine ebraiche*, ed. S. Berti. Torino. [Momigliano, A. (1994) *Essays on Ancient and Modern Judaism*, tr. M. Masella-Gayley. Chicago.]

(1990) *The Classical Foundations of Modern Historiography*, ed. R. di Donato. Berkeley, CA–Oxford.

(1994) *Studies on Modern Scholarship*, eds. G. W. Bowersock and T. J. Cornell, trans. T. J. Cornell. Berkeley, CA–Los Angeles.

(1996) *Pace e libertà nel mondo antico. Lezioni a Cambridge: gennaio-marzo 1940*, ed. R. di Donato. Florence.

Montepaone, C. (1994) 'Proposta per un' ipotesi di applicabilità del "modello tucidideo" mazzariniano all'opera storica di B.G. Niebuhr', in *Tucidide nella storiografia moderna. B.G. Niebuhr, L. v. Ranke, W. Roscher, E. Meyer*, ed. F. Tessitore. Naples: 13–64.

Montiglio, S. (2005) *Wandering in Ancient Greek Culture*. Chicago, IL–London.

Moore, J., Macgregor Morris, I., Bayliss, A. J. (eds.) (2008) *Reinventing History: The Enlightenment Origins of Ancient History*. Institute of Historical Research, School of Advanced Study. London.

Moos, P. van (1988) *Geschichte als Topik: das rhetorische Exemplum von der Antike zur Neuzeit und die 'historiae' im Policraticus Johanns von Salisbury*. Hildesheim.

Morange, J. and Chassaing, J.-F. (1974) *Le mouvement de réforme de l'enseignement en France 1760–1798*. Paris.

More, T. (1965) [1516] 'Utopia', in *The Complete Works of St Thomas More*, eds. E. Sturtz and J. H. Hexter, vol. IV. New Haven, CT–London.

Morley, N. (2009) *Antiquity and Modernity*. Oxford.

Morris, I. (2000) *Archaeology as Cultural History: Words and Things in Iron Age Greece*. Malden, MA.

Morris I. and Powell, B. (2005) *The Greeks: History, Culture, and Society*. Upper Saddle River.

Morrison, J. V. (2004) 'Memory, time, and writing. Oral and literary aspects of Thucydides' *History*', in *Oral Performance and its Context*, ed. C. J. Mackie. Leiden: 95–116.

Mortley, R. (1980) 'The past in Clement of Alexandria: a study of an attempt to define Christianity in socio-cultural terms', in *The Shaping of Christianity in the Second and Third Centuries, vol. I: Jewish and Christian Self-Definition*, ed. E. P. Sanders. London: vol. 1, 186–200.

(1996) *The Idea of Universal History from Hellenistic Philosophy to Early Christian Historiography*. Lewiston, NY.

Mosshammer, A. A. (1979) *The Chronicle of Eusebius and Greek Chronographic Tradition*. Lewisburg.

Most, G. W. (ed.) (2001) *Historicization – Historisierung*. Göttingen.

Muccillo, M. (1996) *Platonismo, ermetismo e 'prisca theologia'. Ricerche di storiografia filosofica rinascimentale*. Florence.

Muckensturm, C. (1993) 'Les gymnosophistes étaient-ils des cyniques modèles?', *in Le cynisme ancien et ses prolongements*, eds. Goulet-Cazé, M.-O. and Goulet, R. Paris: 225–39.

Müller, G., Ries, K., and Ziche, P. (eds.) (2001) *Die Universität Jena. Tradition und Innovation um 1800*. Stuttgart.

Müller, R. (1972) 'Hegel und Marx über die antike Kultur', *Philologus* 118: 1–31.

Müri, W. (1969) 'Politische Metonomasie (zu Thukydides 3, 82, 4–5)', *Museum Helveticum* 26: 65–79.

Muhlack, U. (1978) 'Die Universitäten im Zeichen von Neuhumanismus und Idealismus', in *Beiträge zu Problemen deutscher Universitätsgründungen in der frühen Neuzeit*, eds. P. Baumgart and N. Hammerstein. Nendeln: 299–340.

(1979) 'Zum Verhältnis von Klassischer Philologie und Geschichtswissenschaft im 19. Jahrhundert', in *Philologie und Hermeneutik im 19. Jahrhundert. Zur Geschichte und Methodologie der Geisteswissenschaften*, eds. H. Flashar *et al.*, vol. 1. Göttingen: 225–39.

(1986) 'Historie und Philologie', in *Aufklärung und Geschichte. Studien zur deutschen Geschichtswissenschaft im 18. Jahrhundert*, eds. H. E. Bödecker *et al.* Göttingen: 49–81.

(1988) 'Von der philologischen zur historischen Methode', in *Historische Methode* (Theorie der Geschichte, vol. 5), eds. C. Meier and J. Rüsen. Munich: 154–80.

(1991) *Geschichtswissenschaft im Humanismus und in der Aufklärung. Die Vorgeschichte des Historismus*. Munich.

(1998) 'Johann Gustav Droysen: Das Recht der Geschichte', in *Die 48er*, ed. S. Freitag. Munich: 263–76.

(2006a) *Staatensystem und Geschichtsschreibung. Ausgewählte Aufsätze zu Humanismus und Historismus, Absolutismus und Aufklärung*. Berlin.

(2006b) 'Die Genese eines Historikers. Zur Autobiographie und zur Korrespondenz des jungen Ranke', in *Historie und Leben. Der Historiker als Wissenschaftler und Zeitgenosse. Festschrift für Lothar Gall zum 70. Geburtstag*, eds. D. Hein, K. Hildebrand and A. Schulz. München: 21–40.

Muhlack, U. and Hentschke, A. (1972) *Einführung in die Geschichte der Klassischen Philologie*. Darmstadt.

Muhlberger, S. (1990) *The Fifth-Century Chroniclers: Prosper, Hydatius and the Gallic Chronicler of 452*. Leeds.

Murray, O. (2001) 'Gnosis and tradition', in *Agon, Logos, Polis. The Greek Achievement and its Aftermath*, eds. J. P. Arnason and P. Murphy. Stuttgart: 15–28.

(2002) 'Burckhardt, Nietzsche and Socrates', in *Jacob Burckhardt: storia della cultura, storia dell'arte*, eds. M. Ghelardi and M. Seidel. Venice: 55–61.

(forthcoming) 'Ireland Invents Greek History: The Lost Historian John Gast', *Hermathena*.

Murru, F. (1979) 'La concezione della storia nei Chronica di Sulpicio Severo: alcune linee di studio', *Latomus* 38: 961–81.

Nadel, G. (1964) 'Philosophy of history before historicism', *History and Theory* 3.3: 291–315.

Nelson, E. (2004) *The Greek Tradition in Republican Thought*. Cambridge.

Nestle, W. (1914) 'Thukydides und die Sophistik', *Neue Jahrbücher für das Klassische Altertum* 33: 649–85.

Neugebauer, W. (1990) 'Bildungsreformen vor Wilhelm von Humboldt. Am Beispiel der Mark Brandenburg' *Jahrbuch für Brandenburgische Landesgeschichte* 41: 26–249.

Neumann, U. (1995) *Gegenwart und mythische Vergangenheit bei Euripides*. Stuttgart.

Niebuhr, B. G. (1827) 'Ueber Xenophons Hellenika', *Rheinisches Museum* (vol. 1): 194–8.

(1828) [1812] 'Ueber die Geographie Herodots. (Mit einer Charte)', in *Kleine historische und philologische Schriften*, (vol. 1), Bonn: 132–58.

(1847–51) *Vorträge über alte Geschichte, an der Universität zu Bonn gehalten*, ed. M. Niebuhr (3 vols.). Berlin.

(1926) *Die Briefe Barthold Georg Niebuhrs*, eds. D. Gerhard and W. Norvin (vol. 1). Berlin.

(1981–4) *Briefe. Neue Folge. 1816–1830*, ed. E. Vischer, (4 vols.). Bern–Munich.

Nietzsche, F. (1874) *Vom Nutzen und Nachtheil der Historie für das Leben: Unzeitgemässe Betrachtungen II*, in *Sämtliche Werke: Kritischen Studienausgabe* I, eds. G. Colli and M. Montinari, Berlin (1967–77): 245–334.5.

(1983) [1874] 'On the uses and disadvantages of history for life', in *Untimely Meditations*, trans. R. J. Hollingdale. Cambridge: 57–123.

Nippel, W. (1980) *Mischverfassungstheorie und Verfassungsrealität in Antike und früher Neuzeit*. Stuttgart.

(1990) *Griechen, Barbaren und 'Wilde'. Alte Geschichte und Sozialanthropologie*. Frankfurt.

(1998) 'Von den "Altertümern' zur Kulturgeschichte", *Ktèma* 23: 17–24.

Nipperdey, T. (1983) *Deutsche Geschichte 1800–1866. Bürgerwelt und starker Staat*. Munich.

Nisbet, H. B. (ed.) (1985) *German Aesthetic and Literary Criticism*. Cambridge.

Nisbet, R. A. (1969) *Social Change and History. Aspects of the Western Theory of Development*. New York.

Novick, P. (1988) *That Noble Dream: The 'Objectivity Question' and the American Historical Profession*. Cambridge.

O'Gorman, E. (2000) *Irony and Misreading in the Annals of Tacitus*. Cambridge.

(2007) 'Intertextuality and historiography', in *The Cambridge Companion to Roman Historiography*, ed. A. Feldherr. Cambridge: 231–42.

Oakeshott, M. (1962) *Rationalism in Politics*. London.

(1975) *On Human Conduct*. Oxford.

Ober, J. (1998) *Political Dissent in Democratic Athens. Intellectual Critics of Popular Rule*. Princeton, NJ.

Oesterle, G. (1996) 'Kulturelle Identität und Klassizismus. Wilhelm von Humboldts Entwurf einer allgemeinen und vergleichenden Literaturerkenntnis als Teil einer vergleichenden Anthropologie', in *Nationale und kulturelle Identität. Studien zur Entwicklung des kollektiven Bewußtseins in der Neuzeit*, ed. B. Giesen. Frankfurt am Main: 304–49.

Oexle, O. G. (1996) 'Meineckes Historismus. Über Kontext und Folgen einer Definition', in *Historismus in den Kulturwissenschaften. Geschichtskonzepte, historische Einschätzungen, Grundlagenprobleme*, eds. O. G. Oexle and J. Rüsen. Cologne: 139–99.

Olender, M. (1992) *The Languages of Paradise. Race, Religion, and Philology in the Nineteenth Century*, trans. A. Goldhammer. Cambridge, MA.

Orwin, C. (1988) 'Stasis and plague: Thucydides on the dissolution of society', *Journal of Politics* 50: 831–47.

(1994) *The Humanity of Thucydides*. Princeton, NJ.

Osborne, P. (1995) *The Politics of Time. Modernity and the Avant-Garde*. London.

Osborne R. (1996) *Greece in the Making, 1200–479 BC*. London.

Pagden, A. (ed.) (1987) *The Languages of Political Theory in Early-Modern Europe*. Cambridge.

Page, D. L. (1953) 'Thucydides' description of the Great Plague at Athens', *Classical Quarterly* 47: 97–119.

Paletschek, S. (2001) 'Verbreitete sich ein "Humboldtsches Modell" an den deutschen Universitäten im 19. Jahrhundert?' in *Humboldt International. Der Export des deutschen Universitätsmodells im 19. und 20. Jahrhundert*, ed. R. C. Schwinges. Basle: 75–104.

(2002) 'Die Erfindung der Humboldtschen Idee. Die Konstruktion der deutsche Universitätsidee in der ersten Hälfte des 20. Jahrhunderts', *Historische Anthropologie. Kultur – Gesellschaft – Alltag* 10: 183–205.

Pallantza, E. (2005) *Der Troische Krieg in der nachhomerischen Literatur bis zum 5. Jh. v. Chr.* Wiesbaden.

Parry, A. (1969) 'The language of Thucydides' description of the plague', *Bulletin of the Institute of Classical Studies* 16: 106–18.

Parsons, J. (2001) 'The Roman censors in the Renaissance political imagination', *History of Political Thought* 22: 565–86.

Paulsen, F. (1921) *Geschichte des gelehrten Unterrichts auf den deutschen Schulen und Universitäten vom Ausgang des Mittelalters bis zur Gegenwart – mit besonderer Rücksicht auf den klassischen Unterricht*, 3rd edn. (3 vols.). Leipzig.

Peardon, T. P. (1933) *The Transition in English Historical Writing, 1760–1830*. New York.

Peretti, A. (1943) *La Sibilla Babilonesi nella propaganda ellenistica*. Florence.

Phillips, M. S. (1996) 'Reconsiderations on history and antiquarianism: Arnaldo Momigliano and the historiography of eighteenth-century Britain', *Journal of the History of Ideas* 57: 297–316.

(2000) *Society and Sentiment. Genres of Historical Writing in Britain, 1740–1820*. Princeton, NJ.

Piaia, G. (1983) *Vestigia philosophorum. Il Medioevo e la storiografia filosofica*. Rimini.

Pico della Mirandola, G. (1942) *De hominis dignitate. Heptaplus. De ente et uno*, ed. E. Garin. Florence.

Pocock, J. G. A. (1957) *The Ancient Constitution and the Feudal Law* (2nd edn. 1987). Cambridge.

(1968) 'Time, institutions and actions. An essay on traditions and their understanding', in *Politics and Experience*, eds. P. King and B. Parekh. Cambridge, 209–37.

(1971) *Politics, Language and Time*. London.

(1975a) *The Machiavellian Moment. Florentine Political Thought and the Atlantic Republican Tradition*. Princeton, NJ.

(1975b) 'Early modern capitalism: the Augustan perception', in *Feudalism, Capitalism and Beyond*, eds. E. Kamenka and R. S. Neale. London: 62–83.

(1985) 'The mobility of property and the rise of eighteenth-century sociology', in *Virtue, Commerce and History. Essays on Political Thought and History, Chiefly in the Eighteenth Century*. Cambridge: 103–23.

(1987a) 'The concept of a language and the *metier d'historien*: some considerations on practice', in Pagden 1987: 19–38.

(1987b) *The Ancient Constitution and the Feudal Law. A Study of English Historical Thought in the Seventeenth Century*. 2nd edn. Cambridge.

(1999–2005) *Barbarism and Religion*. Vol. I (1999a) *The Enlightenments of Edward Gibbon, 1737–1764*. Vol. II (1999b) *Narratives of Civil Government*. Vol. III (2003) *The First Decline and Fall*. Vol. IV. (2005) *Barbarians, Savages and Empires*. Cambridge.

(2003) [1975] *The Machiavellian Moment. Florentine Political Thought and the Atlantic Republican Tradition*, 2nd edn. with a new afterword. Princeton, NJ–Oxford.

(2005) *The Discovery of Islands: Essays in British History*. Cambridge.

(2009) *Political Thought and History: Essays in Theory and Method*. Cambridge.

Poliakov, L. (1974) *The Aryan Myth. A History of Racist and Nationalist Ideas in Europe*, trans. E. Howard. London.

Pommier, E. (1991) *L'art de la liberté*. Paris.

Porter, J. I. (2000) *Nietzsche and the Philology of the Future*. Stanford, CA.

Potts, A. (1994) *Flesh and the Ideal: Winckelmann and the Origins of Art History*. New Haven–London.

Prawer, S. S. (1976) *Karl Marx on World Literature*. Oxford.

Preston, R. (2001) 'Roman questions, Greek answers: Plutarch and the construction of identity', in *Being Greek under Rome. Cultural Identity, the Second Sophistic and the Development of Empire*, ed. S. Goldhill. Cambridge: 86–119.

Prete, S. (1955) *I Chronica di Sulpicio Severo: saggio storico-critico*. Vatican City.

(1958) 'Sulpicio Severo e il millenarismo', *Convivium* 26: 394–404.

Price, J. (2001) *Thucydides and Internal War*. Cambridge.

Proß, W. (1996) "Gens sui tantum similis" – Johann Gottfried Herders Beitrag zur Entstehung des deutschen Philhellenismus', *Museum Helveticum* 53: 206–16.

Quillien, G. J. de (1983) *Humboldt et la Grèce. Modèle et histoire*. Lille.

Raines, D. (2006) *L'invention du mythe aristocratique: l'image de soi du patriciat vénitien au temps de la Sérénissime* (2 vols.). Venice.

Rancière, J. (1994) *The Names of History: On the Poetics of Knowledge*, trans. Hassan Melehy. Minneapolis, MN.

Ranke, L. von (1824) *Geschichten der romanischen und germanischen Völker von 1494 bis 1535*, vol. I. Leipzig–Berlin.

(1881) *Weltgeschichte*, vol. 1.1.2, Leipzig.

(1888a) 'Von der historischen Commission bei der Königl. Akademie der Wissenschaften zu München. Rede zur Eröffnung der XII. Plenarversammlung am 27. September 1871', in *Abhandlungen und Versuche* (*Sämmtliche Werke* Vol. 51/52), eds. A. Dove and T. Wiedemann. Leipzig: 567–77.

(1888b) 'Ansprachen, gehalten an persönlichen Feiertagen', in *Abhandlungen und Versuche*. (*Sämmtliche Werke* Vol. 51/52), eds. A. Dove and T. Wiedemann. Leipzig.

(1890) *Zur eigenen Lebensgeschichte* (*Sämmtliche Werke* vol. 53/54), ed. A. Dove. Leipzig.

(1964) 'Tagebücher', in *Aus Werk und Nachlaß*, ed. W. P. Fuchs, vol. I. Munich–Vienna.

(1971) 'Über die Epochen der neueren Geschichte. Historisch-kritische Ausgabe', in *Werk und Nachlaß*, eds. T. Schneider and H. Berding, vol. II. Munich–Vienna.

(1975) 'Vorlesungseinleitungen', *Aus Werk und Nachlaß*, eds. V. Volker Dotterweich and W. P. Fuchs, vol. IV. Munich–Vienna.

(2007) *Gesamtausgabe des Briefwechsels von Leopold von Ranke, vol. 1: 1813–1825*, eds. U. Muhlack and O. Ramonat. Munich. Revised edition in preparation.

Rawlings, H. R. (1981) *The Structure of Thucydides' History*. Princeton, NJ.

Rawson, E. (1969) *The Spartan Tradition in European Thought*. Oxford.

Rebenich, S. (2000) 'Historismus. I. Allgemein' in *Der Neue Pauly* 14, columns 469–85.

(2008) 'Umgang mit toten Freunden. Droysen und das Altertum', in *'Die Ideale der Alten.' Antikerezeption um 1800*, ed. V. Rosenberger. Stuttgart: 131–52.

Regenbogen, O. (1930) 'Herodot und sein Werk. Ein Versuch', *Die Antike* 6: 202–48.

Rehm, W. (1968) [1936] *Griechentum und Goethezeit. Geschichte eines Glaubens*, 4th edn. Berne–Munich.

Reill, P. H. (1975) *The German Enlightenment and the Rise of Historicism*. Berkeley–Los Angeles–London.

Rengakos, A., and Tsakmakis, A. (eds.) (2006) *Brill's Companion to Thucydides*. Leiden.

Repgen, K. (1988) 'Über Rankes Diktum von 1824: "Bloß sagen, wie es eigentlich gewesen"', in *Von der Reformation zur Gegenwart. Beiträge zu Grundfragen der Neuzeitlichen Geschichte*, eds. K. Gotto and H. G. Hockerts. Paderborn–Munich–Zurich: 289–98.

Reumann, O. (2006) 'L'exemplum humaniste comme moyen de légitimation dans la galerie François I', in *L'image du roi de François I à Louis XIV*, eds. T. W. Gaehtgens and N. Hochner. Paris: 131–48.

Rice, E. and Grafton, A. (1994) *The Foundations of Early Modern Europe, 1460–1559*. New York.

Richardson, A. (1965) *History, Sacred and Profane*. London.

Rico, F. (2002) *Le rêve de l'humanisme. De Pétrarque à Erasme*, trans. J. Tellez. Paris.

Ricoeur, P. (1952) 'Christianity and the meaning of history: Progress, ambiguity, hope', *Journal of Religion* 32: 242–53.

(1988) *Time and Narrative*, vol. III, trans. K. Blamey and D. Pellauer. Chicago.

(2004) *Memory, History, Forgetting*, trans. K. Blamey and D. Pellauer. Chicago.

Riedel, M. (1972) 'Bürger, Staatsbürger, Bürgertum', *Geschichtliche Grundbegriffe*, I: 672–725.

Riegl, A. (1982) 'The modern cult of monuments', trans. K. W. Foster and D. Ghirardo, *Oppositions* 25: 21–51.

Rigolot, F. (1998) 'The Renaissance crisis of exemplarity', *Journal of the History of Ideas* 59: 557–64.

(2004) 'Problematizing Renaissance exemplarity: The inward turn of dialogue from Petrarch to Montaigne', in *Printed Voices: The Renaissance Culture of Dialogue*, eds. D. Heitz and F. Jean-Vallée. Toronto: 3–24.

Robbins, J. (2007) 'Continuity thinking and the problem of Christian culture: belief, time, and the anthropology of Christianity', *Current Anthropology* 48: 5–38.

Roberts, J. (1994) *Athens on Trial: the Antidemocratic Tradition in Western Thought*. Princeton, NJ.

Rollin, C. (1728) *De la manière d'enseigner et d'étudier les belles lettres* (3 vols.). Paris.

(1733–39) *Histoire ancienne* (13 vols.). Paris.

Romilly, J. de (1956a) *Histoire et raison chez Thucydide*. Paris.

(1956b) 'L'utilité de l'histoire selon Thucydide', in *Histoire et Historiens dans l'antiquité. Entretiens sur l'antiquité classique* IV. Geneva: 41–81.

(1966) 'Thucydide et l'idée de progrès', *Annali della Scuola Normale Superiore di Pisa. Lettere, storia e filosofia* 35: 143–91.

Roscher, C. (1908) 'Wilhelm Roscher an Leopold Ranke. Ein Stück Wissenschafts-geschichte (1842). Mitgeteilt von Ministerialdirektor Dr C. Roscher – Dresden', *Preußische Jahrbücher* 133: 383–6.

Roscher, W. (1842) *Leben, Werk und Zeitalter des Thukydides. Mit einer Einleitung zur Aesthetik der historischen Kunst überhaupt* (*Klio. Beiträge zur historischen Kunst*, I). Göttingen.

Rösler, W. (1991) 'Die "Selbsthistorisierung" des Autors. Zur Stellung Herodots zwischen Mündlichkeit und Schriftlichkeit', *Philologus* 135: 215–20.

(2002) 'The histories and writing', in *Brill's Companion to Herodotus*, eds. E. J. Bakker *et al.* Leiden: 79–94.

Rossi, P. (1957) *Francesco Bacone. Dalla magia alla scienza* (Bari); Engl. trans. (1968) *Francis Bacon: from Magic to Science.* Chicago, IL.

(1984) *The Dark Abyss of Time. The History of the Earth and the History of Nations from Hooke to Vico*, trans. L. G. Cochrane. Chicago, IL.

Roth, M. S. (1995) *Psycho-Analysis as History. Negation and Freedom in Freud.* Ithaca, NY.

Rousseau, J.-J. (1964) [1755] *Deuxième discours [Discours sur l'origine et les fondements de l'inégalité parmi les hommes], in Oeuvres complètes* (1959–1995), eds. B. Gagnebin and M. Raymond, Bibliothèque de la Pléiade, vol. iii. Paris: 109–223.

Rüegg, W. (1978) 'Die Antike als Leitbild der deutschen Gesellschaft im 19. Jahrhundert', in *Bedrohte Lebensordnung. Studien zur humanistischen Soziologie.* Zurich–Munich: 93–105.

(1985) 'Die Antike als Begründung des deutschen Nationalbewußtseins', in *Antike in der Moderne*, ed. W. Schuller. Constance: 267–87.

(1999) 'Ortsbestimmung. Die Königlich Preußische Akademie der Wissenschaften und der Aufstieg der Universitäten in den ersten zwei Dritteln des 19. Jahrhunderts', in *Die Königlich Preußische Akademie der Wissenschaften zu Berlin im Kaiserreich*, ed. J. Kocka. Berlin: 23–47.

Rüsen, J. (1982) 'Die vier Typen des historischen Erzählens', *Formen der Geschichtsschreibung*, eds. R. Koselleck *et al.* Munich: 514–605.

Saffrey, H. D. (1987) [1952–81] *Recherches sur la tradition platonicienne au Moyen Age et à la Renaissance.* Paris.

(1990) *Recherches sur le néoplatonisme après Plotin.* Paris.

Said, E. (1978) *Orientalism.* New York–London.

Said, S. (2001) 'The discourse of identity in Greek rhetoric from Isocrates to Aristides', in Malkin 2001: 275–99

Saint-Simon, C.-H. de (1966) *Œuvres de Claude-Henri de Saint-Simon.* Paris.

Saladin, J.-Ch. (2000) *La bataille du grec à la Renaissance.* Paris.

Sampson, R. V. (1956) *Progress in the Age of Reason. The Seventeenth Century to the Present Day.* London.

Saure, F. (2006) '"... das ganze Reich der Ideen." Karl Friedrich Schinkels Geschichtsphilosophie zwischen Wilhelm von Humboldts Antikebild und Fichtes Freiheitsmetaphysik', in *Berlin-Brandenburgische Akademie der Wissenschaften. Berichte und Abhandlungen* 10: 307–24.

(2007) '"Körperliche Stärke und Behendigkeit zu ehren" oder Olympia in Berlin. Der deutsche Idealismus, die Sportwettkämpfe im antiken Griechenland und das moderne Deutschland', in *German as a Foreign Language* 2: 7–27.

Sauter, C. M. (1989) *Wilhelm von Humboldt und die deutsche Aufklärung.* Berlin.

Sauter-Bergerhausen, C. (2002) 'Vom "blutigen Krieger" zum "friedlichen Pflüger". Staat, Nation und Krieg in Wilhelm von Humboldts "Ideen zu einem Versuch, die Gränzen der Wirksamkeit des Staats zu bestimmen"', *Forschungen zur Brandenburgischen und Preußischen Geschichte* 12: 211–62.

Savonarola, G. (1955) *Prediche su Ezechiele*, ed. R. Ridolfi. Rome.

(1956) *Prediche sopra l'Esodo*, ed. P. G. Ricci (2 vols.). Rome.

Schadewaldt, W. (1929) *Die Geschichtsschreibung des Thukydides*. Berlin.
  (1982) [1934] *Die Anfänge der Geschichtsschreibung bei den Griechen. Herodot. Thukydides* (*Tübinger Vorlesungen* vol. ii), ed. I. Schudoma. Frankfurt am Main.
Schaumkell, E. (1905) *Geschichte der deutschen Kulturgeschichtsschreibung von der Mitte des 18. Jahrhunderts bis zur Romantik*. Leipzig.
Schiller, F. (1965) [1795] *Über die ästhetische Erziehung des Menschen*. Stuttgart.
Schlobach, J. (1980) *Zyklentheorie und Epochenmetaphorik: Studien zur bildlichen Sprache der Geschichtsreflexion in Frankreich von der Renaissance bis zur Frühaufklärung*. Munich.
Schlözer, A. L. (1979) [1783] 'On historiography', trans. H. D. Schmidt, *History and Theory* 18: 41–51.
Schmale, W. (2005) 'Bürgerliche Gesellschaft', *Enzyklopädie der Neuzeit* 2: 558–64.
Schmitt, A. (2002) 'Querelles des Anciens et des Modernes', *Der Neue Pauly* 15.2: 607–22.
Schmitt, C. (1956) *Hamlet oder Hecuba: Der Einbruch der Zeit in das Spiel*. Düsseldorf.
  (1996) *Politische Theologie II: Die Legende von der Erledigung jeden politischen Theologie*. Berlin.
  (2007) [1975] *Theory of the Partisan: Intermediate Commentary on the Concept of the Political*, trans. G. L. Ulmen. New York.
Schmitz-Kahlmann, G. (1939) *Das Beispiel der Geschichte im politischen Denken des Isokrates*. Leipzig.
Schnabel, F. (1948) *Deutsche Geschichte im 19. Jahrhundert*, vol. i, 4th edn. Freiburg i.Br.
Schneider, H. (1988) 'Schottische Aufklärung und antike Gesellschaft', in *Alte Geschichte und Wissenschaftsgeschichte. Festschrift für Karl Christ zum 65. Geburtstag*, eds. P. Kneissl and V. Losemann. Darmstadt: 431–64.
  (1990) 'Die Bücher – Meyer Kontroverse', in *Edward Meyer: Leben und Leistung eines Universalhistorikers*, eds. W. M. Calder and A. Demandt. Leiden: 417–45.
Schulz, A. (2005) *Lebenswelt und Kultur des Bürgertums im 19. und 20. Jh.*, EDG 75. Munich.
Sedley, D. (1998) *Lucretius and the Transformation of Greek Wisdom*. Cambridge.
Senneville-Grave, G. de (ed. and trans.) (1999) *Sulpice Sévère: Chroniques*. Paris.
Shapiro, S. (1994) 'Learning through suffering. Human wisdom in Herodotus', *Classical Journal* 89: 349–55.
Sharpe, K. (2000) *Reading Revolutions: The Politics of Reading in Early Modern England*. New Haven.
Simonsuuri, K. (1979) *Homer's Original Genius. Eighteenth-Century Notions of the Early Greek Epic (1688–1798)*. Cambridge.
Skinner, Q. (2002) 'From the state of princes to the person of the state', in *idem, Visions of Politics. Volume II: Renaissance Virtues*. Cambridge: 368–413.
Smith, A. (1976) [1776] *An Inquiry into the Nature and Causes of the Wealth of Nations*, eds. R. H. Campbell, A. S. Skinner and W. B. Todd. Oxford.
Soll, J. (2000) 'Amelot de la Houssaie annotates Tacitus', *Journal of the History of Ideas* 61: 167–88.

Solmsen, F. (1982) 'Two crucial decisions in Herodotus', in *Kleine Schriften III*. Hildesheim: 78–109 (Mededelingen der Koninklijke Nederlandse Akademie van Wetenschappen. Nieuwe Reeks 37/6: 139–170).

Solmsen, L. (1944) 'Speeches in Herodotus' account of the battle of Plataea', *Classical Philology* 39: 241–53.

Spitta, D. (2004) *Die Staatsidee Wilhelm von Humboldts*. Berlin.

Spoerri, W. (1959) *Späthellenistische Berichte über Welt, Kultur und Götter*. Basle.

Spranger, E. (1928) [1909] *Wilhelm von Humboldt und die Humanitätsidee*, 2nd edn. Berlin.

(1965) [1910] *Wilhelm von Humboldt und die Reform des Bildungswesen*, 3rd edn. (2nd edn. 1960). Berlin.

Sprinker, M. (ed.) (1999) *Ghostly Demarcations: A Symposium on Jacques Derrida's Specters of Marx*. London.

Stadler, P. B. (1959) *Wilhelm von Humboldts Bild der Antike*. Einsiedeln.

Stadter, P. A. (1992) 'Herodotus and the Athenian arche', *Annali della Scuola Normale Superiore di Pisa* 22: 781–809.

Stahl, H. P. (1966) *Thukydides. Die Stellung des Menschen im geschichtlichen Prozess*. Munich.

(1975) 'Learning through suffering? Croesus' conversations in the *History* of Herodotus', *Yale Classical Studies* 24: 1–36.

(2003) *Thucydides. Man's Place in History*. [trans. of Stahl (1966)]. Swansea.

Stancliffe, C. (1983) *St. Martin and His Hagiographer: History and Miracle in Sulpicius Severus*. Oxford.

Stanyan, T. (1707–39) *Grecian History* (2 vols.). London.

Starobinski, J. (1985) *Montaigne in Motion*, trans. A. Goldhammer. Chicago, IL.

Ste. Croix, G. E. M. de (1972) *The Origins of the Peloponnesian War*. London.

Steenblock, V. (1991) *Transformationen des Historismus*. Munich.

Stern, J. P. (1983) 'Introduction', in *Friedrich Nietzsche: Untimely Meditations*, trans. R. J. Hollingdale. Cambridge: vii–xxxi.

Stern, M. (1974) *Greek and Latin Authors on Jews and Judaism*. Jerusalem.

Stern, M. and Murray, O. (1973) 'Hecataeus of Abdera and Theophrastus on Jews and Egyptians', *Journal of Aegyptian Archaeology* 59: 159–68.

Stewart, A. (1985) 'History, myth, and allegory in the program of the Temple of Athena Nike at Athens', in *Pictorial Narrative in Antiquity and the Middle Ages. Studies in the History of Art 16*, eds. H. L. Kessler and M. S. Simpson: 53–73.

Stierle, K. (1972) 'L'histoire comme exemple, l'exemple comme histoire', *Poétique* 10: 176–98.

(1998) 'Three moments in the crisis of exemplarity: Petrarch, Montaigne and Cervantes', *Journal of the History of Ideas* 59: 581–96.

Stocking, G. W. Jr. (1987) *Victorian Anthropology*. New York.

Strauss, L. (1980) *Persecution and the Art of Writing*. Chicago, IL.

(1997) 'How to study Spinoza's *Theologico-Political Treatise*', in *Jewish Philosophy and the Crisis of Modernity. Essays and Lectures in Modern Jewish Thought*, ed. K. H. Green. Albany, NY: 181–234.

(2002) *The Early Writings (1921–1932)*, ed. and trans. M. Zank. Albany, NY.

Stray, C. (1997) '"Thucydides or Grote": classical disputes and disputed classics in nineteenth-century Cambridge', *Transactions and Proceedings of the American Philological Association* 127: 363–71.

Strong, T. B. (2000) *Friedrich Nietzsche and the Politics of Transfiguration*. Urbana–Chicago.

Sünderhauf, E. S. (2004) *Griechensehnsucht und Kulturkritik. Die deutsche Rezeption von Winckelmanns Antikenideal 1840–1945*. Berlin.

Süßmann, J. (2000) *Geschichtsschreibung oder Roman? Zur Konstitutionslogik von Geschichtserzählungen zwischen Schiller und Ranke (1780 – 1824)*. Stuttgart.

Swain, S. (1994) 'Man and medicine in Thucydides', *Arethusa* 27: 303–27.

(1997) 'Plutarch, Plato, Athens, and Rome', in Barnes and Griffin 1977: 165–87.

Sweet, P. R. (1980) *Wilhelm von Humboldt. A Biography* (2 vols.). Ohio.

Swift Riginos, A. (1976) *Platonica. The Anecdotes concerning the Life and Writings of Plato*. Leiden.

Syme, R. (1939) *The Roman Revolution*. Oxford.

Tanner, R. G. (1989) 'The historical method of Sulpicius Severus', *Studia Patristica* 19: 106–10.

Tarán, L. (1975) *Academica: Plato, Philip of Opus, and the Pseudo-platonic Epinomis*. Philadelphia, PA.

Taubes, J. (1987) *Ad Carl Schmitt Gegenstrebige Fügung*. Berlin.

(2004) *The Political Theology of Paul*, eds. A. Assmann and J. Assmann in conjunction with H. Folkers, W.-D. Hartwich and C. Schulte, trans. D. Hollander. Stanford, CA.

Taylor, C. (1989) *Sources of the Self*. Cambridge, MA.

(1991) *The Ethics of Authenticity*. Cambridge, MA.

(1995) *Philosophical Arguments*. Cambridge, MA.

Taylor, M. C. (2003) Review of L. Kallet (2001), P. Debnar, *Speaking the Same Language: Speech and Audience in Thucydides' Spartan Debates* (Ann Arbor, 2001) and Price (2001), *Phoenix* 57, 3–4: 329–33.

Teich, M. and Müller, A. (eds.) (2005) *Historia Magistra Vitae?*, Special issue, *Österreichische Zeitschrift für Geschichtswissenschaft* 16.2.

Theunissen, M. (2000) *Pindar. Menschenlos und Wende der Zeit*. Munich.

Thiesse, A.-M. (1999) *La création des identités nationales: Europe XVIIIe–XXe siècle*. Paris.

Thom, M. (1995) *Republics, Nations and Tribes*. London–New York.

Thomas, R. (2001) 'Ethnicity, genealogy, and Hellenism in Herodotus', in Malkin 2001: 212–33.

(2006) 'Thucydides' intellectual milieu and the plague', *Brill's Companion to Thucydides*, eds. A. Rengakos and A. Tsakmakis, Leiden: 87–108.

Thompson, E. P. (1978) *The Poverty of Theory and Other Essays*. London.

Thöne, C. (1999) *Ikonographische Studien zu Nike im 5. Jh. v. Chr. Untersuchungen zur Wirkungsweise und Wesensart*. Heidelberg.

Tocqueville, A. de (1985) *De la démocratie en Amérique* (2 vols.). Paris.

Todd, M. (1992) *The Early Germans*. Oxford.

Tourreil, J. de (1701) *Philippiques de Démosthènes avec des Remarques*. Paris.

Trevelyan, H. (1934) *The Popular Background to Goethe's Hellenism*. London.

Trompf, G. W. (1979) *The Idea of Historical Recurrence in Western Thought: From Antiquity to the Reformation*. Berkeley, CA–London.

Trousson, R. (1998) *Voyage au pays de nulle part*. Brussels.

Tsakmakis, A. (1995) *Thukydides über die Vergangenheit*. Munich.

Turner, F. (1981) *The Greek Heritage in Victorian Britain*. New Haven, CT–London.

   (1989) 'Why the Greeks and not the Romans in Victorian Britain?' in *Rediscovering Hellenism. The Hellenic Inheritance and the English Imagination*, ed. G. W. Clarke. Cambridge: 61–81.

Uhlig, L. (ed.) (1988) *Griechenland als Original. Winckelmann und seine Rezeption in Deutschland*. Tübingen.

Ulf, C. (2006) 'Elemente des Utilitarismus im Konstrukt des "Agonalen"', *Nicephorus* 19: 67–79.

Ungern-Sternberg, J. von (2005) 'Wilhelm von Humboldts Bildungsideen. Von der freien Entfaltung des Individuums zum Schulmodell', *Archiv für Kulturgeschichte* 87: 127–48.

Urbinati, N. (2002) *Mill on Democracy: From the Athenian Polis to Representative Government*. Chicago.

Vaesen, J. (1988) 'Sulpice Sévère et la fin des temps', in *The Use and Abuse of Eschatology in the Middle Ages*, eds. W. D. F. Verbeke, D. Verhelst, and A. Welkenhusen. Louvain: 49–71.

Van Andel, G. K. (1976) *The Christian Concept of History in the Chronicle of Sulpicius Severus*. Amsterdam.

Vasoli, C. (2006) *Ficino, Savonarola, Machiavelli. Studi di storia della cultura*. Turin.

Venturi, F. (1989) *The End of the Old Regime in Europe, 1768–1776: The First Crisis*, trans. R. Burr Litchfield. Princeton, NJ.

   (1991) *The End of the Old Regime in Europe, 1776–1789: The Great States of the West*, trans. R. Burr Litchfield. Princeton, NJ.

Vessey, M. (2004) 'Introduction', in *Cassiodorus: Institutions of Divine and Secular Learning and On the Soul*, ed. M. Vessey and trans. J. Halporn, Liverpool: 1–101.

Vessey, M. and Pollmann, K. (1999) 'Introduction', in *History, Apocalypse, and the Secular Imagination: New Essays on Augustine's City of God*, eds. M. Vessey, K. Pollmann and A. D. Fitzgerald. Bowling Green, OH [= *Augustinian Studies* 30:2]: 1–26.

Vick, B. (2007) 'Of Basques, Greeks, and Germans: Liberalism, nationalism, and the ancient Republican tradition in the thought of Wilhelm von Humboldt', *Central European History* 40: 653–81.

Vidal-Naquet, P. (1960) 'Temps des Dieux et temps des hommes', *Revue d'histoire des Religions*, janv-mars: 55–80.

   (1979) 'La formation des Athènes bourgeoise: essai d'historiographie 1750–1870' (with N. Loraux) in *Classical Influences on Western Thought AD 1650–1870*, ed. R. R. Bolgar. Cambridge: 169–222. English trans. in Vidal-Naquet 1995: 82–140.

(1990) 'La place de la Grèce dans l'imaginaire des hommes de la Révolution', trans. in Vidal-Naquet 1995: 141–169.

(1995) *Politics Ancient and Modern*, trans. J. Lloyd. Cambridge.

Vierhaus, R. (1972) 'Bildung', in *Geschichtliche Grundbegriffe. Historisches Lexikon zur politisch-sozialen Sprache in Deutschland*, vol. 1, eds. O. Brunner, W. Conze and R. Koselleck. Stuttgart: 508–51.

(ed.) (1981) *Bürger und Bürgerlichkeit im Zeitalter der Aufklärung*. Heidelberg.

(1987)'Umrisse einer Sozialgeschichte der Gebildeten in Deutschland', in *Deutschland im 18. Jh. Politische Verfassung, soziales Gefüge, geistige Bewegungen*. Göttingen: 183–201.

Vlassopoulos, K. (2007) *Unthinking the Greek Polis. Ancient Greek History beyond Eurocentrism*. Cambridge.

Völler, M. (2002) 'Christian Gottlob Heyne und das Studium des Altertums in Deutschland', in *Disciplining Classics – Altertumswissenschaft als Beruf*, ed. G. W. Most. Göttingen: 39–54.

Wagner, C. (1991) *Die Entwicklung Johann Gustav Droysens als Althistoriker*. Bonn.

Walbank, F. W. (1970) *A Historical Commentary on Polybius*, vol. 1. Oxford.

Walker, D. P. (1972) *The Ancient Theology. Studies in Christian Platonists from the Fifteenth to the Eighteenth Century*. London.

Walther, G. (1993) *Niebuhrs Forschung (Frankfurter Historische Abhandlungen*, vol. 35). Stuttgart.

(1998) 'Adel und Antike. Zur politischen Bedeutung gelehrter Kultur für die Führungselite der Frühen Neuzeit', *Historische Zeitschrift* 266: 359–85.

(2001) 'Theodor Mommsen und die Erforschung der römischen Geschichte', in Most 2001: 241–58.

(2005) 'Bildung', *Enzyklopädie der Neuzeit* 2: 223–42.

Wassermann, F. M. (1954) 'Thucydides and the disintegration of the polis', *Transactions and Proceedings of the American Philological Association* 85: 46–54.

Waszink, J. H. (1979) *Opuscula selecta*. Leiden.

Waterfield, R. (1998). *Herodotus. The Histories*. Oxford.

Watkins, G. (2002) 'The appeal of Bonapartism', in Cowling and Martin 2002: 163–76.

Weber, M. (1971–2) *Gesammelte Aufsätze zur Religionssoziologie*. Tübingen.

(1978) *Economy and Society: An Outline of Interpretive Sociology*, eds. G. Roth and C. Wittich. Berkeley, CA–London.

(1988) *Gesammelte Politische Schriften*, eds. J. Winckelmann and J. C. B. Mohr. Tübingen.

(1992) *The Protestant Ethic and the Spirit of Capitalism*, trans. T. Parsons. London.

Weber, S. (1997) *Die Chronik des Sulpicius Severus: Charakteristika und Intentionen*. Trier.

Weçowski, M. (2004) 'The hedgehog and the fox: Form and meaning in the prologue of Herodotus', *Journal of Hellenic Studies* 124: 143–64.

Wehler, H.-U. (1996) *Deutsche Gesellschaftsgeschichte, vol. 1: Vom Feudalismus des Alten Reiches bis zur defensiven Modernisierung der Reformära 1700–1815; vol. 2: Von der Reformära bis zur industriellen und politischen 'Deutschen Doppelrevolution' 1815–1848/94* (3rd edn). Munich.

Weidauer, K. (1954) *Thukydides und die hippokratischen Schriften*. Heidelberg.

West, M. L. (1971) *Early Greek Philosophy and the Orient*. Oxford.

White, H. (1978) 'The historical text as literary artifact', in White, *Tropics of Discourse: Essays in Cultural Criticism*. Baltimore, MD–London.

(1994) 'Forward: Rancière's revisionism', in J. Rancière, *The Names of History: On the Poetics of Knowledge*, trans. Hassan Melehy. Minneapolis, MN: vii–xx.

Williams, B. A. O. (1985) *Ethics and the Limits of Philosophy*. London.

(1993) *Shame and Necessity*. Berkeley, CA.

(2002) *Truth and Truthfulness: An Essay in Genealogy*. Princeton, NJ.

(2006a) *The Sense of the Past: Essays on the History of Philosophy*, ed. M. Burnyeat. Princeton, NJ.

(2006b) 'What might philosophy become', in *Philosophy as a Humanistic Discipline*, ed. A.W. Moore. Princeton: 200–13.

(2006c) '*The Women of Trachis*: Fictions, pessimism, ethics', in *The Sense of the Past: Essays in the History of Philosophy*, ed. M. Burnyeat. Princeton, NJ: 49–59.

Williams, M. S. (2008) *Authorised Lives in Early Christian Biography: Between Eusebius and Augustine*. Cambridge.

Wilson, E. (2007) *The Death of Socrates*. Cambridge, MA.

Wilson, J. (1982) 'The customary meanings of words were changed – or were they? A Note on Thucydides 3.82.4', *Classical Quarterly* 32: 18–20.

Winterer, C. (2002) *The Culture of Classicism*. Baltimore, MD.

Wiseman, T. P. (1994) 'Monuments and the Roman annalists', in *idem, Historiography and Imagination: Eight Essays on Roman Culture*. Exeter: 37–48.

Wohlleben, J. (1992) 'Germany, 1750–1830', in Dover 1992: 170–202.

Wokler, R. (1987) 'Saint-Simon and the passage from political to social science', in Pagden 1987: 325–38.

Wolf, E. (1982) *Europe and the People without History*. Berkeley–Los Angeles–London.

Wolf, F. A. (1985) *Darstellung der Altertumswissenschaft nach Begriff, Umfang, Zweck und Wert*, ed. J. Irmscher. Berlin.

Woodman, A. (1988) *Rhetoric in Classical Historiography*. London.

Worthington, I. (1982) 'A note on Thucydides 3.82.4', *Liverpool Classical Monthly* 7: 124.

Yates, F. A. (1964) *Giordano Bruno and the Hermetic Tradition*. London.

Yavetz, Z. (1976) 'Why Rome? Zeitgeist and ancient historians in early 19th-century Germany', *American Journal of Philology* 97: 276–96.

Zagorin, P. (1998) *Francis Bacon*. Princeton, NJ.

Zecchini, G. (2003) 'Latin historiography: Jerome, Orosius and the Western chronicles', in *Greek and Roman Historiography in Late Antiquity: Fourth to Sixth Century A.D.*, ed. G. Marasco. Leiden: 317–45.

Index

Lightning Source UK Ltd.
Milton Keynes UK
UKOW031935221012

200984UK00001B/2/P